THE NEW ARAB URBAN

The New Arab Urban

Gulf Cities of Wealth, Ambition, and Distress

Edited by

Harvey Molotch *and* Davide Ponzini

NEW YORK UNIVERSITY PRESS
New York

NEW YORK UNIVERSITY PRESS

New York

www.nyupress.org

References to Internet websites (URLs) were accurate at the time of writing. Neither the author nor New York University Press is responsible for URLs that may have expired or changed since the manuscript was prepared.

Library of Congress Cataloging-in-Publication Data

Names: Molotch, Harvey Luskin, editor. | Ponzini, Davide, 1979– editor.
Title: The new Arab urban : Gulf cities of wealth, ambition, and distress /
    edited by Harvey Molotch and Davide Ponzini.
Description: New York : New York University Press, [2019] | bibliographical references
    and index.
Identifiers: LCCN 2018021510| ISBN 9781479880010 (cl : alk. paper) |
    ISBN 9781479897254 (pb : alk. paper)
Subjects: LCSH: Urbanization—Persian Gulf Region. | Persian Region—Social conditions. |
    Persian Gulf Region—Economic conditions.
Classification: LCC HT147.P35 N47 2019 | DDC 307.7609165/35—dc23
LC record available at https://lccn.loc.gov/2018021510

New York University Press books are printed on acid-free paper, and their binding materials are chosen for strength and durability. We strive to use environmentally responsible suppliers and materials to the greatest extent possible in publishing our books.

Manufactured in the United States of America

Front cover: Doha, 2017.

Photograph by Michele Nastasi

10 9 8 7 6 5 4 3 2

Also available as an ebook

In memory of
Hilary Ballon
Scholar, Teacher, Builder

CONTENTS

List of Figures   ix

Introduction: Learning from Gulf Cities   1
Harvey Molotch and Davide Ponzini

Section I. The Gulf as Transnational

1. Giving the Transnational a History: Gulf Cities across
   Time and Space   35
   Alex Boodrookas and Arang Keshavarzian

2. Problematizing a Regional Context: Representation
   in Arab and Gulf Cities   58
   Amale Andraos

3. Mobilities of Urban Spectacle: Plans, Projects, and
   Investments in the Gulf and Beyond   79
   Davide Ponzini

Section II. Assembling Hybrid Cities

4. A Gulf of Images: Photography and the Circulation
   of Spectacular Architecture   99
   Michele Nastasi

5. Planning for the Hybrid Gulf City   130
   Laura Lieto

6. Planning from Within: NYU Abu Dhabi   147
   Hilary Ballon

Section III. Urban Test Beds for Export

7. Gateway: Revisiting Dubai as a Port City   175
   Mina Akhavan

8. Exporting the Spaceship: The Connected Isolation
   of Masdar City   194
   Gökçe Günel

9. "Two Days to Shape the Future": A Saudi Arabian
   Node in the Transnational Circulation of Ideas
   about New Cities   213
   Sarah Moser

Section IV. Audacity, Work-Arounds, and Spatial
Segmentation

10. Real Estate Speculation and Transnational Development
    in Dubai   235
    Yasser Elsheshtawy

11. Consuming Abu Dhabi   256
    Harvey Molotch

12. A Quest for Significance: Gulf Oil Monarchies'
    International Strategies and Their Urban Dimensions   276
    Steffen Hertog

    Conclusion: From Gulf Cities Onward   300
    Harvey Molotch and Davide Ponzini

    Acknowledgments   321

    About the Contributors   323

    Index   327

LIST OF FIGURES

Figure 2.1. Burj Al Arab in Dubai. 59

Figure 2.2. The Qatar Faculty of Islamic Studies designed by
Ali Mangera and Ada Yvars Bravo. 62

Figure 2.3. Louvre Abu Dhabi designed by Ateliers Jean Nouvel. 63

Figure 2.4. The Solidere area in Beirut. 72

Figure 2.5. Aïshti Foundation designed by David Adjaye, detail. 74

Figure 3.1. Partial map showing holdings currently planned and
managed by QIA, Qatar Diar, and Qatar Holding outside Qatar. 85

Figure 3.2. Partial map of holdings planned and managed by
Emaar Properties outside the United Arab Emirates. 88

Figure 4.1. Burj Khalifa, Dubai, 2010. 101

Figure 4.2. Photograph by Ken Hedrich, 1950s: Mies Van der Rohe,
Lakeshore Drive Apartments. 104

Figure 4.3. Photograph by Jim Hedrich, 1972: SOM,
Sears Towers, Chicago. 105

Figure 4.4. Photograph by Nick Merrick, 2010: SOM,
Burj Khalifa, Dubai. 106

Figure 4.5. A Symphony of Lights, Hong Kong, 2013. 110

Figure 4.6. Hearst Headquarters, New York, 2008. 112

Figure 4.7. Bank of China, Hong Kong, 2013. 113

Figure 4.8. Abu Dhabi National Bank, Abu Dhabi, 2010. 114

Figure 4.9. La Défense, Paris, 2010. 115

Figure 4.10. View of the Gherkin (30 St Mary Axe), London, 2015. 115

Figure 4.11. The Torre Agbar at Glòries, Barcelona, 2011. 116

Figure 4.12. West Bay, Doha, 2013. 117

Figure 4.13. View from Central Market, Abu Dhabi, 2017. 118

Figure 4.14. Capital Gate, Abu Dhabi, 2010. 119

Figure 4.15. Al Bandar, Abu Dhabi, 2010. 120

Figure 4.16. Battersea Reach, London, 2015. 120

Figure 4.17. City Life Hadid Residences, Milan, 2014. 121

Figure 4.18. Marina Bay Sands, Singapore, 2013. 122

Figure 4.19. Gate Towers, Abu Dhabi, 2015. 122

Figure 4.20. View from Sheep Meadow, New York, 2009. 124

Figure 4.21. Dubai Fountains and Burj Khalifa, Dubai, 2010. 124

Figure 4.22. Dubai skyline from Al Satwa, Dubai, 2015. 125

Figure 6.1. The main campus street looking east, with the Experimental Research Building and West Plaza in the foreground, NYU Abu Dhabi. 155

Figure 6.2. The main campus street, with landscaping and seating, and a bridge at High Line level. 157

Figure 6.3. The High Line and undergraduate residences, NYU Abu Dhabi. 161

Figure 6.4. The pedestrian network, NYU Abu Dhabi. 162

Figure 6.5. The ground floor of the Humanities Building and courtyard with a view of the undergraduate residences at the High Line. 163

Figure 6.6. The main entrance of NYU Abu Dhabi, looking toward the Central Plaza and Campus Center. The graduate residences are above the bookstore and welcome center. 167

Figure 6.7. The East Plaza during a concert, with the Arts Center at right, NYU Abu Dhabi. 168

Figure 7.1. The four-phase Dubai port-city development. 181

Figure 7.2. Dubai's value of total foreign trade (1997–2015). 182

Figure 7.3. Dubai's modal split of international trade (based on the value for year 2000). 183

Figure 7.4. Dubai's modal split of international trade (based on the value for year 2015). 183

Figure 7.5. Dubai's top trading partners worldwide (per country) in year 2015. 184

Figure 7.6. Dubai's top trading partners worldwide (per continent) in year 2015. 184

Figure 7.7. Contribution of the main economic activities to the UAE's GDP (2001–2012). 185

Figure 7.8. Contribution of the main economic activities to Dubai's GDP (1997–2015). 186

Figure 7.9. Evolution of the container traffic in UAE, Dubai, Abu Dhabi, and Sharjah (1980–2015). 188

Figure 8.1. The Masdar Institute, a graduate level research center that focuses on renewable energy and clean technology, was designed by Foster + Partners, March 2014.   195

Figure 8.2. A computer rendering of the Masdar City master plan, which was circulated in the media between 2007 and 2010.   196

Figure 8.3. The Masdar Institute campus includes dormitories, a knowledge center, laboratories, and a sports facility, March 2014.   198

Figure 8.4. The laboratory facades at Masdar Institute are composed of insulating cushions that shade the interiors of the building and remain cool to the touch under the desert sun.   201

Figure 8.5. "Man with a brush" clears the thick coatings on solar panels, which result from a mixture of dust and humidity, and ensures their efficacy, April 2011.   206

Figure 9.1. NCF director John Rossant has an onstage conversation with Daniel Libeskind.   219

Figure 9.2. Many networking sessions provide opportunities for leaders, experts, and investors to mingle with builders of new cities.   220

Figure 9.3. Welcome dinner: gourmet dining among luxury villas next to the Red Sea.   222

Figure 9.4. CEOs of new cities start a site tour with an explanation of the master plan.   224

Figure 10.1. Dubai's changing skyline, 2004.   236

Figure 10.2. Dubai's changing skyline, 2015.   237

Figure 10.3. Land use indicators in Dubai's urban area, 2013.   244

Figure 10.4. Developer distribution analysis: state-owned land and property distribution, 2013.   246

Figure 10.5. Developer distribution analysis: private-owned land and property distribution, 2013.   247

Figure 10.6. The al-Shorta neighborhood in 2014, prior to demolition.   251

Figure 10.7. The projected replacement has become reality, May 2016.   251

Figure 11.1. Pork room in rear of Spinney's supermarket, Saadiyat Island, Abu Dhabi, 2016.   267

Introduction

Learning from Gulf Cities

HARVEY MOLOTCH AND DAVIDE PONZINI

To learn from the cities of the Arabian Peninsula, particularly the most controversial and dynamic among them (places like Dubai, Abu Dhabi, and Doha), does not mean celebrating them or ridiculing them either. Instead, the authors in this book follow the intellectual footprints of the architectural scholars Robert Venturi, Denise Scott Brown, and Steven Izenour, who looked at a city nearer at hand and in their own time. In their now classic *Learning from Las Vegas*, they went beyond seeing Las Vegas as tasteless, materialistic, or aberrant and insisted that it had important lessons for all places.[1] According to them, the city needed to be studied on its own terms—an insistence that changed not only future understandings of Las Vegas but also of architecture, planning, and urban thinking more generally. In their view, "Withholding judgment may be a tool to make later judgment more sensitive. This is a way of learning from everything."[2]

Why the Gulf?

In *The New Arab Urban*, with a group of scholars from across many academic disciplines and diverse parts of the world, we strive to learn from the cities of the Persian Gulf—in particular the global showcase cities of Abu Dhabi and Dubai, in the United Arab Emirates (UAE), and Doha, the capital of Qatar—more or less adjoining locales at the mouth of the Gulf. Because of practical limitations, we have given shorter shrift to other parts of the urban Gulf, like Saudi Arabia, Kuwait, and Bahrain, which are also part of the interlinked economies of the Gulf Cooperation Council (GCC). We are also spare in our attention to Riyadh, in

Saudi Arabia—the largest GCC city but one that, in terms of history, ambitions, and contemporary relations with other parts of the world, is in a class distinct from the others. With its (currently) thin political and economic connections to the rest of the Gulf, Iran only occasionally comes into our purview. Recognizing the variation, we avoid thinking in terms of any single "Gulf City model."

To help make the point, we adopt the plural—Gulf *cities*—in the book's title. We do not want to repeat the historically common essentializing error of treating cities, variously "Islamic" or "Arab" or "Middle East," as the same, nor to unthinkingly generalize traits observed at one point in time, whether the sixteenth century or 2018, as true of urban histories, full stop. Especially when dealing with large expanses of geography and peoples, where past scholarship has been radically uneven, we need to avoid falling back on stereotypes, including those academically generated.[3]

We might have even called out the cities of focus as "*our* Gulf cities," to further suggest the limits of the book's reach. They do have things in common. For example, rather than being the important urban centers of surrounding territories, like Cairo was to Egypt (or Chicago to the U.S. Midwest), their centrality is more cosmopolitan. To an increasing degree, they've also escaped dependence on the natural resource most prominent in their region (oil), just as they rely little on any surrounding agriculture or manufacturing. These are essentially city-states with the world as their hinterland. What distinguishes them more markedly compared to all other places is that they are rich and in the hands of people with intense ambitions, not just for themselves as individuals and families, but also for their rising cities. Given their wealth and autonomy, they are important as possible harbingers—as Las Vegas was in the earlier context in the United States.[4] And also like Las Vegas—but more so—their modes of development and ways of life can come to influence the urban world farther afield.

While stressing distinctions, we are also following those scholars striving to "de-exceptionalize"[5] Gulf cities and to, at least, test notions that see them as following economic, political, and cultural trajectories common to other human settlements. To do so means emplacing them in their own histories, as well as in the contemporary world currents in which they now play a significant role. This involves taking on board not only a long history of trade and governance, but also—and to a great degree—

particularities of recent history that do signal a departure from the usual paradigms for understanding urban development. Clearly, these Gulf cities do not conform to anything resembling a "third-world" dependency or, given the world region in which they are located, a postcolonial status.[6] The oil-driven accumulation of capital can be seen in some places in the Gulf, but not in others; and even where oil has been important, it has been important in different ways. Our Gulf cities are, in ways we will be disentangling, following patterns that do not simply recapitulate any single development model of what has come before.

A first declaration and one to which we will eventually return: we are not, in the context of Gulf cities, oblivious to the injustices and dire circumstances that accompany the glamor and fascination of the present day. Indeed, there is a relationship, which is traced in this book, between what appears on the top and what happens lower down, between spectacular wealth and grinding hardship. Appropriately enough, much media and scholarly attention has focused on the social iniquity, as well as the environmental threat, following on from Gulf-style development: surely among the highest levels of world inequality and, as indicated by the best data sources, the highest carbon footprints. As methodological strategy, we sometimes bracket the dystopic as well as the utopian. To build knowledge, we can leverage all the idiosyncrasies, including the distressing features. By restraining judgment (remember Las Vegas), we can come back to the problematics with a greater capacity to understand and strategize. And, at least as aspiration, we can use the Gulf to further think about how the urban works more generally.

Gulf Cities Are Theoretical Puzzlers

Conditions in the Gulf do scramble some of the grand traditions of urban scholarship—indeed of social science in general. They serve notice, in effect, that those traditions may not be sufficient to grasp how societies, cultures, and economies emerge, cohere, and crumble—not just in the Gulf but elsewhere as well. As a first stop, models derived from classical economics do not work. Given the Gulf, it is hard to apply the precepts of classical thinkers like Adam Smith or David Ricardo. Whatever the general propensity to truck, barter, and exchange, in the Gulf, such tendencies are subservient to other forces. Markets are not open and free; information is held close to the vest on vastly unequal playing fields. Crucial principles like comparative advantage as a determinant of price and productivity hardly reign with consistency. The market is not an apparatus to deliver the greatest good for the greatest number. Investments, in real estate or in other sectors, are detached from so-called market discipline.

Based as they are on economistic models, much of land economics and allied approaches in geography and urban sociology lose explanatory power. Across the history of Gulf monarchies, real estate evolved from the outset as monopolistic—explicitly and persistently. Property derives from the birthright of the sheikhs, as modified through truces with the British colonials, and—in varied ways—the playbooks of important merchant families. The bounties of oil followed arrangements of lineage as well, organized at least initially through early-twentieth-century links of favored families with the British colonials and the initiating British, European, and U.S. energy corporations. Together, they constituted parts of what James Bill refers to as "informal empire."[7] Famously and noticeable on the land in the early period, oil companies created gated neighborhoods reserved for Western technocrats and managers. Nelida Fuccaro identifies a section of what became central Manama, Bahrain, as the first of its kind in the Gulf, a "neo-colonial" residential outpost built in 1937 by the American-owned Bahrain Petroleum Company (Bapco).[8] What has evolved in various parts of the Gulf—skyscrapers, resorts, wholesalers, coffee bars, and the whole repertoire of structure and infrastructure—follows in path dependence from monarchical origin and early commercial agreements. Specific to particular Gulf states, in ways our authors indicate, there followed further layerings of privilege and connections.

Vast efforts across the disciplines of urban sociology, geography, and urban economics rely on assumptions Gulf cities do not meet. A scholarly search has been on to determine what best explains the outcomes that maximize efficiency. According to one such foundational perspective (following from the work of the economist Walter Christaller in the mid-1930s),[9] it is geographic centrality that minimizes friction of distance. Many will recognize the centrality model in urban sociology's concentric zone hypothesis, as inherited from the Chicago School of Human Ecology. Centrality also affords agglomeration benefits as similar types of land users end up clustered together in central downtowns, complementing one another's core functions.[10] Other models turn on special geographic features, like the break of bulk points, where, for example, rivers meet up with land transport. These ideas, at least in the terms they were formulated, prove to be poor models for Gulf conditions (as we will see in the volume).

The alternative to conventional economics in any guise is, of course, Karl Marx. But Gulf conditions also challenge Marxian analysis. Along with the continuous potential for intervention through privilege and patronage, the state asserted itself with other traits we associate with feudal monarchies: colossal structures and symbolic showiness. Rather than displaying signs of withering away, the state became a tool for enhancing monarchical rule. Tax-free zones, which might otherwise be thought to have been hatched as capitalist plots, involved "political and economic logics of great powers, regional-rivals, state builders, and local businesses."[11] In other words, the apparently capitalist vehicle was (and is) a tool of the monarchical class, rather than (or at least as much as) vice versa. Far from being mere superstructure, these states have been active agents for furthering the wealth and legitimacy of the royal faction. None of this is to gainsay the authentic advances following from Marxian perspectives regarding the Gulf as in other world settings (or for that matter, the presence of neoclassical markets within specific delimited arenas)—but the application is approximate and, alas, sometimes contorted.[12] We have privileged vassals, favored merchants, and armies of workers—but not a bourgeoisie in service to capitalist rulers or a class proletariat structured through the means of production.

Some contemporary urban theories, Marxian or otherwise, explain cities as following in historic stages, concomitant with shifts in economic base and changes in social organization. Agriculture, itself arising from early sedentary life, provided the surplus to allow urban-based specialization to take root. Or, from a different development paradigm, it can be said that dominant proto-urban elites forced surpluses out of the peasantry. Either way, as Laura Lieto notes (in chapter 5), the classic explanations do not fit the Gulf case. Cities like Abu Dhabi or Doha grew from small settlements with limited preexisting fixed structures or even year-round populations (especially in the case of Abu Dhabi). The open desert provided opportunity for expansion under schemes provided by foreign planners and designers, embraced by local rulers with little regard for what had come before. In this sense, the contemporary urban form of our Gulf cities, professionally hatched and of recent vintage, is visible as an enacted construct, particular to the specificities of time and place. Some of it is surely conjuncture borne out of indeterminacy. The timing of oil and the voluntary British exit, co-occurring in an ideological climate of self-determination, created facilitating state structures.[13] We can term our Gulf nations, borrowing language from Hossein Mahdavy, as instances of "fortuitous étatisme";[14] agencies and structures that follow on lend themselves to having a similar idiosyncratic quality.

In the development of the urban Gulf, hired consultants' grand plans are only loosely followed; they get replaced at fairly short intervals. Real-time development happens through opaque agendas in which even otherwise privileged citizens have little say or advance knowledge. Property owners do not form coalitions to publicly lobby for infrastructures from which they will derive financial benefit—as is so common in a place like the United States, where "growth machines" actively strive to use government for pecuniary advantage.[15] Public plans are drawn up and "visions" for economic and spatial development are enunciated, but they have limited efficacy. There are signs of high-level intraelite bargaining, directly or indirectly, sometimes involving the monarchs themselves.[16] Conditions do vary in these regards, as well as others across the Gulf. Kuwait (and the capital, Kuwait City) has more than symbolic democratic elements; real elections occur. Citizen groups openly and energetically criticize internationally branded projects, arguing instead for expenditures that increase welfare provision or improve citizen services. Frustrated in its capacities to build spectacular structures out of general state revenues, the royal family has had to maintain a separate fund for such purposes, distinct from other public budgets.[17]

What about culture? Might that be a key for understanding Gulf development trends, just as it has been applied—however unevenly and with questionable results—to explain urban shifts elsewhere in the world?[18] A rampant stereotype is that it is "all" indeed fundamentally cultural—with the religion of Islam as a prime proxy. But, of course, religion won't do. Great differences across the Islamic world in doctrine and practice—from Indonesia to Saudi Arabia to Los Angeles[19]—yield up differences, almost surreal in their variation. Similarly, there are obvious distinctions from one Gulf state to another. As with the overstated or just plain empirically false Weberian claim that Protestantism was the launchpad of capitalism or that Europe and North America are bonded as Christian, Islam manifests differently in its intersection with markets, policies, and lives. Two veteran and distinguished researchers of the region flatly summarize the point: " 'Islamic' by itself explains very little indeed."[20] When other informed scholars take up their very different approaches, they rarely—appropriately rarely—invoke religion as a general explanation. Islam is varied and subtle with plenty of room for ambiguity—indeed, indeterminacy—as to what is or is not legitimate.

Even within the same branch or sect, elements can be inconsistent and "co-exist as valid doctrine." They can be allowed to stand, writes Frank Vogel, "without being authoritatively reconciled."[21] Through the various texts and circumstances, there can be innovation in judgments—indeed sometimes necessitated by changing external conditions as well as the evolution of new "learning" among guardians of the faith (uluma).[22] Thus, the "plurality of doctrine" is caused, if in no other way, by the obligation to determine true meanings within texts and also the requirement that believers unendingly search, as a personal obligation, for truth in God's will. Islamic scholars, Vogel asserts, both "modern and classical, benefit from this pluralism of doctrine, since they can shift by various means from one view to the other, sometimes even to suit a particular circumstance."[23]

Skeptical of religion as explainer, we can ask about other, perhaps less doctrinal cultural explanations of how states and societies form up. The economist Alfred Marshall used the term "industrial atmosphere" to invite attention to the nonmaterial aspects (along with the material ones) that make countries and regions productive. The concept has evolved further in more recent thinking, where, for instance, prosperity is grounded in an agglomeration of complementary skills and knowledges, along with mutually understood tacit awareness. Actors' intuitive understandings become the basis for regional economic advantage—like the rise, a generation back, of the "Third Italy" or, more recently, Silicon Valley.[24] Put in the language of economic geographer Michael Storper, these are "untraded dependencies," meaning that the market has no way to affix prices to such assets, but they are of value—economic value—nonetheless. In current discourse, we can cast such qualities as the basis for what makes a place "creative" or "innovative." Jane Jacobs, in her book *The Economy of Cities*,[25] uses something like a Marshallian atmosphere to argue that diverse kinds of people interacting in a common and proximate space (whether like her Greenwich Village neighborhood block or a national region) is the recipe for robust economies. In the Richard Florida argument, creative people are drawn to places that have just such diversity, which then makes them more creative still. (This is indeed the story of how Jane Jacobs got to the Village and then further boosted its worldwide appeal through her own writings.) It is highly dubious—as various of the authors who follow argue—that such ideas make sense when applied to the Gulf. When it comes to Gulf cities' urban and economic development, edict from above is certainly more salient than organic complementarity growing out of the social ground.

Whatever the specifics, the urban Gulf induces, almost as analytic shock therapy, a search beyond the usual urban canons. We have to reach further, or at least differently. Made skeptical of universalistic explanations, we also have to avoid falling back on an outmoded historicism—"things happen"—or a reductionist physicalist gumbo of oil and sand. At the same time, we need to refuse any position asserting that Gulf cities are exceptional, incomparable, or eventually not even "real" cities at all. So, does a nonjudgmental study of Gulf cities make us agnostic of any grand urban theory? Maybe. Whatever "failing" attributed to the dominant paradigms—or alternatively to Gulf cities themselves—something very robust is most certainly happening within and among them. There is durability—literally of buildings and nonliterally of social structures—that are productive and that withstand impacts from the outside. Our job, in effect, is to advance understanding of how the urban whole—a new Arab urban, perhaps—could exist as it does in what might seem unlikely circumstances.

Gulf Cities as Methodological Challenge

Autocratic governance limits access to officials, statistical data, and fieldwork sites. Standard methods like survey, interview, or ethnography are typically not easy or possible at all. Even when data do exist, they might not be made available. A related part of the problem is lack of established traditions of professional, secular scholarship—again, in "our" Gulf, not the region as a whole.[26] As recently as 1957, we should recall, not only were there no universities in Abu Dhabi; there was not a single medical doctor.[27] Scholarship in the UAE locale has thus been especially dependent on outsiders, with all the risks of problematic access and potential for orientalist patronage—including among outside scholars from other parts of the Arab world. Reflecting the troubling state of affairs, one UAE notable put it this way: "For most of the last 200 years, the only existing documentation consists of records and correspondence among British and other colonialists. We are in a lamentable position. We must study the past from the perspective of foreigners, using their old documents and photographs in our research."[28] Those words are from the book *From Rags to Riches*, whose author was an intimate of the ruling sheikh (and holder of the national Mercedes franchise, among other important wealth resources). Substantively informative, it is sincerely hagiographic. Contemporary scholarship by locals needs to respect indigenous figures, especially the monarch.

Our contributors strive to overcome such constraints, emanating from either the past or present. Drawn from diverse parts of the world (including the Gulf and other parts of the Middle East), they are—despite not being native of the Gulf—anything but naïve about such matters. In terms of background disciplines, they come from architecture, sociology, politics, planning, geography, history, and anthropology. Most are experts on particular places in the region, but none of them is knowledgeable about all of it. The knowledge they do have has been formed, at least in part, through reading or close colleagueship with emerging indigenous scholars whose work now gains attention.[29] But given the limits on what is known or knowable, scholars must pick up clues where they can, inevitably shaped not only by their disciplinary base but also the cultures from which they come. Gulf cities need to be explained in terms of their complexities, and part of that complexity is represented by the limits of what has been said and not said.

In part, out of practical necessity but also because of its epistemological virtue, we draw especially on the physical urban apparatus as a strategic way in. We take the city's material instrumentation as a *laboratory* from which to trace larger lessons of politics, culture, and civic life—in this way, following in the tradition of the Chicago school of urban sociology of the mid-twentieth century. Unlike the Chicago setting with its famous plethora of statistical, cartographic, and ethnographic data, we

make do with less, but also with ambitious analytic goals. The buildings, from a research standpoint, have the virtue of being *there*, and in
a big way. Their sponsors avidly promote them. In contexts otherwise
not rich in information, authorities boast and the media report on the
structures and the ambitions of their designers, investors, developers,
and government sponsors. Details of underlying technologies, architectural processes, financing, and roles of specific agencies (and sometimes
even details concerning the suffering of those whose sweat went into
their making) emerge. This is especially true for the major buildings, the
stars of the show that, as opposed to the routine modern structures that
infill around them, get into the books and catch the media eye. Large or
small (but primarily large) buildings provide us, in effect, with *method*.
We deconstruct—reverse engineer—from the physical structures to
better understand the social, political, and cultural realms that gave rise
to them. Using buildings, as we do, is not the only way to proceed along
these lines and carries its own liabilities—risking, for example, un-
derattending to both direct opponents as well as to those not central to
creating the structures. Other researchers will hopefully join us to provide
a more complete picture.[30]

But in the meantime, here are a few preliminary examples of the analytic process. The fabulous buildings suggest high *average* per capita
income, although not necessarily high *median* income. Constructing
them and providing the continuous maintenance they require demands,
besides big money and governmental authority, a massive in-migration
workforce. There is great economic distance between those who might
own or invest in such buildings (high incomes for the average) and those
who build, sweep, and polish them and their contents (the far more numerous who pull down the median figure, if they get counted in official
records at all). Yes, there long has been a significant Arab middle class
of professionals and merchants, augmented by immigrants (over long periods of history) from Iran and the Indian subcontinent. But most no-
toriously there is the presence of those who do the heavy lifting and the
daily servicing. Because of social, political, and consumption differences
(and the status of some at the bottom as virtually untouchable), there is
a need for social sorting: Who will be doing what and where, and how
will they be housed and sustained, even if at barely livable levels? We
can look for the spatial relations that contain such a complex assemblage

and how the diverse elements cohere—through geographic segregation as one element. We can consider the kind of political conditions needed to sustain a stable social and political order under the circumstances. We are on our way to thinking through issues that might otherwise not rise to our attention. The "discovery" invites scholars otherwise attuned to modern Western models to ponder alternative modes of cohesion and varieties of what can appear rational.

An important source of intellectual opening comes, we think, with the notion of *assemblage*, a concept that arises implicitly or explicitly in a number of chapters that follow. (Lieto, in her chapter 5, offers a specific embrace; as do Sarah Moser in chapter 9, and Harvey Molotch and Davide Ponzini in the conclusion.) It derives from the theories of Bruno Latour—along with his colleagues in their school of actor network theory (ANT).[31] It allows at least a bracketing of "cause" to permit the work of looking at what is present and how diverse elements fit together. Applied to the urban bailiwick, assemblage bears resemblance to the older idea of agglomeration. Things happen through complementary linkups that form a historically durable force. This happens even when proponents have different motivations and types of projects. The factors that make up any particular assemblage are heterogeneous and, at least before the fact, significantly indeterminate. It is a modest way to theorize; it can't explain everything, but it tries to take many things—even diverse and apparently inconsistent ones—into account.

Actor network theory is especially useful in the present context because it invites us to see Gulf cities not as bizarre or ironic, but as emerging from their own specific set of actors, resources, and circumstance. Thinking into the future, and about other world regions (emerging cities in China and Africa), one can envision elaborations and departures—different yet again, but open to the same analytic approach. What might appear as a hodgepodge is not a defeat "for theory," but an invitation to find coherence in any given setting or historic episode. Human actors interact with one another and with physical objects (traffic lights, ports, turnstiles, seat belts) and nature as well.[32] Welcome to the city as a network of linkages within and without—busy beehives of projects amounting, in an ongoing way, to *something*.[33]

Whether or not their specifics are bellwethers for what next comes across the world—including what refracts back to change, for example,

London or New York—these are cities that matter in new ways. The assembling and local entangling of urban policy and knowledge in the Gulf clearly shows that such processes are complex and multidirectional. It is unsatisfactory to label them with naive nostrums like "religious," "feudal," "tribal," or "despotic." Nor can Gulf cities be understood as simple recipients of one more or less coherent form of development that is coming in (typically from the West) to transform the destination society. The Gulf is a place where today, as in the long past, the transnational occurs. Ideas and solutions get tested at the urban level through (re)assembling elements, elements with multiple origins. Some such imports, especially if successfully made part of the local assemblage, then move to another region but—as always—with a landing adapted to the new setting. In at least some respects, it is thus made different yet again. We observe transnationality with specific reference to contemporary Gulf urban policy, planning, and culture. But our approach models the transnational urban as a dynamic system, applicable to any system of places and always changing in content.

The Gulf as Transnational

Gulf settlements owe their historic origins to trade, travel, and migrations. Akin to how the Mediterranean shaped the European and North African worlds into a coherent entity, as famously depicted by Fernand Braudel,[34] so it is that the Gulf has not been a barrier, but a content maker—its own cauldron of linkups. These cities are, as articulated by Manuel Castells with respect to essentials of the modern urban, spaces of "flow."[35] Ideas, raw materials, and finished goods moved through towns, villages, and ports, yielding sediments of cultural content and human practice, upstream, downstream, and on all sides. In ways scarcely imaginable in thinking about Braudel's era of focus—centered on the sixteenth century—flows came to operate at a vast scale and volume. In the lead, on a world basis, are Gulf-region initiatives and practices—topics especially central to the chapters in the first section of this book.

The image of a transnational Gulf has long been obscured, of course, by the imposition of political boundaries and other institutional arrangements that give off—or indeed enforce—a misleading fixity.[36] In chapter 1, Alex Boodrookas and Arang Keshavarzian trace back into the prior eras of flows, connections, and commonalities. The authors engage in historical construction, as they urge others to do, in "Giving the Transnational a History: Gulf Cities across Time and Space." Along with contradicting the "time-honored" separation between sides of the Gulf and of the Gulf from the modern world, acknowledging historic fluidity also helps defeat the propensity to see Gulf peoples as trapped in backward and utterly parochial modes of life. They can less easily be seen as forever doomed by their exotic and conflictual primordial ways. A careful examination of the histories of Gulf cities can show, as these scholars do, how particular variants of the transnational have long been in place. Looking at the Gulf this way, we gain some vantage over what hybridity means on the ground, past and present. This Gulf (and its related waterways) constituted a sea of amalgamations, with specific regard to the economic, familial, and religious. The fixity of borders and hostilities—for example, Iran versus Saudi Arabia—is not "ancient" or essential but modern and artefact.

A real past of interconnections and comingling—and a continued presence of variation—is taken up in a very different way by the scholar-architect Amale Andraos in the book's second chapter, "Problematizing a Regional Context: Representation in Arab and Gulf Cities." Through the prism of design and architecture, Andraos calls into question oversimplified contemporary conversations about so-called Arab culture. All over the Middle East, there is verbal respect—even compulsion—for honoring "context," for deference to what has come before and what is left of it. But, as she goes to great lengths to show, context is not simple to determine, and the effort to do so is not at all necessarily innocent. Indeed, it can be quite problematic. What is or is not authentically "Arab" does not come so labeled as a package off the shelf. As we would expect from histories such as those laid out by Boodrookas and Keshavarzian, any current circumstance—and its context—will be heterogeneous in origin.

Using her native Beirut as the primary case of a larger phenomenon, Andraos describes what has been not just a multiplicity of regional impacts, but a collection of eager and crucial absorptions of modern influence from the West. Part of indigeneity has been, in other words, the enthusiastic uptake of the foreign. And, at least for some other cities of the region, this Western impact includes, notably and perhaps unexpectedly, the strong role played by architects and planners from the former Soviet bloc.[37]

Compared to the newly rising cities that strive in their various guises to be conspicuously "Arab," Beirut has long displayed challenging complexities. After the many layers of influence moving to and from Beirut, it becomes difficult to describe, much less proscribe, what is an "Arab" motif or an "Arab" building or an "Arab" material. Does the temporal era of the origin make it more or less Arab? (And if so, which date counts?) Does the national or religious identity of the architect or developer or their funding source determine the answer? How can the modern West be excised given its substantive role in forming what has long been present and (literally) built on? Andraos examines just how particular images, building configurations, and modes of representation might or might not meet the various tests of authenticity. She finds, as per usual, that patterns of Middle East social and physical development are in interaction with urban development elsewhere in the world, altering, in fact, what has been built locally, as well as interpretations made of it. For her part, she is ready and eager to celebrate new buildings in the Arab world that emanate, as they long have, from foreign architects and design influences. As in the past, it is the composing and combining that gives value.

The Beirut case points to dilemmas and problematic outcomes in some of the cities central to our inquiry, like Dubai, which earnestly tears down much of its urban fabric and then rebuilds with mighty spectacles, putatively "Arab." In taking things down or building some up, judgment, Andraos argues, too often does not come from serious inquiry but reflects nationalist ideology or exigencies of tourist appeal—buildings should *look* Arab. To think in terms of a regional past of mixed influences, including modernistic shaping from Europe, risks charges of apostasy. Behind her thinking lie the catastrophic impacts of essentialist perspectives—of declarations that something (or somebody) is or is not truly "Arab" or "Islam" or "colonial" or "Western" or, at the extreme, "infidel."

With the insertion of Middle-East motifs into their buildings, the designers of architectural spectacle are performing a new Gulf context, as Davide Ponzini describes in chapter 3, "Mobilities of Urban Spectacle: Plans, Projects, and Investments in the Gulf and Beyond." Whatever their inspirations or references to an Arab past, the major buildings of our Gulf cities (and the design skills behind them) are heavily sourced from the West. But—and this too repeats a historical phenomenon of the past—these Gulf city designs have their own "legs" that carry them out again to other parts of the world. Ponzini traces some of what is coming and going. With avid Gulf participation, a global elite of "starchitects" are setting the terms of contemporary urban form, often ebullient and, in the Gulf context, made capable of satisfying superlative claims. The tallest building in the world is Dubai's Burj Khalifa (Skidmore, Owings, and Merrill). Doha's spectacular Museum of Islamic Art is by the Chinese American architect I. M. Pei. London's Lord Norman Foster and Paris's Jean Nouvel are all over the spectacular place and come up repeatedly in our chapters. And again, we have fabulous Las Vegas as a precursor place that used superlatives to put itself on the map—albeit primarily the U.S. map.[38]

Whatever the national origins, these projects take form through Gulf-specific conditions and demonstrate that context matters in shaping the process and urban effects of any relevant project. Beyond a common striving—in one way or another, to be Arab-like or to respect some version of context—they also bespeak more concrete common traits: abundant financial resources, strong and monocratic political commitment, weak planning regulation, and great ambition. The "taste" for such structures, hence, follows not from some disembodied aesthetic preference, but from local interpretations of regional goals and, indeed, running global interpretations of them. Such transnational traits are augmented by the presence of skills with which to negotiate, broker, and manage the right linkages between patrons, clients, and professionals of various nationalities and specializations. Together, they bring complex and, at least potentially, inventive projects into being.

Through the speed of such projects' execution and their sponsors' willingness to take risks, the region functions as a "test bed" for projects that then can be picked up, sometimes by the same firms that did the initial versions and executed in other parts of the Middle East and beyond. Gulf-based real estate operators, as Ponzini traces them, have expanded their portfolios beyond the Middle East, to Europe, India, and North America. They also buy existing buildings or new ones being erected, especially those with iconic meaning. The Abu Dhabi Investment Council owns New York's Chrysler Building. Dubai has a dominant stake in the city's Plaza Hotel. Qatar Holding has a 95 percent share of the Shard in London—the tallest building in Europe—and the whole Porta Nuova development in Milan, which includes the tallest building in Italy. These architectural artifacts reflect a newly ambitious mode of financial deployments: not just for real estate, but investments of all sorts (a topic taken up in other chapters). In so doing, Gulf operatives change the world that changes them.

Assembling Hybrid Cities

Such various goals, projects, hybridities, interpretations, and executions have to be developed and implemented in real time in real places by particular people. At a professional level, there is a "crafting," in which particular forms of expertise intersect with an awareness of diverse cultural, political, and material specifics. Sheikhs do not do fenestration or air ducts. Three of our chapters take up how the places they rule nevertheless get built and how the results, including at times innovative solutions, spread to other places.

A scholar as well as a practitioner of architectural photography, Michele Nastasi, in chapter 4, "A Gulf of Images: Photography and the Circulation of Spectacular Architecture," describes how professional photography determines, in part, how the buildings come to be. They come, in a word, from carefully contrived *pictures*. A critical ingredient of design adoption and transfer is the capacity to represent—to show off a project in a way that will win approval, maybe even accolades. This helps build pride, capacity, and profit for its sponsors and induce replication or commissions from other backers, local or distant. Especially for projects like those in the Gulf that are distinctive and often incongruous with what has come before, representation becomes a key aspect. The prevalent tactic, argues Nastasi, is to present buildings as sculpture—in isolation from their physical and social contexts as well as the human beings who otherwise have at least visual connection with them. Conventions of Gulf architectural photography (and this is common in the world) foster monumentality. They do this in part by excluding proximate surroundings and especially the real human beings whose miscellaneous and unscripted stances and gatherings would otherwise distract. The typical result is to present freestanding structures, sometimes as monoliths, abstracted from the urban landscape.

To get across his point, Nastasi compares original and "follow-up" photographs of buildings in Abu Dhabi, Dubai, Doha, London, Paris, and New York, among other sites. He gives us some samples of the artfully "photogenic" commercial pictures that promote a spectacular-ized model. Typically, the sculptural form is enhanced by using an open sky, seductive lighting (often at dusk), and minimal interference from alterations, signage, or human-agent disturbance. To drive home his point, Nastasi also presents some of the building photographs he took not on commission, but for his own research. In such works, he leaves in some of the people and clutter of the real city, allowing them to im-pinge on the iconography. His shots, tellingly, are taken closer to eye level, approximating what an urban pedestrian (or even auto passenger) will more likely experience—a practice that replicates much of Denise Scott Brown's Las Vegas photographic method.[39] The overall result is to document—clearly evident in the Gulf—that architectural photography derives from the commercial (and political) purposes behind it and in ways that sustain selective notions of urban greatness. It is a professional accomplishment—one that takes its place as still another part of the con-temporary practice of urban assemblage.

From a still different vantage point of expert practice, architect-planner-scholar Laura Lieto lays out how professionals accomplish hybridity in interactions with clients. She draws on her work for a Saudi client to plan a new Jubail City Center (as well as on her general familiarity with Abu Dhabi's Masdar City project), describing in "Planning for the Hybrid Gulf City" (chapter 5) what happens. Lieto focuses, in particular, on what she has learned in the micro space of face-to-face interaction between clients and consultants—a type of encounter complicated by the coming together of a Saudi client and an Italian consultant.[40] Lieto hence lays out the trans-fer of ideas across a gap that is geographic, cultural, and gender-specific. The participants joined in bridging disjunctions and creating planning documents that, in effect, enabled them to span the divides. The client and the professionals had somewhat incongruent design wish lists. The client's affection for a traditional European piazza—*not* Lieto's idea—needed to be reconciled with the realities of the extreme heat and the gender segregation of the Saudi city. Far from being instances of mere copycat Western urbanism or rote implementation of "tradition" (Saudi or Italian), the proposals for the public space were carefully (and ardu-ously) worked out. In ways Lieto describes, the professionals make their way toward a deliverable version of the new city that is both an outside and an inside product, both sensible and not so sensible. Whatever the academic debates and definitional struggles, it was their job to do the transnational and it shows in the result.

Lieto plays a special role for two reasons. One is the client's taste for "European style," about which she is perceived as something of an authority, but also through her status as a woman doing work that is associated with men's roles. Her working group had to hold meetings in Dubai, more gender "liberal" than Saudi Arabia. We see still another way, in accommodating different notions of gender propriety as well as different views of urbanism, in which Middle-Eastern/Western hybridity can take form. In this case, the job breakdown is geographically distributed, like parsing out design to one city and production to another, with gender playing an evident role.

In chapter 6, "Planning from Within: NYU Abu Dhabi," we come to another case study of professional amalgamations, one that aligns with the New York University institutional home base of several authors in the volume. The late Hilary Ballon, a historian of urban architecture and planning, was herself directly involved in the design and construction (as well as academic functioning) of the university's Abu Dhabi campus. Ballon, as one of the key participant-administrators of the project, explains in firsthand authoritative language the process therein. Through her account, we witness the coming together of architectural practice with unusual climactic conditions and, of course, the particular social conditions of the region. The challenge was to establish a contemporary and ambitious university in a mixed Arab-U.S. milieu. The project was financed by the Abu Dhabi government, with the patronage of the country's crown prince, made possible by linkages and face-to-face assurances—carefully tended across multiple fronts, including at the highest levels of NYU administrators and trustees. The campus was built by the country's strong development arm, Mubadala, a company formed initially by the ruler and later expanded into a vast array of worldwide operations with assets valued at $122 billion.[41] Mubadala's chief executive was to become a member of the NYU Board of Trustees in New York. We can see Abu Dhabi reaching back into the cosmopolitan center, thereby increasing the NYU board's transnationality while also occasioning the UAE elite access to the important group of alumni, donors, and Wall Street figures who govern the university. Perhaps just as significant, the creation of NYU Abu Dhabi (NYUAD), along with the founding of NYU Shanghai, helped prompt an administrative reconfiguration of NYU overall as the "global network university."

Besides institutional hybridity, something that occurs at levels far lower than the NYU trustees, an effort was made with this project to enact a physical embodiment of Gulf-U.S. combining. A concrete example was the way the NYUAD campus designers, led by Uruguay-born, New York–based Rafael Viñoly, configured the campus to relate to the city of Abu Dhabi. Although NYUAD is a stand-alone campus (with clear and evident borders), it does not, as Ballon explains, "stand against" the city, present or future. It has ungated openings, a departure from some local design orientations that emphasize walled-in compounds. The designers strove to enhance pedestrian interaction, both within the university and with the now emerging development in the surrounding area. These qualities differentiate the campus not only from building patterns in Abu Dhabi, but also as found in other new universities and cultural centers recently built in the Gulf region. But it also has the Gulf in it, if in no other way than the amazingly rapid speed with which it went up—far faster than any project could at NYU in New York. In Ballon's chapter, we can look for clues as to how development and urban decision making occurs in the Gulf more generally.

Urban Test Beds for Export

In the Gulf, assemblage can happen faster than elsewhere. There is less blockage from planners, regulations, or workplace rules. Historic preservation seldom arises as a challenge; nor does the need for the meaningful mitigation of environmental impact. Gulf cities are investment-friendly. This means they can function as test beds where designs, structures, and technologies can fast-track into implementation. The resulting outcomes can then serve as precedent for replication, sometimes under Gulf sponsorship, sometimes under sponsorship of the foreign actors who participated in initiating the Gulf arrangements. Because of what is now happening in the Gulf, we can move beyond the orientation of seeing the West (or the North) as the source and learn how things happening in the Gulf move *out* of the Gulf.

The test bed phenomenon also means that the Gulf can teach, within the Gulf but also to those outside, about negative impacts. We can learn what happens when projects are misguided and how, at least potentially, future correctives can be made. In civic terms, we can also learn what happens when projects are executed without citizen surveillance or traditional market discipline.[42] Elites sometimes construct buildings that will remain mostly (or completely) empty, even causing bankruptcy for a participating investor or at least an embarrassing need to reschedule payments. The negatives are made less noticeable by the immense wealth liquidity that cushions mistakes. Buildings operating at severe cash-flow deficits can be maintained ("patient money" as it is sometimes termed) as development regimes move forward to their next projects, perhaps gaining knowledge or techniques through the failed precedent.[43] Even if dramatically inefficient in the short term, they can become functional at a broader transnational scale or over the longer haul. (Of course, efficiency can be found after the fact, offered up as an ex post rationalization.) Or, as with chain restaurant operators in the West who envision replication from the start, the ambition to reproduce is a built-in feature. This can change the calculus of what profit level the first implementation needs to provide. The same kind of logic can be used to explain—at least to investors—complexes built at a far larger scale, even as entire new cities.

In the three chapters that address this test bed urbanism, we see the potential for diverse outcomes. One case involves the creation of the vastly significant port of Dubai; another takes up the audacious high-tech compound of Masdar City in Abu Dhabi. A third case is the Saudi-based Cityquest, an effort to systematically discover the right formula for packaging up large-scale urban systems—whole cities of hundreds of thousands—with the potential for replication *de nouveau* elsewhere.

First, Mina Akhavan explains the test bed success of Dubai's ports in chapter 7, "Gateway: Revisiting Dubai as a Port City." Akhavan analyzes the evolution of that city from fishing village into transportation and logistics world hub. The Dubai port (actually several proximate facilities) has the largest manmade harbor in the world in its Jebel Ali installation. From the Dubai base, DP World—as the overall operating company is now known—encompasses a total of seventy-seven marine and inland terminals across the world. These are sometimes the largest ports in the countries of their location. As a global operator, DP World now is third in world ranking for container throughput.

Ancillary facilities, like warehousing and logistical services, are intrinsic for port functioning, making them an aspect of ports everywhere. But under the Dubai regimen, ports push inland to organize or reorganize urban territory at increasingly distant locations, utilizing rail, highway, and air facilities as means for intermodal logistics systems. The deliberate instituting of multimodality thus goes beyond the limited physical infrastructure of what is needed for shipping per se and includes free-trade zones and other governance arrangements. The innovations move beyond the Gulf, with hardware and software aligning and coordinating across global sites. DP World also represents a great success in fostering UAE diversification away from oil and gas.

Driven by a set of even more radical industrial and economic ambitions, Abu Dhabi moves forward with the "zero-carbon" Masdar City project, as described by author Gökçe Günel in chapter 8, "Exporting the Spaceship: The Connected Isolation of Masdar City." The project aims to create a climactically neutral mode of urbanization in a region otherwise so massively contributing to carbon-rich environmental disaster. With an investment estimated at $16 billion,[44] ambitions include breakthroughs in solar, pollution-free driverless vehicles, and self-sufficient cooling technologies. With the Massachusetts Institute of Technology as a research and training partner, success would yield hyperadvanced goods and services for export. Günel takes stock of the project's accomplishments and shortcomings or failures. The grand internal transit scheme ended with one origin point and one destination—the parking lot adjacent to the complex. Looking back, one can interpret the project as too much tied into a scenario of technical breakthrough—without attending to social, economic, or political transformations that might have, in Günel's opinion, made innovation more viable. This may be a general lesson coming out of Gulf technology ventures. Weakness on the social and political side hinders the chance for technology to be effectively implemented. (This theme, both concerning Masdar and as a more general note, also comes up in Lieto's discussions of hybridity in chapter 5.)

Although more oriented toward "soft" infrastructure rather than hard, the Cityquest KAEC Forum is also in the running as the most ambitious among current Gulf-region urban initiatives. The geographer Sarah

Moser reports on her experience at the hyperelite event, held yearly in Saudi Arabia, in chapter 9, "Two Days to Shape the Future." Cityquest takes lessons from development initiatives in the Gulf, combining them with others, to yield up optimum strategies for creating a new genre of city. Hosted by the King Abdullah Economic City (KAEC)—the first of Saudi Arabia's four new cities—the event was cosponsored by the Paris-based NGO New Cities Foundation. Moser offers a close-up examination of this new node in the circulation of urban strategies, supplanting what now appear to be almost antique forms of urban conferencing that otherwise exist. Amid an over-the-top luxury environment, the author was among the technologists, architects, planners, CEOs, politicians, and visionaries exchanging views on how to master plan new cities in the world. (It is worth noting that even more ambitious Saudi plans have since been put forward.)

Aligning with recent critical geographic scholarship, Moser strives to identify how, why, where, and with what consequence urban policies circulate globally—in this case, emanating from and taking at least initial form in the Gulf. In the eyes of Asian and African urban policy makers in particular, projects like King Abdullah Economic City (and others to be discussed in this volume) have become the touchstones in shaping world urbanism, inspiring with a mantle of utopian boldness—one that Moser tries to balance against questionable social and ecological consequences.

Audacity, Work-Arounds, and Spatial Segmentation

Actual and existing Gulf cities have settled into patterns that could not have been envisioned by autocracy or any version of technocratic planning. Before "disruption" became a fashionable term in Western policy circles, cities of the Gulf engaged in the practice—without using the term—to a high degree. Desert ecologies, trade relations, migration streams, and neighborhood residential patterns were arranged and rearranged through dictum, segregation, and abrupt transformation. On a continuous basis, parts that would appear inconsistent, even mutually contradictory, were made to cohere and, in ways made evident in this book's chapters, were made durable as cities. Challenges came and some are still present, but they have been, at least thus far, held in check. In part, but only in part, because of the long-term upward trend in world oil markets, regimes survived even risky maneuvers.

Gulf cities remain famous in their contradictions, the most often cited being the tension between cosmopolitan reach and fealty to some envisioned Arab or Islamic tradition. Evident in a number of chapters in this book is the solution of what we term the "work-around." They are makedo arrangements to bypass awkward or "rigid" legal, social, and cultural proscriptions. Both in daily life and in the history of peoples, we have to see such creative moves as normal and indeed necessary[45]—and a presence in societies of every kind. Here the work-around presses in, making itself evident in land use, law, and custom. It can carry into virtually all spheres, including the social-psychological, what one observer terms "an ideology of daily adjustments."[46]

In urban land use, one work-around mainstay is spatial separation. Whatever their etiology in other parts of the world, in the Gulf, the separations are frequently mandated—as when certain residential areas are set aside for citizens only or for particular groups of manual workers. The outcome represents a kind of "urbanism as a way of life" different from that empirically observed by past urban analysts. It is also distinct from the colonial or postcolonial cities of the Americas, Asia, or Africa. With their capacity to adapt and invent as they go, the Gulf regimes foster something new again in the urban world.

The veteran Gulf city researcher and professor of architecture Yasser Elsheshtawy gives us a view of the Dubai version. He concentrates on tracing how Dubai managed to roar back from overextension, severe debt, and world humiliation. Aptly titled "Real Estate Speculation and Transnational Development in Dubai," Elsheshtawy's chapter documents the way Dubai's massive infrastructural investments (spelled out in part by Akhavan in her chapter on Dubai's ports) facilitated the country's rebound from its 2008 financial crisis. This only furthered the national zeal for the spectacular and a leadership role in regional construction, transportation, tourism, and consumption. There has been a reemergence of megaprojects (in part through financial rescue by neighboring Abu Dhabi), a return to sale of real estate units in advance of construction, and bidding wars for condo and townhouse units seen only online. Developers have revived projects that had been halted earlier. All kinds of affluent people, including well-off expats or foreign buyers, have gotten in on the speculation. This has also furthered a burgeoning cross-ethnic expat community life.

A downside of the hectic tearing down and building back is, as Elsheshtawy laments, the continuous displacement of residents, destruction of "traditional" neighborhoods, and imposition of a fragmented urban form. It also means a loss of history, including modernist structures (albeit some very ordinary and nondescript), that bespeaks actual lives, tastes, and crafts of the past.[47] Dubai acts as a showcase for the downside of turning urban environments into mechanisms for generating rent. There is a cautionary note for governments that strive to emulate the Dubai model but with weaker resources for dealing with the negative economic and social aftermath. This too constitutes a learning from the Gulf.

Often overlooked in accounts of urban regime functioning, goods consumption plays an outsized role in shaping the urban Gulf—a topic taken up by the sociologist Harvey Molotch in "Consuming Abu Dhabi" (chapter 11). Those with ancestors living in what became the UAE before 1925 (as evidenced by lineages recorded in their "Family Book") are citizens with whom the largess is, by rights, to be shared. As a mainstay of the "contract" between the sheikhdom's inner circle and its other citizens comes the wherewithal for the massive purchase of goods, with houses and cars (both with air conditioning) at the core. Extreme urban sprawl derives in good part from these twin elements, made especially evident given the flat topography. Building and maintaining the consumption infrastructure requires extensive and ongoing labor, performed—in lieu of an indigenous working class—by foreigners. Absent democracy, high levels of consumption yield a specific substitute form of political and social stability among the beneficiaries.

Consumption also arguably includes, in ways that are historically distinct, the import of prestige cultural institutions like the Louvre, Sorbonne, and eventually the Guggenheim. They are part of the work-arounds that enable modernization, globalization, and permissive practices—among certain types of people in demarcated zones—toward sexuality, food, finance, alcohol, and artistic representation. Among the most important tools is separation into special geographic spaces, conceptually similar to free ports that exempt shippers and merchants from duties and other taxes. But these are places that permit exception for activities like Western-style education (allowing a high degree of academic freedom) as well as easy social mixing, particularly across genders. Tourist service zones also cater to special tastes and pleasures—providing, in effect, a kind of "morality zoning"[48] familiar enough in the West (e.g., as red-light districts). In the Gulf, a specific mode of spatiality similarly reflects the attempt to reconcile contradictory goals—further specified and elaborated by Steffen Hertog's chapter near the end of the book.

Hertog sees the Gulf monarchies as engaged in what he terms a "quest" in the title to his chapter 12, "A Quest for Significance: Gulf Oil Monarchies' International Strategies and their Urban Dimensions." The oil elites have been using their wealth to buy the accoutrements of "good citizenship" and apparent "progressiveness" on the world stage. Their very costly projects—undertaken through the heavy involvement of international partners—have an audience, regardless of where they are specifically located, that is almost exclusively international. There is evidently a desire to acquire international recognition independent of hydrocarbon plutocracy. The result is a proliferation of global-elite institutions and displays, serviced by specific infrastructures, both bureaucratic and physical, with the cumulative result, in governmental terms, that state apparatuses are highly segmented not just spatially but organizationally as well. Specific elite agencies run separately from the rest of the state bureaucracy. They sometimes operate their own—what they term—"cities" (actually more akin to districts in Western terminology[49]) or other types of enclaves operating independent of other physical and regulatory entities.

The underlying strategies are thus anchored in the monarchies' local political economy, rather than, for example, international civil society or substantive emulation of outside forms of governance. This is all in line with a general pattern of rent-financed state building that is both top-down and deeply fragmented. While the ideas and language informing these regimes' international strategies are often borrowed from the West, their roots are very specific—as Hertog articulates—to the Gulf situation.

The intersection of the specifics of the urban local and the patterns of the general has been one of our major themes and one we will take up again in the concluding chapter of the book. As stressed by Hertog, the segmented patterns in Gulf cities are closely grounded in arrangements of land development and spatial form (as some of our other authors also make clear). Urban studies—whether critical or celebratory—tend to assume, at least in classic formulations, something like democratic capitalism, which then enables so much study of cities to remain Western-based, even when in a critical vein. Exceptions have, of course, been noted and even made the basis of "special" studies ("area studies" in a prior time). But the Western intellectual pattern is to presume a background familiar in the experience of Europe and North America.

Such patterns and their intellectual depictions, as we have already argued and as our authors will further elaborate, are greatly challenged by dynamics in the Gulf. Gulf city arrangements, something like them, or something else again—as in China or Asia[50]—are in increasing contemporary evidence. They have always been around in some variant, providing anomalies indeed to our West-based paradigms that, however awkwardly, reach for generalizability. But modes of inclusion and exclusion—distinctive assemblages of peoples, capital, and spatial arrangements—however "arbitrary" to contemporary Western sensibilities, need to be taken on board as their own kind of normal, maybe even of the ordinary. Where there are "issues," there are work-arounds that have at least the potential to manage them. As Gulf cities further evolve with their own sets of mix, they make spectacle, inequality, and authoritarianism all the more available for emulation, export, and disquiet.

NOTES

1   Venturi, Scott Brown, and Izenour 1972.
2   Venturi, Scott Brown, and Izenour 1972, xvii. It came to our most recent attention through Stierli 2013, 35 and 36.
3   Edward Said's *Orientalism* and the sagacious essay by Janet Abu-Lughod 1987.
4   Some indeed thought of Las Vegas as "the prototype of the American city of the future." See Stierli 2013, 90, citing Fielden 1970, 64.
5   For a first example, see Fuccaro 2001.
6   Fuccaro 2009.
7   Bill 1996, 106, as cited in Keshavarzian and Hazbun 2010, 270.
8   Fuccaro 2009, 191.
9   Berry and Pred 1961.
10 Alonso 1964.
11 Keshavarzian and Hazbun 2010, 208.

12 For a strong and strongly informed effort, see Kanna 2011. For further critique, see Farías and Bender 2010.

13 See Sato 2009 for details on the British exit.

14 Mahdavy 1970. This discussion benefits from Hanieh 2011, 10.

15 Logan and Molotch 1987.

16 Ponzini 2011.

17 Farah al-Nakib brought this point to our attention. We thank her for this and other valuable comments.

18 Hannerz 1990 and 1996.

19 For an edifying view of young Muslim peer group life in Los Angeles, see O'Brien 2017.

20 Mottahedh and Fandy 1997, 298.

21 Vogel 1997, 263.

22 Woolfhart 2016, 251.

23 Vogel 1997, 263–264.

24 See, for example, Putnam 1994; Piore and Sabel 1984; Saxenian 1996.

25 Jacobs 1969.

26 Kolo (2016, 164) remarks on the common characterization of the Gulf region as having a "limited indigenous capacity in virtually all professions."

27 Al-Fahim 1998.

28 Al-Fahim 1998. This passage is also quoted in Thompson 2016, 211.

29 See, in particular and highly relevant to the intent of this volume, Fuccaro 2009.

30 Alternative strategies, like "bottom up" research, are especially useful, in part to avoid reifying the "tangible effects of empire." See Elsheshtawy 2010; Hourani and Kanna 2014, 603; Kanna 2014; Menoret 2014; Al-Nakib 2014 and 2016; Beaugrand 2014.

31 For example, Michel Callon, John Law, Leigh Star, and Geoffrey Bowker.

32 Molotch 2011.

33 For prior examples of ANT in explaining urban outcomes, see Beauregard 2015; Lieto and Beauregard 2015; Farías and Bender 2010.

34 Braudel 1996.

35 Castells 1996.

36 See, for example, Thiollet and Vignal 2016.

37 See, for example, Stanek 2015.

38 Beauregard 2003.

39 See Venturi, Scott Brown, and Izenour 1972 and Stierli 2013 (especially 109–114). As Stierli observes, this is an intensely considered "deadpan," something Scott Brown took from the Los Angeles artist Ed Ruscha. See Stierli 2013, 137.

40 In attending to the significance of sustained interpersonal relations between agents coming from the West with agents "on the ground" in places like Saudi Arabia, Lieto reinforces the emphasis on "political and sociological complexity" involved in the conjoining. See also Peck and Theodore 2012, 23, as discussed in Khirfan and Jaffer 2014.

41 According to the Mubadala website: "Who We Are," www.mubadala.com (accessed September 4, 2017).

42 Lindblom 1965.

43 Again, we can caution against simplistic characterization: monied interests in other parts of the world also may tolerate empty buildings or even build into unfavorable markets when they think markets will eventually rebound. Almost drawing from the Gulf playbook, many owners of downtown U.S. real estate would rather maintain empty storefronts than sign long-term leases at lower rent levels; Bagli 2017.

44 Carlisle 2010.

45 See, for example, Garfinkel 1967; Zimmerman 1970.

46 Brorman Jensen 2014, 49.

47 Elsheshtawy 2008; 2016. See Menoret 2014.

48 Fuccaro 2009, 231.

49 The names given to these "cities"—for example, Economic City, Education City, Internet City—do not necessarily describe what goes on within them. Dubai's Internet City, for example, is the location of many non-Internet companies. See Keshavarzian 2010, 274. An extensive discussion of the issue can be found in Easterling 2014.

50 Roy and Ong 2011.

REFERENCES

Abu-Lughod, Janet L. 1987. "The Islamic City—Historic Myth, Islamic Essence, and Contemporary Relevance." *International Journal of Middle East Studies* 19, no. 2: 155–176.

Al Fahim, Mohammed A. J. 1998. *From Rags to Riches: A Story of Abu Dhabi*. Abu Dhabi: Makarem.

Al-Nakib, Farah. 2014. "Towards an Urban Alternative for Kuwait: Protests and Public Participation." *Built Environment* 40, no. 1: 101–117.

Al-Nakib, Farah. 2016. *Kuwait Transformed: A History of Oil and Urban Life*. Stanford, CA: Stanford University Press.

Alonso, William. 1964. *Location and Land Use: Toward a General Theory of Land Rent*. Cambridge, MA: Harvard University Press.

Bagli, Charles V. 2017. "In a Thriving City, SoHo's Soaring Rents Keep Storefronts Empty." *New York Times*, August 23, 2017. www.nytimes.com.

Beaugrand, Claire. 2014. "Urban Margins in Kuwait and Bahrain: Decay, Dispossession and Politicization." *City* 18, no. 6: 735–745.

Beauregard, Robert A. 2003. "City of Superlatives." *City and Community* 2: 183–199.

Beauregard, Robert A. 2015. *Planning Matter: Acting with Things*. Chicago: University of Chicago Press.

Berry, Brian J. L., and Allen Pred. 1965. *Central Place Studies: A Bibliography of Theory and Applications*. Philadelphia: Regional Science Research Institute.

Bill, James A. 1996. "The Geometry of Instability in the Gulf: The Rectangle of Tension." In *Iran and the Gulf: A Search for Stability*, ed. Jamal S. al-Suwaidi, 99–117. Dubai: The Emirates Center for Strategic Studies in Research.

Braudel, Fernand. 1995 (1949 French edition). *The Mediterranean and the Mediterranean World in the Age of Philip II*. Berkeley: University of California Press.

Brorman Jensen, Boris. 2014. "Masdar City: A Critical Retrospection" In *Under Construction: Logics of Urbanism in the Gulf Region*, ed. Steffen Wippel, Katrin Bromber, and Birgit Krawietz, 45–54. Aldershot, UK: Ashgate.

Carlisle, Tamsin. 2010. "Masdar City Clips Another $2.5bn from Price Tag." *National*, December 1, 2010. www.thenational.ae.

Castells, Manuel. 1996. *The Rise of the Network Society: The Information Age: Economy, Society, and Culture*, vol. 1. London: John Wiley & Sons.

Easterling, Keller. 2014. *Extrastatecraft: The Power of Infrastructure Space*. New York: Verso Books.

Elsheshtawy, Yasser. 2008. "Transitory Sites: Mapping Dubai's 'Forgotten' Urban Spaces." *International Journal of Urban and Regional Research* 32, no. 4: 968–988.

Elsheshtawy, Yasser. 2010. *Dubai: Behind an Urban Spectacle*. New York: Routledge.

Elsheshtawy, Yasser, ed. 2016. *Transformations of the Emirati National House*. Abu Dhabi: Catalogue of the UAE National Pavilion of the 15th International Architecture Biennale of Venice.

Farías, Ignacio, and Thomas Bender, eds. 2010. *Urban Assemblages: How Actor-Network Theory Changes Urban Studies*. New York: Routledge.

Fielden, Robert. 1970. "In Defense of the Strip." *AIA Journal* 54, no. 6: 64.

Fuccaro, Nelida. 2001. "Visions of the City: Urban Studies on the Gulf." *Review of Middle East Studies* 35, no. 2: 175–187.

Fuccaro, Nelida. 2009. *Histories of City and State in the Persian Gulf: Manama since 1800*. Cambridge: Cambridge University Press.

Garfinkel, Harold. 1967. *Studies in Ethnomethodology*. Englewood Cliffs, NJ: Polity Press.

Hannerz, Ulf. 1990. "Cosmopolitans and Locals in World Culture." *Theory, Culture, and Society* 7, no. 2: 237–251.

Hannerz, Ulf. 1996. *Transnational Connections: Culture, People, Places*. New York: Taylor & Francis.

Heinrichs, Woolfhart P. 2016. "On the Figurative (Majaz) in Muslim Interpretation and Legal Hermeneutics." In *Interpreting Scriptures in Judaism, Christianity and Islam: Overlapping Inquiries*, ed. Mordechai Z. Cohen and Adele Berlin, 249–265. Cambridge: Cambridge University Press.

Hourani, Najib B., and Ahmed Kanna. 2014. "Arab Cities in the Neoliberal Moment." *Journal of Urban Affairs* 36, no. 2: 600–604.

Jacobs, Jane. 1969. *The Economy of Cities*. New York: Vintage Books.

Kanna, Ahmed. 2011. *Dubai: The City as Corporation*. Minneapolis: University of Minnesota Press.

Kanna, Ahmed. 2014. "'A Group of Like-Minded Lads in Heaven': Everydayness and the Production of Dubai Space." *Journal of Urban Affairs* 36, no. 2: 605–620.

Keshavarzian, Arang. 2010. "Geopolitics and the Genealogy of Free Trade Zones in the Persian Gulf." *Geopolitics* 16, no. 2: 263–289.

Keshavarzian, Arang, and Waleed Hazbun. 2010. "Re-Mapping Transnational Connections in the Middle East." *Geopolitics* 15, no. 2: 203–209.

Khirfan, Luna, and Zahra Jaffer. 2014. "Sustainable Urbanism in Abu Dhabi: Transferring the Vancouver Model." *Journal of Urban Affairs* 36, no. 3: 482–502.

Kolo, Jerry. 2016. "Accidental or Envisioned Cities: A Comparative Analysis of Abu Dhabi and Dubai." In *Gulf Cities as Interfaces*, ed. George Katodrytis and Sharmeen Syed, 161–180. Cambridge: Gulf Research Center.

Lieto, Laura, and Robert A. Beauregard, eds. 2015. *Planning for a Material World*. London: Routledge.

Logan, John, and Harvey Molotch, 1987. *Urban Fortunes: Toward a Political Economy of Place*. Berkeley: University of California Press.

Lindblom, Charles Edward. 1965. *The Intelligence of Democracy: Decision Making through Mutual Adjustment*. New York: Free Press.

Mahdavy, Hossein. 1970. "The Pattern and Problems of Economic Development in Rentier States: The Case of Iran." In *Studies in the Economic History of Middle East*, ed. M. A. Cook, 428–467. Oxford: Oxford University Press.

Menoret, Pascal, ed. 2014. *The Abu Dhabi Guide: Modern Architecture, 1968–1992*. Abu Dhabi: NYUAD/Find.

Menoret, Pascal. 2014. *Joyriding in Riyadh: Oil, Urbanism, and Road Revolt*. Cambridge: Cambridge University Press.

Molotch, Harvey. 2011. "Objects and the City." In *The New Blackwell Companion to the City*, ed. Gary Bridge and Sophie Watson, 66–78. London: Blackwell-Wiley.

Mottahedh, Roy P., and Mamoun Fandy. 1997. "The Islamic Movement." In *The Persian Gulf at the Millennium: Essays in Politics, Economy, Security and Religion*, ed. Gary G. Sick and Lawrence G. Potter, 297–318. New York: Palgrave.

O'Brien, John. 2017. *Keeping It Halal: The Everyday Lives of Muslim American Teenage Boys*. Princeton, NJ: Princeton University Press.

Palermo, Pier Carlo, and Davide Ponzini. 2015. *Place-Making and Urban Development: New Challenges for Contemporary Planning and Design*. London: Routledge.

Peck, Jamie, and Nik Theodore. 2012. "Follow the Policy: A Distended Case Approach." *Environment and Planning A: Economy and Space* 44, no. 1: 21–30.

Piore, Michael, and Charles Sabel. 1984. *The Second Industrial Revolution*. New York: Basic Books.

Ponzini, Davide. 2011. "Large Scale Development Projects and Star Architecture in the Absence of Democratic Politics: The Case of Abu Dhabi, UAE." *Cities* 28, no. 3: 251–259.

Putnam, Robert D. 1994. *Making Democracy Work: Civic Traditions in Modern Italy*. With Robert Leonardi and Raffaella Y. Nanetti. Princeton, NJ: Princeton University Press.

Roy, Ananya, and Aihwa Ong, eds. 2011. *Worlding Cities. Asian Experiments and the Art of Being Global. Chichester: Blackwell.*

Said, Edward. 1978. *Orientalism: Western Representations of the Orient.* New York: Pantheon.

Saxenian, Anna. 1996. *Regional Advantage: Culture and Competition in Silicon Valley and Route 128.* Cambridge, MA: Harvard University Press.

Stanek, Lukasz. 2015. "Mobilities of Architecture in the Cold War: From Socialist Poland to Kuwait and Back." *International Journal of Islamic Architecture* 4, no. 2: 365–398.

Stierli, Martino. 2013. *Las Vegas in the Rearview Mirror: The City in Theory, Photography and Film.* Los Angeles: Getty Research Institute.

Thiollet, Hélène, and Leïla Vignal. 2016. "Transnationalising the Arabian Peninsula: Local, Regional and Global Dynamics." *Arabian Humanities* 7: n.p. doi:10.4000/cy.3145.

Thompson, Seth. 2016. "Digitally Preserving the Heritage of the Arabian Peninsula: Al Jazeera Al Hamra Considered." In *Gulf Cities as Interfaces*, ed. George Katodrytis and Sharmeen Syed, 211–228. Cambridge: Gulf Research Center.

Venturi, Robert, Denise Scott Brown, and Steven Izenour. 1972. *Learning from Las Vegas.* Cambridge, MA: MIT Press.

Vignal, Leïla, ed. 2016. *The Transnational Middle East: People, Places, Borders.* London: Routledge.

Vogel, Frank E. 1997. "Islamic Governance in the Gulf: A Framework for Analysis, Comparison, and Prediction." In *The Persian Gulf at the Millennium: Essays in Politics, Economy, Security and Religion*, ed. Gary G. Sick and Lawrence G. Potter, 249–296. New York: Palgrave.

Wippel, Steffen. 2016. *Salalah: The Economic Development and Social Fragmentation of a Globalized Port City in Southern Oman.* Cambridge: Gulf Research Center.

Zimmerman, Don H. 1970. "The Practicalities of Rule Use." In *Understanding Everyday Life*, ed. Jack D. Douglas, 221–238. Chicago: Aldine.

SECTION I

The Gulf as Transnational

1

Giving the Transnational a History

Gulf Cities across Time and Space

ALEX BOODROOKAS AND ARANG KESHAVARZIAN

In the familiar trope, Gulf cities are flashy boomtowns of hype and sand. Somehow less organic or more absurd than their counterparts elsewhere, they are often described as either lodestars or nightmares of urban modernity and capitalist development. Prominent historian of the Gulf Nelida Fuccaro has critiqued such narratives as examples of "Gulf exceptionalism."[1] Ubiquitous in both popular and scholarly discourses, exceptionalist narratives elide the role of Gulf cities as lived urban spaces while sidelining their historical significance. They have also contributed to a tendency critiqued by Ahmed Kanna in the opening to his seminal work on Dubai: "Today it still seems acceptable to represent the Arab Gulf, in ways no longer so acceptable in the case of other postcolonies, ahistorically and apolitically, as a region somehow exempt from the structural constraints of empire and capital."[2]

Even as Kanna wrote those words, however, a wave of innovative and critical scholarship on social history, political economy, and, in particular, urban space was challenging this paradigm. This chapter traces the ways in which this emergent literature has been generative for new directions in research, reconfiguring popular conceptions of Gulf cities. Scholarship on urbanism in the Gulf is a useful corrective to portrayals that misconstrue and dehistoricize these urban spaces, which are too often framed unproblematically as "cities of the future." While commentators describe Gulf cities as the "brand new" cultural centers "filling in the leadership vacuum" left by the stagnant capitals of Cairo, Beirut, and Damascus, Gulf cities have, in fact, been central to global capitalism, urban planning, and architecture since at least the middle of the last century. And, contrary to the oft-repeated story of skyscrapers emerging out of empty desert, their form is the result of a historical trajectory that long predates the hydrocarbon age.[3]

Narratives about the exceptionalism of Gulf cities have been particularly alluring to journalists and architectural practitioners working in and on the region. Rem Koolhaas and his colleagues—including those at AMO, his research and branding unit—have been at the forefront of somewhat hysterical accounts of Gulf cities as a frontier for urban possibility. Critics have also represented Gulf cities as extreme neoliberal dystopias or cases of globalization run amok. In a typically hyperbolic piece, for example, Mike Davis dismisses Dubai as a "hallucinatory pastiche of the big, the bad and the ugly" that has become "a new Mecca of conspicuous consumption and economic crime."[4]

Flattening representations of Gulf cities have persisted with remarkable tenacity, in large part due to their value to Gulf regimes. Often with singular and instrumental purpose, royal families have sought to reify a binary between heritage and modernity, positioning themselves as guardians of the former and vanguards of the latter. They construct narratives of the past that stress Bedouin austerity or Arab tribal solidarity, framing their dynastic rule as the "authentic" mode of governance for their traditional, patrimonial society.[5] In so doing, they sideline the history of trade and migration that has long connected the Persian Gulf to the port cities of the Indian Ocean and the caravan routes of Asia.[6] They also elide the crucial role of British imperialism in concentrating previously fluid sovereignty into unitary sheikhly authority.[7] Long ruling as firsts among equals and dependent on the capital of powerful and mobile merchant families, most ruling dynasties wrested total control of sovereignty only through their role as British intermediaries. Thus, the concept of heritage, bereft of historical contingency and laden with connotations of timeless primordialism, both silences the diversity that has long characterized Gulf cities and naturalizes ethnocratic monarchy.

Gulf states have mobilized an array of resources to buttress their preferred visions of the past. Heritage tourism often orients visitors toward the desert and away from the sea. A visitor navigating the standard orientalist array of falcons, camels, wind towers, and Bedouins is unlikely to suspect that long-distance trade long provided essential staples of everyday life for the region's inhabitants. When the maritime past does emerge, a diverse and fluid history of pearl divers, merchants, and date growers is boiled down to picturesque sailboats, "Arab" dhows, and their pioneering crews that supposedly signify precursors to a contemporary entrepreneurial spirit. The many Persian speakers, enslaved people, non-Muslim communities, and influential merchants and moneylenders from the Indian subcontinent who played a crucial role in the region's history are subject to erasure. As the work of Neha Vora makes clear, "foreigners" are presumed to be a necessary evil that emerged from the oil boom, rather than an integral part of the history of the port cities of the Gulf from their inception.[8] Adorning everything from malls to postage stamps, desert tropes are as ubiquitous as they are obfuscating.

If heritage is a reservoir of static images in need of protection, modernity is simultaneously a threat and an opportunity that must be tamed by a visionary patriarch. With modernity and tradition positioned as simultaneous and antagonistic, the ruler becomes the arbiter uniquely capable of harnessing both. Some of the most effective conduits of this narrative are hired "urbanists," in Ahmed Kanna's terminology. These high-flying architects, planners, and consultants lend their names to the battery of prestige projects that have transformed the Gulf into a hub for cutting-edge design. Architecture has become a pillar of branding campaigns that are often described as means of attracting foreign expertise, tourists, and businesses but simultaneously serve the purpose of framing ruling families as farsighted, modernizing technocrats, depoliticizing and naturalizing their rule.

Recent works on Gulf cities can be grouped into three broad categories. While these are by no means mutually exclusive and do not do justice to the complexity of the works they describe, they provide a broad outline to the field. The first to have appeared is the literature on oil states. Largely the provenance of economists and political scientists, these works have used rentier state theory to examine how oil wealth enables state elites to forge broad coalitions with social forces and deflect dissent through the strategic redistribution of resources to its citizenry.[9] The second is a group of rich ethnographic works that highlight the multifaceted modes of identification and belonging that crisscross the Gulf and Indian Ocean littoral, complicating the commonplace binaries of resident and nonresident, migrant and citizen.[10] The third, largely the province of urban historians, is a dynamic and growing literature on Gulf cities. By creatively drawing on the archives of architecture and consulting firms, these historians use the built environment as a lens for investigating the intertwined and interrelated processes of urbanization, political control, and conceptions of self.[11]

These different strands of scholarship on the Persian Gulf and Arabian Peninsula illustrate the historical and translocal processes that manufactured these cities as "global" objects. Contrary to top-down narratives that stress the visionary role of rulers and starchitects, urban space in the Gulf has long been defined by logics of capitalism, shifting legal regimes, and everyday struggles in which non-elites negotiated structural inequities to emerge as crucial actors. Gulf cities have been a means to selectively distribute oil wealth and forge lasting categories of differentiation. They have shaped personal identities and legal categories, and challenges even the most seemingly rigid binaries between citizen and noncitizen, resident and migrant, nomadic and urban. As in other historical moments and places, buildings and infrastructure became crucial locations for the fixing of surplus capital.[12] Finally, and most importantly, studies of urban space have served as a means for de-exceptionalizing Gulf cities, which are too often framed as illogical, ephemeral, or unreal. Instead, even the most spectacular spaces in Gulf cities can be seen to reflect global patterns, be they flows of capital or sovereign power, manifesting themselves in particular local and historical circumstances.

Urban Fragmentation across the *Longue Durée*

Far from emerging on a tabula rasa, contemporary urban forms in the region have been built on—and informed by—intertwined legacies of imperial rule and extractive capitalism. Drawing on the technologies of architecture and city planning, a new cadre of urban experts etched colonial hierarchies deep into the structure of Gulf cities, as British officials and transnational corporations used urban space to divide, control, and mobilize populations. In turn, these populations pushed back, challenging or appropriating spaces in new and unexpected ways. Group formation and individual identification thus shaped and were shaped by the very fabric of urban space in the Gulf.

The link between political power, extractive capitalism, and urban differentiation long predates the oil age. The Gulf has been an entrepôt for centuries, its residents reliant on trade, brought by the annual monsoon winds, for basic necessities of daily life.[13] Port cities emerged around the mainstays of the Gulf economy until the early twentieth century—pearls, dates, and slaves—creating a wealthy class of mobile merchants.[14] Cross-class, communal, and vertical solidarities were crucial, even as they enforced a multitude of hierarchies and exclusions. Writing in the middle of the twentieth century, the anthropologist Peter Lienhardt recorded nostalgic tales of the pre-oil merchants, who would care for their pearl divers in the off-season and pay off the debts of compatriots who faced unexpected setbacks.[15] If political conditions turned unfavorable, merchants reserved the right to move elsewhere, limiting the ability of political authorities to collect taxes or build strong states.[16] Contemporary distinctions between the "Arab" and "Persian" sides of the Gulf would have made little sense to these multilingual merchants, many of whom strategically scattered family members across the Gulf littoral and Indian Ocean world.[17] Cosmopolitan "golden age" narratives remain ubiquitous, even if they tend to gloss over the often vicious inequalities that underpinned the region's port economy.

This picture of the Gulf was not timeless, however. In her groundbreaking work on Bahrain, Nelida Fuccaro notes that "family traditions portray the second half of the nineteenth century as a major rupture in the history of Manama," as emerging global markets and changing fashions in Europe and the United States triggered unprecedented demand for pearls and dates.[18] Fuccaro traces how the ruling family leveraged its position as an imperial intermediary to consolidate its control over urban marketplaces and pearl banks and, in so doing, positioned itself as the arbiter of the island's economy. British officials formalized the tribal division of pearl banks, thus establishing offshore property rights and sovereign control of natural resources.[19] Likewise, land emerged as a central generator of value. By ruthlessly enforcing the payment of shopkeeper fees, the family guaranteed a steady stream of revenue, while the property market of Manama turned into a hub of speculation that foreshadowed the transformations of the oil years. Established urban centers, though diverse, were also divided. Fuccaro describes turn-of-the-century Manama as "the archetype of a segmentary urban system," with local institutions divided by class, religion, or place of birth.[20] In many ways, the segmented, boom-and-bust "oil cities" of the Gulf are not, in fact, the work of oil.

As pearling (which collapsed in the 1930s) gave way to hydrocarbon extraction during the early twentieth century, new urban spaces emerged to enable the subsequent accumulation of wealth. These were exemplified by the segregated enclaves designed and built by oil companies, most notably Abadan, Ahmadi, and Awali, in present-day Iran, Kuwait, and Bahrain, respectively. Taking the form of the "colonial city" or the "garden city," they represented the cutting edge of imperial urban modernity. Abadan provides a useful example. Like Ahmadi (its counterpart in Kuwait), Abadan was designed by James Wilson, who, after serving as the assistant to Sir Edwin Lutyens during the planning of colonial New Delhi during World War I, founded the Iraqi Public Works Department and served as its first director from 1920 to 1926.[21] Wilson helped transport the urban forms of the Raj into the Gulf, replicating and updating their symbolic hierarchies in a new context. While "senior" employees—almost exclusively white—enjoyed the amenities of lush suburbs and bungalows, other workers were housed in a parallel form: the labor camp. Some labor camps were unplanned, emerging as shantytowns for workers who were coming to be seen as both foreign and temporary; indeed, the towns' very ramshackle informality reinforced perceptions of their occupants as transient interlopers.[22] Corporations sought to cut costs by framing workers as part of a temporary "construction phase" that would soon be over, and that therefore the construction of durable housing was unnecessary and wasteful.[23] As non-white employees were often forbidden from living with their families, the labor camp became a location where narratives of race and gender crosshatched and reinforced each other. Non-elite workers were, and sometimes still are, described as "bachelors," a term that legitimizes their segregation from middle- and upper-class family suburbs while reinforcing masculinist conceptions of labor. Urban space was thus mobilized by transnational corporations in attempts to segregate noncitizen workers in isolated enclaves from the early years of the twentieth century.[24]

Projects like Ahmadi and Abadan were simultaneously colonial cities and "company towns," designed to address the specific concern of managing large numbers of workers in an isolated region. With roots in corporate paternalism, Fordism, and colonial hierarchy, they provided housing, education, recreation, and transport facilities for their employees.[25] They were often strategically isolated from preexisting urban areas, which were themselves often labeled "native towns." Most importantly, these services and spaces were deeply unequal. Blending imperial strategies of governing through difference and corporate techniques of dividing workers, the amenities and spaces of company towns reflected a strict racial and economic hierarchy.[26] In Abadan, "native" labor communities, consisting of an Iranian and South Asian workforce, were located on the alternate side of the mammoth refinery and originally in tents and self-built huts. In Ahmadi, meanwhile, urban space "replicated the company's policy of ethnic segregation" down to the minutest details.[27] Visiting Ahmadi in the 1950s, the anthropologist Peter Lienhardt noted that even "the domestic furniture provided for each family correspond[s] to the householder's grade of employment in the company. Any wife invited out for a cup of coffee would be reminded by the furniture how much higher or lower than . . . her hostess's husband rated."[28] Backed by public relations campaigns, gendered civilizing missions, and the rhetoric of corporate paternalism, oil companies embraced the role of urban space as a mechanism of division and differentiation.[29]

As these examples make clear, colonial cities and company towns were not mutually exclusive; indeed, the forms influenced each other, evolving simultaneously across metropole and colony. This corporate and imperial production of space was instrumentally linked to the production of particular subjects. Nelida Fuccaro has written extensively on oil company public relations in Bahrain, where technologies of film and advertising were mobilized to shape "new urban and suburban lifestyles."[30] Positioning itself as a vanguard of modernization, the company "construed and popularized two contrasting profiles: that of the expatriate housewife of suburban Awali as shopper and the urbanite oil worker as the accomplished company employee."[31] Similar campaigns are a reminder that urbanists often directed their energies squarely at women, or explicitly sought to enforce normative gender roles. The suburban single-family dwelling is, of course, itself a symbol of—and an invitation to—particular kinship structures and gendered divisions of labor.

Such projects were also intimately linked to processes of class formation. Mark Crinson, for instance, frames Wilson's urban plan in Abadan as a mechanism for the production and control of an industrial proletariat.[32] A similar desire for proletarianization drove the creation of the Arab Village near Ahmadi in Kuwait.[33] To control ethnically segmented towns, police forces drew on and enforced group differences by deploying minority populations to man security forces and preserve a sense of enclosure.[34] Sometimes, spatial layouts reproduced divisions that are often thought to be far older. Farah al-Nakib has traced how state housing policies reified a divide between Kuwaitis who were formerly considered "nomadic" or "settled," long after the country was entirely urbanized. She argues that the process resulted in the political inclusion but social marginalization of Bedouin Kuwaitis, who were instrumentally retribalized in order to create a political base of support for the regime.[35] Thus, by isolating nuclear families in suburbs of single-family dwellings, physically and morally separating spaces of work and leisure, and reifying categories of identification through careful zoning, states and corporations sought to shape not just urban space, but the individuals that lived in it.[36]

These hierarchical visions did not go unchallenged. Indeed, from the 1920s to the 1970s, successive waves of protest swept across the region, explicitly confronting the exclusivist paradigms that were shaping urban growth. As John Chalcraft notes, noncitizen residents were crucial actors in this process, often forging coalitions that crossed boundaries of language, citizenship, and place of birth.[37] In his work on Saudi Arabia, Robert Vitalis traces how Aramco replicated the Jim Crow segregation of copper mines in the American Southwest in the oil towns of Saudi Arabia's Eastern Province. Its racially segregated wage structures and housing policies were only changed due to the collective resistance of outraged Saudi and Italian workers in the late 1940s and 1950s, who appropriated the American suburb as a new symbol of Saudi modernity.[38] In Abadan, labor protests in the 1920s led the Anglo-Iranian Oil Company's management to view "the bazaar" and "town" as threatening and unruly, and forced the commissioning of a new housing plan for the emergent local working class.[39]

As struggles over urban space bled over into questions of oil nationalization and anti-imperialism, Gulf cities became fields on which wider questions of equality were contested. Ironically, strict regimentation opened unforeseen opportunities for residents of these company towns, planned townships, and model homes to make them their own, reconfiguring what companies, urban planners, and rulers had imagined. Reem Alissa traces how Ahmadi's racially segregated modernity was upended as Kuwaiti employees moved from an unplanned space named the Arab

Village to a formerly white suburb.[40] With its green spaces, spacious homes, and array of domestic amenities, Ahmadi was transformed from a segregated enclave into a nostalgic symbol of oil-driven Kuwaiti modernity.[41] Simultaneously, as Farah al-Nakib again notes, the urban core of Kuwait was emptied of its historic residents and replaced with migrant workers.[42] More recently, Yasser Elsheshtawy has shown how the Emirati "national house" (or "people's house"), which was originally commissioned in the early 1970s, has been reconfigured in unforeseen and unintended ways by Emiratis who have been living in them.[43] In this sense, battles over "the right to the city" were transfigured into wider movements for participation and appropriation in emerging national polities.[44]

A Forever "New Frontier"

Gulf cities are often portrayed as youthful debutantes or precocious youngsters, as if they are late bloomers scrambling to catch up to a global standard of maturity. Anthropomorphism and developmentalism are ubiquitous tropes in the accounts of both optimists and pessimists. Supporters see Gulf cities as glamorous paragons of modernity finally having their "moment," while critics disdainfully dismiss their "hormonally adolescent urban growth."[45] Both critiques, however, miss that the Gulf has been the "new frontier" for architects and planners since the early twentieth century (see Andraos in the chapter that follows). As Tanis Hinchcliffe has astutely commented in his historical survey of British architects in the midcentury Gulf, "At the same time the Middle East was seeking to transform its physical fabric with modern buildings, America—and to a certain extent Europe—were also changing the face of their own cities." The Gulf states were not trying to keep up with an already well-established modernism but were an integral part of its emergence. In fact, in 1975, a feature story in the *Architectural Record* was already asking if the Middle East was indeed the "new frontier".[46]

Scholarship on cities and urban planning under colonial rule has acknowledged that conceptions of modernity and the management of space were products of a dialogical exchange between the imperial metropole and the colonized periphery.[47] In fact, urban planning in colonies was often carried out coeval with, or even prior to, planning in the metropole.

As Anthony King observes, "Colonial planning affords an example of a comprehensive and positive planning theory put into practice by government many decades before this became feasible in the metropolitan society."[48] As early as the 1920s, comprehensive urban planning was articulated and implemented in the Persian Gulf region, a move that followed the establishment of municipal government in Manama in 1919 and Kuwait in 1930.[49] But the role of planning bodies, which had become forums for elite landowners to defend their propertied interests, shifted dramatically as colonial officials and corporations built freestanding enclaves from the ground up. With these new towns, planners sought to produce modern subjects who could be disciplined by the state and available for labor and consumer markets, simultaneously drawing on and informing similar projects in metropolitan Britain. To design Abadan, Wilson was inspired by the "garden city movement," which was being developed by social reformers and urban planners simultaneously in Hampstead and New Delhi as a means to generate social harmony while spatially reifying social distinctions of class and race. Abadan's bungalows were themselves enmeshed within colonial networks. Originally developed in British India and then adopted in Britain in the 1890s "as a cultural model of living in *non-urban*, or *ex-urban* areas," the bungalow was adopted in Abadan for managers and technicians, who, at least initially, were exclusively British.[50] Far from being "blank slates" on which European specialists could practice their already tested craft, Gulf cities were integral laboratories that shaped the field of urban planning itself.

After World War II and with the process of decolonization, the dynamics of this translocal urban design shifted. The British were in a strong position to win commissions in the Gulf. Not only could they build on connections to the colonial administration, but British firms had become pioneers in town planning by the 1950s. Thus in 1951, when the Kuwaiti government commissioned its first comprehensive city plan, it turned to a British firm closely associated with the postwar new-town planning movement in England (as set forth by the New Towns Act 1946)—Minoprio, Spencely, and Macfarlane. Kuwait, which would be a protectorate of Britain for another decade, was offered a "new vision for Kuwait City . . . based on the British New Town precedent, with a comprehensive road network, clear zoning for different uses, and a protective 'green belt.'"[51] Minoprio, Spencely, and Macfarlane had recently completed the plan for Crawley in West Sussex and would go on to offer plans for Baghdad and Dhaka. The colonial city was evolving into the model suburb.

John Harris serves as a prime example of this generation of architects who made their careers on the shores of the Gulf. In 1952, he and Jill Harris (a fellow architect and wife of John Harris), were both fresh out of the Architectural Association of London. They had failed to win a competition to build the Nairobi Town Hall.[52] But the pair quickly recovered from this setback by winning the competition for the Doha State Hospital, which "ensured that a struggling young practice survived the adverse post-war economic conditions."[53] By the end of the decade, Harris drafted the first town plan for Dubai, designed six hospitals, and opened offices in Kuwait and Tehran, which would serve as their headquarters as they worked on projects for the National Iranian Oil Company. Harris's architectural firm flourished in the Gulf for several decades, establishing a presence across the littoral.

The tendency of architectural firms to work simultaneously in the Gulf and the industrialized nations of Europe and North America continued, and even accelerated, after the 1960s. Pioneering urban and architectural forms sprouted across the Gulf, often prefiguring developments elsewhere. Victor Gruen, the "father of the mall," who would later become a prominent critic of shopping centers, won the contract for the master plan for Tehran in 1966[54] in the midst of the peak of his career as a planner of cities and malls in the United States.[55] Gruen's "dumbbell plan" for malls as "a pastoral alternative to perceived ills of urbanity" was adopted initially in Dubai and across the region[56] only to be supplanted by the latest models that simultaneously appeared in London and Dubai in the 2000s.[57] Other notable planners and architects of this period that were commissioned to draft urban plans, design palaces, and offer models for free-trade zones (see chapters by Hertog and Akhavan respectively, in this volume) included firms headed by Louis Kahn, Kenzo Tange, Richard Llewelyn Davies, and Frank Lloyd Wright.[58]

These architects and engineers were also learning while they worked in the Gulf region. They soon discovered that a number of ecological factors combine to accelerate the deterioration of concrete in the Gulf region. After trial and error in the region and beyond, solutions were devised to increase the longevity of concrete structures, with one study concluding "that the experience gained has greatly increased understanding of concrete durability, the benefit of which will be felt worldwide."[59] Other engineering and architectural innovations, including ones that were "not the most economic," or "gambles," were developed in the context of the large-scale and interrelated construction projects built under extreme environmental conditions and stringent timetables.[60] Thus, the particularities of the Gulf, from the harshness of its ecology to the frenetic pace of its building boom, were literally incorporated into the fabric of the world's cities.

Such globalizing trends were not limited to the capitalist world. Łukasz Stanek has found that Polish architects "were crucial, if rarely accounted for, agents of globalization of architectural practice" in Kuwait in the 1970s and 1980s, when Kuwait City was considered to be at the forefront of avant-garde architecture in the Gulf.[61] By tracing the backlash against modernist trends that evolved simultaneously across the Gulf and Poland, and by highlighting the role of Kuwait as an influential proving ground for new design software, Stanek traces how Kuwait emerged as a central location for the formation of new trends and technologies, some of which are associated with postmodernism in architecture.

In recent years, it has become increasingly common for commentators to describe contemporary architecture and urban development in Europe and North America as bearing the imprint of the spectacular cities of the Persian Gulf. The *Financial Times*, for instance, offered its readers a scathing critique of the architecture on the banks of the Thames River, which, alas, "closely resembles Dubai."[62] The debates over if the Dubai model exists, if it can be replicated, and if it is normatively attractive have spilled into academic literature.[63] It is not commonly acknowledged that many of the construction firms and architectural imaginaries that are now (re)making cities, ports, and skylines—which seemingly ape Dubai and Doha—were some of those involved in fashioning these Gulf cities in the first place.

Urbanism and the Formation of the State and the Global

Over the course of the twentieth century, urban space in the Gulf emerged as a central node for the accumulation, circulation, and redistribution of capital. By leveraging their connections to the state, pre-oil elites were often able to maintain their wealth and influence through construction contracts and land speculation ventures, while British design and construction firms found a valuable client base during a period of austerity at home. The oil-fueled boom that swept across the Gulf, whose effects were anything but uniform, was shaped by the historical outlines of previous settlements, patterns of land ownership, class coalitions, and technological transformations, lavishing fabulous wealth on some cities and individuals while bypassing others.[64] The unevenness produced by urban space eventually spread across the region, as Gulf elites and state corporations invested surplus capital in urban hubs beyond their immediate locales.[65]

Renewed focus on urban space has added valuable nuance to work on the political economy of the Gulf. While it is tempting to see oil as the force that transformed land into a generator of value, it was the imperial imposition of unitary sovereignty that enabled both the creation of a market in land and the dominance of ruling families and their allies. Farah al-Nakib traces how, at the turn of the twentieth century, Sheikh Mubarak of Kuwait freely distributed land, only to turn around several years later and demand that occupants repurchase their own plots, with prices determined by the ruler's own appraisers.[66] Thus, it was Mubarak's absolute control of sovereignty, secured by his compact with British imperialism, that enabled the Kuwaiti ruling family to secure the land that became a key source of income in the pre-oil era. In Saudi Arabia, the state expropriated massive swaths of land from its nomadic population in a nationalization program that was legitimated by international development consultants and models of urbanization that valorized automobiles.[67] Finally, in Iran's province of Khuzestan, the Anglo-Persian Oil Company's intervention eventually enabled the centralized state to sweep away its local competitors.[68] Thus, while oil certainly raised the stakes of land speculation, the commodification of both relied on the imposition of totalizing territorial sovereignty across the Gulf, a process that long predated the hydrocarbon age.

With their hold on land secure, merchant families and members of ruling families jockeyed to profit through every phase of the development process. This began with planning, which transformed land into a tool of capital recycling. Several recent case studies trace how this process worked by drawing on the archives of planning firms. As soon as plans were announced in Dubai, Riyadh, and Kuwait, speculators with inside information, many of whom were ruling family members, would rush to buy up empty plots to resell to the government. Alternatively, after learning that a planning scheme would increase the value of their land, original owners would hold out until their plots were purchased at astronomical prices. In Kuwait, several rounds of planning were rendered financially impracticable as the announcement of new planning schemes triggered waves of land speculation.[69] In the explosive building boom of the immediate post-oil period, land speculation and construction in Kuwait City (as in Riyadh) became so profitable that they crowded out other investments and deincentivized economic diversification, compounding the deleterious monetary effects of oil exportation.[70] Land purchasing soon became the single largest expenditure in the Kuwaiti budget, transforming royal and merchant family members into spectacularly wealthy rentiers. Stephen Ramos's study of Dubai uncovers how planning and land laws were growth strategies that were schematic, flexible, and never fully implemented.[71] Therefore, the monarch, his mercantile allies, and a cadre of advisors from international firms could propose and implement new proposals and large infrastructural projects, such as the Jebel Ali manmade port or land reclamation schemes. Ultimately, Ramos concludes that this pattern of urban development—hampered by neither democratic participation nor technocratic adherence to "the plan"— allowed Dubai to be "reactive," "swift," and "nimble," characteristics that were present in other locations in the region, to some extent or another.

Citizens of the Gulf states were not the only beneficiaries of this process. The building boom that started in the late 1940s came as a godsend to British international construction and consulting firms struggling to survive in a domestic environment of postwar fiscal austerity. As Egypt, Iraq, and Sudan gained independence in the 1950s, consulting and engineering firms redirected their energies to the capital-rich Gulf region.[72] As one scholar of the construction industry has noted, "Leafing through the architectural magazines, particularly those of the 1970s, it is not unusual to find articles chronicling the activities of numerous British firms working in the Gulf, and it could be claimed that this work kept the architectural profession in this country afloat, especially during the recurring periods of recession in the post-war era."[73] British firms continue to reminisce about the ease with which projects were managed and profits accumulated in the early oil years. Sir William Halcrow and Partners, which enjoyed a near-monopoly over construction projects in Dubai, stated in their brochure celebrating the partnership's 125th anniversary, "All approval was verbal, a far cry from the cut-throat post-war arena of Europe."[74]

The British government was deeply invested in firms winning contracts and projects, as its current and former protectorates were the largest holders of sterling. While after World War II, the British government focused on Iran as a source of sterling reserves, attention soon shifted elsewhere.[75] In 1967, Kuwait, despite gaining independence in 1961, became the single largest foreign holder of sterling.[76] This financial incentive for urban development was only enhanced after the oil shock of the 1970s: "In 1976 Edmund Dell, the British Secretary of State for Trade, compared the expansion of the Arab countries as 'the nearest modern industrial equivalent to the booming days of the American gold rush.'"[77] The concentration of expertise in metropolitan Britain was redeployed to combat the sterling crisis: "The architect Raglan Squire recounted that in the 1950s, when his practice needed a boost, he read a paper that commented on the fact that there were 22,000 fully qualified architects in England, while in the Commonwealth countries the numbers could still be counted on the fingers of one hand."[78] Squire ended up opening an office in Baghdad and was commissioned to draw the master plan for Mosul. Other British firms received contracts for Baghdad and Basra. While the Iraqi revolution of 1958 overturned the prominent position of British firms, other Western architects, including the legendary architect-planner Constatinos Doxiadis, stepped in. Many British engineers and planners saw "a great opportunity which is opening up for a whole range of British expertise to be applied to a large number of building programmes in a way which will ensure that *our knowledge and expertise is used to solve the problems of the countries concerned* and not to saddle them with inappropriate buildings." Yet, as Hinchcliffe himself comments, this was a prescription for the perpetual British "quest to run other peoples' lives for them," one that would be appropriated, adapted, and reconfigured by a new generation of Gulf elites.[79]

Conclusion

The discursive framework around many of the region's new prestige projects highlights the dangers of ahistorical or teleological narratives of urbanization. Abu Dhabi's Masdar, for example, is framed as a universal model for the future, but its physical and institutional separation from city and region mean that it functions as an enclosure and has had a negligible impact on the massive carbon footprint of most Gulf cities (as explained in chapter 8 by Gökçe Günel). The Louvre and Guggenheim projects in Abu Dhabi are framed as opportunities to make art accessible in the Middle East, yet on closer examination other purposes become evident. It is clear that at the local scale, the museums—cloistered on Saadiyat Island, the flagship quasi-state-development project of Abu Dhabi Emirate—are designed to add value to an elite real estate endeavor reserved for those sufficiently cosmopolitan and global to exploit its particular benefits. By neglecting to take into account their different scalar and distributional effects, flagship projects can reinforce the paradigm of a desert-like tabula rasa blooming with wonders, thereby failing to acknowledge their role in reinforcing the established networks of power and wealth. Like prestige projects, Gulf cities cannot be understood as objects isolated from relationships of complexity and historical depth.

This perspective is essential for disrupting journalistic and academic representations that frame Gulf cities as artificial or top-down impositions by foreign city planners or authoritarian states. Architects' renditions too often stand in for the actual lived urban spaces. Projects such as Dubai's Palm Islands are visible to air travelers and make for attractive magazine photography (see more examples and reasoning in Michele Nastasi's chapter 4) but are frequently hidden behind gates and imperceptible from the ground.[80] Seemingly influenced by critiques of high modernism, these impositions are contrasted with "organic" cities, which are presumed to grow naturally and thus to better represent the social relations of ordinary residents. While one should not minimize the often explicitly imperial intentions of oil companies and hired urbanists, this dichotomy threatens to resurrect the binary of the pre- and post-oil boom by other discursive means, glorifying a past in which Gulf cities were supposedly kinder, more cohesive systems untouched by "outside" forces and enforced hierarchies. The productive question, however, may not be whether cities are sufficiently organic or overly artificial. Rather, it is a question of tracing the ever-present networks of power and privilege that have always shaped Gulf cities—and indeed, all cities—and the forms of resistance and collective action that opposed them. Few, if any, cities anywhere can be said to have been built democratically, with the needs of all of their residents taken into account. The "right to the city" has always been unevenly distributed, with residents battling powerful structural forces of capital and coercion. How this struggle unfolded, from global networks of oil production to quotidian details of everyday life, is the question that scholars of the region have begun to address.

NOTES

The authors thank Harvey Molotch, Davide Ponzini, and Ahmed Kanna for their constructive feedback on earlier drafts of this essay. Portions of this essay appear and are developed in Alex Boodrookas and Arang Keshavarzian, "The Forever Frontier of Urbanism: Historicizing Persian Gulf Cities," *International Journal of Urban and Regional Research* (forthcoming).

1   Fuccaro 2009, 5.
2   Kanna 2011, 1.
3   Abdulla 2013.
4   Davis 2006, 54.
5   Cooke 2014.
6   Onley 2005; Bose 2006.
7   Onley and Khalaf 2006; Commins 2012; Said Zahlan 1989; Takriti 2013.
8   Vora 2013.
9   Herb 2014; Mahdavy 1970; Beblawi 1987.
10 Vora 2013; Nga Longva 1997; Gardner 2010; Nadjmabadi 2010; Dresch 2006; Limbert 2010.
11 Khalaf 2006; Kanna 2011; Elsheshtawy 2008; Al-Nakib 2013; Menoret 2014; Ehsani 2003.
12 Harvey 1982.
13 Fattah 1997.
14 Fuccaro 2009.
15 Lienhardt 1993.
16 Crystal 1990.
17 Keshavarzian 2016; Potter 2009.
18 Fuccaro 2009, 97.
19 Fuccaro 2009, 60.
20 Fuccaro 2009, 110.
21 Crinson 1997, 348; Alissa 2013, 43.
22 Seccombe and Lawless 1987.

23 Seccombe and Lawless 1987; Ehsani 2003.
24 Ahmed 2012.
25 Grandin 2009; Vitalis 2009; Ehsani 2003.
26 Alissa 2013; Vitalis 2009; Seccombe and Lawless 1987.
27 Alissa 2013, 45.
28 Lienhardt 1993, 31.
29 Damluji 2013; Alissa 2013; Fuccaro 2013.
30 Fuccaro 2013, 60.
31 Fuccaro 2013, 70.
32 Crinson 1997.
33 Alissa 2013.
34 Crystal 2005; Eamon 2015.
35 Al-Nakib 2014.
36 Alissa 2013.
37 Chalcraft 2011.
38 Vitalis 2009; Seccombe 2010.
39 Cronin 2010; Ehsani 2003.
40 Alissa 2013.
41 Alissa 2013.
42 Al-Nakib 2013.
43 Elsheshtawy 2016.
44 Mitchell 2003.
45 Abdulla 2012; Parker 2005.
46 Hinchcliffe 2013, 27.
47 Rabinow 1989; Celik 1997.
48 King 1999, 24.
49 Fuccaro 2009; Al-Nakib 2016.
50 Crinson 1997, 345. Even gardeners were imported to Abadan from New Delhi and
    Kew.
51 Jones 2013, 41.
52 Morris 1984.
53 Hinchcliffe 2013, 27.
54 Emami 2014.
55 Wall 2006.
56 Jewell 2013, 175.
57 Jewell 2013,176.
58 Mohajeri 2015; Keshavarzian 2010.
59 Roberts and Flower 1995, 68.
60 Roberts and Flower 1995, 143; Ramos 2010.
61 Stanek 2015, 366.
62 Heathcote 2016.
63 Hvidt 2009.

64 Keshavarzian 2016.

65 Hanieh 2013.

66 Al-Nakib 2016. For a discussion of this process in Dubai, see Ramos 2010.

67 Menoret 2014.

68 Cronin 2004.

69 Al-Nakib 2016.

70 Menoret 2014.

71 Ramos 2010.

72 Ramos 2010.

73 Hinchcliffe 2013, 23.

74 Roberts and Fowler, 138.

75 Bostock and Jones 1989, 55.

76 Fain 2008, 3.

77 Hinchcliffe 2013, 31.

78 Hinchcliffe 2013, 24.

79 Hinchcliffe 2013, 34 (italics added).

80 Ramos 2010. On the visibility and invisibility of capital and labor in Dubai, see Kanna 2007.

REFERENCES

Abdulla, Abdulkhaleq. 2012. "The Arab Gulf Moment." In *The Transformation of the Gulf: Politics, Economics, and the Global Order*, ed. David Held and Kristian Ulrichsen, 106–124. New York: Routledge.

Abdulla, Abdulkhaleq. 2013. "Khaleej Cities are Present and Future." *Al-Monitor*, October 20, 2013. www.al-monitor.com.

Ahmed, Attiya. 2012. "Beyond Labor: Foreign Residents in the Gulf States." In *Migrant Labor in the Persian Gulf*, ed. Mehran Kamrava and Zahra Babar, 21–40. New York: Columbia University Press.

Alissa, Reem. 2013. "The Oil Town of Ahmadi since 1946: From Colonial Town to Nostalgic City." *Comparative Studies of South Asia, Africa and the Middle East* 33, no. 1: 41–58.

Al-Nakib, Farah. 2013. "Kuwait's Modern Spectacle Oil Wealth and the Making of a New Capital City, 1950–90." *Comparative Studies of South Asia, Africa and the Middle East* 33, no.1: 7–25.

Al-Nakib, Farah. 2014. "Revisiting Hadar and Badu in Kuwait: Citizenship, Housing, and the Construction of a Dichotomy." *International Journal of Middle East Studies* 46, no. 1: 5–30.

Al-Nakib, Farah. 2016. *Kuwait Transformed: A History of Oil and Urban Life*. Stanford, CA: Stanford University Press.

Al-Rasheed, Madawi, ed. 2005. *Transnational Connections and the Arab Gulf*. London: Routledge.

Beblawi, Hazem. 1987. "The Rentier State in the Arab World." In *The Rentier State*, ed. Hazem Beblawi and Giacomo Luciani, 49–71. London: Croom Helm.

Bose, Sugata. 2006. *A Hundred Horizons: The Indian Ocean in the Age of Global Empire.* Cambridge, MA: Harvard University Press.

Bostock, Frances, and Geoffrey Jones. 1989. "British Business in Iran, 1860s–1970s." In *British Business in Asia since 1860*, ed. R. P. T. Davenport-Hines and Geoffrey Jones, 31–67. Cambridge: Cambridge University Press.

Celik, Zeynep. 1997. *Urban Forms and Colonial Confrontations: Algiers under French Rule.* Berkeley: University of California Press.

Chalcraft, John. 2011. "Migration and Popular Protest in the Arabian Peninsula and the Gulf in the 1950s and 1960s." *International Labor and Working-Class History* 79: 28–47.

Commins, David. 2012. *The Gulf States: A Modern History.* New York: I. B. Tauris.

Cooke, Miriam. 2014. *Tribal Modern: Branding New Nations of the Gulf.* Berkeley: University of California Press.

Crinson, Mark. 1997. "Abadan: Planning and Architecture under the Anglo-Iranian Oil Company." *Planning Perspectives* 12, no. 3: 341–359.

Cronin, Stephanie. 2004. "The Politics of Debt: The Anglo-Persian Oil Company and the Bakhtiyari Khans." *Middle Eastern Studies* 40, no. 4: 1–31.

Cronin, Stephanie. 2010. "Popular Politics, the New State and the Birth of the Iranian Working Class: The 1929 Abadan Oil Refinery Strike." *Middle Eastern Studies* 5: 699–732.

Crystal, Jill. 1990 (first paperback edition 1995). *Oil and Politics in the Gulf: Rulers and Merchants in Kuwait and Qatar.* Cambridge: Cambridge University Press.

Crystal, Jill. 2005. "Public Order and Authority: Policing in Kuwait." In *Monarchies and Nations: Globalization and Identity in the Arab States of the Gulf*, ed. James P. Piscatori and Paul Dresch, 158–181. London: I. B. Tauris.

Davis, Mike. 2006. "Fear and Money in Dubai." *New Left Review* 41 (September/October): 47–68.

Damluji, Mona. 2013. "The Oil City in Focus: The Cinematic Spaces of Abadan in the Anglo-Iranian Oil Company's Persian Story." *Comparative Studies of South Asia, Africa and the Middle East* 33, no. 1: 75–88.

Dresch, Paul. 2006. "Foreign Matter: The Place of Strangers in Gulf Society." In *Globalization and the Gulf*, ed. John W. Fox, Nada Mourtada-Sabbah, and Mohammed al-Mutawa, 200–222. London: Routledge.

Eamon, Jeff. 2015. "Policing the Bahrain Islands: Labor, Race, and the Historical Origins of Foreign Recruitment." Unpublished MA thesis, Program in Near Eastern Studies, New York University.

Ehsani, Kaveh. 2003. "Social Engineering and the Contradictions of Modernization in Khuzestan's Company Towns: A Look at Abadan and Masjed-Soleyman." *International Review of Social History* 48, no. 3: 361–399.

Elsheshtawy, Yasser, ed. 2008. *The Evolving Arab City: Tradition, Modernity, and Urban Development.* London: Routledge.

Elsheshtawy, Yasser. 2016. "Transformations: The Emirati National House: Inside UAE's Pavilion at the 2016 Venice Biennale." *ArchDaily*, August 22, 2016. www.archdaily.com.

Emami, Farshid. 2014. "Urbanism of Grandiosity: Planning a New Urban Center for Tehran." *International Journal of Islamic Architecture* 3: 69–102.

Fain, W. Taylor. 2008. *American Ascendance and British Retreat in the Persian Gulf Region*. New York: Palgrave Macmillan.

Fattah, Hala. 1997. *The Politics of Regional Trade in Iraq, Arabia, and the Gulf 1745–1900*. Albany: State University of New York Press.

Fuccaro, Nelida. 2009. *Histories of City and State in the Persian Gulf: Manama since 1800*. Cambridge: Cambridge University Press.

Fuccaro, Nelida. 2013. "Shaping the Urban Life of Oil in Bahrain: Consumerism, Leisure, and Public Communication in Manama and in the Oil Camps, 1932–1960s." *Comparative Studies of South Asia, Africa and the Middle East* 33, no. 1: 59–74.

Gardner, Andrew M. 2010. *City of Strangers: Gulf Migration and the Indian Community in Bahrain*. Ithaca, NY: Cornell University Press.

Grandin, Greg. 2009. *Fordlandia: The Rise and Fall of Henry Ford's Forgotten Jungle City*. New York: Metropolitan Books.

Hanieh, Adam. 2013. *Lineages of Revolt: Issues of Contemporary Capitalism in the Middle East*. Chicago: Haymarket Books.

Harvey, David. 1982. *The Limits of Capital*. Oxford: Blackwell.

Heathcote, Edwin. 2016. "How Lookalike Riverside Architecture Is Drowning Out the Thames." *Financial Times*, October 3, 2016. www.ft.com.

Herb, Michael. 2014. *The Wages of Oil: Parliaments and Economic Development in Kuwait and the UAE*. Ithaca, NY: Cornell University Press.

Hinchcliffe, Tanis. 2013. "British Architects in the Gulf, 1950–1980." In *Architecture and Globalization in the Persian Gulf Region*, ed. Murray Fraser and Nasser Golzari, 23–36. Farnham, UK: Ashgate.

Hvidt, Martin. 2009. "The Dubai Model: An Outline of Key Development-Process Elements in Dubai." *International Journal of Middle East Studies* 41: 397–418.

Jewell, Nicholas. 2013. "Shopping Malls in Dubai." In *Architecture and Globalization in the Persian Gulf Region*, ed. Murray Fraser and Nasser Golzari, 173–195. Farnham, UK: Ashgate.

Jones, Gwyn Lloyd. 2013. "Kuwait City, Kuwait." In *Architecture and Globalization in the Persian Gulf Region*, ed. Murray Fraser and Nasser Golzari, 37–56. Farnham, UK: Ashgate.

Kanna, Ahmed. 2007. "Dubai in a Jagged World." *Middle East Report* 243: 22–29.

Kanna, Ahmed. 2011. *Dubai: The City as Corporation*. Minneapolis: University of Minnesota Press.

Keshavarzian, Arang. 2010. "Geopolitics and the Genealogy of Free Trade Zones in the Persian Gulf." *Geopolitics* 16, no. 2: 263–289.

Keshavarzian, Arang. 2016. "From Port Cities to Cities with Ports: Towards a Multiscalar History of Persian Gulf Urbanism in the Twentieth Century." In *Gateways to the World: Port Cities in the Persian Gulf*, ed. Mehran Kamrava, 19–41. Oxford: Oxford University Press.

Khalaf, Sulayman. 2006. "The Evolution of the Gulf City Type, Oil, and Globalization." In *Globalization and the Gulf*, ed. John W. Fox, Nada Mourtada-Sabbah, and Mohammed al-Mutawa, 244–265. London: Routledge.

King, Anthony D. 1999. *Colonial Urban Development: Culture, Social Power and Environment*. London: Routledge.

Lienhardt, Peter. 1993. *Disorientations: A Society in Flux: Kuwait in the 1950s*. Edited by Ahmed Al-Shahi. Reading, UK: Ithaca Press.

Limbert, Mandana E. 2010. *In the Time of Oil: Piety, Memory, and Social Life in an Omani Town*. Palo Alto, CA: Stanford University Press.

Mahdavy, Hossein. 1970. "The Pattern and Problems of Economic Development in Rentier States: The Case of Iran." In *Studies in the Economic History of Middle East*, ed. M. A. Cook, 428–467. Oxford: Oxford University Press.

Menoret, Pascal. 2014. *Joyriding in Riyadh: Oil, Urbanism, and Road Revolt*. Cambridge: Cambridge University Press.

Mitchell, Don. 2003. *The Right to the City: Social Justice and the Fight for Public Space*. New York: Guilford Press.

Mohajeri, Shima. 2015. "Louis Kahn's Silent Space of Critique in Tehran, 1973–74." *Journal of Society of Architectural History* 74 (December): 485–504.

Morris, A. E. J. 1984. *John Harris Architects*. Westerham, UK: Hurtwood Press.

Nadjmabadi, Shahnaz R. 2010. "Cross-Border Networks: Labour Migration from Iran to the Arab Countries of the Persian Gulf." *Anthropology of the Middle East* 5, no. 1: 18–33.

Nga Longva, Anh. 1997. *Walls Built on Sand: Migrant, Exclusion, and Society in Kuwait*. Boulder, CO: Westview Press.

Onley, James. 2005. "Transnational Merchants in the Nineteenth-Century Gulf: The Case of the Safar Family." In *Transnational Connections and the Arab Gulf*, ed. Madawi Al-Rasheed, 59–91. London: Routledge.

Onley, James, and Suleyman Khalaf. 2006. "Shaikhly Authority in the Pre-Oil Gulf: An Historical-Anthropological Study." *History and Anthropology* 17, no. 3: 189–208.

Parker, Ian. 2005. "The Mirage." *New Yorker*, October 17, 2005. 128–143.

Potter, Lawrence, ed. 2009. *The Persian Gulf in History*. New York: Palgrave.

Rabinow, Paul. 1989. *French Modern: Norms and Forms of the Social Environment*. Cambridge, MA: MIT Press.

Ramos, Stephen. 2010. *Dubai Amplified: The Engineering of a Port Geography*. Burlington, UK: Ashgate.

Roberts, Gwilym, and David Flower. 1995. *Built by Oil*. Reading, UK: Ithaca Press.

Said Zahlan, Rosemarie. 1989. *The Making of the Modern Gulf States*. London: Unwin Hyman.

Seccombe, Ian J. 2010. "'A Disgrace to American Enterprise': Italian Labour and the Arabian American Oil Company in Saudi Arabia, 1944–54." *Immigrants and Minorities: Historical Studies in Ethnicity, Migration and Diaspora* 5, no. 3: 233–257.

Seccombe, Ian J., and R. I. Lawless. 1987. "Work Camps and Company Towns: Settlement Patterns and the Gulf Oil Industry," working paper. Durham: University of Durham, Center for Middle Eastern and Islamic Studies.

Stanek, Łukasz. 2015. "Mobilities of Architecture in the Global Cold War: From Socialist Poland to Kuwait and Back," *International Journal of Islamic Architecture* 4, no. 2: 365–398.

Takriti, Abdel Razzaq. 2013. *Monsoon Revolution: Republicans, Sultans, and Empires in Oman 1965–1976*. Oxford: Oxford University Press.

Vitalis, Robert. 2009. *America's Kingdom: Mythmaking on the Saudi Oil Frontier*. London: Verso Press.

Vora, Neha. 2013. *Impossible Citizens: Dubai's Indian Diaspora*. Durham, NC: Duke University Press.

Wall, Alex. 2006. *Victor Gruen: From Urban Shop to New City*. Barcelona: Actar.

2

Problematizing a Regional Context

Representation in Arab and Gulf Cities

AMALE ANDRAOS

The term "Arab city" immediately evokes particular images, whether of large-scale constructions of national or civic identity or more finely grained architectures that attempt to represent so-called Arab identity in gestural form. The term is as much aspirational as it is indicative of particular anxieties. Looking closely at the Arab city today requires that we also attend to the various historical constructions of the term in the hopes of facilitating Arab urban futures that are both true to historic realities and produce authentically positive prospects. The potential exists for an irreverent optimism—looking forward toward a secular, transnational, progressive, and intellectual "Arabism" that articulates modernity, and indeed politics, on its own terms. Sketching the basis for such a reconciliation in the Arab city—historical and prospective—is my present goal. The events of the Arab Spring and its "retaking of the public square" awakened this hopeful ambition in many. However discouraging the subsequent events on the ground may have been, these thoughts have continued to live and grow, if not in the realities of the "Arab street" (now sadly bloodier and more repressive than ever), then in the minds and work of a new generation of highly engaged architects, historians, and scholars.

Another reason for taking up the Arab city as a focus is to probe the underexamined issues that are raised by the notion of global practice in architecture and urbanism today and, relevant to the purposes of this volume, the manner in which architectural practices travel and yield alternatives as they land in different places. Such a perspective—one of synthesis but also of local distinctiveness—has been stymied by clichés that assume the opposition between "local" and "global" and the parallel dichotomy between "traditional" and "modern." No matter how complex and contradictory the environment in which we work is, architecture is often entrusted with the role of somehow bringing it all together, uniting local and global, tradition and modernity. But this formulation, ironically, conceals the reality that tradition is itself a modernist construction.[1] Such a realization invites, maybe even necessitates, solutions that refuse to be thwarted by the putative divide between the modern and (typically) some ersatz version of tradition.

Efforts to reconcile the modern and the traditional—however partial, tentative, or awkward—have given us some of the most impressive icons in the architectural imagination of the early twenty-first century. Many such works, found in Gulf cities, are often conceived and interpreted as built metaphors—consciously and powerfully deployed with the power to brand.[2] Dubai's spectacular Burj Al Arab Hotel is a strong case in point (fig. 2.1), famously given the form of a dhow, a well-known type of sailing vessel that has been in use in the region since, perhaps, 600 B.C.

Bespeaking such design strategies, contemporary global practice has reintroduced the question of architecture as symbolic form, focused on

Figure 2.1. Burj Al Arab in Dubai. Photograph by Michele Nastasi.

representation in addition to performance. This return is rooted in Robert Venturi and Denise Scott Brown's endorsement of the pleasures of signs and symbols in architecture in the 1970s and onward. Today, these modes of representation appear largely in the form of branding—a strategy imported from graphic and product design that enabled the expediency required to serve the speed and scales of global practice and global capitalization, as well as the production of architectural icons.

Wherever we arrive, and whatever the origin or our acknowledgment is of the aesthetic accomplishment, we are left to question the meanings being produced. Whether for a corporate client, an institution, a city, or a state, we can question what kind of identity architecture is being called on to produce, what identities are being constructed, and how that knowledge can allow us—here I speak as an architect—some margins to resist what we deem inappropriate given our larger values and hopes for the future.

There is probably no context more appropriate to investigate imagination and projection, fear and exotic anxiety, than the cities of the Arab world. The old centers—Beirut, Baghdad, Damascus, Cairo—represent a long, rich, and complex dialogue with, struggle over, and acceptance of modernity, not only through art, literature, poetry, and intellectual and political thought, but also through the architecture and urban experiments launched during the last stretch of Ottoman rule. In contrast, the emergence of new urban centers offers a seeming blank slate with "no context," as some architects have claimed. Frank Gehry spoke of his Guggenheim Museum on Abu Dhabi's Saadiyat Island as constructed in a kind of void: "like a clean slate in a country full of resources . . . it's an opportunity for the world of art and culture that is not anywhere else because you're building a desert enclave without the contextual constraints of a city."[3] This seeming absence of urban constraint (as well as the presence of rich financial backing) fuels fast-track development, embodying an image of modernity and facilitating architectural experiments and breakthroughs. (For additional examples, see Ponzini, chapter 3.)

Imagery of the void—ignoring centuries of urban settlement across the Gulf (in Dubai, Manama, and Kuwait City, for example)—perpetuates a widely-circulated larger narrative: while recently inhabited by fishermen and Bedouins roaming the desert and living in tents, today's instant cities boast the financial skyscrapers, luxury lifestyles, and cultural centers of advanced urbanism, and are led by visionary rulers, who are single-handedly lifting their citizens and their cities toward the future while respecting the traditional and religious values of the past. (See the preceding chapter by Boodrookas and Keshavarzian.) This tale of harmonious coming together is often set in contrast to a politicized Islam and the violent clash of civilizations said to be taking place elsewhere.

The challenge, then, is to avoid simplistic explanations of any sort. In fact, in the rise of these new cities, we can glimpse a struggle for both regional power and the nature of its makeup.[4] We are presented with ways to engage modernity but with a conservative underpinning that circumvents democracy. In this struggle, ethnicity, tradition, and religious identity are set as the foundation for new transnational formations, variously moderate or extreme as they may be. Using form and content, architecture is expected to reconcile competing forces. Buildings must go up and their forms must, by necessity, involve some kind of settlement.

As a way to meet such expectations, the proliferation of architectural metaphors invokes traditional life in the desert and on the sea. Well-known examples include the building of a super-luxury seaside hotel in the form of a sail (the Burj Al Arab mentioned above). A second prominent (and more recent) example is Jean Nouvel's National Museum of Qatar, which "crystallizes" the Qatari identity into a building that, like a desert rose, "appears to grow out of the ground and be one with it."[5] The Jeddah International Airport—designed by OMA, the global firm led by Rem Koolhaas—is another attempt at making a meaningful blend: "both the main terminal and Royal pavilion with their crescent-like shape enclose an internal oasis that can accommodate different forms of use."[6] Urban master plans follow suit. Los Angeles–based practice Morphosis's King Abdullah Petroleum Studies and Research Center proposes a "master plan . . . rooted in the historical model of the oasis village."[7] Similar language was used for Zaha Hadid's Dubai Opera House and Cultural Centre ("the gentle winding form evokes images of mountains or sand dunes"[8])—a design that, alas, failed to survive a severe Dubai budgetary cutback.

Some projects merge symbolism with functional goal. Among the most notable are the parallel projects of Foster + Partners' Masdar City in Abu Dhabi and OMA's new eco-city for Ras Al Khaimah. In both symbolic and functional terms, each was designed to echo the traditional medina, with its high-density and low-rise built form. Masdar in particular presents a sophisticated language of traditional Islamic architectural motifs—forms that also help it function with high-tech devices for green energy performance. The designers seamlessly integrate the use of the *mashrabiya*—traditional lattice-wood screening—to filter sunlight and handsomely serve as building facades. (On Masdar's actual—mixed— technological accomplishments, see Gökçe Günel, chapter 8.) Other strategies involve layering calligraphy onto the bold forms of contemporary expression, such as for the new Qatar Faculty of Islamic Studies designed by Ali Mangera and Ada Yvars Bravo (a collaboration based in London and Barcelona)—reaching far beyond surface emblems to create bold forms and volumes (fig. 2.2).

The most undeniably successful architectural synthesis of the traditional and the modern in the Gulf is Jean Nouvel's Louvre Abu Dhabi.[9] Although it is a building surrounded by water, the design takes inspiration from the organic patterns of traditional medinas. The complex forms a landscape of building-scaled rooms, whose nonhierarchical relationships are made legible by a shallow dome (with a diameter close to that of the Louvre's Cour Carrée in Paris). As a layering of fractal three-dimensional patterns, the dome filters light to create microenvironments of dreamy

Figure 2.2. The Qatar Faculty of Islamic Studies designed by Ali Mangera and Ada Yvars Bravo. Photograph by Michele Nastasi.

mist—referencing both the rays of sunlight that trickle through the palms of an oasis and the refraction of light produced by the ornate surfaces of mosques. There is modulation of light and shade as characteristic of Islamic structures, comparable to other sensitively informed projects that reinterpret the mashrabiya.[10] As in many of Nouvel's projects, the architecture here is almost immaterial, blending in with the scenarios and atmospheres of its context, both real and imagined (fig. 2.3). Nouvel, a self-declared contextual architect,[11] is a no-kitsch designer; his sophisticated knowledge insulates him from any charge of simplistic orientalism. The seeds were sown with his Institut du Monde Arabe building in Paris (designed in partnership with Architecture-Studio), where the mechanical facade of sun-sensitive diaphragms technologically interprets the Islamic geometric pattern that calibrates light to render vision as both optics *and* experience—in a multilayered and complex configuration.

It would be disingenuous to ignore the architectural power and success of some of these projects—the Louvre Abu Dhabi, Skidmore, Owings & Merrill's Burj Khalifa, or even the sailboat-like Burj Al Arab. The realities of their form and content move these buildings beyond the slogans of

Figure 2.3. Louvre Abu Dhabi designed by Ateliers Jean Nouvel. Photograph by Michele Nastasi.

their renderings; they are complex material and lived experiences. They show how, at best, concepts such as context and heritage can open up new territories for the architectural imagination and for the architect to knowingly produce invention, architectural and otherwise. In the process, these projects successfully introduce tensions and hold together contradictions. Yet, along with such dynamic and hybrid accomplishments, it is important to note another fundamental and intractable contradiction: that this striving for a new cosmopolitanism accompanies an aim to shape a national identity that is exclusive and exclusionary.

Building Identity between a Mythical Past and Futuristic Utopia

Through purposive efforts, the goal has been to create an Emirati identity narrowly defined as stemming from the pure lineage of Bedouins, constructed as the only original inhabitants of the *witan* (homeland). In this imagination, Bedouins are the bearers of an "authentic" culture, to the exclusion of many of the other populations and cultures that historically constituted the hybrid populations of the Gulf states (as documented by Boodrookas and Keshavarzian in the prior chapter; see also Lieto, chapter 5). This mythical narrative also serves as a political and cultural performance intended to reassure Emirati nationals, who are now a small minority of the population. Set against the reality of a highly diverse people—from young Western expats, to Arab refugees, to Southeast Asian construction workers—is the representation of authentic cultural heritage that groups all non-Emirati together as a never-to-be-integrated "other." Among some of these enactments of heritage, tradition, and authenticity is the revival of sports such as falconry and camel racing (albeit, with mechanical robots sitting as jockeys) designed to ratify regime and citizenship.

Through statecraft and modes of building construction, the UAE's ruling families energetically challenge past depictions—often demeaning in fact—of themselves and their citizens. As Edward Said famously argued in his *Orientalism*,[12] a favored trope in the West has been to depict people elsewhere, particularly those in the Middle East, as stuck in static religious beliefs and cultural practices, as well as lacking history and context. In a distinctive twist, the anthropologist Ahmed Kanna renders Dubai and the Gulf states as, in their own self-representations, similarly (and miraculously) suspended outside of history or politics.[13] It is, says Kanna, a kind of "reverse Orientalism."[14] Yet this time the essentialist reduction takes the form of hypermodern states inspired by futuristic and visionary development.[15] In this narrative, Gulf cities become the fantastical and glittery city-as-spectacle, emerging from the desert like the twenty-first-century incarnation of *One Thousand and One Nights*.[16] As the old centers of the Arab world continue to struggle for modernity, with every new conflict another devastating setback, they make way for the new centers of global entrepreneurial neoliberalism. Dubai, in particular, asserts the promise of a new future that constitutes a radical break from "Arab traditions and pathologies," the *New York Times* columnist Thomas Friedman's term for the so-called backward past.[17]

The result invites bringing together, both in building form and historical narrative, two fanciful descriptions of the Arab context: the golden age of mythical Islamic empire and the promise of technological utopia. In its looking back, it does not differentiate across space or time but esteems together and at once the traditional medinas of Fez and Aleppo, the lush palaces of Andalucía, the golden buildings of the caliphate of Baghdad, and the domes and pixelated refracting surfaces of the mosques. The new is also mostly undifferentiated as up-to-the-minute mastery of global starchitecture. At once nostalgic and futuristic, it produces a powerful narrative: Islam cannot be understood as against progress because it was itself once the driver of progress. What we are witnessing, goes the line, is in fact a new Islamic renaissance: a society at once deeply religious and mindful of belonging to a broad "Islamic nation" while committed to achieving the most visionary, global, urbanized future.

Other than historic analysis, what problems do these naïve notions produce—when combined with influences from the technocratic West and its various aesthetic locutions? One problem is that this montage of signs and symbols, in building form or otherwise, risks manufacturing reductive meanings and experiences—or essentializing an entire society (or group of societies)—which then become embedded into the urban fabric and other narratives. The orientalism described by Said was not only offensive in its representations but also instrumental in advancing the colonial project—British imperialism in particular in the Gulf region. Too often reduced to and misconceived as a simplistic identity in opposition to and at the exclusion of others, such cultural specificity risks reinforcing architecture's inherent tendency to reductiveness, given the physical durability of the artifacts that it creates.

A second and possibly larger problem lies in the tendency toward a misleading type of pan-Islamism. Not only is there little need to differentiate Islamic places from one another, there is little need to differentiate Islamic places across time. While art historians like Oleg Grabar have thoughtfully probed differentiations within Islamic art,[18] others still believe that if particular architectural features were developed during the technological advancement that took place in sixteenth-century Istanbul under the genius of the architect Mimar Sinan, they are equally contextual in the desert of Qatar or Abu Dhabi. They belong, after all, to a unified history. Regardless of place and time, politics and economics, material advances and changing technologies, Islamic architecture is constructed as the principal unifier, a fixed representation of the "Arab world." This is a form of cultural displacement that, however ironically, makes possible the conception of a romanticized, cohesive Islamic people, nation, or empire. At its most dystopic, this is the same mythical Islamic empire claimed by—and marked by—the horrific violence of an ISIS. An overgeneralized idea of Islamic culture is used to legitimize the brutal murder of innocent others as well as the destruction of any symbol of ancient architectural hybridity or anything contaminated by progressive modernity.

This kind of generalized and reduced identity should in fact be seen as the construction of a doctrine that renders it difficult, if not impossible, to reconstitute alternatives that are more fine-grained, subtle, and historically aware. The endless focus on the expression of Islamic culture in all its forms (whether in scholarship, in popular culture, in architecture, or urban boosterism) drowns out knowing and uncovering another past—that of the endlessly rich and varied intellectual, political, literary, and artistic Arab record. Buried in the process are discourses for building a modern, progressive (and secular) Arab nation. It is those two visions—one open and varied, the other absolute and closed—that collided in the streets of Cairo with the Muslim Brotherhood's singular Islamic vision winning out, albeit (as events were to unfold) only temporarily due to a series of lamentable regressive outcomes.[19]

Although unfolding at a flashpoint, the so-called Arab Spring emerged after a two-decade-long period (at least) of questioning "identity" as an interpretive lens. A seminal recent account of this is that of the historian and political economist Georges Corm in his *Pensee et Politique dans le Monde Arabe* (*Thought and Politics in the Arab World*). Starting from his disappointment with the outcome of the Arab Spring, Corm insightfully and comprehensively traces the evolution of Islamic and Arab intellectual and political thought in its encounter with modernity from 1850 to today. Looking to early religious reformists, such as Sheikh Tantawi and Taha Hussein from Al-Azhar University in Cairo, and early Arab secular thinkers—such as Yassin El-Hafez, Mahdi 'Amel, the poet Adonis, the economist Samir Amin, and the feminist poet May Ziade, to name but a few—Corm generates an archive that counteracts the dominant and destructive "Jihad vs. McWorld" phantasmagoria.[20] Arab nationalism was not only antiimperialist but often Marxist in its critique, socialist in its ambitions, and nonaligned in general. Nasserian thought was also an aspect of Arab Spring mobilization; portraits of Nasser were visible during demonstrations. Given its long and complex development, Corm's line of critical engagement with an Arab modernity should constitute an alternative standpoint from which to construct architectural possibilities. Just as with its twin appendage of trivia kitsch, the conservative social and political structures that architects are so often invited to serve should not be the only guiding option.

Representing Images for the Arab City

There are institutions engaged in this very project of fostering historical memory *and* Arab modernity. They include the Arab Image Foundation (AIF) and the Arab Center for Architecture (ACA), both based in Beirut. While the advancement of disciplinary knowledge sits at the heart of their cultural mission—architecture for the ACA and photography for the AIF—both institutions are nevertheless deeply engaged in the question of identity, religious and otherwise. Founded in 1997, the AIF houses a unique collection of over 600,000 photographs taken between 1850 and 1950 by professional, amateur, and anonymous photographers. The images encompass a wide range of subjects, genres, and styles that capture everyday life during an age of transformation, progressive thinking, and optimism about the future of Arab nations. These images make evident the multiplicity of influences that constitute Arab urban life.

The AIF acknowledges that "inevitably, its research projects raise questions about how images connect to notions such as identity, history, and memory." Clearly evident in the archive is "the infiltration of modernity into the Arab world," in both mundane and extraordinary ways. One powerful collection, published also as an ambitious book volume, is Akram Zaatari's *The Vehicle*. Going through family albums, the project links representation of the vehicle—cars and trucks—to modernizing trends of culture and domestic life.[21] The AIF project "Arts et Couleurs" similarly reveals larger lessons of modernism in Arab urban life, depicting as it does "a time of economic growth, hula hoop parties, beehive hairdos and the Beatles."[22] With these projects taken together, the AIF presents modernity in its multifaceted and complex layers—vividly contrasting the notion of a region stuck in time and in senseless conflict.

For architecture, the AIF's Chadirji collection is particularly important. It documents Baghdad's ebullient intellectual and artistic renaissance in the 1950s, a time when Iraqi architects, poets, and writers were welcoming modernist ideas and styles, hybridizing them not only with Islamic references but also with a playful mix of Babylonian ancestry and contemporary political discourse. This was a time that brought talented architects like Mohammed Makiyo and Hisham Munir together with European eminences like Walter Gropius, Josep Lluis Sert, and Marcello d'Olivo. Besides his work with other European architects, Munir became close friends with d'Olivo, with whom he collaborated on the Unknown Soldier Monument in Baghdad. Even Hassan Fathy, whose language has come to embody the quintessential regionalist architecture, never referenced Islamic motifs in his seminal 1958 New Gourna project (Luxor, Egypt) but rather wove together abstract modernist forms with pharaonic imagery.

This creative and resilient embrace of modernity helped Arab nations shed the shackles of colonialism and build new, independent institutions. The writing of certain architects, urban theorists, and scholars thus resists the notion that modernity was experienced as a simple imposition, arguing instead that it gave rise to a unique form (architectural and otherwise) in every city in which it took root.[23] This narrative is one that Beirut's Arab Center for Architecture painstakingly traces through photography, drawing, and texts. Besides their availability at the center in Beirut, these documents are becoming available in an online archive.

As with the Arab Image Foundation, the archive collapses the distinctions between generic structures and exquisite buildings, private houses and public monuments, local designers and international figures. In so doing, it strives to make palpable the many-layered complexities of the region's modernist project. Like the AIF, the ACA archive also carefully traces authorship, documenting collaborations between local and international architects, as well as temporary and permanent residents. CETA, a collaborative effort of French and Lebanese architects and engineers—J. Reacting, J. N. Conan, J. Nassar, P. Neema—is well represented. This is the collaboration that was responsible for the design of the perfectly proportioned Electricité du Liban building (1965–1972) in Beirut. Alas, many of these jewel-like buildings have been destroyed by either conflict or development, fallen into complete disrepair or "dressed" with orientalizing arches and the depressing pastiche surface Arabism that passes for "identity."

Old Centers and New Centers in the Arab Modernization Process

Arab urbanization—as now should be obvious—is far from being a unitary and geographically homogenous process. A visit to the old centers of Cairo, Beirut, Damascus, or Baghdad even today provides evidence of how these cities have embraced modernism. There are the less noticeable features, like crumbling modernist old towns, new shopping malls (by no means all spectacular), and the relentlessly generic housing and commercial buildings of prebranded neighborhoods. However much or little these structures are now valued, they signal varieties of the Arab modern; and they document, once again, the ways that Arab cities were not simply sites where an "authentic" culture was brutally displaced by an encounter with modernity.

An example of an imposed "outside" design, but one that would also—albeit awkwardly—take root, was the suburban-style gated communities established in the 1930s by oil companies as "company towns" for their employees. The goal was to attract middle-class Americans, among others from the West, by providing a comfortable enclave for them to spend a few years in suburban familiarity, albeit in places like the Saudi desert. These detached homes and surrounding yards inverted the local courtyard housing typology, which connected rooms and houses around extended kinship and tribal relationships. Aramco built suburban-style compounds for its Arab staff as well, though segregated from its American employees. The consumerist lifestyle that marked these environments was less appealing to Arab women in particular, who found the arrangements socially isolating.[24] Today, as the Gulf states' sprawling, luxurious gated communities are built with imported labor located in invisible camps, one is reminded of the oil company's original experimentation with arbitrary separations and enclosures running counter to most versions of urbanistic cosmopolitanism.

In addition to involving European and American planners and architects, Saudi development also involved collaborations with Japanese architects—whose respect for tradition, awareness of cultural specificity, and commitment to a specific national architectural identity rendered them desirable partners for major projects. Kenzo Tange, for example, built numerous state buildings including the Royal State Palace in Jeddah (1980–1983) and the King Faisal Foundation (1976–1984) in Riyadh. Minoru Yamasaki, the Seattle-born Japanese American architect designed the original World Trade Center towers in New York and the elegant Dhahran International Airport in Saudi Arabia (1961).

Successive collaborations with American oil and construction companies (such as Bechtel) led to increased commissions for U.S. design and engineering firms. These projects borrowed Western modernist, Far East, and Bedouin motifs of patterned surfaces, arched openings, courtyards, medina-like cityscapes, and tent-inspired structures. They simultaneously represented origin stories blended with statehood and adhered to modernist principles of form and massing. Their architectural language, restrained and reticent, aligned with conservative social and political values and readily incorporated modern technologies.

Today, an emboldened version of this narrative can be read across buildings such as Skidmore, Owings & Merrill's National Commercial Bank of Jeddah (1977–1984), which weaves together strong modernist abstraction with orientalized patterns and courtyards. Similar types of fusion show up in the firm's Abdul Aziz International Airport in Jeddah, also known as the Hajj Terminal (1982); and in the King Saud University (1984) designed by U.S.-based HOK architects, who also designed the King Khaled International Airport (1975–1984) in Riyadh. These projects represent a synthesis between tradition and modernity rather than an actual mediation of past and future.

Parallel versions were manifest in urban planning: from Constantinos Doxiadis's plan for Riyadh (1971) to Georges Candillis's plans for Dhahran and Al Khobar (1974) developed for Aramco. In urban planning projects, modernist approaches to zoning and infrastructure incorporated restrictions on height and setbacks to address privacy concerns appropriate to gender issues, in particular.[25]

The Bahrain Pavilion at the Fourteenth Venice Architecture Biennale in 2014 was itself a narrative of conflicting modernities, of uneasy cultural heritage, and of political, socioeconomic, and technological anxieties. Designed by the Lebanese architects Bernard Khoury and George Arbid, the pavilion staged a rotunda of shelves: a library, but one filled with thousands of copies of the same book. Consisting of seminal architectural buildings from the Middle East and North Africa built between 1914 and 2014, the book stood as a manifesto for the region's ability to not only "absorb modernity," as the overall theme for the national exhibits announced, but to find in modernism's generic and abstract nature universal qualities of the region's social ambitions, inventions, and adaptations. As visitors flipped through books while seated around a large circular table at the center of the space, an animated video played on a loop above them. In it, a man dressed in all white recited what would seem a trancelike prayer in Arabic. The speaker was in fact simply reciting the names of the nations from which the archived buildings had been selected. The pavilion's scenography depicted, in effect, the longstanding opposition between an Arab progressive identity—as represented by the exhibited buildings and the map on the table—and an Islamic conservative nationalism as suggested by the speaker's incantation, even as that incantation was utterly innocuous. As a whole, the project undermined the simplicity of binary oppositions (modern vs. traditional, Jihad vs. McWorld).

A less artful but far more consequential intervention is being radically played out on the ground in the reconstruction of Beirut—while it is not a city on the Gulf, it is a place that reveals what can go wrong (or potentially, at least, go right) when particular versions of heritage meet up with vicissitudes of contemporary ambitions. Here the city's most important urban development project, Solidere—named after the

Figure 2.4. The Solidere area in Beirut. Photograph by the author.

public-private corporation that continues to oversee the development of the heart of the Lebanese capital—has fallen woefully short in its attempt to valorize the country's actual traditions. Solidere was founded in 1994 by Prime Minister Rafik Hariri, a self-made businessman who rose to fortune and power as Prince Fahd's personal contractor in Saudi Arabia. Under Hariri's direction, Solidere's mode of development has become a model for the region and beyond, inspiring new projects from Mecca to Mumbai. Within Beirut, Solidere's operations generated intense opposition, mostly to little avail. The company made extensive use of eminent domain, as per the pattern of the legal tool, forcing owners to forfeit their property rights. In redrawing ownership lines and combining parcels of land, Solidere enabled its favored large-scale projects to move forward (fig. 2.4).

Like the iconic buildings that have emerged as part of the Gulf's architectural landscape, Solidere poses for Beirut and Lebanon a complex conundrum. On the one hand, the heart of the city was rebuilt with incredible speed and with the greatest architectural and urban intentions (often with undeniably striking results). On the other hand, as many architects noted at the time, the planned reconstruction also destroyed significantly more of the urban fabric than had fifteen years of war.[26] And while this material destruction—as with most any act of preservation—represented a political editing of history as it demolished certain buildings and recast the importance and meaning of others, the more significant erasure was that of the city's social fabric. The combined effect is the ushering in of a new narrative for the city's formation and the formation of its people's identity. With the goal of reviving Beirut as a tourist destination and as the "Paris of the Middle East," Solidere turned the buzzing, tight-knit, and messy fabric of downtown into a city of icons. Mosques, churches, and a single temple were excavated and preserved as ruins. Transformed into freestanding objects, these religious buildings became at once monuments and meaningless clichés, standing in for religious pluralism—but gutted of the real life and endless daily transactions that had shaped their prior existence.

Using as pretense the preservation of memory, Solidere constructed a fiction instead—a picture-book religious assortment to serve as the only possible foundation of the national identity. As the critic Assem Salam observed, "To pretend to protect this memory by preserving a few monuments while obliterating the context onto which they were inscribed can only diminish their real nature. They will be like desecrated tombs, witnesses to the death of the city." As religious icons punctuate shopping streets with alternating Haussmanian and Ottoman flavors, downtown Beirut has today become successful as a tourist destination for wealthy Gulf and Saudi nationals. Emptied of a local population, it becomes a ghost town the minute those countries declare its grounds unsafe for their citizens to visit.[27] In actuality, downtown Beirut's legacy as the social condenser for the city beyond was ignored.

Nor was the opportunity taken, as a result of the terrible events of war and then misconceived land clearance, to reflect more deeply on the city's history and its years of conflict. One exception that engaged in this reflection (and maybe also an example of a "real Beirut" in all its layers, contrasts, and contradictions) is the surviving 1920s-era complex repurposed by the talented architect and Lebanese national Bernard Khoury as the Centrale restaurant and bar. The project captures the intensity, fragile beauty, and raw history of downtown Beirut in all its complexity. By layering a steel girding and metal mesh onto the bullet-ridden and peeling facade of what had been a ruined private residence, Khoury both fulfills a modern functionality and actively reflects on the question of war, memory, and preservation. The project invites future generations to not only remember but also construct new possibilities for civic engagement that avoid disheartening clichés about received and reductive identities. Rather than building new fantasies or tearing down what was there before, this kind of creative adaptation displays the power of more radical forms of preservation to engage with history and to contribute varied texture and meaning to the urban and social fabric of a city.

Perhaps the best example of a wholly new construction that also fits into the inventive multilayered "tradition" of hybridity and contrast for which Beirut's actual history bespeaks, is the David Adjaye–designed Aïshti Foundation. Adjaye, born in Tanzania but with part of his life lived in Egypt, Yemen, and Lebanon—as well as many years in the United Kingdom—is now renowned for projects like the celebrated National Museum of African American History on the Washington Mall. In the earlier Beirut project, Adjaye seamlessly integrated an important private art collection with an everyday shopping experience. In so doing, he created a unique basis for the Aïshti art spaces. Architecturally, the treatment of both the facade's perforated screen—now a well-known Adjaye device—and the interior's Piranesian commercial space is nothing but contemporary in its expression (fig. 2.5). In reviewing the

Figure 2.5. Aïshti Foundation designed by David Adjaye, detail. Photograph by the author.

project, a Western critic described the aluminum tubular structure facade as "a scrim of multiple layers and patterns, reminiscent of the perforated woodwork typical of traditional Arabic architecture"[28]— falling into the trap of one-dimensional dictums of nativist identity, as many critics often do. Instead, the Aïshti Foundation's radical proposition reflects the city's resilient life, unique contrasts, and multilayered complexities. It presents a polemical juxtaposition of programs and contexts: art and commerce, the sea and the highway. We have, based on this successful project, further evidence that restriction to "local" architects (or local authors or local anything else) does not secure meaningful authenticity. Well beyond misconceived monumentality and surface trivia, there are ways to engage history and reflect on the lived and complex realities of place while also constructing unexpected and possible futures.

As in the past, the Arab city can produce audacious and complex constructions going forward. More than ever, we need to understand, in architecture and in the realms to which it is related, all the possibilities for respecting the past while charting a meaningful future. It is a challenge that can only be met by embracing our shared responsibility to consider the ways in which, as Bernard Tschumi once insisted, the concepts we enlist, the contexts we shape, and the content we produce matter in the world. A site at once imaginary and real, the Arab city embodies much of what is at stake today for architects and for architecture—and beyond. To engage in its complexity is to acknowledge the renewed urgency of historical knowledge while also embracing the responsibility to project much needed alternate possibilities.

NOTES

Some segments of this chapter have appeared in my introductory essay to the volume *The Arab City: Architecture and Representation* (New York: Columbia Books on Architecture and the City, 2016), Graduate School of Architecture, Planning, and Preservation (GSAPP), Columbia University.

1 For a critique of the constructed opposition of "tradition versus modernity," situating tradition as an effect of modernity, see Mitchell 2000.

2 Klingmann 2007.

3 Kanna 2011, 89.

4 See Mitchell 2011.

5 Etherington 2010.

6 "Jeddah International Airport," retrieved from http://oma.eu. For a convincing snapshot of the cliché, as of 2013, see Artemel 2013.

7   "King Abdullah Petroleum Studies and Research Center," retrieved from http://morphopedia.com.

8   Fairs 2008.

9   Ponzini 2011.

10 Balbo 2014.

11 Nouvel 2008. See the rehabilitation of orientalism post-Said in the work of Georges Corm, among others.

12 Said 1968.

13 Kanna 2011.

14 Besides Kanna, see Davis 1991.

15 Ackley 2005; Kanna 2011, see especially the chapter "Going South with the Starchitects: Urbanist Ideology in the Emerati City."

16 Bernhardsson 2008, 88.

17 Thomas Friedman (2006, online) on the Arab world: "The problem is much deeper—we're dealing with a civilization that is still highly tribalized and is struggling with modernity. Dubaians are building a future based on butter not guns, private property not caprice, services more than oil, and globally competitive companies, not terror networks. Dubai is about nurturing Arab dignity through success not suicide. As a result, its people want to embrace the future, not blow it up."

18 Gabar 1987.

19 Corm 2015, 178.

20 Barber 2010.

21 Zaatari 1999.

22 "The Vehicle: Picturing Moments of Transition in a Modernizing Society," Arab Image Foundation, retrieved from www.fai.org.lb; "Arts et couleurs," Arab Image Foundation, retrieved from www.foi.org.lb.

23 See Tabet 1998. Too often, "traditional" and vernacular styles have been indexed, codified, and then hijacked, moving to a more assimilative form of occupation, as brilliantly described in Wright, 1991.

24 Citino 2006.

25 Al-Hathlool 1996, especially 195–235.

26 Kassir 2003, especially 630–640.

27 As Salam has elaborated: "Effectively, a fatal blow has been dealt to the memory of this very ancient city, one better suited for oil-rich Arab countries, with a wealth of new buildings, perhaps, but a dearth of architectural traditions" (Salam 1998, 132).

28 Stevens 2015. See also the mission of the Ago Khan Architecture Award, which while promoting the important work of preservation and preserving heritage works to move beyond the criteria of Islamic identity. See also Holm and Kalle-hauge 2014.

REFERENCES

Ackley, Brian. 2005. "Permanent Vocation: Making Someplace out of Non-place." *Bidoun* 4: n.p. http://bidoun.org.

Al-Hathlool, Saleh. 1996. *The Arab-Muslim City: Tradition, Continuity, and Change in the Physical Environment*. Riyadh: Dar Al Sahan.

Artemel, A. J. 2013. "Hey Middle East: Enough with the Regional Architectural Clichés, Already." *CityLab*, August 16, 2013. www.citylab.com.

Balbo, Laurie. 2014. "Modern Mashrabiya Is Arab Architecture Made in the Shade." *Greenprophet*, June 26, 2014. www.greenprophet.com.

Barber, Benjamin. 2010. *Jihad vs. McWorld*. New York: Ballantine Books.

Bernhardsson, Magnus. 2008. "Modernizing the Past in 1950s Baghdad." In *Modernism and the Middle East, Architecture and Politics in the Twentieth Century*, ed. Sandy Isenstadt and Kishwor Rizvi, 81–96. Seattle: University of Washington Press.

Citino, Nathan. 2005–2006. "Suburbia and Modernization: Community Building and America's Post-World War II Encounter with the Arab Middle East." *Arab Studies Journal* 13–14: 39–64.

Corm, Georges. 2015. *Pensée et Politique dans le Monde Arabe*. Paris: La Découverte.

Davis Eric. 1991. "Theorizing Statecraft and Social Change in Arab Oil Producing Countries." In *Statecraft in the Middle East: Oil, Historical Memory, Popular Culture*, ed. Eric Davis and Nicolas Gavrielides, 1–35. Miami: Florida International University Press.

Etherington, Rose. 2010. "National Museum of Qatar by Jean Nouvel." *Dezeen*, March 24, 2010, www.dezeen.com.

Fairs, Marcus. 2008. "Dubai Opera House by Zaha Hadid." *Dezeen*, June 6, 2008, www.dezeen.com.

Friedman, Thomas. 2006. "Dubai and Dunces." *New York Times*, March 15, 2006. http://query.nytimes.com.

Grabar, Oleg. 1987. *The Formation of Islamic Art*. New Haven, CT: Yale University Press.

Holm, Michaeljuul, and Mette Marie Kallehauge, eds. 2001. *Arab Contemporary: Architecture and Identity*. Humblebaek, Denmark: Louisiana Museum of Modern Art, 2014.

Kanna, Ahmed. 2001. *Dubai: City as Corporation*. Minneapolis: University of Minnesota Press.

Kassir, Samir. 2003. *Histoire de Beyrouth*. Paris: Fayard.

Klingmann, Anna. 2007. *Brandscapes: Architecture in the Experience Economy*. Cambridge, MA: MIT Press.

Mitchell, Timothy. 2000. "The Stage of Modernity." In *Questions of Modernity*, ed. Timothy Mitchell, 1–34. Minneapolis: University of Minnesota Press.

Mitchell, Timothy. 2011. *Carbon Democracy*. New York: Verso.

Nouvel, Jean. 2008. *Louisiana Manifesto*. Humblebaek, Denmark: Louisiana Museum of Modern Art.

Ponzini, Davide. 2011. "Large Scale Development Projects and Star Architecture in the Absence of Democratic Politics: The Case of Abu Dhabi, UAE." *Cities* 28, no. 3: 251–259.

Said, Edward. 1968. *Orientalism*. New York: Pantheon Books.

Salam, Assem. 1998. "The Role of Government in Shaping the Built Environment." In *Projecting Beirut: Episodes in the Construction and Reconstruction of a Modern City*, ed. Peter Rowe and Hashim Sarkis, 122–134. New York: Prestel.

Stevens, Philip. 2015. "First Images of David Adjaye's Completed Aishti Foundation Revealed." *Designboom*, October 30, 2015. www.designboom.com.

Tabet, Jad. 1998. "From Colonial Style to Regional Revivalism: Modern Architecture in Lebanon and the Problem of Cultural Identity." In *Projecting Beirut*, ed. Hashim Sarkis and Peter Rowe, 83–105. New York: Prestel.

Wright, Gwendolyn. 1991. *The Politics of Design in French Colonial Urbanism*. Chicago: University of Chicago Press.

Zaatari, Akram. 1999. *The Vehicle: Picturing Moments of Transition in a Modernizing Society* (Arabic). Beirut: Arab Image Foundation.

3

Mobilities of Urban Spectacle

Plans, Projects, and Investments in the Gulf and Beyond

DAVIDE PONZINI

The Gulf is not just reconfiguring itself; it's reconfiguring the
world. The Gulf's entrepreneurs are reaching places that
modernity has not reached before . . . from Morocco in
the West, then via Turkey and Azerbaijan to China in the
East. . . . The Gulf's developers operate on a scale that has
completely escaped "our" attention. This burgeoning campaign to export a new kind of urbanism . . . may be the final
opportunity to formulate a new blueprint for urbanism.
—Rem Koolhaas

In the face of the 2007–2008 financial crisis, some cities in the Western
world and in Asia nevertheless kept investing in large-scale and spectacular projects, cities of the Gulf prominent among them. Spectacular
skyscrapers assert international presence, part of the recipe for putting a
place "on the map."[1] Even Mecca, the very word already signifying all that
is most valuable about a site, added in some spectacle with construction
of what is now the third highest building in the world —the Royal Clock
Tower, right at the holy site. Saudi Arabia has other skyscrapers under
way—the Kingdom Tower in Jeddah—at 1,008 meters is to be completed
in 2020 and eventually become the tallest in the world. Some record-
breaking buildings now exist in the Gulf, of course, with Dubai's Burj
Khalifa the world's highest structure. As with Qatar (of which Doha is
the capital), Dubai UAE uses a worldwide portfolio of real estate investments as a part of economic strategy toward diversifying the national
economy.

Some developmental initiatives also involve mega events like sports championships and world-class art and cultural festivals, with iconic buildings as part of the same branded venue. Qatar sponsored the 2006 Asian Games and the 2011 Pan Arab Games. Bahrain began hosting a Formula One grand prix in 2004; Abu Dhabi followed in 2009. The FIFA World Cup is set for Qatar in 2022. The 2020 Universal Exposition, a kind of world's fair of futuristic programs and building projects, will take place in Dubai—under the motto "Connecting Minds, Creating the Future." Besides their immediate venue, each event has its own related infrastructure and spectacular development stratagem.

Architectural and Urban Spectacles

Spectacle, when referring to objects or activities in relation to a specific place, often connotes something that *disconnects* from the locale and indeed may achieve its impact by standing out and going beyond. Spectacles provide an element that transcends local conditions and the interconnections of day-to-day operations. For Jean Baudrillard,[2] who can be considered a theorist of the disconnect, the Centre Georges Pompidou in Paris (known as Beaubourg because of its location in that neighborhood) exemplifies the phenomenon. He uses the term "Beaubourg effect" to call attention to the architectural and urban features of the Pompidou Museum, which utterly betrays the urban texture of what came before. Derived from top-down decision making, it was designed as a machine for hosting massive numbers of visitors, separated physically and socially from the surrounding lively neighborhood. It is a superblock of modernism, meant to connote the latest trends in museology. For intellectual followers of Baudrillard, this is a recurrent cultural condition of contemporary cities: symbols have substituted for contents entirely. Spectacular city symbols exhibit connectivity with one another, but on Internet websites or through tourist travel routes and guidebooks—not through the realities of actual urban places and the lives of people who use them.[3] Although Gulf cities are extreme manifestations, some of the same tendencies are to be found in other cities in the world, where urban problems and challenges of the importing and exporting of spectacular projects are clearly discernible.

Certainly in the Gulf, the Baudrillard critique rings true. For most of the population, many such buildings are at best backdrops, at worst the very structures whose construction exploited their labor and whose maintenance relies on their (underpaid) efforts. Some of them are available only to a small elite; they stand as reminders of others' wealth and power. In still other cases, their very creation was never meant to imply routine access. Formula One circuits operate only a few days per year. The grounds that host an expo or sport mega events are difficult to reconnect to the city fabric and functioning. Typically, the images of stadia or race-tracks are placeless: rankings of winners and losers, records, and prizes connect to the events (and their stars) and not the host places. As with ranking cities themselves—which has the tallest buildings, for example—judging is not about how they serve their urban contexts or their residents. Instead, the criterion is about how a given isolated architectural item compares with a different one, however distant, with which it is taken to be in competition.

These culturally powerful images and spectacles now circulate at an unprecedented pace, in part through Internet visual representations.[4] They are consciously and explicitly used for economic and political aims. In this sense, one can see how urban spectacles are concrete ways of representing, strengthening, and even establishing social and power relationships internationally. "Putting the city on the map" thus involves accumulating wealth and power that advantages a particular group of actors in the global urban competition. Spectacularizing and decontextualizing are often shortcuts for helping to obscure the contradictions of specific urban processes and policy making. The greatness of the building can lessen attention to context, or to the liabilities of the project. This is especially useful in conditions of low political legitimization and uneven distribution of the benefits that will result. The whole phenomenon of spectacularization has general relevance, not just pertaining to architectural and urban projects per se. For the French theorist Guy Debord,[5] spectacles are ways of communicating, of fostering messages and understandings of the world—a basis for perpetuating given power structures.

The worldwide flow of real estate finance, city competition to attract it, and indulgence of mobile design professionals are an increasing part of the worldwide city-building recipe.[6] Projects already seen as successful can be duplicated as investment packages capable of generating good returns.[7] This often means repeating similar building types or master plans and applying similar technologies for spectacular effects—but adapted to new places. Exact duplication is rarely the aim; some adjustments are typically made to handle topography, adapt to the client's requests, or allow the passing of time to bring some shift in detail. Although there are changes in consumption and taste,[8] the original template serves as a master guide. Overall, these processes involve the mobility of international experts, designs, and aesthetics stimulating a degree of global urban homogeneity in the race to keep up with the evolving newness.[9]

Although the content of their work may be recognizable and in fact admired, the starchitects provide the element that is perhaps the most crucial for communication: their name. The big name is a brand that invokes past glories of international prizes and, quite often, past commercial success. Not only will the name attract tenants and consumers, but also it will help sell the project as it moves through the government planning process, such as it may be. High design makes the real estate product more visible and authoritative for global investors. For these reasons, and given the limited presence of specialized design expertise historically available from within the Gulf, the region's development actors have depended on the intense importation of outsiders.[10] But those outsiders then change what they do elsewhere based on what they take away from their Gulf city experience. All this coming and going yields stumbles as well as stunning accomplishments. In application at the local level, the recurrent potential for disconnect remains, as is sometimes apparent in the various spectacular Gulf cases.

From a Tower in Barcelona to a Tower for Doha

Given that the same architects who are active in the Gulf are also active in Europe (and other parts of the world as well), we have a chance to see how projects, of similar design, do or do not change as the they "travel" across distant countries and regions and how they impact context when they land. Our primary case at hand involves a comparison of two buildings in close resemblance but separated not only by geographic space but also by the types of urban governance that produced them.

With the highest GDP per capita in the world, Qatar has the capacity to implement significant architecture. In Doha, the capital city, we have the building that truly is a stand-alone accomplishment, the Museum of Islamic Art designed by the U.S.-based architect I. M. Pei. Other projects from international designers in Doha include the Hamad International Airport (HOK), National Museum (Jean Nouvel), and National Library (OMA). In each case, the architects' renown is beyond dispute. Beyond that, as is common with other projects in Doha, they emanate from planning and permit regimes that provide fast approvals, and which encourage construction speed.

With dozens of high-rise buildings built within the last fifteen years on the waterfront of the West Bay Central Business District (CBD), the Doha skyline has itself become an icon for the city. Although recent strategies envision a core role for public transit[11] (and massive investments in railways and subways), highways remain the key transportation reality and affect the ambiance and viewscapes surrounding any project. Contrary to the classical features of central business districts in the West—accessibility, density, concentration of retail and office space, and multiple transportation modes—the Doha CBD relies on stand-alone buildings, with little attention to the public realm except car access, parking, and traffic movement.[12]

One of the West Bay skyscrapers offers up the Doha "side" for a more or less matched comparison with a Barcelona version of implementation. The same French architect, Jean Nouvel, designed towers of strong resemblance to one another. The Doha Tower completed in 2012 followed seven years after the opening of the Spanish one in 2005. The Agbar Tower in Barcelona's Poblenou District was part of a complex process of urban renewal. Since the mid-1990s, Barcelona's planners had been aiming to convert Poblenou from an obsolete light-industrial and residential zone to a "new-economy" higher-density and mixed-use area.[13] Nouvel's Agbar Tower was to represent a pinnacle, a landmark for the newly conceived district. Sited at the crossing of three main road axes, the 142-meter-high building, although among the tallest in the city, respects the surrounding low-rise urban landscape. Given height limits for the district overall (and the rest of Barcelona), Agbar Tower could stand out as a symbol of the district's renewal. Its specific siting derives from the competence of the democratically controlled local planning apparatus and a participating public, albeit one contentious at times.[14]

The much taller Doha Tower (231 meters) came about through a very different institutional apparatus, with an absence of public participation or binding regulatory framework. Other skyscrapers, each with striking aesthetics on its own (e.g., the Tornado Tower and Palm Towers), crowd it in. It means that each building loses its individual readability, certainly when perceived in situ—as opposed to idealized architectural renderings before the fact (a distinction spelled out by Michele Nastasi in chapter 4). The presence of so many wannabe spectacular buildings reduces the impact of any one of them.

Thus, despite the similarities in building aesthetics, architecture, and building function, the relationship between the towers and their urban contexts is radically different. In the Barcelona version, the building has strong visibility and makes a clear contribution. The goal was accomplished through coordinated land-use planning (including that of the adjacent district), a planning system that gained both from local and international professional competence and from the discipline of democratic agency.

Qatar Capital Migration: To the Shard in London and UniCredit Tower in Milan

Echoing the domestic investment policy leaning toward iconic sites and landmarks, Gulf-based developers and investors have become active in foreign real estate ventures in the West, both importing and exporting urban spectacles (notably to and from Doha, Dubai, and Abu Dhabi). In 2005, the government of Qatar created the Qatar Investment Authority (QIA), which was to coordinate a number of agencies and subsidiaries oriented toward investment both nationally and in what was to become operations in over twenty foreign countries. Adding to its visibility, and eventual profitability, Qatar was conspicuously bullish during the global economic crisis of the late 2000s. As stated by the Emir of Qatar, "With the current crisis, many countries prefer to keep their money instead of investing it abroad. For us, though, this is an opportunity that will not be repeated in the next 20 years."[15] QIA has developed a significant

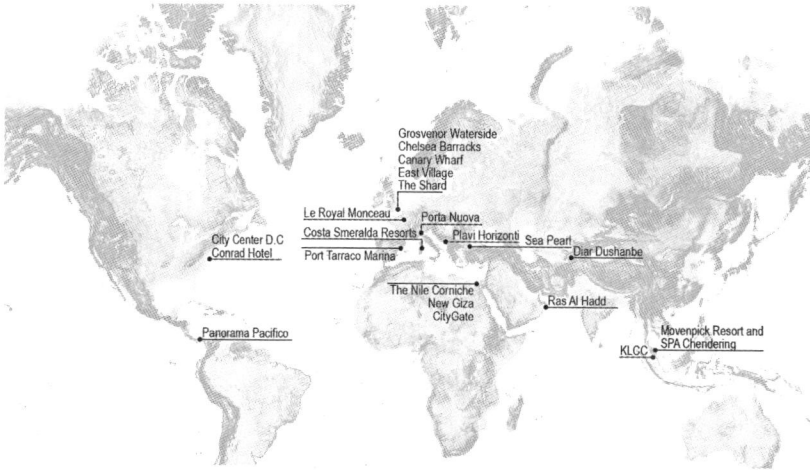

Figure 3.1. Partial map showing holdings currently planned and managed by QIA, Qatar Diar, and Qatar Holding outside Qatar. Source: elaboration of data retrieved from www.qataridiar.com and www.qia.qa in September 2015.

network of partnerships with large planning and construction firms in Europe and beyond,[16] with major investments in Turkey, Montenegro, and Malaysia, as well as countries in the West (fig. 3.1). Consistent with its strategy of favoring megaprojects, its subsidiary Qatari Diar took a large-scale position in financing the CityCenterDC project in downtown Washington, DC.

London is the city with the greatest number of Qatari projects and largest amount of capital invested outside Doha. In the decades before the new millennium, the few London high-rises that had been completed were built outside the most central areas—like Canary Wharf. But in the 2000s, iconic buildings (branded by the usual cast of international designers, like Norman Foster, Richard Rogers, Rafael Viñoly, and others) started to rise in the financial district ("the City") and in central London. The Shard skyscraper (designed by Renzo Piano), on top of the London Bridge multimodal rail station, was in line with then-mayor Ken Livingstone's call for densifying infrastructure nodes by "creating new architectural icons for the new century," as he put it.[17] British organizations—the Commission for Architecture and the Built Environment, English Heritage, and still other local groups—opposed its scale and impact. The original design was adjusted to a somewhat lower height along the way. But at ninety-five stories, it remains Europe's tallest building since its completion in 2012.

At the building's 2012 inauguration, praise for the project came from Prince Andrew, the new mayor Boris Johnson, and the Emir of Qatar, who were all in attendance. According to its British developer, it was made possible only through financing from the Qatari state (eventually to have a 95 percent share of the property). At a time of great world economic uncertainty,[18] Qatar's patient money thus likely played a role in accepting near-term low or perhaps negative returns. The building soon became a new icon in the urban landscape, reinforcing a long-term transformation for the South Bank of the Thames.

Either because of design, height, or some aspect of cultural anxiety, Qatari projects in London are, as evidenced in opposition to the Shard, not without controversy. Prince Charles (the Prince of Wales), a consistent critic of untraditional London projects, became a vociferous public opponent of Qatar's later efforts to redevelop the site of the historic Chelsea Barracks. London's Deputy Mayor Kit Malthouse (during Mayor Boris Johnson's term in office) also condemned the Barracks plan (designed by Lord Richard Rogers) as "nothing short of urban vandalism."[19] The opponents forced a redesign. Other controversies evolved over development of the East Village in the 2012 Olympic area. The recent control gained by QIA over Canary Wharf—another mega investment—has similarly met with some concern.

A second European skyscraper that has involved crucial Qatari investment is Milan's UniCredit Tower—Italy's tallest (231 meters). In terms of large-scale sites available for real estate development in the 2000s, the Porta Nuova area surrounding the Garibaldi railway station was the most central. Authorities had long envisioned it for a new business headquarter and public administrative district. Located only a few hundred meters from the historic city center, it had been underutilized and mostly vacant since the Second World War. In the mid-2000s, the Italian branch of a multinational real estate development company, Hines, bought the land and development rights and assembled some surrounding lots to form a single large-scale development site. Under design direction of the starchitect Cesar Pelli, the project gained some momentum, including a commitment by the large international bank UniCredit as the anchor tenant. In the planning phase, and as a means of building political support for the project, there was supposed to be a fashion museum and a large public park.

The global financial crisis threatened the capacity to build most any project variant. As with the Shard, rescue came from the Qatari authorities. In 2013, Qatar Holding acquired 40 percent of the development company. This enabled coverage of the debts of Hines Italy and permitted the project's partial completion. In 2015, Qatar Holding bought out all remaining shares; currently it owns the entire Porta Nuova development. In all the stops and starts, the museum project was lost, and the promised parkland, at the time of this writing, has been only partially implemented. But the spectacular tower is distinctive on the Milan landscape, along with some other showy high-rise buildings constructed nearby. Whatever worth it provides to the city's planning system (and there remains controversy on that front), the project offers further testimony of the potential for Gulf capital to make a difference in a Western metropolis.

Dubai-Based Emaar: Importing and Exporting Master Plans and Projects

Dubai is the great exemplar of urban spectacularization, and Dubai's Emaar Properties is the Emirates' most visible and resource-rich commercial sponsor and project exporter. Dubai authorities are clear about using spectacle for attracting international attention and amazing the public.[20] Like Qatar and other governments in the Gulf, Dubai stresses the goal of economic diversification, here necessitated by the fact that the emirate does not have access to significant oil and gas resources—hence the high priority for other sectors, including trade, tourism, and business services.

Even when a Dubai project design might come from a foreign source, it undergoes local adaptation as it transfers in. One such instance— unlikely as it may seem, was from Vancouver's False Creek to Dubai.[21] In the process of planning and creating the Dubai version, the developer, Emaar, trimmed away some key features of the Canadian original, like its emphasis on public space, green areas, and social inclusion.[22] Such features fell to the developer's financial priorities and, on the design front, favor for high-rise and iconicity.

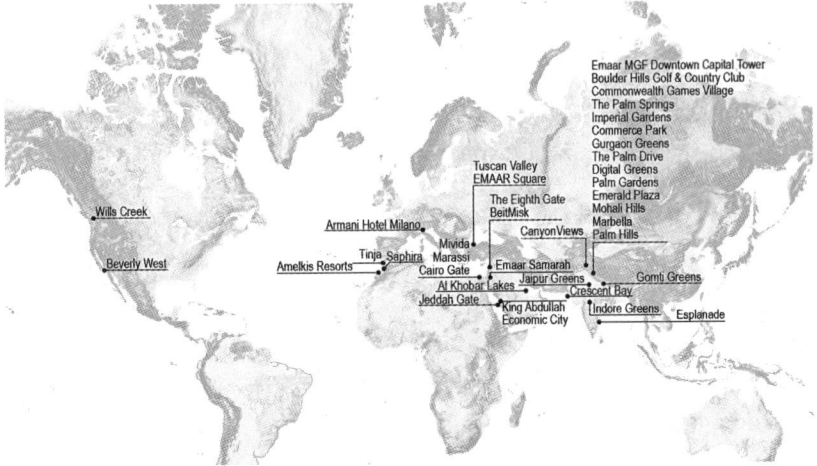

Figure 3.2. Partial map of the holdings planned and managed by Emaar Properties outside the United Arab Emirates. Source: elaboration of data retrieved from www.emaar.com in September 2015.

On a more giant scale is Emaar Square in Dubai, adjacent to the iconic Skidmore, Owings & Merrill's–designed Burj Khalifa, now with the largest and most visited mall in the world—Dubai Mall—adjacent to the tallest building in the world. But some of Emaar's operations abroad are arguably equally impressive. The company now has thirty-three out of its fifty-three major projects located outside of the United Arab Emirates—in North Africa, Asia, Europe, and North America (fig. 3.2). In most cases, Emaar's projects follow (albeit at a varied scale and diversified according to geography and partnership arrangements) mixed-use residential and retail forms. Taking from the Dubai original, it has used the brand Emaar Square for successive projects in Istanbul, Cairo, and Jeddah. Emaar is also involved in developing the extreme megaproject King Abdullah Economic City in Saudi Arabia.[23] Overall, Emaar has a stated strategy: "To replicate our Dubai business model and practices in international markets."[24] In some contrast to its local projects, in international operations Emaar looks to partner with other investors, sometimes limiting its role to land acquisition and basic infrastructure-related interventions. Additional funds are raised project by project. Emaar benefits from its "headlining accomplishment"—the Burj Khalifa—to reassure decision makers and investors. When viewed from this perspective, the risks involved in constructing spectacular buildings in Dubai are compensated by the business opportunities gained by operating internationally.

Abu Dhabi's Central Market to Abu Dhabi Plaza in Astana, Kazakhstan

On a more limited scale of engaging in other parts of the world, the major operator in Abu Dhabi is Aldar Properties, established in 2005 (according to its official website profile) "primarily to create world-class real estate developments for the nation of Abu Dhabi."[25] It only recently has made moves abroad.

A prominent and consequential example of its domestic work is the firm's redevelopment in the mid-2010s of the city's Central Market project designed by Foster + Partners. The site had once been the city's central souk, a lively center of small entrepreneurs, which somehow came to be considered incompatible with the city's ambitions to modernize. The new project, also known as the World Trade Center Abu Dhabi, consists of what remains the tallest building in Abu Dhabi (at 381 meters), the Mohammed bin Rashid Tower. Besides office space, the complex includes luxury residences, a hotel, and shopping. According to the designers, it represents, particularly in the layout and materials of its shopping mall, a contemporary reinterpretation of the traditional bazaar.[26] The development required demolishing the preexisting popular market and replacing shopkeepers with more upmarket merchants. While no doubt adding to the spectacle of Abu Dhabi's skyline, it surely falls short of maintaining the traditional atmosphere of a souk.[27] Few would be convinced it provides, as in the Foster + Partners prospectus, "a new civic heart for Abu Dhabi." This civic heart has gone upmarket but barely gets a mention in tourist guidebooks and, indeed, does not appear to attract many visitors, local or otherwise, to its designed spaces.

Aldar's single significant project outside of the UAE is Abu Dhabi Plaza in Astana, capital of Kazakhstan. For this fast-growing city fueled by its own booming hydrocarbon economy (primarily natural gas), Aldar has created a complex of luxury hotels, retail, office, and housing, following quite literally—right down to its name—the Abu Dhabi format, as taken from the Central Market project. The project has received the avid support of and participation from the country's longstanding autocrat, Nursultan Nazarbayev, who has been in office since the country's independence from the USSR in 1990. He now holds the title "Leader of the Nation" and is the main promoter, decision maker, and financier in Astana city planning. Astana was the designated host of the 2017 Expo, with new developments making use of transnational designers and spectacular forms. Norman Foster is again a key figure, as architect of the Palace of Peace and Reconciliation (also known as the Pyramid) and the Khan Shatyr entertainment and shopping center. Other spectacular projects, also under patronage of the president, revolve around the central Millennium Axis, grandly laid out to maximize monumental views.

Referring to the Abu Dhabi Plaza, the Foster + Partners press release confirms that "the scheme is inspired by its sister project in Abu Dhabi— the Central Market Redevelopment."[28] It has the goal of "creating a new landmark on Astana's skyline"[29] with, if completed as planned, the tallest building in Central Asia, at 382 meters. In further reference to its antecedent, parts of the mall are touted as drawing on the traditional Kazakhstani bazaars—in the firm's now familiar message, a "reinvention of a traditional marketplace."[30] There are also claims for implementing cutting-edge technologies, in particular for maximizing gain from solar light during the city's freezing winter. Astana and Abu Dhabi have almost opposite climates but similar urbanistic rhetoric. The economic goals are also familiar. The chairman of Aldar, Ahmed Ali Al Sayegh, commented: "The Abu Dhabi Plaza development is a catalyst for the city of Astana to further develop its economy and bring business interest into the nation. We hope that this development will be viewed as an icon for Astana as well as a landmark for Kazakhstan on an international level."[31] To further enhance commercial prospects, the authorities designated the project's district as a "special economic zone." The Astana planning scheme reproduces UAE and Gulf tactics in myriad ways: architectural ambition, advanced indoor climate technologies, and juxtaposition of mixed uses—all through similarly autocratic political and economic arrangements.

After the grand public and international announcement of the Astana plaza's design, implementation was handed over to the British-based HKR Architects, a lesser-known firm than the eminent Foster +

Partners. HKR describes itself as "an architectural consultancy for the new global economy . . . Our network of offices in the United Kingdom, Turkey, Russia, Kazakhstan and the UAE enables us to offer a full scope of services to our clients, delivering international experience and local knowledge to each project, *regardless of location*."[32]

Mobilities of the Spectacular: Some Early Learnings

Gulf cities play an origin role for spectacular projects. Agents in European and North American global capitals are involved as both senders and receivers of ideas, competences, plans, and architectural projects. Rem Koolhaas had an insight, as quoted in the chapter's introduction, in pointing to the Gulf as an urbanistic force. There are multiple reasons why urban and architectural spectacularization is amplified in the Gulf. Although the Middle East has an extremely rich historical layering, the newness of most of the Gulf's cities is perceived and managed, in land-use terms, as a tabula rasa. In the fast-expanding cities of Doha, Dubai, and Abu Dhabi, a basically weak planning system relies on schemes and visions that designate megaprojects but not precise uses, procedures, or controls. Concentration of land holdings also facilitates development options. Financial, political, and legal resources are similarly in the hands of a few decision makers. A shared consensus and political orientation among national and city authorities toward economic diversification and internationalization further guide development toward the spectacular and the mega scale. Into the mix come transnational architects who can exercise their fame or career-building design imaginations. It makes for speed, but it impairs the building of strong urbanistic structures.[33]

Part of the symbolic value of spectacularization has been to signal cultural worth and status both to national citizens and international observers (a theme further developed by Steffen Hertog in chapter 12). Besides some vague symbolic gain, having the tallest—the largest or the most splendid—distinguishes Gulf projects in a crowded global real estate market. Gains in technology, most conspicuously displayed in the Foster-designed Masdar City (described by Gökçe Günel in chapter 8), have the potential for replication elsewhere. Otherwise risky projects—conceived and managed through the favorable Gulf-city conditions—can be exported in adapted forms to other markets (where they may or may not fail). Dramatic displays of construction capacity can induce confidence among developers in other cities in the world to proceed with similar design models and hence spread the gospel of spectacle even when Gulf entrepreneurs are not involved.

A consistent element in all the Gulf examples of this chapter is the depoliticization of local planning and designs—the other side of the spectacle coin. In the Gulf, this depoliticization has also involved social exclusion and an uneven distribution of costs and benefits. There is surely a gap between the rhetoric and the actual urban effects, a tendency spreading out to other cities, West and East. The depoliticization of urban and architectural projects is problematic not only because democratic involvement is of value and a worthy end in itself (even in places that bypass it), but also because having information from multiple parties helps bring more sensible outcomes into being. It is unwise to disable what has been called "the intelligence of democracy"[34] in individual projects, as well as in broader urban policies.

Even within the competitive logic so prevalent among today's cities, spectacularization can induce paradoxical effects. The multiplication of places vying for consumers' attention tends to lower the potential for any one place to stand out. In their prodigal reach, redundant spectacles tend to homogenize. At the aggregate international scale, it is even possible that the creation of parallel pieces of architecture will reduce tourist flows to any one of them—people may instead stay home or at least travel within a narrower range of destinations. The ironic antidote, one can posit, is to pay more attention to contextual aspects—but attending to the warnings offered by Amale Andraos (in chapter 2) to be wary of the kitsch that might substitute for the authentic complexity of tradition. Better planning would require fuller and more intensive interaction with local actors and places.[35] Developing place-sensitive projects implies awareness on the side of developers and designers toward local richness, even regarding spectacle. In furtherance of such awareness, it is not absurd to say that transnational elites would be better off, in the long haul, supporting stronger planning and design power at the local level. Reaching a higher public good would mean, of course, thinking beyond spectacle as desirable in itself. Decency and social justice have an aura only of goodness.

NOTES

I would like to acknowledge Fabio Manfredini's and Liana Mandradzieva's kind research support for data collecting and mapping and Jill Diane Friedman's support for English-language editing.

1 Urry 2007a.
2 Baudrillard 1982.
3 Baudrillard (1994) presciently called this condition "hyperreality."
4 See Nastasi, in this volume.
5 Debord 1970.
6 Knox and Pain 2010.
7 Gotham 2006.
8 Siemiatycki 2013.
9 As we know, cities tend to generate policies by using antecedent cases in terms of prototypical examples and paradigmatic and successful models (Urry 2007b; Guggenheim and Söderström 2009; McCann 2011).
10 See, among others, Aoun and Teller 2016.
11 See the Qatar Development Framework, www.mdps.gov.qa.
12 Mirincheva, Wiedmann, and Salama 2013.
13 Ajuntament de Barcelona 2011.
14 Ponzini and Arosio 2017; Palermo and Ponzini 2015.
15 Windfuhr and Zand 2009, para 1.
16 Djermoun and Hersant 2013.
17 GLA 2001, 14.
18 Ruddick 2012.
19 Cited in Adams 2009.
20 Elsheshtawy 2010.
21 Lowry and McCann 2011.
22 Ponzini, Fotev, and Mavaracchio 2016.
23 See Moser, Swain, and Alkhabbaz 2015; Moser's chapter in this volume. Emaar n.d.
24 Emaar 2014, 4.
25 Retrieved from www.aldar.com (accessed May 28, 2009).
26 In the firm's words: "Central Market will be a reinterpretation of the traditional market place and a new civic heart for Abu Dhabi." Cited in Elsheshtawy 2008b and retrieved from "Abu Dhabi Central Market to Be Transformed," www.foster andpartners.com (accessed April 29, 2012).
27 See Elsheshtawy 2008b.
28 Foster and Partners 2007.
29 Foster and Partners 2007.
30 Foster and Partners 2007.
31 "Aldar, Al Maabar launch project in Kazakhstan," Trade Arabia (website), November 1, 2007, www.tradearabia.com.
32 "About Us," www.hkrarchitects.com (accessed April 12, 2015; italics added).

33 Ponzini 2013.
34 Lindblom 1965.
35 Palermo and Ponzini 2015.

REFERENCES

Adams, Stephen. 2009. "Chelsea Barracks Plan Is 'Urban Vandalism' Says Boris Johnson's Deputy." *Telegraph*, April 8, 2009. www.telegraph.co.uk.

Ajuntament de Barcelona. 2011. *22@: 10 Years of Urban Renewal*. Barcelona: Mimeo.

Aoun, Oula, and Jacques Teller. 2016. "Planning Urban Megaprojects in the Gulf: The International Consultancy Firms in Urban Planning between Global and Contingent." *Frontiers of Architectural Research* 5, no. 2: 254–264.

Baudrillard, Jean. 1982. "The Beaubourg-Effect: Implosion and Deterrence." *October* 20: 3–13.

Baudrillard, Jean. 1994. *Simulacra and Simulation*. Ann Arbor: University of Michigan Press.

Commins, David. 2014. *The Gulf States: A Modern History*. London: I. B. Tauris.

Djermoun, Soraya, and Emmanuel Hersant. 2013. *Qatar(isme)? Essai d'analyse du mode de fonctionnement d'un système*. Paris: Editions L'Harmattan.

Elsheshtawy, Yasser. 2008a. "Transitory Sites: Mapping Dubai's 'Forgotten' Urban Spaces." *International Journal of Urban and Regional Research* 32, no. 4: 968–988.

Elsheshtawy, Yasser, ed. 2008b. *The Evolving Arab City: Tradition, Modernity and Urban Development*. London: Routledge.

Elsheshtawy, Yasser. 2010. *Dubai: Behind an Urban Spectacle*. London: Routledge.

Emaar Properties PJSC. (n.d.) "Corporate Presentation March 10th, 2014." www.emaar.com.

Emaar Properties PJSC. (n.d.) "King Abdullah Economic City Is the Largest of Its Kind Private Sector Development." www.emaar.com.

Foster and Partners. 2007. "Designs Unveiled for a New Mixed-Use Development in Astana, Kazakhstan." www.fosterandpartners.com.

GLA [Greater London Authority]. 2001. *Interim Strategic Planning Guidance on Tall Buildings, Strategic Views and the Skyline in London*. London: Mimeo. http://legacy.london.gov.uk.

Gotham, Kevin Fox. 2006. "The Secondary Circuit of Capital Reconsidered: Globalization and the US Real Estate Sector." *American Journal of Sociology* 112, no. 1: 231–275.

Guggenheim, Michael, and Ola Söderström, eds. 2009. *Re-shaping Cities: How Global Mobility Transforms Architecture and Urban Form*. London: Routledge.

Kamrava, Mehran. *Qatar: Small State, Big Politics*. 2013. Ithaca, NY: Cornell University Press.

Knox, Paul L., and Kathryn Pain. 2010. "Globalization, Neoliberalism and International Homogeneity in Architecture and Urban Development." *Informationen zur Raumentwicklung* 5/6: 417–428.

Koolhaas, Rem. 2007. "Last Chance?" In *Al Manakh*, ed. Ole Bouman, Mitra Khoubrou, and Rem Koolhaas, 7. Amsterdam: Stichting Archis.

Lindblom, Charles Edward. 1965. *The Intelligence of Democracy: Decision Making through Mutual Adjustment*. New York: Free Press.

Lowry, Glen, and Eugene McCann. 2011. "Asia in the Mix: Urban Form and Global Mobilities–Hong Kong, Vancouver, Dubai." In Roy, Ananya, and Aihwa Ong. Worlding Cities. Asian Experiments and the Art of Being Global, 182–204. Malden: Wiley-Blackwell.

McCann, Eugene. 2011. "Urban Policy Mobilities and Global Circuits of Knowledge: Toward a Research Agenda." *Annals of the Association of American Geographers* 101, no. 1: 107–130.

McNeill, Donald. 2009. *The Global Architect: Firms, Fame and Urban Form*. London: Routledge.

Mirincheva, Velina, Florian Wiedmann, and Ashraf M. Salama. 2013. "The Spatial Development Potentials of Business Districts in Doha: The Case of the West Bay." *Open House International* 38, no. 4: 16–26.

Moser, Sarah, Marian Swain, and Mohammed H. Alkhabbaz. 2015. "King Abdullah Economic City: Engineering Saudi Arabia's Post-oil Future." *Cities* 45: 71–80.

NLA [New London Architecture]. 2014. *London's Growing Up!* London: NLA Insight Study. www.newlondonarchitecture.org.

Palermo, Pier Carlo, and Davide Ponzini. 2015. *Place-Making and Urban Development: New Challenges for Contemporary Planning and Design*. London: Routledge.

Ponzini, Davide. 2013. "Branded Megaprojects and Fading Urban Structures in Contemporary Cities." In *Urban Megaprojects: A Worldwide View*, ed. Gerardo Del Cerro Santamaria, 107–129. New York: Emerald.

Ponzini, Davide, and Prisca M. Arosio. 2017. "Urban Effects of the Transnational Circulation of Branded Buildings: Comparing Two Skyscrapers and Their Context in Barcelona and Doha." *Urban Design International* 22, no. 1: 28–46.

Ponzini, Davide, Stefan Fotev, and Francesca Mavaracchio. 2016. "Place-Making or Place-Faking? The Paradoxical Effects of Transnational Circulation of Architectural and Urban Development Projects." In *Reinventing the Local in Tourism: Travel Communities and Peer-Produced Place Experiences*, ed. Greg Richards and Antonio Paolo Russo, 153–170. Bristol, UK: Channel View.

Ponzini, Davide, and Michele Nastasi. 2016 (second edition). *Starchitecture: Scenes, Actors, and Spectacles in Contemporary Cities*. New York: Monacelli Press.

Ruddick, Graham. 2012. "The Shard Developer Says London 'Owes a Debt' to Qatar." *Telegraph*, July 5, 2012. www.telegraph.co.uk.

Siemiatycki, Matti. 2013. "Riding the Wave: Explaining Cycles in Urban Mega-Project Development." *Journal of Economic Policy Reform* 16, no. 2: 160–178.

Sklair, Leslie. 2017. *The Icon Project: Architecture, Cities, and Capitalist Globalization*. Oxford: Oxford University Press.

Urry, John. 2007a. "The Power of Spectacle." In *Visionary Power: Producing the Contemporary City*, ed. Christine de Baan, Joachim Declerck, and Veronique Patteeuw, International Architecture Biennale Rotterdam, 131–141. Rotterdam: Nai Publishers.

Urry, John. 2007b. *Mobilities*. New York: Polity Press.

Windfuhr, Volkhard, and Bernhard Zand. 2009. "Interview with the Emir of Qatar: We Are Coming to Invest," *Der Spiegel*, March 29, 2009, www.spiegel.de.

SECTION II

Assembling Hybrid Cities

4

A Gulf of Images

Photography and the Circulation of Spectacular Architecture

MICHELE NASTASI

As a professional practitioner, I have photographed many buildings designed by so-called starchitects as well as by other major architectural offices who have hired me for that purpose. My interest is also as an academic, urban researcher, who is focused on larger issues of context and patronage. Besides cities in the Gulf—Abu Dhabi, Dubai, Riyadh, Kuwait City, Manama and Doha—other places covered by my work include New York, Paris, London, Hong Kong, Barcelona, Singapore, and Milan. In examining and engaging architectural works in such places, one can make comparisons in how context alters design; it also becomes possible to "follow" projects, building types, and their designers as they move across different parts of the world.

High-design buildings now attract a great deal of attention, sometimes globally, often becoming icons of the cities in which they are located. One important and prevalent convention of architectural representation leads photographers—including sometimes myself—to deliberately exclude buildings' surroundings, including the humans who might otherwise be present. The exclusion of context facilitates the spectacle of the building form in itself, now constituting a global scenario of what cities can and should become. Decontextualization of images instills a simplified idea of the city, incapable of encompassing the complexity of contemporary urban landscapes or the lives of their residents and visitors. This is particularly evident in photographs of the cities of the Gulf, which do not just represent buildings but serve as normative inspiration for what cities can be. Whether in celebratory or critical analysis, these images (and their aftermath) influence architectural and urban debates that shape, in turn, developments on the ground.

My research,[1] both practical and theoretical, has been carried out in parallel with my professional work as a photographer of contemporary architecture and also as editor of the architecture magazine *Lotus*. Through various commissions and assignments, I often end up spending a lot of time in the vicinity of buildings, providing me opportunity to look at them from perspectives different from that of pure formal representation. Spending time with buildings allows a broader view outward to the surrounding city, adjacent and otherwise, and the many different populations that inhabit it. As editor of *Lotus* I must deal with the large number of pictures that come to the magazine every day. This encourages me to reflect on the recurrent characteristics of these images and on their implicit premises. As happens with other genres of photography, there are noticeable patterns and photographic conventions that come into play.[2] Searching for these patterns and their wider origins and consequence make up my PhD project as well my effort in this chapter.

For the more limited purpose here at hand, I intend to sketch out some of those recurrent modes of architectural representations, both of individual buildings and of ensembles. Then, I will draw on my photographs to demonstrate that these processes of representation, however much they lead to emulation, reveal what are only surface similarities between buildings across the world. The varied contexts in which the buildings exist in fact transform them. This gets effaced through those particular practices of spectacularization involving the careful choices of photographic siting, handling of light, and other details of professional practice. None of this alters how the building in fact connects (or fails to connect) with other buildings and populations. But in the way that projects' images and their designers travel, we can witness the movement of ideas to and from the Gulf. Whatever degree of truth there may have been to the idea that Gulf cities are the recipient of exports from the West, the Gulf can be now considered its own kind of leading force, in terms of assembling and circulating both images and actual designs—something I will try to show with the photographs that follow.

Figure 4.1. Burj Khalifa, Dubai, 2010. Photograph by the author. An actual photograph, not a rendering, shows Dubai's Burj Khalifa at dusk against the backdrop of the city, characterized by groups of high-rise buildings scattered all over the place while the air is thick with humidity. In the lower section of the photograph, a cluster of buildings in Neo-Moorish style is visible, facing the "waterfront" of the Dubai Fountain, the largest choreographed fountain system in the world.

Learning from Images

In part inspired by the goals of the current volume, I took another look at *Learning from Las Vegas* (1977). The Las Vegas book reintroduced into architectural debate the theme of the relationship between the physical building and its symbolic significance, something relevant for all spectacular and iconic architecture and especially so in emerging cities like those in the Gulf that aim to express an identity through architecture. As a photographer and student of images, I consider *Learning from Las Vegas* particularly important precisely because it is a research project based largely on images, carried out in the context of a living city.[3] It takes a phenomenological approach that is very close to my way of looking at urban architecture.

The Venturi–Scott Brown project took seriously ideas and images neglected in mainstream architectural criticism and scholarship, ideas and images that were (as with their subject matter) considered at best to be insignificant, shallow, or backwardly kitsch. Looking further at the original volume, there is the simulation of a genuine treatise on architecture, like the venerated discourse of Sebastiano Serlio or Andrea Palladio's. Both in the book's organization and in its polemical language—not without irony—the Las Vegas authors present contrasting architectural images and informal line drawings. These are mixed in with examples of historic buildings, the work of great modern architects, and with a collection of their own designs. They use large format, with an imposing title in serif typeface. In part, perhaps because of its provenance as a studio at the elite Yale School of Architecture, the book—in the manner perhaps of a Las Vegas scandal—caused something of a sensation. Robert Venturi, Denise Scott Brown, and Steven Izenour had turned the modernist canon on its head, making a case for spectacle as played out on the desert sands, including what they called "the ugly and ordinary."

My own method thus runs in parallel. I process what I find in the field in a heuristic, intuitive, and analogical manner. It is a more holistic practice as opposed to the conventional representation of architecture, which generally tends to illustrate solely the formal aspects of a building and to reproduce the idea of whoever has realized and promoted it. My perspective also differs from the didactic and illustrative use of images typical of academic writing. In contrast to both, photographs for me are a genuine "text," or rather a layering of texts, that concern not just architecture and city planning, but other social dimensions as well. Just like a text, a sequence or montage of photographs can propose a thesis and have programmatic value. But it is an open program in which the argument does not take the form of a classical syllogism. It is never a question of arriving at a conclusion that will reduce the complexity of the phenomena observed to unity, but instead it makes that complexity apparent through the suggestion of alternative interpretations.[4] So the photographs and images presented here should be seen as an investigation of imagery that, intersecting with other areas of research, brings up topics and raises questions.

Rhetorical Figures

Whether in branding a city, gaining an architectural commission, or leasing a building, the rhetorical devices of architects and photographers are rarely questioned. Over time, they become embodied in professional practice and publishing formats. These rhetorical devices are nevertheless not at all neutral; rather, they trigger mechanisms that, repeated on innumerable occasions, have helped advance spectacularization as ideology. Abstracting buildings from their contexts "smooths out" some of their idiosyncratic contradictions, as well as their problematic fit with their sites or social context.

Broadly speaking, we can trace the diffusion of professional architecture photography, as we understand it today, to the middle of the last century, and to a generation of photographers that shaped the image—and with it the myth—of American modernism in architecture (figs. 4.2 and 4.3).[5] For decades, photographs of modern buildings have followed those early conventions, some originating due to technical issues of their time and some arising from particular characteristics of the architecture itself. For example, the building is often presented in a three-quarter view taken with a wide-angle lens, in order to boost its volume and three-dimensionality. Many of these photographs make dramatic use of light and shade, to emphasize the modulation of the facades rather than the nature of the space. The buildings are photographed as autonomous objects, abstracted—as sculptures must be—from puzzling or befuddling extraneous elements. The long exposure times of the large-format cameras

Figure 4.2. Photograph by Ken Hedrich, 1950s: Mies Van der Rohe, Lakeshore Drive Apartments. Chicago History Museum, Hedrich-Blessing Collection.

generally in use did not permit the capture of movement—hence, people are commonly omitted. The sky is always blue, perhaps flecked with a few picturesque clouds. The photo is often taken at sunset so as to simultaneously show the building's outside and, with interior lights just on, at least a glimpse of the inside as well. This is not so much to document the features of the building, but to build image qua image (fig. 4.4). The majority of these photo shoots are commissioned by the architects of the buildings; hence, the picture tends to reflect principally the formal conception of the building, to be promotional, and to emphasize positive aspects and play down negative ones.

Figure 4.3. Photograph by Jim Hedrich, 1972: SOM, Sears Towers, Chicago. Chicago History Museum, Hedrich-Blessing Collection. Hedrich Blessing is one of the most prestigious photographic studios in the United States. Founded in Chicago in 1929, the studio's name is associated with American modernism, Blessing having long worked with some of its most important exponents and having been involved in constructing their iconography.

Figure 4.4. Photograph by Nick Merrick, 2010: SOM, Burj Khalifa, Dubai. © Hedrich Blessing Photographers. As with others of its genre, this photograph emphasizes verticality and minimizes contextual elements that might interfere with image qua image. It aims to reproduce, in effect, the architect's concept that lies behind the project, rather than a representation of what has come to be.

Many spectacular buildings do have their critics, with complaints against their excessive formalism, the incongruities of their scale, and a general indifference to their location. In part responding to the critique, there are a few examples of a deconstructive use of architectural photography. Most such examples that do exist are linked to specific publications or their editor's special interests in just these topics I have been taking up.[6] But this kind of representational departure, modest though it may be, is itself under threat given declines in editorial revenues. Budgets for architectural features have been hard hit, making photographers even more dependent on commissions from large architectural firms. This decreases the capacity of photography to serve as a means of critical interpretation of architectural design, even while the images become more important—thanks to the web—in circulating design outcomes. Increasingly, professional architectural photographs must adhere to the usual conventions and hence conform even closer to stereotype—further reducing the potential for alternative ways of looking at buildings and the city.

Renderings Unbound

Beyond the circulation of actual photographs, computer-generated images are no longer just a way of presenting architectural ideas, but a genuine tool used by architects during the different design phases of a project. Among all kinds of architectural representation, renderings are the ones closer to what Leigh Star and James Griesemer refer to as "boundary objects,"[7] which are artifacts and documents that can travel from one actor to another, one office to another, as a common reference point for further action, creation, or discourse.[8]

Computer-based images are means of seeking approval for the various agents involved—as those images travel over time and space. On some occasions, a persuasive rendering can decisively help an architect win a competition. Developers systematically use renderings in funding and selling a project, and public administrators also strategically utilize them to interact with citizens. Once again, however, these are not neutral objects. As spectacle becomes a lingua franca of prized buildings, renderings need to be "readable" as achieving just that goal. As they are passed from one office, agency, or actor to another, the spectacle part must come through. Renderings must thus further emphasize the characteristics of the photographs that I analyzed above, serving as the vehicle for a conception of architecture and of site that in renderings can be simplified, schematized, or idealized. All these developments are now even more evident in relation to the recent turn to photo-realism, which has become so accurate that it is almost impossible to distinguish certain renderings from an actual photograph.[9]

A significant part of any project remains based on the communicative power of images, especially if it is public or involves a high level of speculative investment. In various realms, cities of the Gulf have provided some of the most over-the-top examples of these types of fictional representation. There are several critical issues connected with the photorealistic rendering, the first of which is the tendency for it to be confused with the photograph and to be interpreted in a literal and objective sense, even though it represents a project that has not yet been realized. In addition, notwithstanding the photo-realism, which is generally associated with an idea of objectivity, renderings—often as deliberate choice—conceal the more problematic aspects of the projects they represent.

Paradoxes of the Skyline

Another typical representation of cities, beyond a particular building or its immediate context, is the skyline—representing something physical and substantial but experienced only in an abstract way, from a distance and "all at once." A key aspect is that—in real experience—as one goes closer in, the skyline recedes and then disappears. It can thus function, intended or not, as a veil over what goes on within cities, in both their physical and social qualities. Skylines seem a special obsession within the Gulf.

As a photographer and editor, but also as an ordinary citizen and tourist, I am often confronted with this kind of image, which is by now so well established and widespread in the world that, for many places, it has become the main urban symbolic form. Skyline images are the most common way to succinctly represent a place, skipping over the details of mess and complexity. Beyond issues like circulation, waste, or public amenity, they generate an easily read message. They are often used to promote internal consensus and affirm prosperity, including by developers and architects striving to create single buildings or groups of them. The skyline as representational device is thus the fruit of an effective and locally oriented mobilization. The skyline replaces other possible forms of representing life in cities, with a potential impact on the political and social functioning within them.

The word "skyline," now only about a hundred years old, was coined in New York at the end of the nineteenth century.[10] It was not initially picked up by architects, city planners, or even by critics. Instead, it was artists, photographers, and writers who put it to use in popular, literary, and journalistic images.[11] The first case in which the words "sky line" were utilized in relation to a picture dates from 1896, when the *New York Journal* included a pictorial supplement with a color lithograph of a panoramic view of the lower section of Manhattan, from the Brooklyn Bridge to the Battery.[12] Later it was photographers, of every kind, who replicated this type of representation and followed the evolution of the city's profile. The skyline transforms the city into a stage for architecture, which is sometimes spectacularized through the ensemble. Today, in an age in which everyone has a camera and is able to publish his or her own pictures instantaneously online, the skyline is everywhere.[13]

From early on, there was appreciation for the skyline as important for guiding urban impressions—"city branding," in today's language. In an article published in *Harper's Weekly* in 1897,[14] its prominent author, Montgomery Schuyler, compares two drawings of the city, one made in 1881 and one in 1897, to illustrate the vertical growth of the lower section of Manhattan. Recounting his arrival in New York by ship, Schuyler describes the appearance of the southern tip of Manhattan as a "confused mass of erections of various form and formlessness," a comment that could be applied today to the waterfront of any city in the Gulf. As his journey continues, the author describes the panorama to the east as a staggering mountain range running north for over a mile. He notes with satisfaction that the majority of visitors from Europe would get their first impression of New York from that point of view. In addition to grasping the touristic function of the skyline far ahead of his time, Schuyler links the skyline image to its constituent characteristic of the skyscraper, something about which he has overwhelmingly positive sentiments but with a note also of concern. He is anxious that the constant competition for height will unleash the skyscraper's "unneighborly" impacts and defeat the potential for urban "concert" that he imagines would come with some appropriate regulation.

Figure 4.5. A Symphony of Lights, Hong Kong, 2013. Photograph by the author. A crowd of tourists observes and photographs the sound-and-light show staged every evening for the Hong Kong skyline. The buildings are animated, like characters in a theatrical production, by patterns of light and laser beams. Spectacles of this kind were once staged only on special occasions.

Representing cities through imageries of their skylines, most famously in the case of Manhattan, has been replicated for many cities. It is a modern tool to signal power, achievement, and progress. But unlike prior representations of urban significance—for example, of the baroque square or the nineteenth-century boulevard—the skyline is not a tangible, physically experienced urban element. The skyline is inherently ephemeral; it fades with proximity.[15] Not a stand-in for busyness and concentrated interaction, it is a mere image for metropolis rather than a symptom of it. In places like Manhattan or Hong Kong (as depicted in fig. 4.5), skylines result from social and economic density that drive architecture upward. In contrast, the skylines of cities like Dubai or Doha correspond to a socially sparse city—where buildings are conceived and implemented in isolation from one another, creating alienating stretches in between. In other words, the image of the skyline in such cities is essentially misleading.[16]

Identity of Images, Difference of Places

In my photographic practice, I have investigated the relationship that actually exists between each work of architecture and the place in which it is located, showing the building in use, the city inhabited by different populations at different times of day and night, and the variety of the urban landscapes that result. This enables comparison between the landscapes of cities in different parts of the world and reveals the distinctive aspects of buildings, even as they follow similar sculptural forms or share similar skins or are designed by the same architect. Once again, context matters.

In terms of form and image, buildings (and skyscrapers especially) tend to repeat themselves across very different and distant places, appearing to create a sort of single undifferentiated place that is rootless and estranging, what Yasser Elsheshtawy has characterized—with the oxymoron—in a recent seminar on Dubai urbanism, "placeless geography" (see also his and Davide Ponzini's chapters in this volume). Taken as a whole and observed in sequence, these spectacular landscapes seem to closely resemble one another. But a closer examination of pairs or groups of them reveals that, despite a studied exuberance they tend to share, they are not, in urbanistic terms, at all the same.

The photograph taken at the Hearst Tower (designed by Norman Foster) in New York (fig. 4.6) shows how New York is itself part of the building's presentation. It cannot be seen as simply a global starchitect's imagining of a particular form—as a "Norman Foster" as it might exist in another city, Abu Dhabi for example. A first and strong element of the composition is the legally preserved six-story Joseph Urban-designed historic element—the prior Hearst Building. The new forty-six-story Foster tower stands on top of it. Above all in importance are the vitality of the immediately surrounding area and the cacophony of abutting buildings, pedestrians, cars, taxis, and bicyclists.

The I. M. Pei–designed Bank of China Tower, Hong Kong (fig. 4.7), displays a system of triangular frameworks comparable to the facade of the Hearst structure and hence carries an element of visual resemblance. But it also shows an impact from topography, including the kind of hills and lush landscape far less probable for a New York setting. The Hong Kong building also appears in context of other high-modern structures: on the

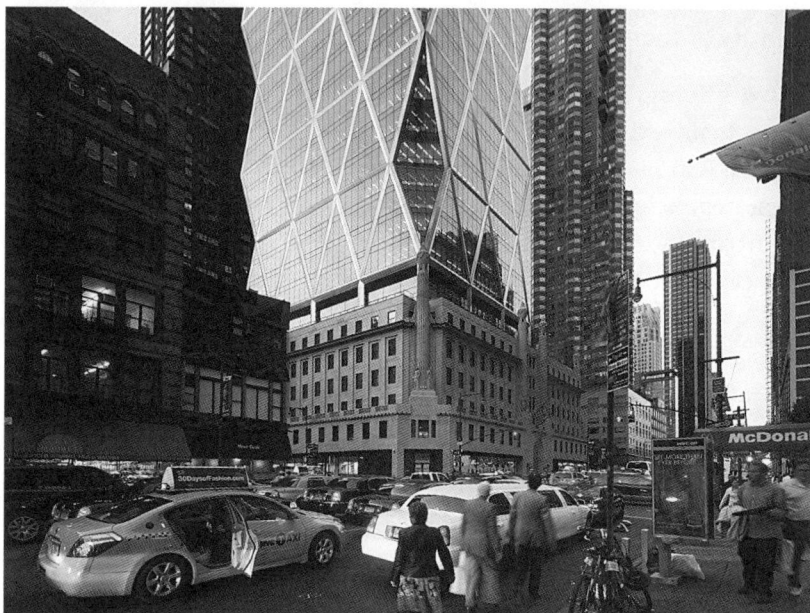

Figure 4.6. Hearst Headquarters, New York, 2008. Photograph by the author.

right, we can see César Pelli's Cheung Kong Center and Norman Foster's HSBC; on the left, we see Rocco Yim's Citibank Plaza. All are connected at road level, along with a dense network of elevated passageways for pedestrian and vehicular traffic. No matter the architect or its specific design, this could not be a Manhattan building.

The National Bank of Abu Dhabi, shot from the same street-level perspective, is something else again. The photograph shows a building at the intersection of two major traffic arteries with six lanes each (fig. 4.8). The city has clearly been structured to give highest priority to cars. In the foreground, we can see a group of people crossing the road, a contingency that has not been at the center of the region's urban planning schemas. Their mode of dress identifies them as workers, likely from India and Southeast Asia. Although making up a majority of the urban population, they often move about on foot. The bank is a design by the globally renowned Uruguayan-Canadian architect Carlos Ott, designer of the Bastille Opera in Paris and other buildings in Dubai.

Figure 4.7. Bank of China, Hong Kong, 2013. Photograph by the author.

Although punctuated with spectacular structures in various parts of the city, and concentrations in several districts, Abu Dhabi is composed largely of generic buildings being put to prosaic uses. While the presence of people, as in New York or Hong Kong, might well challenge conventions of architectural photography, the presence of these people in Abu Dhabi—and the low-rise buildings scattered sometimes nearby—is especially out of synch pictorially.

I have shown the photograph in figure 4.9 many times at conferences and seminars—two men in business attire walking along a pedestrian bridge between the towers of La Défense in Paris—but only rarely has someone been able to identify where it was taken. People cannot do so because the visible buildings are "anywhere" structures. There is no "known Paris" in the photograph—no Eiffel Tower, no Louvre pyramid, nor other usual icons. Just as consequential, there are no localistic elements that might give it away, like vendors, booksellers, shop signage, gendarmes, or uniformed schoolchildren. Stripped of any such context, the buildings themselves become anonymous. These are structures that do have significant architectural pedigree—the building at the center is

Figure 4.8. Abu Dhabi National Bank, Abu Dhabi, 2010. Photograph by the author.

Kohn Pedersen Fox Associates' Tour CBX. But that is not enough to give it distinction. Lack of contextual specifics yields a placeless architecture that also resurfaces—to different degrees—in many cities in the Gulf and beyond.

Another way for me to establish the salience of context is by taking up four otherwise "matched" buildings from European (and Middle Eastern) designers, made different from each other by the specificities of sites. In terms of form and prominent design elements, they might appear to be outright replicas of one another.

The first is Norman Foster's celebrated building in the city of London (fig. 4.10) that everyone calls the Gherkin (a.k.a. 30 St Mary Axe). The building strongly contrasts with the dense texture of the surrounding area, one that is highly varied in architectural style and typically of lower heights. (I shot all these buildings from the same perspective.) The Gherkin stands different, but it does not stand alone. The ground level is dense with pedestrians and London bric-a-brac.

The second photograph shows Jean Nouvel's Torre Agbar in Barcelona (fig. 4.11). It is on the edge of the large Plaza Glòries that, despite being

Figure 4.9. La Défense, Paris, 2010. Photograph by the author.

Figure 4.10. View of the Gherkin (30 St Mary Axe), London, 2015. Photograph by the author.

Figure 4.11. The Torre Agbar at Glòries, Barcelona, 2011. Photograph by the author.

in the middle of a long-term major transformation, is frequented by a variety of populations with pedestrian access at several levels. Urban uses are in strong evidence. The square is an important infrastructural node, and the building has become a specific landmark both for the transformation of the surrounding neighborhood and for the city of Barcelona in general.

The strong contrast comes with the Doha West Bay project (fig. 4.12)—an exuberant set of towers in a landscape made up entirely of tall buildings. The ensemble was evidently conceived as isolated objects. The public space is not much more than a leftover, a waste product of the architectural scheme. In the right side of the image are large multi-lane streets that seem to run into a white building, which is a nine-story parking structure. There are commodious walkways internal to the project, but not very useful given their surplus scale and lack of sun protection, so, as is characteristic of the site, only a few pedestrians are present. To the left in the photo, we can see, albeit mostly hidden in the background, the Gherkin-like tapered form of Jean Nouvel's Doha Tower, so very similar to Barcelona's Torre Agbar—also designed by Nouvel. Both of the Nouvel's are regularly compared, in turn, with London's Foster-designed

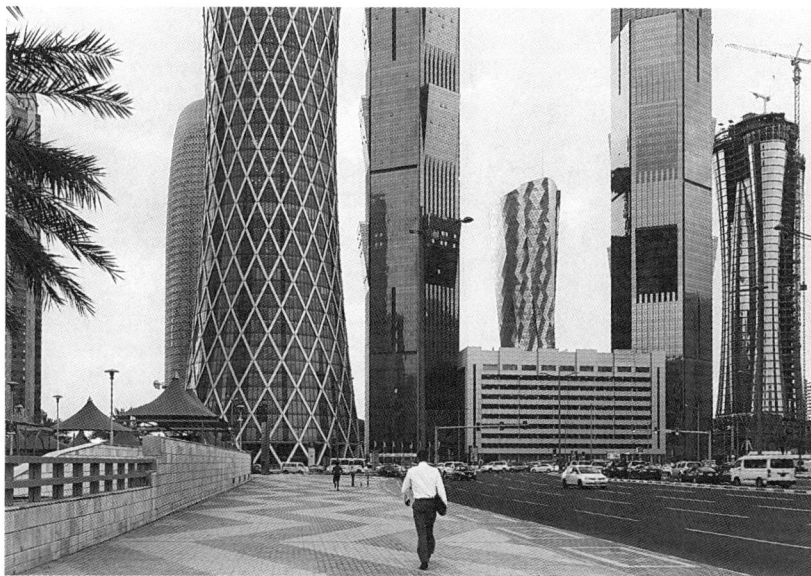

Figure 4.12. West Bay, Doha, 2013. Photograph by the author.

Gherkin. Although it uses a different structural technique, the Barcelona building was certainly the model for the Doha version, enlarged in scale.[17]

In the foreground and in full view (toward the left) is the so-called Tornado Tower, designed by MZ Architects, a firm founded in Qatar with offices in Lebanon and the UAE. It again repeats the diagrid design of the Gherkin. Such elements translate well as images that can travel and, given globally available technologies, can be replicated. We see the diagrid design in other recent spectacular buildings as well—besides the Hearst Tower in New York, the Aldar Headquarters in Abu Dhabi (also designed by MZ Architects but not pictured here), and the Capital Gate in Abu Dhabi (designed by the British-based firm RMJM [fig. 4.14]).

Another factor in the iconographic life of the New York skyline is the fact that new buildings are typically quite sober—sometimes as a result of constraints imposed by public agencies—again compared to their Gulf counterparts.[18] Quite in dissimilarity with most of commercial Manhattan, Abu Dhabi gained its supertall buildings without direct pressure from market demand and in a more permissive planning environment. Figure 4.13 shows Norman Foster's Abu Dhabi Central Market

Figure 4.13. View from Central Market, Abu Dhabi, 2017. Photograph by the author.

when under construction, with what remains the tallest building in the city, the Mohammed bin Rashid Tower. The complex was initially designed as three towers, the tallest of which is at the center of the photograph. Only two were built: one at ninety-two stories (381 meters), one meter higher than the Empire State Building; the other at sixty. The picture reveals the glaring disproportion between the height of the new group and the surrounding city, made up chiefly of generic buildings that do not exceed fifteen stories.

While some buildings can vie for height superlatives, others compete in terms of formal eccentricity, at times measured against some bizarre benchmark. The photograph in figure 4.14 shows, in the midst of a desolate landscape, the Abu Dhabi building called Capital Gate, a 160-meter tower designed by UK-based RMJM, boasting the record for being the "world's furthest leaning man-made tower." We see a contrived repetition of an image, but on a larger scale: the original leaning iconic tower in Pisa—the precarious result of human error—is here made taller and still more tilted. It anchors—if that is the right word—the scheme for the new Abu Dhabi National Exhibition Centre, intended to be a sort of gateway to the city.

Figure 4.14. Capital Gate, Abu Dhabi, 2010. Photograph by the author.

Buildings can take on phantasmagoric forms through various architectural strategies, such as those appreciated by Venturi and Scott Brown, which involved shaping a building as a duck—to sell eggs. Boat shapes are not an uncommon form for large projects—residential, touristic, and commercial. Even the heavy concrete Brutalist style of the 1960s and 1970s had marine-like manifestation, as with the "Vele" housing project at Scampia, Naples, which suggests huge urban ships that somehow make it to land. In Abu Dhabi, the massive structures of Al Bandar on the waterfront (Al Raha Beach), designed by the British group Broadway Malayan, are inspired by the "sails" of Marina Baie des Anges at Villeneuve-Loubet in Côte d'Azur. Here they appear as great ships stranded on the desert shore. The buildings' emphasis on terraces and balconies on all the facades further helps recall the decks of a cruise liner (fig. 4.15). But these are luxury apartments of permanent residence. The same nautical reference image reappears in a London version by the same designers, at Battersea Reach on the South Bank of the Thames (fig. 4.16). Here again the buildings' balconies and terraces simulate decks at sea.

Ships and their decks have also come to Milan, built as part of the City Life scheme to include the Hadid Residences, named for their

Figure 4.15. Al Bandar, Abu Dhabi, 2010. Photograph by the author.

Figure 4.16. Battersea Reach, London, 2015. Photograph by the author.

Figure 4.17. City Life Hadid Residences, Milan, 2014. Photograph by the author.

starchitect, the late Zaha Hadid (fig. 4.17). The cruise ship aesthetic here yields results—given the Milan context—that radically differ from the stand-alone beachfront environment of Abu Dhabi. The project is over-scaled in its context and abruptly creates a visual stop for the surrounding streets. With walls and fences that separate the buildings from the city, both visually and physically, the result is a closed and introverted complex that flies in the face of the traditional permeability of Italian cities.[19] The style travels and lands as contradiction, itself the urban fixture.

We also see signs of architectural travel involving Asian locations. Miami-based Arquitectonica's Gate Towers in the Al Reem district of Abu Dhabi (fig. 4.19) and Singapore's new landmark, Marina Bay Sands (fig. 4.18), show strong similarity in iconicity. The latter was designed by Moshe Safdie, himself a global hybrid—Syrian, Israeli, Canadian, and American.[20] But again, context matters, with the Abu Dhabi project being distinctive in its impermeability. Its buildings are residential towers mounted on a commercial podium that contains a mall and parking garage, while the upper bridge holds private penthouses. The mall is the only accessible element of the complex—part of Al Reem Island, a new district of Abu Dhabi that so far is composed of detached buildings

Figure 4.18. Marina Bay Sands, Singapore, 2013. Photograph by the author.

Figure 4.19. Gate Towers, Abu Dhabi, 2015. Photograph by the author.

scattered in the desert, reachable only by car. The Singapore counterpart is Marina Bay Sands—a hotel, a mall, and a casino. It stands in a central area, with an open scheme that leaves the buildings publicly accessible by walking and public transport—a gesture to urbanistic values. The sky deck on top contains a swimming pool reserved for hotel guests, but also an open-to-the-public observatory to view the city and its surroundings.

Besides site-specific impacts, an accumulation of buildings made fantastic by height, shape, or use cumulate as urban form that, especially when given drama through viewing platforms and photographs, become the city—at least in circulating imagery and as well as on-the-spot observation. It happens to a strong degree, as I have previously discussed, through the skyline, whether deliberately or accidentally created. Beyond the Gulf region, emerging countries in Asia—not just China but also Malaysia, Indonesia, Taiwan, and India—push toward the skyline to affirm their prosperity and prospects. The United States (and Manhattan) can no longer be assumed as the only source of spectacle for emulation. As with other parts of the world, the UAE is no longer the simple recipient of American (or European) architectural ideas; some of the influence goes in the reverse direction (as Ponzini details in chapter 3).[21]

The impact of skyline also depends on its "place" within the larger arena that provides viewing location and the range of what can be included. Viewing London from within London, with its own jumble of buildings and uses, is not like being "in the view" of Dubai. Nor is the experience of open space in Manhattan like experiencing open space in Dubai (or Doha or Abu Dhabi). Perhaps the greatest contrast is in how the New York skyline appears from within Central Park (fig. 4.20); there is no parallel viewing site within UAE cities. Besides the fact that New York's buildings are shorter and more mixed in age and style, the park's vastness as public amenity matches the scale of the buildings on the horizon. It is also its own exhibition space of diverse peoples doing diverse things; it is a recreation zone of people and whatever might cross their minds to do in public. That too is part of what is glimpsed and noticed as scene.

Figures 4.21 and 4.22, images from Dubai, feature two distinct population groups. These images show spaces that are—in social, physical, and symbolic terms—profoundly different both from one another as well as from New York. The first (fig. 4.21), at the foot of the Burj Khalifa, is a space of visual entertainment that is the product of a large-scale

Figure 4.20. View from Sheep Meadow, New York, 2009. Photograph by the author.

Figure 4.21. Dubai Fountains and Burj Khalifa, Dubai, 2010. Photograph by the author.

development project related to the skyscraper and the massive commercial activities of Downtown Dubai. People are programmed by the changing colors and "dancing" of the fountain they face, as well as the shops and restaurants adjacent. The second image (fig. 4.22) captures the skyline and a place of spontaneous aggregation by those who are essentially excluded from the rituals of consumption. They have very little

Figure 4.22. Dubai skyline from Al Satwa, Dubai, 2015. Photograph by the author.

to work with other than the omnipresent sand and views of the backdrop buildings to which they have limited access, if indeed any access at all. In the photo, they can be seen playing a semi-improvised game, making creative use of a leftover (for now) piece of the urban fabric. These photographs document, once again, how spectacles of architecture and skyline shift in their meaning, in this case by the way their adjacent urban spaces come to be used and who is using them.

Conclusion

This analysis of photographs has shown architecture's global visual spread, and not just regarding particular buildings, but to whole swaths of cities. The characteristics of urban development in Gulf cities like Doha, Dubai, and Abu Dhabi—large in scale, deliberately iconic, and given to extravaganza—are advanced through photographic conventions that are very partial representations. The Gulf cities are now part of global imagery and a common visual language.[22] They are increasingly relevant for discovering and thinking about architectural trends, visual and otherwise, happening in any city in the world. As in those other places, common and persistent problems remain unaddressed—or are made even worse—by the skewed agendas: congestion, waste, and social deprivation. In examining specifics of site, as well as other urbanistic dimensions, the analysis has reinforced the finding that the logic of spectacle does not ensure positive outcomes for urban life, resource use, or civic governance.

NOTES

1   The first part of the photographic research was published in the volume Ponzini and Nastasi, 2016, in which the case studies of Abu Dhabi, Paris, and New York are compared. Most ideas in this chapter have been discussed in depth with Harvey Molotch and Davide Ponzini in the process of developing and curating the exhibition *Learning from Gulf Cities*, held in New York (March–April 2016) and Abu Dhabi (November–December 2017); the research and exhibition indeed integrated a number of the following images of mine and related comparisons between cities in the Gulf and in other world regions.

2   See, for example, Ford 1998.

3   See Stadler and Stierli 2008.

4   The reflections on the status of images, their montage, and their function made here draw on the chapter devoted to Warburg's atlas, "Le montage Mnemosyne: tableaux, fusées, détails, intervalles," in Didi-Huberman 2002.

5   Two recently published volumes are particularly interesting for the breadth of their treatment of the relations between photography and architecture: Higgott and Wray 2012; Zimmerman 2014.

6   Ideas on photography as a critical tool in the representation of architecture were discussed in a seminar that I organized at the Politecnico di Milano with Davide Ponzini (*Fotografia critica d'architettura: vedute e riflessioni*, 2011) and then published in Ponzini 2012. See also Nicolin 2006 and the texts by Paolo Rosselli, Luigi Ghirri, and Lewis Baltz in Galbiati 1991, and the recent article Wilkinson 2015.

7   Star and Griesemer 1989.

8   See Rose, Degen, and Melhuish 2014, on the case of the 310,000-square-meter Msheireb Downtown project in Doha, Qatar.

9   For an in-depth analysis of architectural rendering and the recent turn to photorealism, see my article Nastasi 2016a.

10 Taylor 1992.

11 "The Sky Line" is the name used by the *New Yorker* magazine for its architecture column, from 1925 by George Shepard Chappell, then by Lewis Mumford, 1931–1963, then again Brendan Gill, 1987–1997, and currently by Paul Goldberger. It was also the name of a militant architectural journal, edited in New York by the Institute for Architecture and Urban Studies from 1978 to 1984.

12 Kouwenhoven 1972.

13 For detailed examples and interviews with internationally known architectural photographers, see my PhD dissertation: Nastasi, 2017.

14 Schuyler 1987.

15 As a formula of representation, the skyline can be associated with the concept of the polarity of the image—that is, the possibility that the same figure can be interpreted in different and contrasting ways. Didi-Huberman (2002) discusses the principle of "antithesis" or "inversion of meaning" of the image, which on the one hand intensifies its effect formally and, on the other, leads it to abandon the meaning that is commonly associated with it in order to assume the opposite one. See also Ginsburg 2015.

16 In Lindner 2015 the city is seen through an interesting opposition of the two conceptual categories of "skylines" and "sidewalks." On the skyline as a powerful image, see also Nastasi 2016b.

17 For a more detailed comparative analysis of these two buildings, see Ponzini and Arosio 2017. The theme of "traveling buildings" was one of the topics of the exhibition *Learning from Gulf Cities* curated by Harvey Molotch and Davide Ponzini displaying my work.

18 Erich Mendelsohn, in his famous 1926 book *Amerika*, entitled two of his chapters "The Gigantic" and "The Grotesque," referring to New York building types that now seem innocent compared to the showiest part of today's global architectural production, much of it located in the Gulf. See Mendelsohn 1926.

19 A further example of the ambiguity of images, but also of their pervasive character, is provided by the article on City Life published in *Architect Magazine*, the organ of the American Institute of Architects, in May 2014, illustrated with my photographs. In the article the scheme in Milan was indicated as a possible model of urban development for the United States, and on the cover of the magazine, there was a photo of a detail of the Hadid Residences accompanied by the title "Learning from Milan" (Russell 2014).

20 At the time of writing, a very similar project, again by Moshe Safdie, is being built in Chongqing. A comparison of the Singapore and Chongqing projects can be found in Ponzini, Fotev, and Mavaracchio 2016.

21 For London, see Booth 2013. For Milan, see Bocconi 2016. This subject has been treated in the exhibition *Learning from Gulf Cities* (see note 1). See also Ponzini's chapter, this volume. Some parts of the last paragraphs of the present chapter are quoted from the exhibition's texts.

22 See Yasser Elshashtawy's website www.dubaization.com.

REFERENCES

Bocconi, Sergio. 2016. "L'uomo che Cambia lo Skyline di Milano, il Ritratto di Manfredi Catella." *Corriere della Sera online*, January 11, 2016. http://milano.corriere.it.

Booth, Robert. 2013. "Boris Johnson May Regret Portraying London as the 'Eighth Emirate.'" *Guardian*, April 17, 2013. www.theguardian.com.

Didi-Huberman, George. 2002. *L'Image Survivante: Histoire de l'Art et Temps des Fantômes selon Aby Warburg*. Paris: Éditions de Minuit.

Ford, Edward. 1998. "The Inconvenient Friend." *Harvard Design Magazine* 6: 12–22.

Galbiati, Marisa, ed. 1991. *Lo Sguardo Discreto. Habitat e fotografia*. Milan: Tranchida.

Ginsburg, Carlo. 2015. *Paura Reverenza Terrore*. Milan: Adelphi.

Higgott, Andrew, and Timothy Wray, eds. 2012. *Camera Constructs: Photography, Architecture and the Modern City*. Burlington, VT: Ashgate.

King, Anthony D. 1996. "Worlds in the City: Manhattan Transfer and the Ascendance of Spectacular Space." *Planning Perspective* 11, no. 2: 97–114.

Kouwenhoven, John A. 1972. *The Columbia Historical Portrait of New York: An Essay in Graphic History*. New York: Columbia University Press.

Lindner, Christoph. 2015. *Imagining New York City: Literature, Urbanism, and the Visual Arts, 1890-1940*. New York: Oxford University Press.

Mendelsohn, Erich. 1926. *Amerika. Bilderbuch eines Architekten*. Berlin: Rudolf Mosse Buchverlag.

Nastasi, Michele. 2016a. "The City of Renderings: Photorealism, Spectacle and Abstraction in Contemporary Urban Landscapes." In *Inter—Photography and Architecture* (Proceedings of the International Conference, University of Navarra), ed. Rubén A. Alcolea and Jorge Tárrago Mingo, 274–285.

Nastasi, Michele. 2016b. "Skyline rêverie." *Lotus international* 159: 72–87.

Nastasi, Michele. 2017. "Image Cities: Skylines, Renderings, and Icons, Transforming Urban Landscapes" PhD diss. (Italian), Ca'Foscari University of Venice.

Nicolin, Pierluigi, 2006. "Architecture and Photography: Three Histories." *Lotus international* 129: 4–8.

Ponzini, Davide. 2012. "Photographers: Architecture Critics of Today?" *Domus* 961: 86–91.

Ponzini, Davide, and Prisca M. Arosio. 2017. "Urban Effects of the Transnational Circulation of Branded Buildings: Comparing Two Skyscrapers and Their Context in Barcelona and Doha." *Urban Design International* 22, no. 1: 28–46.

Ponzini, Davide, Stefan Fotev, and Francesca Mavaracchio. 2016. "Place-Making or Place-Faking? The Paradoxical Effects of Transnational Circulation of Architectural and Urban Development Projects." In *Reinventing the Local in Tourism: Travel Communities and Peer-Produced Place Experiences*, ed. Greg Richards and Antonio Paolo Russo, 153–170. Bristol, UK: Channel View.

Ponzini, Davide, and Michele Nastasi. 2016 (second edition). *Starchitecture: Scenes, Actors, and Spectacles in Contemporary Cities*. New York: Monacelli Press.

Rose, Gillian, Monica Degen, and Clare Melhuish. 2014. "Networks, Interfaces, and Computer-Generated Images: Learning from Digital Visualisations of Urban Redevelopment Projects." *Environment and Planning D: Society and Space* 32, no. 3: 386–403.

Russell, James. 2014. "CityLife." *Architect Magazine*, May, 86–91.

Schuyler, Montgomery. 1987. "'The Sky-Line of New York, 1881–1897." *Harper's Weekly*, March 20, 1987, 295.

Stadler, Hilar, and Martino Stierli, eds. 2008. *Las Vegas Studio*. Zurich: Scheidegger & Spiess.

Star, Leigh S., and James R. Griesemer. 1989. "Institutional Ecology, 'Translations' and Boundary Objects: Amateurs and Professionals in Berkeley's Museum of Vertebrate Zoology, 1907–39." *Social Studies of Science* 19, no. 3: 387–420.

Taylor, William R. 1992. *In Pursuit of Gotham: Culture and Commerce in New York.* New York: Oxford University Press.

Wilkinson, Tom. 2015. "The Polemical Snapshot: Architectural Photography in the Age of Social Media." *The Architectural Review* 1415: 91–97.

Zimmerman, Claire. 2014. *Photographic Architecture in the Twentieth Century.* Minneapolis: University of Minnesota Press.

5

Planning for the Hybrid Gulf City

LAURA LIETO

The hybrid city, an emerging process of transnational urbanism, exists where global networks of power and knowledge hold together (and are reshaped by) transforming material resources and social structures in specific contexts. These can be described as metabolic processes. The Gulf region is one of the most prominent contexts for witnessing such a process: new cities are being built at the intersection of different urban ideas, political visions, technologies, and actors traveling worldwide, and they are developing by means of a massive transformation of material settlements and exploitation of natural resources.

Gulf cities have been invested with different political tasks over the past few years, according to a general strategy that has mainly knowledge-based targets and aims to create alternatives to the oil economy. As such, they must offer new, competitive "world-class" environments that mix "the best of" architecture, technology, comfort, and lifestyle. In their aspiration to be considered world or global cities, these cities are also among the most important destinations of massive labor migration flows. Dependence on foreign labor, which started in the 1970s after the oil boom, is still one of the main features—as well as political concerns—of this urban region. In this milieu, an increasingly fragmented labor structure consisting of a transnational elite of professionals and "a vast army of low skilled workers"[1] is contributing to the formation of a multicultural society, where a formal capitalist economy overlaps with the spaces of an informal or illegal economy.[2]

The urbanization process in the Gulf is also quickly transforming the land and its material structures, given the rapid growth of major cities in the region—Dubai and Abu Dhabi in particular, but Doha, Muscat, and others to different extents. High-density as well as sprawling urban formations entail high-energy costs, massive land consumption, and consistent alterations of desert habitats. These two merging facets of urbanization—the social and the material—allow us to understand the transfer process of policies, actors, ideas, and values as a networked mobilization of people, natural resources, technologies, places, and norms. Within such a socio-material process, "environmental and social change co-determine each other,"[3] giving rise to a hybrid metabolism processing energy, labor flows, human settlements, and natural resources.[4]

Using this perspective, one can view transnational and hybrid urbanism as a process unfolding through different stages of the global travel of urban ideas, "born" somewhere (in the West, at least in the past) and "landing" somewhere else (in the Gulf region, in this case), with a more or less windy trajectory in between.[5] These stages are the decontextualization of ideas, as a symbolic and technical process of "reflexive extraction" from an origin context, and their recontextualization, as both a political and material assembling process within a new context.

Examining two primary cases—a planning experience with which I was involved in Saudi Arabia, the Jubail City Center Plan; and findings from current literature about a major sustainable project in the United Arab Emirates, Masdar City (discussed in further detail by Gökçe Günel in chapter 8)—brings this process into focus in different but complementary ways. The Saudi planning experience, a plan for a city-to-be, provides insights on the symbolic dimension of sociocultural hybridity; Masdar City, as an ongoing urban transformation, can help us reflect on the political implications and massive transformations of an arid environment into a specifically high-tech settlement aiming for primacy in the sustainable cities network worldwide.

Hybridity and the Urban

In the Gulf context, planning can be understood as a transnational, networked enterprise.[6] Ideas are exchanged and confronted as different actors, things, technologies, norms, and contracts gather in a new context and produce contingent associations—be it a new plan, an international conference, a policy-making initiative. Behind my understanding of this process—on the ground—are certain conceptual advances from social science that can be fruitfully merged to help explain the processes I have witnessed and taken part in.

Hybridity

The idea of the hybrid city as the outcome of transnational relations is not new. Cities in history are the long-term results of networked relations of power and trade crossing cultural and political borders: the Mediterranean urban civilization, exemplarily depicted by Fernand Braudel, is one outstanding example.[7] Notwithstanding the ample precedents, the hybrid and the urban have been progressing on rather analytically separate tracks for a long time, following different intellectual traditions that can now be brought closer together.

Starting at the biological beginning, hybridity historically involves a crossbreeding of two different organisms, fused to form a "third." In the nineteenth century, the notion surfaces in genetic studies to create the essentialist social category of mulatto—the outcome of the mixing of different races. Through postcolonial studies, the notion of the hybrid, in the past a rationale for domination, gains a more liberatory connotation, indeed one that is valorized. The notion of a "mongrel city"[8] migrates to the planning field to incorporate difference and heterogeneity as assets for a new "inter-cultural coexistence in shared spaces."[9] The racialized background of such a notion is still present, but it bolsters a political claim for more just cities based on cultural diversity and respect for variation. This marks a first and important convergence between the hybrid and the urban, opening a new line of inquiry about transnational flows and their effects on city life and civil coexistence. The postcolonial discourse here is a powerful lever to unsettle inequalities and inspire a transformed kind of urban politics.

A second type of rather recent conceptual advance adds to hybridity in a different way, from science and technology studies (STS) and the related field of actor network theory (ANT). STS and ANT are all about mixture. Writers in this tradition use the word "hybrid" as an explicit reference to physical and social worlds as a unity with any component being a quasi-object,[10] a "cyborg" in some conceptual treatments.[11] STS/ANT rejects the exclusive priority attributed to human actors as causal force over physical matter, falsely understood as brute and inert. It rather maintains that humans always act in concert with things that are also "actants"—be it water, electrons, trees, pipelines, or digital technologies. So we have sociotechnical interfaces that form a hybrid ensemble. Such a formulation now restates the role of the actor as someone or something that changes relations within a network of people and things. When things have equal weight in determining actions and change within assemblages, then the key figure in action is not the human individual, but the actor-network—a hybrid object-subject.

Referring specifically to the urban, hybridity now opens new perspectives on the mutuality of society and physicality (space and its artifactual and natural elements) and ups the stakes in what gets created as buildings, infrastructure, and components. Such so-called objects themselves partake in causal efficacy. The concept of hybridity—as I use it—works in the frictional space between discourses and material processes of urban transformation. Analytically, it operates as a lever over heterogeneous elements that unsettles otherwise fixed notions of urbanization. Empirically, hybridity is assembled through both local and transnational networks, crystallizing[12] within a specific context—the Gulf in this instance.

Origin Stories and Myths

In the context of all the unsettling that goes on in the urban realm, the human condition is open to, perhaps even requires, appropriate narratives to overcome what would otherwise appear as chaos. To understand the city, as a professional matter, various parties introduce narratives of idealized fixity. They may proffer a normative vision of the "good city," replete by its nature with specific cultural biases and perhaps a policy design method for it to be established in a particular political context. Also offered up may be benign "antecedents" or "origin stories": a best practice successfully experienced somewhere, an educational regimen from a specific country or planning school.

The origin issue is a problem not to be underestimated. In the debate on transnational planning, some authors[13] maintain that planners, before applying an idea to a new context, should know where and how that idea came about and why it succeeded in its "origin site." But ideas do not arise ahistorically; when they land in a new destination, they have been already decontextualized. To be recontextualized, they go through a process of translation that makes them different from the "original version." They will be differentially validated by social actors and thus work in uneven ways across sites. Allies may or may not come forward. The risk of copycat urbanism and cultural flattening is clearly in play.[14] In such a critical perspective, I have maintained, planning ideas are similar to other myths that round-off exceptions and nuances, and are made durable only through something like faith.[15]

Within modernity, mythology becomes inherently political.[16] Political myth is a symbolically structured narrative whose power does not derive from tight logic, but instead from emotional force.[17] As a particular form of ideological belief, political myth can be aimed at political integration, as well as at domination and populism.[18] Following Roland Barthes and Michel Foucault, myth is caught between a "depoliticized speech"[19] and a "strategically polyvalent discourse":[20] it can be a device of control and subjection or a means to open new perspectives, to refresh old ideas and provide stronger social cohesion in critical times.

When planners are engaged in a context different from their homeland—as is so often the case in the Gulf—they are contending with their own myths (as perhaps modified by interactions and sense making in the adopted environment).[21] A planning mythology can be, for example, the idea that the gridiron city would provide clear and fair rules for a real estate market and for the efficient circulation of people and goods regardless of world region or culture, or that "well-designed" public spaces (e.g., well equipped with street furniture, artworks, and appropriate lighting) would provide a "vibrant and lively" social environment. An ongoing assumption valorizes participation of a particular sort—the idea that respect and fair dialogue with all parties affected by a new plan would create planning solutions superior to authoritarian, top-down decision making.

Such embedded ideas, once decontextualized from their origin site, undergo a complex process of translation.[22] Sometimes they are used just as labels to popularize a forthcoming project having nothing in common with an original model (perhaps merely retaining the architectural surface). Other times, they can prompt intense negotiations that play a strong mediating role to build up new communities of practice and thus different outcomes, involving both new modes of decision making and built forms that arise from them.

For Western planners—and this is an aspect of the orientalist posture— the Middle East consists of "mythical regions," held as exceptional in urbanistic terms, as well as other regards. Part of the mythology is prompted by an imagined void: the desert land. I want to reflect about this "empty context." One needs to challenge the common sense that, in the Gulf, the global phantasmagoria of high-rise architecture is happening because that region is a land of unlimited possibilities, a physical and social tabula rasa in a ready and open setting.[23] What is this *desert*—provided that I am not thinking of sands and dunes? There are some extreme conditions in the Gulf region that indeed make its current urbanization quite different from other known, historical processes related to capital accumulation in Western cities. These Gulf cities have relevant histories but no "post" to share with Western cities: no post-Fordism, no postindustrialization, no postwelfare state. They are indeed postnomadic; perhaps that is a "post" that might, in some meager sense, fit—and one that is disappearing in the Gulf as in other parts of the world, where urbanization has replaced it. As for colonialism, there is no close commonality with modes of resource exploitation carried out by European exploiters: Belgians in the Congo, Spaniards in South America, the British most everywhere. After the rapid development of oil starting in the 1960s, resource exploitation in the UAE "did not contribute to the underdevelopment of the region,"[24] as most of the sheikhdoms' affairs were quite independent from colonizing powers. There was not a replication of the "resource curse" afflicting other world subaltern territories.

There were other distinctive aspects not only new to the region but also different from conditions otherwise commonly faced by professional consultants working in the Middle East since the "building frenzy"[25] started in early 2000s. There was not the need to protect (or overcome) structures against intrusion on natural areas otherwise in the path of urban growth. They were planning new cities where no brownfield had to be adapted or prior pollutions abated. In social terms, what otherwise would have been claims to the right to the city were not development impediments. Historic preservation or cultural rights groups were not insistent on protecting vestiges of tangible memory. More broadly, in an urban context where notions such as postmodernity or post-Fordism do not make much sense, a whole set of urban ideas and strategies lose their relevance. Issues like urban revitalization and gentrification, and a host of others from contemporary urban studies, have little bearing.

Instead, from the perspective of Western professional elites (and the entrepreneurs associated with them), the Gulf offers the galvanizing idea of a "land of freedom"—from building regulations and other normative constraints.[26] The vista opens for architectural creativity and the crafting and construction of whole new urbanscapes. On the side of the local leading class, it caters to the aspiration for a "world-class urbanism" where everything is brand new, unique, and iconic. Risks are taken, and claims to be respecting tradition, religion, and cultural patterns are routinely made as part of business and professional practice. The hybridity in play takes in all such considerations, as it is given shape from local rulers and their circles—along with the Western transnational business class of professional and managerial workers who gain presence and voice.[27]

On the ground, a whole related urban-design syntax arises—from the business downtown to the revitalized waterfront, from the sustainable urban village to the pedestrianized street. Developed out of historic contexts that gave rise to their "original" prototypes in the West, they are emplaced as deliberate artifacts, emptied of social and political implications. Such figurations carry the risk of being pure forms—simulacra of urbanisms gone by in other places under altogether different conditions.

Nonetheless, the transnational urbanization process is not limited to a symbolic construction: it also deals with action and change, with concrete metabolic processes, associating ideas, people, norms, and technologies formed into socio-material assemblages. Out of the matrix of interests and proclivities that are present in the Gulf come their own versions of hybridity, as in the urban design of Jubail City and the master planning for Masdar—the two projects to which I now, in succession, turn my attention. They display, albeit in somewhat contrasting ways, both socio-materiality and mythmaking as they enter into the construction of urban assemblage.

Urban Form and the Political Meaning of a "European-Style" Piazza for Jubail City

A few years ago, I was involved in a planning experience in Saudi Arabia, where an international team of Western professionals was hired to provide technical consulting to the Royal Commission of Jubail and Yanbu, a regional development agency tasked by the Saudi government with creating a plan for the new center of Jubail City. In the Gulf, developers typically enlist ambitious designs to compete for international attention.[28] Planning, in absolute monarchies like Saudi Arabia, is an authoritative action of the state. State agencies hire external consultants to develop plans and projects under the supervision of top officials and counselors, and such a relationship is mostly of a client/professional kind.[29] This means that consulting planners do not have much political power; nor can they play a mediating role between the government and the citizens—much less between the government and the disenfranchised expats and workers. Still planners can make a difference, and—as in the case at hand—hybridity is a challenge and a possibility, an alternative strategy to just "doing what the client wants." It becomes possible to open a space of dialogue about values and differences beyond what is a business opportunity for contractors and consulting firms.

It was within such a context that project sponsors asked our consultancy to design a European-style plaza for a new central business district. Aligned with what we thought were project goals, we worked up a scheme that would provide attractive features resembling the pleasant and human-scale environment of traditional Euro-Mediterranean towns, but appropriately adapted to the new setting. That strategy, iconic in its own way, would—in our thinking—differentiate the new urban center from other more Manhattan-style Gulf city landscapes.

We felt a need to elaborate our concept into an "origin narrative" of the European square, to explain to our interlocutors how it "came to life" in a specific historical context. Our narrative spanned the Greek agora and the Roman forum, from the medieval open market to the Renaissance square and up to the nineteenth-century square of the modern, bourgeois city. The richness of the story would thus provide help to win allies for the project. But, of course, a plaza invokes traditions of living outdoors and using open spaces for sociality and business dealings. When climate conditions are so different—as in the case in point—where temperatures in summer can reach unbearable highs, the urban outdoors need to be completely revisited as a socio-spatial consideration. A main public space in the Islamic city is the mosque, offering protection against the sun through systems of covered porticos (*riwaq*) and courtyards.[30] The souk, typically covered, similarly offers potential for year-round social, civic, and business functioning.

To design a big square for an Arab city, a new, hybrid myth had to be worked out—and formed through mutual learning and negotiation. In the beginning of the process, each party had its own set of myths to bring to bear, including notions of what a modern Arab urban space could, climatically and spatially, actually be. For the planners, the square was the idealized place for social encounters and mixing. For the client, it was mostly an iconic space, featuring arcades, fountains, artworks, with the necessity of ensuring clear patterns of spatial and sexual segregation. If left unconfronted and unhybridized in the transfer process, both myths would have possibly led to decontextualized, copycat projects of some already existing versions in Europe or the Middle East. Following Roland Barthes's critique of modern mythology—aimed at controlling masses by depriving them of history, conflicts, and contingencies[31]—these different "square myths" would have conflated into a "depoliticized speech" about public space. The result could have been some mechanistic "compromise" or, if one party or the other had simply prevailed, a materialization of a vacuous contradiction, making little sense to any of the involved participants.

Heading off such an outcome, meetings were held with agendas that took up the practices and traditions of the local society, as well as realistic assessments of climate. Learning about praying, feasts, and social rituals (like weekend outdoor family reunions) helped give shape to specific layouts of the new square. At the same time, sexual segregation norms and religious concerns for privacy led to specific technical requirements. The distances between buildings were precisely measured, and the views in and out were closely considered, of facades especially. A whole series of design features were to provide shade and comfort. For client and professionals, the square became an arena of synthesis, of collaboration, of hybridity.

From my perspective, the contending myths were repoliticized as a matter of mutual adaptation. We were confronting an oxymoron—a European square in the Saudi desert. The knowledge of Western planners merged with the knowledge of local public officials and counselors, who were asked to revise their initial request for an iconic space. They were encouraged to draw on their practical and traditional knowledge, while being open to innovative socio-spatial performances. Whereas nothing like a European square exists in the traditional Arab city, there could emerge, as we came to propose, a typological innovation with the potential for achieving similar results of sociality and commerce.[32] Commenting on Foucault's discussion about the mythical, *Society Must Be Defended*, Stuart Murray highlights how mythical discourse is capable of opening "onto something new . . . to allow for something to be created out of old forms."[33] I liken this to our endeavor.

Our negotiation for dealing with this not-yet-realized project—whose socio-material effects were unknown—occurred through the "microspace" of face-to-face interactions between client and planner, as is typical in professional practice.[34] This communicative effort, as it is made possible by the tradecraft of planning practice, mobilized materiality as an essential medium for dialogue and confrontation.[35] In the meetings, there were countless physical representations at hand—drawings, site plans, photos, and renderings. These functioned as "boundary objects"[36] (in the ANT lexicon)—items that diverse parties can reference, discuss, and elaborate on an ongoing basis. They get returned to, passed around, and cited. In the "swim" of so much that tends not to stay the same, they remain as quasi-durable common points of departure for discussion and alteration. These boundary objects provided a powerful mediating role in the planning process.[37] Things, ideas, experiences, and skills were all circulated—materially and virtually—in the process of hybridizing "the square" into a common accomplishment. They were in service to defeat the supposedly empty space and to avoid the temptation of viewing the process as beginning with the tabula rasa, "starting with nothing."

Some prior colonial trope, either to mimic or through which to construct a postcolonial response, was also not available for us as a point of departure. This is where the no-"post" issue, discussed above, comes into concrete force as a design resource. "Post" always implies a "pre-" and thus a way to suggest some form of historical continuity for designers who might wish to replicate or at least "quote" from its traditions. Similarly, there is an absence of something to oppose, to tear down, reverse, or reject. In this Gulf context, the only thing left was to engage in intensive consideration of an alternative urban tradition and its severe climate condition: we had the opportunity to rethink our "origin narrative" of the square, focusing on features we usually take for granted (circulation, accessibility, security, exposure to light and ventilation) and recontextualizing any and all solutions. Our plan proceeded on that basis.

This example should help us understand the hybrid city as a field where knowledge transfer, bracketed and pervaded by power asymmetries and cultural prejudices, occurs also with patterns of mutual learning. A heterogeneous assemblage of people, things, ideas, skills, and political and economic interests is always in play in transnational work settings, replete as well with misunderstandings, false starts, but also with the potential for productive dénouement. Hybridity is not a peaceful merging of discourses but a controversy-rich culture-nature processing of ideas and things according to a specific sociopolitical context.

The Hybrid Urban Metabolism of Masdar City

As a response to the unsustainable UAE "petro-urbanism,"[38] the country has launched very ambitious programs for sustainable best practices. This becomes still another realm in which Gulf cities enter the global competition to be famously best at something, in this case for being "green" and in a wondrous way. Described and evaluated by Günel (in chapter 8), Abu Dhabi's Masdar project was heralded by the international media as the world's first "sustainable city." Now being master planned for about 48,000 inhabitants, it has opened the way for many other claims for "eco-city" status around the world. Unlike most projects "still on paper," Masdar has been partly developed. The casual visitor can take a tour, ride in one of several self-driving electric vehicles (so-called personal rapid transit—PRT), and experience some urban cooling from the smart massing of close-in buildings. There is lunch and espresso. Masdar makes provisions not only for reduced carbon emission, but also for use of waste, smart grids for energy efficiency, and inventive modes of transportation.

The project holds a strong techno-utopian charge—a kind of futuristic world's fair of coming adventure. In this, it follows in a long tradition of Western utopian thinking that invests technology as a messianic problem solver. In the face of big problems, urban planning in particular has always turned to utopian thinking—mobilizing a space of thought and innovation to put forward bold, cutting-edge solutions sufficiently disentangled from mundane facts to ease them into acceptance.[39] In the Gulf, the tabula rasa imaginary beckons along with the particularly wicked problem of environmental disaster. The UAE's status as the worst carbon footprint in the world (along with Doha) and the highest rate of greenhouse emissions per capita[40] creates a fact on the ground (and in the atmosphere) that further induces big thinking. Moreover, the vast

economic investments in the region will likely fuel increased industrial production, massive seawater desalination, and further population
growth. (Saudi Arabia has a high, although now declining, birthrate.)

From this perspective, the Masdar City project unfolds as a logical
yet emotional and aestheticized response. It also fulfills another "best
of" for the UAE, encasing ideas and technological solutions accumulated
through research and experimentation in architecture, urban design, and
engineering from all over the world, a traveling "superidea" aimed to be
implemented in the Abu Dhabi transnational space. But in urbanistic
terms, it is precisely in its enactment of such a visionary and ultimately
technological project that it is alien to any historic experience of city
building. Emblematic, in this perspective, is the contrast between projects
like Masdar and the growing awareness, in the Arab world (if not in the
UAE), of the importance of urban heritage, not just in terms of preserving the past or reappropriating it by means of architectural decoration,
but also of maintaining traditional knowledge for coping with climate and
resource challenges.[41]

The initial Masdar City project has suffered major cuts due to the recession of the late 2000s and the fall of oil prices in the early 2010s.[42]
The zero-carbon slogan was walked back to something more modest.
The PRT system has been greatly scaled back, probably abandoned as a
meaningful concept. Energy has started to come in from offsite, no longer relying on the pioneering photovoltaic solar installation. A number
of firms withdrew from the project after the first enthusiastic gathering
of major smart technology companies, and the major carbon-reduction
deadline—scheduled for 2016—has been postponed to 2025. As always,
the Masdar enterprise undergoes all the vagaries of financial markets,
and so its high-expenditure-based structure is exposed to fluctuations
that are hardly predictable. The major social partners of such a new
enterprise—investing global firms, technology partners, and research
organizations—may or may not be able to attract appropriate professionals or people who want to move into such a high-tech environment. The
usual social incentives—cultural opportunities and lively surroundings—
are yet to come.

Into this assemblage of smart technologies, institutions, and corporate
firms, a hybrid socio-natural metabolism struggles to come into being.
Paternalistic structures—transmuted through local institutions—are

reworked by means of imitative actions and projects that strive to transform external pressures over sustainability into the usual types of local
development ambitions.[43] Natural resources are being intensively exploited (water, electricity) and at the same time—almost as trading on
the disaster—using technological innovation as the come-on for global
firms and researchers. The quest for mega-level novelty overlaps with a
growing awareness—and story—of dire circumstance made useful.

Masdar City is part of a worldly process of assemblage where
materialities—from harsh climate conditions to the abundance of oil—
play a decisive role in how human and nonhuman actors move and
change within transnational networks. We are far from dealing with a
win-win game; as always, when it comes to socio-material metabolism,
there is the potential for both enabling and disabling political and environmental conditions. The experimental, techno-utopian society
forming around Masdar City may offer an extreme test of how future
citizenship, in times of climate change, might fare. In Abu Dhabi, it is a
techno-feudal institution with only very limited evidence of emancipatory
shift. The earth's environmental problems are kept outside the wealthy
citizens' lives of excess consumption, just as the workforce needs are
similarly provided by outsiders who are also kept beyond meaningful
societal membership.

Conclusion: Hybrid Cities in the Gulf and Beyond

In its own distinctive ways, Gulf urbanism carries asymmetric relations
into the "broader totality" of capitalism—the "context of context," as it has
been termed.[44] As with any precept based in historical shifts, its mode of
difference and variation is not to be considered as a "final destination,"
but rather a stage where traveling "universals"[45] hybridize and incarnate
into a region and its specific cities. For economic, environmental, social,
and cultural reasons, Gulf cities—extreme compared to more ordinary
and familiar cases in the West—further illuminate the range of what can
happen under the overall process of capital accumulation.

The frame of hybridity can help planning scholars understand current projects and transformations, focusing on the constant reworking
of forms, patterns, and models that are transferred from one place to
another—not just as the effect of large, impersonal forces or top-down

policies, but also as step-by-step negotiation among intersecting urban visions, cultures, and traditions. The mediations conducted in the Gulf, whether built out or simply maintained as plans, models, and images, can enter into circulation in other locales and regions. However myth-based they may have been, they have the potential to "work again"—to become in turn physical, economic, and social assemblages that enter into projects elsewhere and into the future.

NOTES

1   Friedmann 1986, 73.
2   Malecki and Ewers 2007.
3   Swyngedouw 2006, 118.
4   Swyngedouw 1996 and 1998; Gandy 2004 and 2005.
5   Lieto 2015; Healey 2011.
6   Lieto 2015, and as further described in Sarah Moser's Saudi case, in this volume.
7   Braudel 1966.
8   Sandercock 2003.
9   Sandercock 2003, 319.
10   Serres 1982.
11   Haraway 1991.
12   Brenner and Schmid 2015.
13   Healey and Upton 2010; Healey 2011.
14   Roy 2010.
15   Lieto 2015.
16   Edelman 1964; Derrida and Moore 1974.
17   Ohana 1991.
18   Tudor 1972.
19   Barthes 1991.
20   Foucault 1998.
21   This conceptualization of mythology is quite in tune with its combinatory and controversial nature. Rejecting hybridity as panacea, as harmonization of differences, we need to be aware that—in the planning and as well as in other domains—fusing diverse or even antithetical issues into new practices or forms also implies reducing heterogeneity into a new form of homogeneity. In this sense, the oscillation between depoliticization and social cohesion strategy is always at stake.
22   Law 1997.
23   Lieto 2012.
24   Coles and Walsh 2010, 1320.
25   Ong 2011, 11.
26   Imrie and Street 2011.
27   Malecki and Ewers 2007, 470.

28 Lieto 2012 and 2015.

29 Friedmann 2010.

30 Hathloul 1981; Bianca 2000; Elsheshtawy 2008; Abu-Lughod 1987.

31 It is useful here to quote Barthes: "What the world supplies to myth is an historical reality, defined . . . by the way in which men have produced or used it; and what myth gives in return is a natural image of this reality. And just as bourgeois ideology is defined by the abandonment of the name 'bourgeois,' myth is constituted by the loss of the historical qualities of things: in it, things lose the memory that they once were made" (1991, 142).

32 Although completely different from the task at hand, the example of Tahir Square in Cairo shows how some crucial elements of "square life," as Europeans know it, have been emerging recently in the Arab urban world, and this reinforces the idea that a change in the conception and use of public space is possible even in those traditions that do not share similar outdoor cultures.

33 Murray 2003, 216.

34 Harris and Moore 2013.

35 Beauregard 2013.

36 Star and Griesemer 1989.

37 Vicari-Haddock and Vanhellemont 2016; Beauregard and Lieto 2016.

38 Crot 2013.

39 Choay 2000.

40 World Wide Nature Fund 2008.

41 Elsheshtawy 2008.

42 Cugurullo 2013.

43 Crot 2013.

44 Brenner, Madden, and Wachsmuth 2011.

45 Tsing 2009.

REFERENCES

Abu-Lughod, Janet. 1987. "The Islamic City: Historic Myth, Islamic Essence, and Contemporary Relevance." *International Journal of Middle East Studies* 19, no. 2: 155–176.

Bakhtin, Mikhail. 1981. *The Dialogic Imagination.* Austin: University of Texas Press.

Barthes, Roland. 1991. *Mythologies.* New York: Noonday Press.

Beauregard, Robert A. 2013. "The Neglected Places of Practice." *Planning Theory and Practice* 14, no. 1: 8–19.

Bhabha, Homi. 1996. "Culture's In-Between." In *Questions of Cultural Identity*, ed. Stuart Hall and Paul du Gay, 53–60. London: Sage.

Bianca, Stefano. 2000. *Urban Form in the Arab World: Past and Present.* London: Thames & Hudson.

Braudel, Fernand. 1966. *The Mediterranean.* New York: HarperCollins.

Brenner, Neil, David J. Madden, and David Wachsmuth. 2011. "Assemblage Urbanism and the Challenges of Critical Urban Theory." *City* 15, no. 2: 225–240.

Brenner, Neil, and Christian Schmid. 2015. "Towards a New Epistemology of the Urban?" *City* 19, no. 2: 151–182.

Choay, Françoise. 2000. *La Città, Utopie e Realtà*. Turin: Einaudi.

Coles, Anne, and Peter Jackson. 2006. *Windtower*. New York: Stacey International.

Coles, Anne, and Katie Walsh. 2010. "From 'Trucial State' to 'Postcolonial' City? The Imaginative Geographies of British Expatriates in Dubai." *Journal of Ethnic and Migration Studies* 36, no. 8: 1317–1333.

Crot, Laurence. 2013. "Planning for Sustainability in Non-democratic Polities: The Case of Masdar City." *Urban Studies* 50, no. 13: 2809–2825.

Cugurullo, Federico. 2013. "How to Build a Sandcastle: An Analysis of the Genesis and Development of Masdar City." *Journal of Urban Technology* 20, no. 1: 23–37.

Derrida, Jacques, and F. T. C. Moore. 1974. "White Mythology: Metaphor in the Text of Philosophy." *New Literary History* 6, no. 1: 5–74.

Edelman, Murray J. 1964. *The Symbolic Uses of Politics*. Urbana: University of Illinois Press.

Elsheshtawy, Yasser. 2008. *Evolving Arab City: Tradition, Modernity and Urban Development*. London: Routledge.

Foucault, Michel. 1998. *Bisogna Difendere la Società*. Milan: Feltrinelli.

Friedmann, John. 1986. "The World City Hypothesis." *Development and Change* 17: 69–83.

Friedmann, John. 2010. "Similarity or Differences? What to Emphasize Now for Effective Planning Practice." In *Crossing Borders: International Exchange and Planning Practices*, ed. Patsy Healey and Robert Upton, 313–328. London: Routledge (kindle edition).

Gandy, Matthew. 2004. "Rethinking Urban Metabolism: Water, Space and the Modern City." *City* 8, no. 3: 363–379.

Gandy, Matthew. 2005. "Cyborg Urbanization: Complexity and Monstrosity in the Contemporary City." *International Journal of Urban and Regional Research* 29, no. 1: 26–49.

Haraway, Donna. 1991. *Simians, Cyborgs and Women: The Reinvention of Nature*. London: Routledge.

Harris, Andrew, and Susan Moore. 2013. "Planning Histories and Practices of Circulating Urban Knowledge." *International Journal of Urban and Regional Research* 37, no. 5: 1499–1509.

Harvey, David. 1990. *The Condition of Postmodernity*. Malden, MA: Basil Blackwell.

Hathloul, Saleh Al A. 1981. "Tradition, Continuity and Change in the Physical Environment: The Arab-Muslim City." PhD diss., MIT.

Healey, Patsy. 2011. "The Universal and the Contingent: Some Reflections on the Transnational Flow of Planning Ideas and Practices." *Planning Theory* 11, no. 2: 188–207.

Imrie, Rob, and Emma Street. 2011. *Architectural Design and Regulation*. Chichester, UK: Blackwell Publishing.

Law, John. 1997. "Traduction/Trahison. Notes on ANT." http://cseweb.ucsd.edu.

Lieto, Laura, ed. 2012. *Americans. Città e Territorio ai Tempi dell'Impero*. Naples: Cronopio.

Lieto, Laura. 2015. "Cross-border Mythologies. The Problem with Traveling Planning Ideas." *Planning Theory* 14, no. 2: 115–129.

Lieto, Laura, and Robert A. Beauregard, eds. 2016. *Planning for a Material World*. London: Routledge.

Malecki, Edward J., and Michael C. Ewers. 2007. "Labor Migration to World Cities: With a Research Agenda for the Arab Gulf." *Progress in Human Geography* 31, no. 4: 467–484.

Murray, Stuart J. 2003. "Myth as Critique? Review of Michel Foucault's 'Society Must Be Defended.'" *Qui Parle* 13, no. 2: 203–221.

Ohana, David. 1991. "Georges Sorel and the Rise of Political Myth." *History of European Ideas* 13, no. 6: 733–746.

Ong, Aihwa. 2011. "Worlding Cities or the Art of Being Global." In *Worlding Cities: Asian Experiments and the Art of Being Global*, ed. Aihwa Ong and Ananya Roy, 1–26. Hoboken, NJ: Blackwell Publishing.

Roy, Ananya. 2010. "Poverty Truths: The Politics of Knowledge in the New Global Order of Development." In *Crossing Borders: International Exchange and Planning Practices*, ed. Patsy Healey and Robert Upton, 27–46. London: Routledge (kindle edition).

Sandercock, Leonie. 2003. *Cosmopolis II: Mongrel Cities of the 21st Century*. London: Continuum.

Serres, Michel. 1982. *The Parasite*. Baltimore: Johns Hopkins University Press.

Star, Susan L., and James R. Griesemer. 1989. "Institutional Ecology, 'Translations' and Boundary Objects: Amateurs and Professionals in Berkeley's Museum of Vertebrate Zoology, 1907–39." *Social Studies of Science* 19, no. 3: 387–420.

Swyngedouw, Eric. 1996. "The City as a Hybrid: On Nature, Society and Cyborg Urbanization." *Capitalism Nature Socialism* 7, no. 2: 65–80.

Swyngedouw, Eric. 1999. "Modernity and Hybridity: Nature, Regeneracionismo, and the Production of the Spanish Waterscape 1890–1930." *Annals of the Association of American Geographers* 89, no. 3: 443–465.

Swyngedouw, Eric. 2006. "Circulation and Metabolism: (Hybrid) Natures and (Cyborg) Cities." *Science as Culture* 15, no. 2: 105–121.

Tsing, Anna. 2009. "Supply Chains and the Human Condition." *Rethinking Marxism* 21, no. 2: 148–176.

Tudor, Henry. 1972. *Political Myth*. London: Pall Mall.

Vicari-Haddock, Serena, and Linus Vanhellemont. 2016. "Minutiae: Meeting Minutes as Actors in Participatory Planning Processes." In *Planning for a Material World*, ed. Laura Lieto and Robert A. Beauregard, 102–120. London: Routledge.

World Wide Fund for Nature. 2008. *Living Planet Report*. Gland, Switzerland: World Wide Fund for Nature.

6

Planning from Within

NYU Abu Dhabi

HILARY BALLON

The start of the twenty-first century has seen a quantum leap in the number of American university programs started abroad. These initiatives vary considerably in scope and approach and mark an experimental phase in the globalization of higher education, as American universities test different strategies to deepen connections to other parts of the world. The export of American higher education is not new. Going back to the mid-nineteenth century, universities were established in foreign lands based on American models of education, with American faculty and presidents, American donors and trustees, American charters, and English as the language of instruction. Robert College in Istanbul (now Boğaziçi University), founded in 1863, and Syrian Protestant College (now the American University of Beirut), founded in 1866, were the earliest examples. Since then dozens of universities, often called the "American University of (or in) . . . ," have been founded around the world based explicitly on the American research university or liberal arts college.

One factor that distinguishes the early twenty-first-century initiatives is the direct involvement of American universities, although the nature of their participation ranges considerably from advisory work, primarily in academic planning and faculty hiring, to the creation of branch campuses that are part of the American institution. The University of Pennsylvania helped to establish the Singapore Management University in 2000. MIT was involved in the establishment of the Masdar Institute of Science and Technology in Abu Dhabi in 2009 and the Singapore University of Technology and Design in 2012. Yale participated in the creation of Yale-NUS College (cofounded with the National University of Singapore), which opened in 2011. None of the above institutions grants American degrees. New York University established campuses in Abu Dhabi in 2010 and in Shanghai in 2013. Texas A & M (2003), Carnegie Mellon (2004), Georgetown (2005), and Northwestern (2008) are among the American universities that opened branch campuses in Education City, Doha, Qatar. The branch campuses offer American degrees.

Over the course of this 150-year history, the foreign ventures have faced the same basic challenge in defining their institutional identity: Where on the spectrum from faithful transfer of the American model to integration in the foreign location does the new entity sit? This issue is, however, more acute with branch universities, where the foreign branch is an integral part of the parent university. How does the branch campus relate to its American parent and to its new host society? Should all practices, policies, and instruction reproduce those at the main campus or diverge in response to local conditions? In 2007, the government of the emirate of Abu Dhabi invited New York University to establish a comprehensive, degree-granting branch campus in Abu Dhabi, the capital of the United Arab Emirates. During the creation of NYU Abu Dhabi, the question of institutional identity emerged in nearly every dimension of university planning, including admissions standards and procedures, the composition of the student body and faculty, the design of the curriculum, governance, and accreditation.

The Abu Dhabi government turned to NYU in part because it wanted a university that departed in some basic respects from Emirati norms. The government wanted an American-style liberal arts curriculum, whereas its own national universities offered professionally oriented programs on the British model. NYU Abu Dhabi would be coeducational with an international student body; the national universities had a majority of Emirati students who study in gender-separated facilities. NYU Abu Dhabi would develop a residential campus typical of American colleges, whereas the national universities were largely commuter schools. An inviolable principle was that NYU Abu Dhabi would enjoy academic freedom and be exempt from some restrictions that applied to other institutions. Thus, it was determined that NYU Abu Dhabi would be American in its basic contours.

Yet despite these differentiating features, the aspiration in planning the new university was to integrate in Abu Dhabi and give new meaning to the NYU motto "in and of the city." The symbol of the university was emblematic of the integrative aspiration. NYU's icon is a single large torch. For NYUAD, the torch was miniaturized and arrayed in a traditional arabesque pattern. This fusion of NYU and the visual culture of Abu Dhabi in the new university's logo, designed by Michael Beirut of Pentagram, symbolized the aspirations to bridge two cultures.

As NYUAD came into being, it also changed NYU. A new conception of NYU as a "global network university" took shape and encompassed the branch campuses in a centralized structure. In the traditional hub-and-spoke model of international study, students enroll in a main campus but have the opportunity to spend a semester or year at a foreign study site. In NYU's "network" construct, students can matriculate at one of three degree-granting campuses—in New York, Abu Dhabi, and Shanghai. While students spend the majority of their college years at their home campus, they can also study at any of NYU's fourteen locations.[1] A premise of the NYU global network was containment within an NYU system: the curriculum is aligned so you can pursue your major at multiple sites, high academic quality is assured, your ID works wherever you go, the library resources are shared, and comparable NYU student services are provided. Regardless of where students matriculate, students receive an NYU degree.

The simultaneous emergence of the global network university and NYUAD (as well as NYU Shanghai) revealed certain tensions in building out a unified network and distinctive branch campuses. How, on the one hand, to provide enough cross-campus standardization, such as in the curriculum, to foster student mobility, while enabling the new campuses in Abu Dhabi and Shanghai to become embedded in their host cities and develop unique features responsive to their contexts? To what extent should NYUAD copy NYU in New York or develop its own approach, in response to its environs, student body, and historical moment? For example, should literary instruction in the twenty-first century look the same in Abu Dhabi as in New York, where it is divided by language in a half dozen departments, particularly given that NYUAD would be very much smaller than NYU in New York?

The history of well-established institutions like the American University of Beirut, as well as youthful start-ups like NYU Abu Dhabi, demonstrates that there is no fixed answer to the question of institutional identity. Rather, there are contingent responses that shift over time as historical circumstances change, experience is acquired, and goals are adjusted. At NYUAD, forces pull simultaneously toward consistency and standardization within NYU's global network and toward independence, differentiation, and local integration.

But one manifestation of institutional identity is less mutable—the architecture of NYUAD. The campus would play an important role in conveying the vision of NYU Abu Dhabi. What could its architecture say about the university, its belonging to both NYU and to Abu Dhabi, and its dual attachments to New York and Abu Dhabi? This essay reflects on these questions by examining the design of the campus. After three years of planning, the university opened to students in September 2010, and during the first four academic years (2010–2014), students completed their studies at interim facilities while a permanent campus was under construction on Saadiyat Island. The permanent campus was completed in time to host the first graduation, in May 2014, and officially opened for the academic year 2014–2015. (As I was a participant in the process of planning NYUAD, both the academic programs and the facilities, this essay employs the personal pronoun in recounting this history.)

The Local Framework

In the UAE, relationships are considered especially important, which means that it matters who sponsors a project. NYUAD was established under the patronage of the crown prince of Abu Dhabi, Sheikh Mohammed bin Zayed al Nayhan, with whom NYU president John Sexton established a personal relationship. Those planning NYUAD perceived the bond between those two individuals as a significant factor in the university's start-up phase and the ruler's commitment for a special endowment. Whereas other UAE projects were affected by the global recession of 2008, NYUAD continued on an aggressive development path, which we attributed to the crown prince's patronage.

The development of NYUAD should be seen in the context of a national policy to promote education from the time the country was founded in 1971. As the UAE underwent rapid transformation from a Bedouin society to an oil-rich, urbanized culture, it was dependent on a foreign workforce of both highly skilled professionals and unskilled laborers. The UAE leadership saw investment in education as a pathway to develop Emirati capacity. The founding father of the country, Sheikh Zayed bin Sultan al Nahyan (the crown prince's father), established three Emirati universities: the United Arab Emirates University in Al Ain in 1976; the Higher Colleges of Technology in 1988, which expanded to encompass seventeen campuses throughout the country; and Zayed University in 1998, with campuses in Dubai and Abu Dhabi.

After his father's death in 2004, the crown prince expanded the higher-education sector in the emirate of Abu Dhabi, sometimes in foreign partnerships. A branch of the Sorbonne opened in 2006. The Masdar Institute of Science and Technology, a graduate school focused on renewable energy, was started with MIT in 2007 (see Günel, chapter 8), and Khalifa University, an engineering school, was also founded in 2007.[2] New campuses were built for Zayed University in both Dubai (2006) and Abu Dhabi (2011), and the UAE University was expanded at the same time. The wealth and ambitions of the UAE fueled other initiatives elsewhere in the country. The emirate of Sharjah has two universities, both founded in 1997 by its learned ruler, Sheikh Dr. Sultan bin Muhammad Al-Qasimi: the University of Sharjah, an Islamic institution, and the coeducational American University of Sharjah, which draws an international student body. These institutions are supplemented by other, smaller entities across the UAE, including branch programs of various foreign schools in the emirates of Dubai and Ras Al Khaimah.[3]

As a result of the crown prince's patronage, NYUAD directly interacted with two powerful entities in Abu Dhabi. The Executive Affairs Authority (EAA) develops and implements the ruler's policy objectives and was NYUAD's governmental partner until a dedicated, quasi-governmental organization called Tamkeen was formed to oversee construction of the campus and other nonacademic matters that fell within its managerial scope. The second entity, Mubadala, was tasked with building the campus. Whereas the EAA develops policy, Mubadala is the development arm charged with executing the emirate's strategic initiatives to diversify its economy. Its expansive portfolio encompasses industrial, technological, health care, infrastructure, and real estate projects, including universities. Mubadala built new campuses for the UAE University, Zayed University, the Sorbonne, and the Masdar Institute (and Masdar City), as well as NYUAD.

Planning NYUAD coincided with the establishment of a planning process in the emirate of Abu Dhabi. Before 2007, Abu Dhabi did not have a comprehensive system of land use. The municipal Department of Buildings reviewed individual plans, but there was no policy framework that addressed, for example, maximum densities, building heights, permissible uses, and environmental standards—that is, a context in which to consider the impact of individual buildings. Absent growth controls, individual developers sought to maximize the profit on their building sites, driving up building heights without regard for their impact. Following the death of Sheikh Zayed in 2004, several properties in Abu Dhabi were opened for development. Development fever was high; Abu Dhabi experienced a surge of high-rise construction, with many big projects on the drawing boards. In 2006, having observed unregulated growth in Dubai and concerned with projects arising in Abu Dhabi, the Executive Affairs Authority launched an urban planning initiative.

A taskforce led by Larry Beasley, the former codirector of planning in Vancouver, was charged to develop a strategic urban plan for Abu Dhabi. A gathering of international planners produced Plan Abu Dhabi 2030 (also known as the Urban Structure Framework Plan), which was issued in September 2007. But more important than a master plan, Beasley argued, was developing a planning process. Embracing this recommendation, in 2007, the government of Abu Dhabi created the Urban Planning Council to govern land use decisions in the emirate of Abu Dhabi, akin to the planning commission in American cities. The 2030 plan included five principles or values to inform the Urban Planning Council's work. These principles included a commitment to "measured growth reflecting a sustainable economy, rather than an uncontrolled growth"; respect for the "sensitive coastal and desert ecologies"; and the identity of Abu Dhabi as "a contemporary expression of an Arab city."[4] From the start, Sheikh Mohammed bin Zayed served as chairman of the new planning agency. His leadership was essential because so much property was controlled by other members of the royal family, and placing constraints on the traditional prerogatives of the sheikhs to capitalize on the land was a considerable political challenge.

In its infancy, the Urban Planning Council had to establish its authority, develop and enforce land use controls, and review a tremendous number of projects. It faced a stream of large projects in Abu Dhabi: Saadiyat Island; Reem Island, where the Sorbonne was located; Masdar City, the mile-square, carbon-neutral city where the Masdar Institute was built; Al Raha Beach Development; the Capitol District; and many building projects distributed across the main island. In the case of large projects, the Urban Planning Council delegated authority to the master developer. Thus, for Saadiyat Island, the primary agency with authority to review the NYUAD campus designs was the master developer of the island, the Tourism Development and Investment Company, or TDIC. TDIC had developed a master plan for the island that incorporated land use and height restrictions with which the university had to comply or obtain waivers.

In addition to the two local planning authorities, a variety of municipal agencies had to review construction drawings and eventually issue certificates of occupancy; these included the agencies responsible for electricity, water, and fire and life safety. Building codes raised an interesting question: what happens when the local codes differ from those of the foreign institution, for example, regarding fire safety or handicapped accessibility? We had encountered some disparities between NYU and Abu Dhabi building codes when the downtown campus was built in 2008–2009, but by the time the standards for the Saadiyat campus were set, Abu Dhabi had adopted the International Building Code, which resolved most disparities. For example, the International Building Code essentially incorporates the requirements of the Americans with Disabilities Act, so that the imperative of universal accessibility shed its specifically American character.

Speed

The creation of NYU Abu Dhabi was announced in October 2007.[5] The site was determined in spring 2008, following which Mubadala and NYU jointly selected Rafael Viñoly Architects for the master plan through an invitational request-for-proposals process. The Viñoly firm completed the space plan, a component of the master plan, in January 2009. The space plan defined two phases of campus development: phase 1 with 2,600 students and phase 2 with 4,000. Phase 1 encompassed academic, recreational, dining, cultural, and residential life in a variety of buildings that added up to a total of 425,000 gross square meters, in addition to the landscaped outdoor public realm that knits the buildings together. Phase 2 buildings would provide residences for the incremental growth of the student body, expanded research space, and buildings for graduate study. The master plan reserved two parcels, at the east and west ends of the campus, for phase 2 expansion, but it was too remote to dwell on its details. The master plan focused on defining phase 1.

Mubadala decided to build the 2,600-student campus at once, even though at opening the population would be well below capacity, closer to 700 students. There can be a great impatience for results in the UAE, yet money can also be patient—at least for strategic initiatives. It is not uncommon in the region to build ahead of demand; this is evident in commercial and residential construction, hotels, and infrastructure, and while there may be disadvantages to this approach in some sectors (empty buildings, unprofitable investments), for the university it was greatly advantageous to be built at once. Mubadala concluded that one construction campaign would provide efficiencies and cost economies. This approach would also improve the quality of life on campus: it would not be a construction site over an extended period, and a complete campus would create a sense of place, increase the appeal of the university, and counteract the isolation of the site. The challenge would be to animate a campus that would be underoccupied for approximately a decade.

We did not yet have a mature vision of the university in fall 2008, when the space plan was worked out. What fields would the curriculum cover, especially in space-hungry fields such as science and engineering, and how large would they be? How many faculty were needed in each area, since space needs vary by discipline? What was the research profile of the university, and how much research space would the scientists and engineers require? These were some of the questions that had to be answered prematurely in order to keep pace with the fast-moving construction project. The vision of the university was continually evolving, but NYU had to stay within the parameters of the 2009 space plan, since it was a key driver of the construction budget.

The Viñoly firm completed the master plan in June 2009. A five-hundred-page document, it covers everything from lighting to water use to landscape, but the core of it lays out the design vision of the campus. Although the design matured considerably during the subsequent phases,

Figure 6.1. The main campus street looking east, with the Experimental Research Building and West Plaza in the foreground, NYU Abu Dhabi. Photograph by Andrew Moore, 2014.

it stayed true to the master plan, realizing the concept principles with greater clarity and simplicity.

The master plan was followed by the development of the employer's requirements. This stage, more common in British than U.S. building projects, involves defining detailed performance specifications for each type of room. The specifications included such elements as acoustics, furniture and equipment, finishes and fixtures, audio visual and computational requirements, wall systems, and wayfinding. The employer's requirements, which preceded detailed design, were completed in a mere three months (summer 2009). It was difficult to anticipate all the needs of the university at that early stage, let alone approve furniture, equipment, finishes, and fixtures before the university had been designed. But this information was needed because contractors bid for the contract to build the campus based on the master plan and the employer's requirements, right down to the details of desks and wall switches.

Mubadala structured the construction project as design-build. In design-build contracts, the contractor is responsible for cost control; thus, the contractor hires the architect and is responsible to deliver the project on time and on budget. Design-build is less common in the United States, where owners more typically contract separately with the designer and builder, although design-build is growing in favor for infrastructure projects, where it is credited with saving time and money. Mubadala selected Al-Futtaim Carillion to build the campus, who in turn hired Rafael Viñoly Architects for design development. Typically, big contractors would not hire star architects; they are risk factors, perceived as driving up costs. The norm would have been for Al-Futtaim Carillion to hire a large architectural firm without design pretensions and high profile and geared to low-cost construction to interpret the Viñoly master plan. However, because the Executive Affairs Authority shared NYU's commitment to design excellence and considered it essential for Viñoly to develop the master plan, his appointment was secured. It should be noted that NYU was not party to any contracts and had no commercial responsibility; the campus, like all aspects of the university, was funded entirely by the government of Abu Dhabi.

Design development proceeded in fall 2009 and continued on a fast track in parallel with construction. Construction of the pilings began in summer 2010, just before the university opened to students at its interim downtown campus in September. The new campus was completed four years later, in spring 2014. The speed was astonishing. Generally speaking, development in the Gulf has happened quickly, but speedy construction cannot be assumed, and projects are often delayed by financial pressures or changes in strategic priorities. To cite a prominent example, the museums planned for Saadiyat Island—the Louvre Abu Dhabi, Guggenheim Abu Dhabi, and Zayed National Museum—were announced years before the university and were subject to multiple delays. The Louvre Abu Dhabi eventually opened in 2017; as of 2018, construction of the other two museums has not yet begun.

Several factors accounted for the speed of building NYUAD, including high-level government support, the design-build contract, and Abu Dhabi's streamlined governmental review processes. Unlike New York, Abu Dhabi does not have local community boards that weigh in on build-

Figure 6.2. The main campus street, with landscaping and seating, and a bridge at High Line level. Photograph by Tom Rossiter, 2014.

ing plans nor an extensive impact-review process. The Saadiyat campus was built in about the same time that it took NYU in New York to complete preliminary planning and the uniform land use review procedure (ULURP) for expansion on its two Greenwich Village superblocks—a smaller area and fewer buildings than the Abu Dhabi campus.

Gratifying though the speed was, it imposed pressures on the design process. For example, the two basement parking levels with the structural grid to support the upper floors were built before those buildings were designed. Construction proceeded so quickly that decisions were sometimes made in the field, outside the formal framework of decision making and documentation.

Site

Saadiyat Island had been chosen at the highest level as the site of the university. Plans to develop the island, which was located just off the coast of the main island of Abu Dhabi, were announced in 2007 and immediately established Saadiyat as a prestige location. Planned for a residential population of 120,000, Saadiyat was also intended to play a key role in lifting the profile of Abu Dhabi and attracting international tourism by serving as a resort and culture destination. Taking advantage of its splendid beaches, the north coast was reserved for luxury hotels and a golf course, while the east side of the island was programmed as a cultural district. The original plans included four museums, a performing arts center, and a circuit of small art pavilions arranged around a canal.[6]

The island's master developer, TDIC, situated the university in the Marina District, which was conceived as the island's most urban zone. The Marina District was laid out on a grid plan and zoned for mid- and high-rise buildings with a marina as the signature feature. Given NYU's urban identity, the Marina District seemed the right fit for the university, even if it would take decades for the island to urbanize and for the university to be "in and of the city."[7] In order to determine how much land was needed, the university engaged in a high-level space planning analysis with the help of Sasaki Associates from November 2007 to March 2008. NYU then submitted a request for 16 hectares, not including athletic fields, to accommodate a university for 4,000 students. TDIC had commercial objectives in developing the island; it had already provided substantial land for the cultural institutions, and thus the prospect of giving substantial territory to another noncommercial venture could not have been appealing. They granted the university 15.4 hectares, but this included athletic fields. The site was divided into two parcels by a highway that was planned to loop through the Marina District and connect to Reem Island. (As of 2018, that highway had not yet been built.) The university was not allowed to build on the 4-hectare parcel to the north; it was reserved for the athletic fields. The university buildings were restricted to the 11.4-hectare parcel, south of the highway. The parcels would be connected by two bridges across the highway.

There was some disappointment with the site, because, first, the campus would be split by a highway and, second, the area seemed small to contain our ambitious vision. Comparing buildable area, the university had requested 16 hectares and was granted 11.4. To address both problems, Viñoly had the brilliant idea of building a wide platform across the highway not only to link the two parcels and enclose the highway but also to create more territory for the university. The idea was rejected, but in the future, as the university seeks to expand, a platform may have more appeal. As to the second problem, the relatively small buildable area, it led us toward density, which we realized was a great asset. Density became a defining feature of the design.

We envisioned NYUAD as an open campus, with a seamless connection with the city, in contrast to the national universities, which are more like enclaves. The national universities are primarily commuter schools. To accommodate the large number of day commuters, the campuses are surrounded by large parking lots, and the perimeter is sometimes enclosed by a wall. Access to the campus is regulated, and the university is set apart from its environs. The aspiration to embed the NYUAD campus in the city may seem unrealistic given that the location was an undeveloped island, but eventually the campus will be surrounded by buildings and the Marina District will be built out.

To be prepared for that future stage of urbanism, the campus was designed with the latent potential to connect. Toward that end, every campus street is open; there are no gates. Visitors are welcome on campus; indeed, there is extensive programming—public lectures, art exhibitions, performances—to attract Abu Dhabi residents to the campus. In addition, many of the public-facing activities were placed along the perimeter of the campus to accommodate future city residents as well as campus dwellers. Those uses include retail shops, the bookstore, art gallery, and conference center. Yet the intrinsic connectivity and openness of the campus will only be realized over time, as the neighborhood takes shapes.

Anticipating that the university would be isolated upon opening, it was imperative for the campus itself to create a sense of place, since we could not depend on any surrounding context to provide it. The Marina District had been planned with a street grid, and our site (the southern, buildable parcel) was divided into several rectangular blocks. Our architect recommended merging them into one superblock in order to create a unifying public realm and sense of place that separate blocks of buildings would not allow. The master developer, TDIC, granted this request. Like density, the superblock, with the possibility it afforded of a unifying public realm, was essential to the concept of the campus.

A Pedestrian Campus

We conceived of the campus as an urban fragment—mixed-use buildings in a dense and walkable environment. Abu Dhabi is not generally considered a walkable city because it can be boiling hot. The temperatures soar to 110 degrees Fahrenheit and higher during the summer months (June–August), when the desert heat combines with heavy humidity. Walking outdoors even short distances is onerous. For this reason, the two Zayed University campuses have fully enclosed, air-conditioned indoor streets. But, however punishing the summer, the weather is temperate for most of the academic year; from October through April, the outdoors is habitable. Moreover, the university's compact site made it easier to imagine a walkable, outdoor campus. To walk from one end of the campus to the other takes no more than ten to fifteen minutes.

The university's desire to create a walkable campus initially met with considerable skepticism. Some parties thought we were uninformed about local conditions and misguidedly seeking to import a New York idea. The old cities of the Islamic world developed a walkable, street-centered urbanism with strategies to mitigate the heat, but when Abu Dhabi was laid out in the 1970s, it was planned for automobile convenience, with a large-scale grid of superwide streets of eight lanes or more, and that automobile orientation has become only more pronounced with recent construction. Notwithstanding the dominant car culture, the vernacular urbanism of the 1970s and 1980s also fostered a pedestrian street life, with continuous ground-floor retail establishments, sidewalks partially shaded by overhanging apartment buildings, and dense development within each block. Early buildings, such as the Central Market (demolished), the old Fish Market (demolished), and the Madinat Zayed Mall and Gold Centre, incorporated colonnades to provide shade in an outdoor zone around each building. There are also sophisticated reinterpretations of traditional design in modern terms, notably the National Theater and Cultural Center, designed by Rifat Chadirji in 1977, and the Cultural Foundation, designed by the Architects Collaborative also in 1977.[8] An artful fusion of modern and Islamic elements, the Cultural Center is fronted by a monumental colonnade, adorned with colorful tiles in geometric patterns, that provides a shaded and well-ventilated social space and walkway, and an amphitheater was built for outdoor

Figure 6.3. The High Line and undergraduate residences, NYU Abu Dhabi. Photograph by Tom Rossiter, 2014.

programs. The strategy for NYUAD was to make intelligent environmental adaptations, some derived from traditional Islamic architecture, to shade the outdoors and temper the heat so that it was possible to walk and socialize outdoors the better part of the year.

To meet this objective, the orientation of the campus and size of the plazas were influenced by climate modeling. Given the goal of a habitable outdoors, it was important to optimize shading provided by buildings, benefit from prevailing northwest winds and natural ventilation, and allow for local wind steering by building form. In addition to these low-tech strategies of climate adaptation, all hardscapes were light colored and low luster to limit glare. Large, open spaces were not desirable because of sun exposure. The open spaces—plazas at the ground level and quads at the upper circulation level—were scaled to take advantage of shading from the surrounding buildings, and judicious placement of trees provided additional relief from the sun, notably the stand of palm trees in the relatively large Central Plaza.

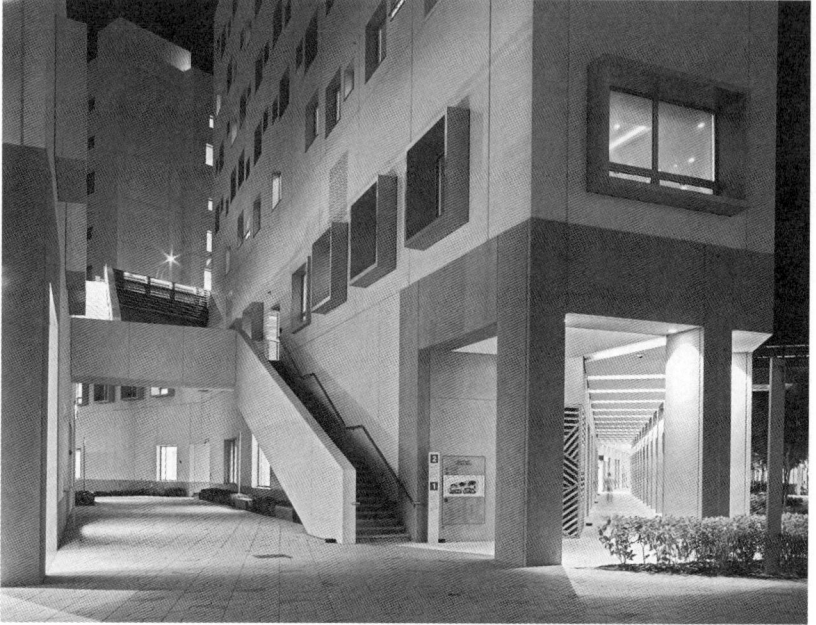

Figure 6.4. The pedestrian network, NYU Abu Dhabi. Photograph by Andrew Moore, 2014.

Density

Density and walkability go hand in hand. The campus is structured around a pedestrian circulation plan. No cars are allowed at ground level; parking and service vehicles are accommodated in two basement levels. The main campus street runs along the middle of the superblock, with three plazas defining its middle and end points. The main street is flanked on both sides by a covered colonnade, which makes it possible to walk the length of the campus in shade (see figs. 6.1 and 6.2). The street is also bordered by plantings and a channel of water, a reference to the traditional *falaj* of Islamic gardens. The gurgling sound and cooling properties of the water enhance sitting areas that are set in this landscape.

Secondary streets connect the plazas to the perimeter of the campus, where they meet the surrounding street grid.[9] When approaching the university from the surrounding streets, the diagonal orientation of the campus streets will signal a shift to a pedestrian environment. Except for the main entrance, the streets are not straight; they are all slightly kinked, so you cannot see from one end of a street to the other. The angling of the streets evokes the organic street patterns in old Islamic cities while creating the illusion of greater distance on this very compact campus. The streets are narrow so they are always shaded by their buildings. The new campus of the American University of Cairo is also organized around a zigzagging main street. Although much larger in extent than NYUAD, the Cairo campus reflects a similar principle of Islamic urbanism, organized by the spine of a pedestrian street, which opens up into plazas and provides access to smaller, lateral spaces.

A hallmark of the NYUAD campus is its split-level circulation: there is, in effect, a second ground plane at the second level, which is called the High Line. Although not directly inspired by the High Line in New York, the name was proposed during the design process (in the master plan, it was called the Garden Level), and it stuck because it perfectly captures the idea of fusing New York and Abu Dhabi in NYUAD. Whereas the plaza level provides access to classrooms (on the ground level) and faculty and staff offices (on the first floor), the High Line belongs to the residential zone (fig. 6.3). The High Line circumnavigates the campus, meandering through the student quads and connecting

Figure 6.5. The ground floor of the Humanities Building and courtyard with a view of the undergraduate residences at the High Line. Photograph by Will Pryce, 2014.

to the faculty residences. As in a city, there are multiple routes between any two points, due to the split-level circulation, the many vertical connections, bridges between buildings, and indoor pathways.

Rather than traditional single-use areas, such as a precinct for dormitories and another for academic facilities, all the NYUAD buildings mix uses, which is another driver of density. Consider two examples: the Campus Center and so-called A blocks on the south side of the main street. The Campus Center, the biggest building on campus, faces the Central Plaza. It combines the library and gym as well as the other components of student life—rooms for student government and clubs, the health and wellness center, a game room, dining areas, study space, and relevant administrative offices. Normally the library and gym are considered programmatically incompatible and located in different buildings, and in early designs of NYUAD, they were housed in two separate structures. But the functions were ultimately combined in a single building in order to create greater convenience and social activity around the Central Plaza. Given that the campus would be underpopulated for some time, it was desirable to create a magnet that would attract students and other community members to the Central Plaza and set it abuzz with social life.

The A blocks work differently: the residences sit above academic podiums, but circulation between them is blocked so that they seem like separate, monofunctional buildings rather than the mixed-use structures they are. The split-level circulation does not allow you to access the residential floors from the ground level. It is necessary to ascend to the High Line, where you encounter low-rise residential buildings, each front door leading to a series of student life spaces. The High Line creates a residential domain that feels intimate, small scale, and domestic, while the plaza level is more formal and geared to academic functions. The student residences form six quads (four undergraduate and two graduate). The undergraduate quads are roughly triangular in shape, with three wings separated by the High Line. Each wing houses about 200 to 250 students and rises five or six stories. The campus is an off-white color, with accents in gray, but there is a surprising burst of color inside the undergraduate quads, which are clad in earth-colored tiles that change appearance depending on the fall of light. The use of color helps to reinforce the distinctive identity of each residential quadrangle. We wanted to avoid New York–style dormitory apartment buildings; how could we recreate the appealing human scale of the residential buildings typical of American liberal arts colleges, with their formation in community clusters? NYUAD did not have a sufficiently large site to match that low-density arrangement. The solution was provided by the split-level circulation: it achieves higher density by stacking different uses while ingeniously forming a domestic, human scale on the residential High Line.

The density of the campus inherently promotes interaction, but specific design strategies give it deeper salience. First, the large floor plates of the academic buildings encourage faculty interaction and serendipitous encounters. Disciplines are not siloed in different buildings or separated on different floors. The faculty offices are arrayed on the first floor (what would be "second floor" in U.S. nomenclature) of the interconnecting A blocks, with each building hosting a cluster of related disciplines.[10] The possibility of randomly distributing faculty so that disciplines did not establish footprints was briefly considered. This bold approach was executed at the new campus of Singapore University of Technology and Design, developed in partnership with MIT, which opened in 2012. But the academic leadership at NYUAD favored groupings by domains (social sciences, humanities, computational fields, lab-based science and engineering), with office assignments often mixing up faculty in related disciplines. The A blocks are also connected by first-floor bridges, which provide shortcuts between buildings, especially useful during the heat of summer (fig. 6.4).

Transparency is another design strategy that reinforces the campus density and converts it to a visual drama by bringing different environments together in a single view—indoor and outdoor spaces, academic and residential zones, the campus and the skyscraper city, the campus and the sand fields and villas of Saadiyat. The A blocks have open-air, circular courtyards in the center that establish a strong indoor-outdoor connection. The courtyards are enclosed by slanted glass walls that form dramatic cones. Light pours through the glass walls to illuminate the large floor plates of the academic podiums. The cones ascend into the High Line, where the glass walls provide a protective enclosure around the courtyard opening. The glass walls afford views between academic space below and the student quads above, a visual representation of the integration of living and learning on the university campus and demonstration of the mixed uses in these buildings (figs. 6.5 and 6.6). Such visual connections proliferate across the campus, even in the large Campus Center, where you can look clear through the building to the city beyond on either side.

Fabric, Not Objects

Abu Dhabi abounds with spectacular buildings, buildings that claim attention for themselves through dramatic shapes and other formal features and physically stand apart from neighboring buildings as self-contained objects. The recent construction along the Corniche, the city's main waterfront boulevard, is illustrative. While the beachfront has an inviting pedestrian path, the opposite side presents a series of new sky-scrapers that ignore the street. These buildings are designed to facilitate vehicular access, disregard pedestrians, reduce outdoor exposure, and maximize indoor, climatized space. The campus may be seen as a form of counterurbanism, exemplifying an alternative model of humble build-ings that eschew special effects and work together to create a fabric where the whole is far more important than any individual part. The buildings seem plain; clad with precast concrete panels, the ground-floor colon-nade is gray and the upper floors off-white. Nothing is flashy. The sense of fabric, of continuity, is achieved in part through the use of common materials, the visual harmony of the buildings, their compact spacing, and shared circulation at plaza level and the High Line. The buildings have unity but are not uniform.

The variety achieved within a limited language can be seen in the housing. The campus has three types of residences, each with a differ-ent exterior treatment. The undergraduate housing appears to have thick masonry walls. In fact, the walls are of modern construction, not any thicker here than elsewhere on campus, but the treatment evokes a tradi-tional style of construction in hot climates where thick walls offer cooling properties. The heritage district in Sharjah, the old fort in Abu Dhabi, and the traditional housing in Sana'a, Yemen, are reference points. The undergraduate residences have punched windows of two different sizes. The limited glass exposure reduces heat gain, while the irregular pattern of large and small windows gives a surprising degree of variety to what is after all the repetition of standard cellular housing units. The vari-ety is enhanced by projections and recesses in the wall surfaces and

Figure 6.6. The main entrance of NYU Abu Dhabi, looking toward the Central Plaza and Campus Center. The graduate residences are above the bookstore and welcome center. Photograph by Tom Rossiter, 2014.

the irregular, triangular geometry of the blocks. The graduate residences have more glass, with gray and white precast panels that create a lighter impression. The faculty apartments have yet more glass—floor-to-ceiling walls of glass—with balconies and patterned metal screens that work like mashrabiya, traditional Islamic screens used to provide privacy and here also to block the sunlight. The punched windows, evocation of thick masonry walls, and mashrabiya screens are not deployed in a historicizing manner; rather, they reference the region within a context of otherwise abstract, nondecorative design. The approach at NYUAD contrasts with that at the American University of Cairo, where many buildings feature the traditional architectural forms of wind towers, mashrabiya screens, and domes. Instead of quoting decorative elements, Viñoly's strategy was to borrow the logic of Arabic design—narrow streets, courtyards, irregular geometry, visual complexity, colonnades, water channels, colored tile—but to express them in a contemporary mode.[11]

The emphasis on fabric does not mean the absence of monumental or dramatic spaces, but they are contained inside buildings, where their impact is heightened by a sense of surprise. This design strategy is deployed in the Campus Center, which contains an oval core that rises the full height of the building. The oval form is evident upon entering the building, and it is always in sight as you ascend the stairs, which seem to float in a soaring, vertical open space around the oval core. This core comprises three double-height spaces: the pool (basement and ground level), the gym (levels 1–2), and the library (levels 3–4), where the main reading room expresses the oval shape. It is a vast and majestic clear-span space, the largest room on campus. Three oculi penetrate the ceiling and floor of the library and channel natural light into the gym and pool below. The oval arises from the building mass to crown the Campus Center. Imprinted with the NYU torch, this metal-clad crown shimmers in daylight but dematerializes at night, appearing like a halo with its nocturnal illumination (fig. 6.7). The crowning oval form gives the traditional symbolic and physical centrality to the library, emblematic of the pursuit of knowledge.

The Arts Center also combines a modest, even unimpressive exterior with dramatic interior spaces. In addition to the academic facilities for a

Figure 6.7. The East Plaza during a concert, with the Arts Center at right, NYU Abu Dhabi. Photograph by Christopher Pike, n.d.

multimedia arts curriculum, the Arts Center contains three theaters that you encounter as distinct volumes upon entering the lobby. The three boxes are each clad in colored metal panels that give the theaters their names (Black Box, Blue Hall, Red Theater). The boxes penetrate the ceiling of the Arts Center and emerge in the roofscape, where they are legible as different volumes but clearly embedded in a bigger container.

Public Access and Security

The open campus design was inspired by NYU's situation in New York City, where the buildings are organized by the city's grid plan and do not form a campus at all. Whatever security was deemed appropriate, the idea was to make it unobtrusive so that visitors would feel welcome. Thus, rather than secure the perimeter of the campus with a hard edge, security checks would be located within buildings as needed.[12] Late in the design process, this approach was questioned. The UAE is a very safe country and has no recent history of terrorism. Nevertheless, it was not unreasonable to imagine the university as a target. The idea of enclosing the perimeter of the campus was briefly considered but was rejected for various reasons, including the likely inefficacy of a wall in the event of an attack.

Soon after the campus opened, the U.S. State Department in Abu Dhabi issued a security warning and an American schoolteacher was killed in a Reem Island mall restroom by an Emirati woman, a very surprising and shocking event. These events led the university to open a checkpoint along the road leading to the campus. Since nothing else was built yet in the vicinity, the road only serviced the university. Drivers were required to show identification to proceed. The checkpoint unleashed a campus debate: some felt it provided necessary protection, others that it primarily served to alienate visitors and convey an antisocial message of isolation. Before long, the security alert was withdrawn and the checkpoint was dismantled, but the question of how to balance openness and security on the campus persists.

Another dimension of this issue relates to campus life. Visitors are welcomed to the campus for a variety of public events, including performances at the Arts Center, exhibitions at the Art Gallery, and lectures at the NYUAD Institute (fig. 6.7). There is nothing to stop visitors from strolling the grounds, as happens at most U.S. campuses. The university teaches respect for local laws and values, but as at most universities, a community of inquisitive, bold young people from around the world will involve experimentation, the testing of limits, and self-expression. What if a visitor is offended by something seen on campus? An open campus can mean a potentially risky degree of exposure, but closing the campus and adopting an isolationist stance is not a desirable solution. Negotiating the cultural friction points between the university and the community is a productive challenge, inherent in the mission of NYU Abu Dhabi to provide an alternative model of education.

***

The architect Rafael Viñoly described the NYU Abu Dhabi campus as a village, intentionally playing on the reference to Greenwich Village, NYU's home in New York, but with a twist. "The scheme is essentially a New Village, neither replicating the image of the traditional Islamic neighborhood, nor the character of Greenwich Village, but instead an amalgam of both, as a metaphor for the central idea of the institution."[13]

The physical form of the university draws on a variety of sources—traditional Islamic architecture, American campus planning, modern design. Inspired by the pedestrian urbanism of New York as well as traditional Islamic cities, the campus creates a walkable environment with a dense building fabric, in contrast to the approach to city building that now prevails in Abu Dhabi. The result is an original melding of Abu Dhabi and New York, traditional and modern, local and Western. The NYU Abu Dhabi campus embodies the aspiration to bridge cultures.

NOTES

1   These locations are Abu Dhabi, Accra (Ghana), Berlin, Buenos Aires, Florence, London, Madrid, New York, Paris, Prague, Shanghai, Sydney, Tel Aviv, and Washington, DC.

2   In 2016 it was announced that the Masdar Institute and Khalifa University, both focused on science and technology, and the Petroleum Institute would merge.

3   On the tremendous growth of higher-education programs in the UAE, see Donn and Al Manthri 2010; UAE Ministry of Higher 2006.

4   Abu Dhabi Urban Planning Council 2007, 15–16.

5   An announcement in New York in October was followed by one in Abu Dhabi in November 2007.

6   Over time, three museums were staged for phase 1: the Louvre Abu Dhabi, Sheikh Zayed Museum, and Guggenheim Museum Abu Dhabi. The Maritime Museum, performing arts center, and art pavilions were grouped in a second phase, which has been indefinitely delayed. The museums were launched by TDIC, but it has been reorganized several times and its scope narrowed since its establishment in 2006. TDIC now manages only their construction, while the development of the museums as cultural institutions is overseen by the Abu Dhabi Tourism and Culture Authority (TCA), which was formed in 2012.

7   In addition to the Saadiyat Beach, Cultural, and Marina Districts, the original master plan for the island included the Lagoons District, programmed for villas and townhouses; South Beach, a somewhat denser residential area; and Eco Point, an ecological sanctuary.

8   See Menoret 2014.

9   The plan of the Marina District has changed since the campus was designed, and some of the streets south of the campus have been eliminated.

10 Not all faculty offices are located in the A blocks. Some are located in the Arts Center, which combines several disciplines: art, film and new media, interactive media, music, and theater. The Experimental Research Building houses faculty who work in its wet and dry labs. The labs were designed to allow the easy formation of multidisciplinary teams around changing research questions.

11 It should be noted that planning policy in Abu Dhabi favors historicizing elements. The sustainability requirements established by the Urban Planning Council, called the Estidama Program, not only address water and energy use, but also award points for traditional Arab architectural forms, such as ornate roof lines and domes.

12 It was decided that security checkpoints, in the form of ID-operated turnstiles, were needed only in the student residences and the Experimental Research Building.

13 Rafael Viñoly Architects 2009, 71.

REFERENCES

Abu Dhabi Urban Planning Council. 2007. *Plan Abu Dhabi 2030: Urban Structure Framework Plan.* Abu Dhabi: Mimeo.

Donn, Gari, and Yahaya Al Manthri. 2010. *Globalisation and Higher Education in the Arab Gulf States.* Oxford: Symposium Books.

Menoret, Pascal, ed. 2014. *The Abu Dhabi Guide: Modern Architecture 1950s–1990s.* Abu Dhabi: NYU Abu Dhabi. www.f-in-d.com.

Rafael Viñoly Architects. 2009. *NYU Abu Dhabi Master Plan*, internal document, June 24, 2009.

UAE Ministry of Higher Education. 2006. *Educating the Next Generation of Emiratis: A Master Plan for the UAE Higher Education.* Abu Dhabi: UAE Ministry of Higher Education.

SECTION III

Urban Test Beds for Export

7

Gateway

Revisiting Dubai as a Port City

MINA AKHAVAN

Through a close tracing of a truly remarkable kind of infrastructural growth, Dubai's experience can more generally expand our notions of how cities and their ports develop together. Dubai shows us—in part through its speed of evolution and also the eventual scale of its operations—a particular port-city dynamic outside of conventional industrialization, colonialism, postcolonialism, or other familiar development paradigms.

Both in preindustrial cities[1] and under conditions of modern industrialization, ports have been considered pivotal.[2] Beyond their obvious function of linking parts of the global system to one another (as in colonial, industrial, and tourist trade), they also finance and give shape to their respective metropoles. For entrepôt cities, patterns of internal transit and communication were heavily oriented toward getting raw materials—natural resources and agricultural goods—to points of export. For the colonial and "first-world" centers, warehousing and related "break of bulk" activities evolved with port development. The port-hinterland linkage—one of the most important concepts in transport geography[3]—suggests that the land located in the vicinity of a port, where a port has a monopolistic position, follows a dynamic of dual growth. Given that the transport and transshipment activities need certain types of manufacturing operations to locate close by, the combination generates new employment, economic investments, and related activities. Transportation proximity similarly stimulated the import of raw materials and export of finished goods, as well as agricultural yields from the hinterlands. This gave rise to adjacent or nearby administrative and commercial undertakings, sometimes merged into other types of "downtown" support. Further distant hinterlands were themselves shaped through networks of roads, rail systems, and canals ultimately oriented to shipping.

The dominant models in modern thinking heavily derive from nineteenth-century industrialization, particularly from North America. New York, a prototype, is often depicted as achieving its prominence through an optimal natural port configuration, including multiple shelters from winds and swells, as well as links into the U.S. heartland. The other most prominent American examples are New Orleans and Baltimore, with the latter's deep-water harbor sometimes referred to as "the port that built a city."[4] Liverpool and Rotterdam are European examples of port-based metropolitan growth. Even where, as in much of Europe, urbanism came in the form of interior cities (e.g., Paris, London, and Berlin), rivers played a significant role. Ports were labor intensive. There was thus an organic mutuality between transportation, population, commerce, and industry. Residential settlements similarly arose in relation to the other uses. Considered noxious, both in physical and social terms, close-in port districts tended to repulse residential use—except for those with the least amount of choice.

With late modernity, however, the model loses its power for all places, including those, like in nineteenth-century Europe and North America, from which it originated. Triggered by intensified global trade, containerization, and megaships, the dominant trend has been a growing disconnect between the port and its (deindustrializing) city.[5] Container shipping radically decreases the number of workers needed per tonnage. Another shift has been the rise of airfreight and highways, which create new forms of multimodal transit. Increases in scale reward operators who can readily function in diverse port environments across the world, both in technical and administrative terms. In order to enter the global supply chain and enhance its competitiveness, a port has to provide infrastructure for logistic clusters.[6] There is also an advantage for port operators who have interport capacities—the ability to function across regions and to themselves implement interlocal standardization of technologies and procedures.

Advancing the Free-Trade Zone

Starting with fifteenth-century Venetians and then Portuguese, the Dutch, and finally the British, the Persian Gulf region was important for trade routes to and from India and other eastern regions.[7] To protect the passageways as part of the colonial regime, Britain secured—from about 1763 until 1971—dominance over territories that would come to include the states of the UAE, Bahrain, Kuwait, Oman, and Qatar.[8] Other than as points of transit, refuge, and incidental trade, port-hinterland interactions were modest. Dubai's creekside trade was as fishing village and pearling center. By the 1930s, Dubai had become, under British tutelage, one of the busiest ports in the Persian Gulf, including the transshipment of goods to other parts of the region.

The coming of a regional oil economy in the mid-1970s brought vast change. To accommodate more and larger vessels, the creek was repeatedly widened and dredged, eventually supplanted by a new artificial port, Port Rashid, constructed adjacent to a historical core of the city. Moving well beyond oil, Dubai's shipping became in fact transshipping: the same goods that come in then go out, with no change in substance. It is an infrastructure of distribution, not production. Success led to still deeper dredging and capacity building. Dubai authorities constructed, starting in the late 1970s, a second and eventually much larger port, at Jebel Ali (thirty-five kilometers [km] from the historical city center). There arose a division of roles between the two facilities (Port Rashid and Jebel Ali), with container activities transferred to the Jebel Ali Port, destined to take on the global role at a massive scale (see below). The two places were later to be administratively conjoined.

Along with changes in physical apparatus and shifts in landscape came institutional alteration. As early as the turn of the twentieth century, Dubai had decreased taxation and enacted other inducements to win favor with traders to settle in Dubai, particularly in competition with locations across the Gulf in Persia (see Boodrookas and Keshavarzian, this volume[9]). Such arrangements, including tax exclusion, were to evolve into a new kind of jurisdictional manipulation, growing in practice across the world. The rubrics are alternatively "free port," or "free zone," or "free-trade zone"—often abbreviated as "FTZ," which I will also sometimes use.[10] Keller Easterling refers to the whole process as a move toward "extrastatecraft," calling it an "evacuation of the state."[11] There is a selective weakening of governmental authority in favor of private and "off-the-books" decision making. Authorities exclude certain favored geographic areas from tax and other forms of regulation but with offsetting gains from rents, construction profit, and a share in profits from associated enterprises. FTZs are thus a tool to attract outside capital and to segregate generated revenues from absorption for other public purposes. Authorities decrease regulation on commerce and labor to enhance investment and goods' transit from local to global and vice-versa. They thus facilitate the interface of "territoriality" and "transnationalism." All along, we need to remind ourselves, the Dubai sheikhdom and its governmental apparatus played an active role of management, subsidy, rulemaking—and income gaining.

As one of the first efforts to develop the port hinterland and logistics activities in Dubai, the government established, in 1985, the Jebel Ali Free Trade Zone (hereinafter JAFZA). Although not invented at Jebel Ali, the free-trade zone model has had no bigger success, helping the concept travel the world. The zone began initially with only nineteen companies (in 1985); by the end of the 1990s, it had attracted over two thousand, employing about 35,000 people. It has now come to host more than seven thousand companies—from one hundred countries—with 135,000 workers.[12] Dubai now has more than twenty of such free zones, completed or under construction; they come with rules and regulations adapted to their intended function. They fit within a larger strategy of megaproject "cities within the city."[13]

The Dubai Model

The Dubai model, as I use the term, refers not to the overall ambitions and accomplishments of the emirate[14] but instead to the particular port-city linkage that has evolved. Compared to other cases, it represents a different scale and mode of geo-interaction between port and city. The guiding substantive urban concept at least implicit in the model is to create logistical clusters that enhance internal and external efficiencies beyond what is present even in world cities. Port activities are not left to organic evolution; they are planned to gain development synergies. The key concept is to create logistics clusters, complementary functions for global competition. To represent its extent and growth, I rely on the standard data classification "Transportation, Storage and Communication." This sector contributed close to 12 percent of overall Dubai GDP in 2015 (fig. 7.8). It plays the key role in making the UAE the only country in the

Middle East to rank among the top fifteen in the World Bank's Logistics Performance Index in 2016.[15]

Formally inaugurated in 2010 (with an area of approximately two hundred square kilometers),[16] the Dubai Logistics Corridor is one of the world's largest multimodal logistics platforms. In legal terms, it forms a single custom-bonded zone. In functional terms, it links sea, land, and air.[17] Joining with what is already the third busiest airport in the world— Dubai International—a still larger airport is being added, Al Maktoum. It will have the capacity for 160 million passengers per annum and will take over as the world's busiest. Heathrow by comparison handles 73.4 million annual passengers. The new airport carries a government build-out cost estimate of $82 billion; the "old" airport will remain in service, and indeed is itself being expanded. The new airport is part of a mega complex, the Dubai World Central (hereafter DWC), a multiphase development launched in 2006. Spanning more than 140 square kilometers, it is almost twice the size of Hong Kong Island. DWC is slated for a resident and working population of 750,000.

Besides the new airport, other project elements will include Dubai Logistics City, Central Residential City, Commercial City, Enterprise Park, Central Commercial City, Central Aviation City, Central Staff City, and Central Staff Village. Everything will be connected by rapid transit links, including between airports. Extensive facilities for manufacturing, production services, and parts assembly—all in a free zone environment—are also in the planning stages. Table 7.1 summarizes the key government-led port-building initiatives from the 1900s onward.

TABLE 7.1. Dubai's key government-led port-building initiatives.

Main Trade-Based Infrastructures	Ancillary Trade and Logistics Infrastructure	Trade- and Logistics-Based Institutions
1900s—The creek as a free port	1983—Dubai Dry Dock	1957—Dubai Municipality
1959—Dubai International Airport	1985—Jebel Ali Free Zone (JAFZA) opened	1985—Dubai Sky Cargo
1961—Dredging Dubai Creek	1990—ZAFZA expanded	1991—Dubai Port Authority (DPA[18]) established
1972—Port Rashid opened	2006—Dubai World Central (DWC)	1999—Dubai Port International (DPI[19]) established
1978—Port Rashid expanded	2008—Maritime City	2001—Ports Customs and Free Zone Corporation (PCFC) established
1979—Jebel Ali Port	2009—Industrial City	
2007—Jebel Ali Port expanded	2010—Dubai Logistics Corridor	2005—DP World established
2010—Al Maktoum Airport		

Source: author, drawing from various sources.

The relevant auxiliary functions for these Dubai-based trade centers are made part of the infrastructural scheme in the first place. Compared to past port-city evolutions, this is a different type of co-development. Manufacturing, for example, is opportunistically provisioned only given perceived complementarity with the port. All this is facilitated by the specific conditions of the Gulf, including the capacity to plan and implement the largest-scale, highly complex synergies—and to pay for them, on a very short time schedule.

Giant Diversifier: Growth and More Growth

Scholars have sought to lay out various "stages" of world port-city development, a prominent example of which is Brian Hoyle's: beginning with the period of antiquity, moving through nineteenth-century industrialization, and ending (albeit with certain variations) with the contemporary era of containerization. At each stage, industrial growth pushes port activity toward increases in infrastructural scale and spatial extent.[20] In contrast, based on Asian cases, particularly Singapore and Hong Kong, scholars show an alternative picture, with the need for concentration being more apparent at earlier points in the evolution.[21] Although Dubai is sometimes referred to as the "Singapore of the Middle East," it differs from Singapore (and Hong Kong) given the open-space desert environments that provide a more open field for infrastructure and complementary functions. This is, of course, in sharp contrast with the intense densities with which the Asian exemplars must deal. Furthermore, Dubai's characteristic access to capital with minimal red tape or governmental or market constraint sets it apart. It also operates, as with other Gulf enterprises, through the massive importation of labor, under conditions judged unacceptable in many other parts of the world, including (at least in recent times) Hong Kong and Singapore.

Seeking to set up analytic stages that might particularly fit with Dubai, I see progression through four main phases (see fig.7.1):[22] phase 1, the fishing village emerges into a free port (1900s–1950s); phase 2, the entrepôt port city (1960s–1970s); phase 3, the regional transshipment hub port city (1980s–1990s); phase 4, the logistics global hub port city (2000s–present). At each stage, there is a relevant institutional intervention. Each appears,

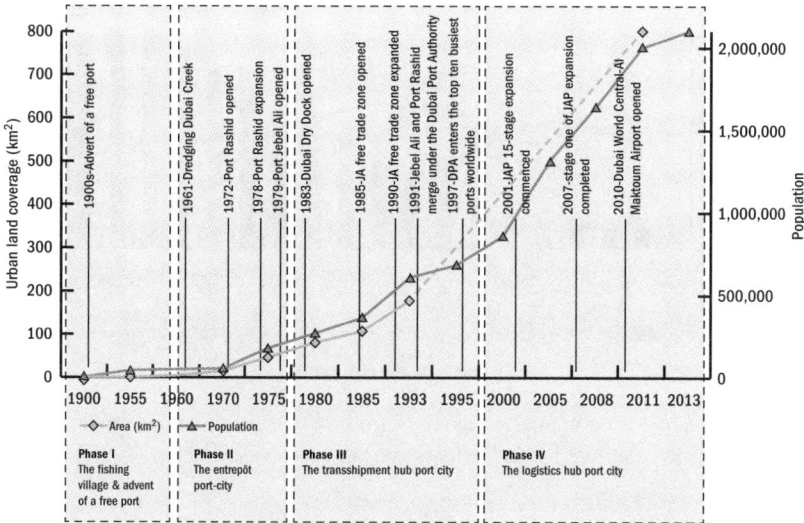

Figure 7.1. The four-phase Dubai port-city development. Source: Akhavan 2017, 350.

based on the data, to effectively usher in concomitant growth both in port-sector urbanization and the rise in Dubai's overall population.

The Dubai port complex, increasingly by explicit design, has embedded its operations in the broader global supply chain. Well before Dubai became globally recognized for its urban spectacle, the city was already an important center of trade—a status that, unlike a museum or skyscraper, does not lend itself to iconic representation. In 2015, the value of its non-oil freight trade added up to about $354 billion, amounting to a quarter of GDP. Imports are the lion's share of traded goods—62 percent—while exports and re-exports accounted for 10 and 28 percent, respectively.[23]

Figure 7.2 shows, over the period 1997–2015, that the year-by-year growth in international trade has been in sync with Dubai's impressive GDP growth. Although there was a sharp decrease in trade during the 2009 economic crisis, data indicate recovery in the subsequent years—part of the trend observed by Yasser Elsheshtawy, as well (see chapter 10). There has been obvious movement toward an economy based on foreign trade, as well as some other (related) economic sectors (see fig. 7.8). Dubai is the main non-oil exporter in the UAE. It is also, by a wide

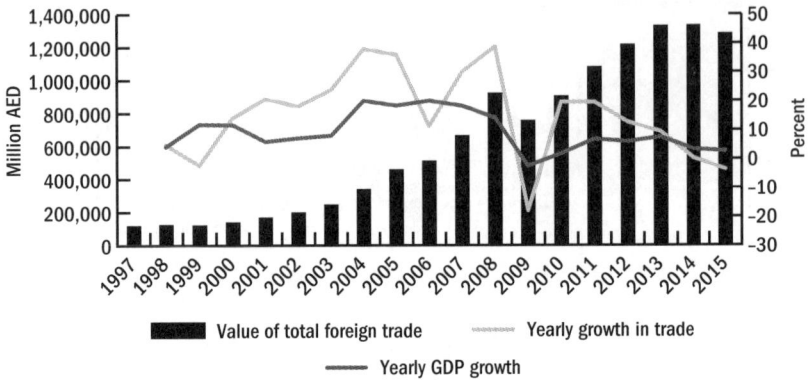

Figure 7.2. Dubai's value of total foreign trade (1997–2015). Source: author's own computation based on data from Dubai Customs and Dubai Statistics Center.

margin and in keeping with its historic role, responsible for most of the country's re-exporting activities—77 percent of the national volume.[24]

While earlier gains in trade came from seaport operations (70 percent of foreign trade value in 2000), over time there has been a growing shift toward air. So, for the year 2000, about a fourth (27 percent) of international trade was by air (with a negligible 3 percent by land). But by 2015, air cargo had overtaken freight via sea, with a share of, respectively, 44 percent and 40 percent (transit by land showed modest growth). Evident in figures 7.3 and 7.4, Dubai is moving toward a more intermodal transportation system, even as its seaports continue to grow as well.

Over time, Dubai also has widened in geographic linkage. Figures 7.5 and 7.6 show the geographic distribution of Dubai's non-oil foreign trade by country and continent for year 2015. Asia, with 64 percent, is by far the most important trade connection, with the rest divided between Europe (18 percent), Africa (9 percent), and North America (7 percent). At the global scale, China (13.8 percent), Saudi Arabia (12.5 percent), and Germany (10.1 percent) are the main national trading partners (non-oil again). Almost half of Dubai's regional trade is carried out with Saudi Arabia, followed by Oman (19 percent), Kuwait (16 percent), Qatar (12 percent) and Bahrain (8 percent). In most any sense, Dubai is now a logistics hub port city par excellence, obviously different from the Western model[25] but also, with some variation, from large port cities of Asia.

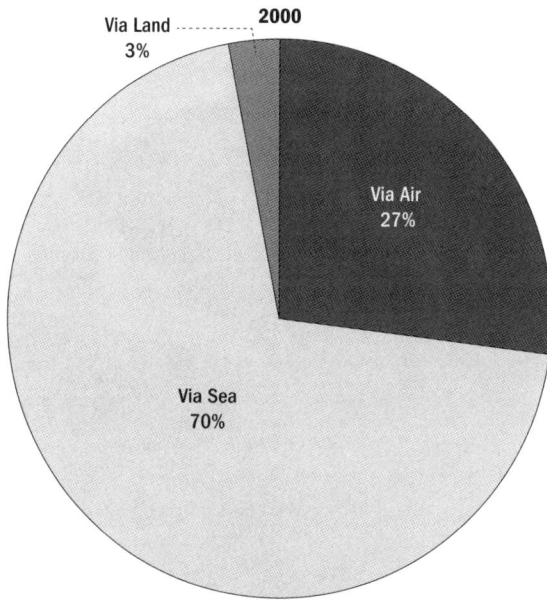

Figure 7.3. Dubai's modal split of international trade (based on the value for year 2000). Source: author's own computation based on data from Dubai Statistics Center and Dubai Customs.

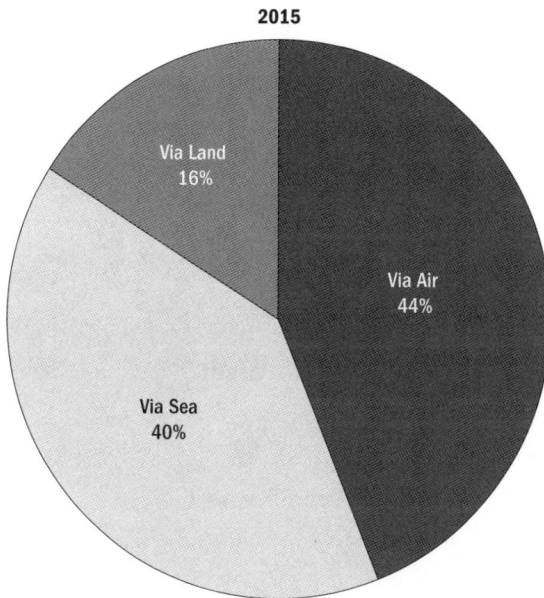

Figure 7.4. Dubai's modal split of international trade (based on the value for year 2015). Source: author's own computation based on data from Dubai Statistics Center and Dubai Customs.

Per Country

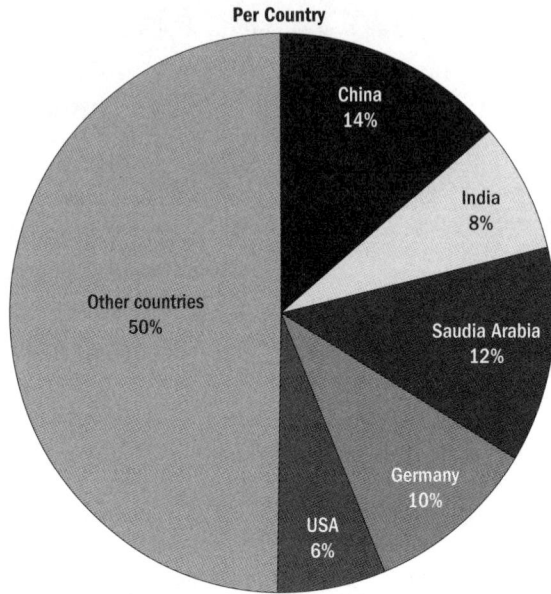

Figure 7.5. Dubai's top trading partners worldwide (per country) in year 2015. Source: author's own computation based on data from Dubai Customs.

Per Continent

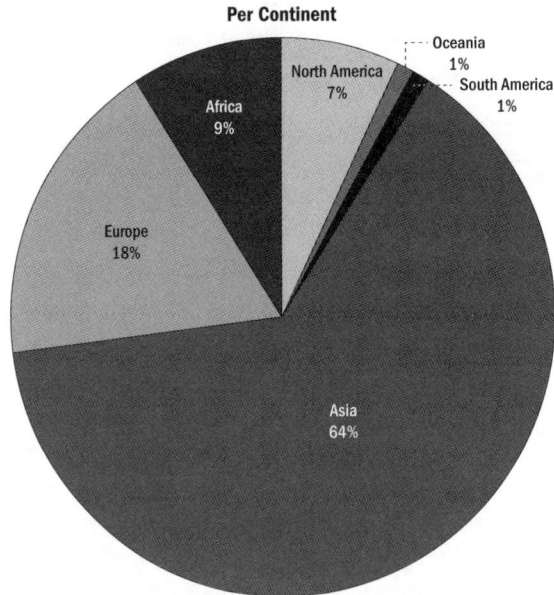

Figure 7.6. Dubai's top trading partners worldwide (per continent) in year 2015. Source: author's own computation based on data from Dubai Customs.

Dubai's Dominion

Dubai's evolution occurs within the context of UAE national growth, but it follows a different pattern than the other emirates. Since its creation, the UAE has had a GDP compound annual growth rate of around 60 percent over a forty-year period (1975–2015), from $14.7 billion to $370.29 billion.[26] This makes UAE the second-largest economy in the Arab world, after Saudi Arabia. But, in contrast to the Saudi situation—as well as some other parts of the UAE—trade and transportation in Dubai figure large. Dubai has led the UAE's economic diversification and is still the only emirate with a diversified economic structure and with almost no direct dependence on oil. About half of Abu Dhabi's GDP is based in oil; for Dubai it is less than 2 percent. As depicted in figure 7.7, oil and gas still comprise a large share of the national UAE GDP.

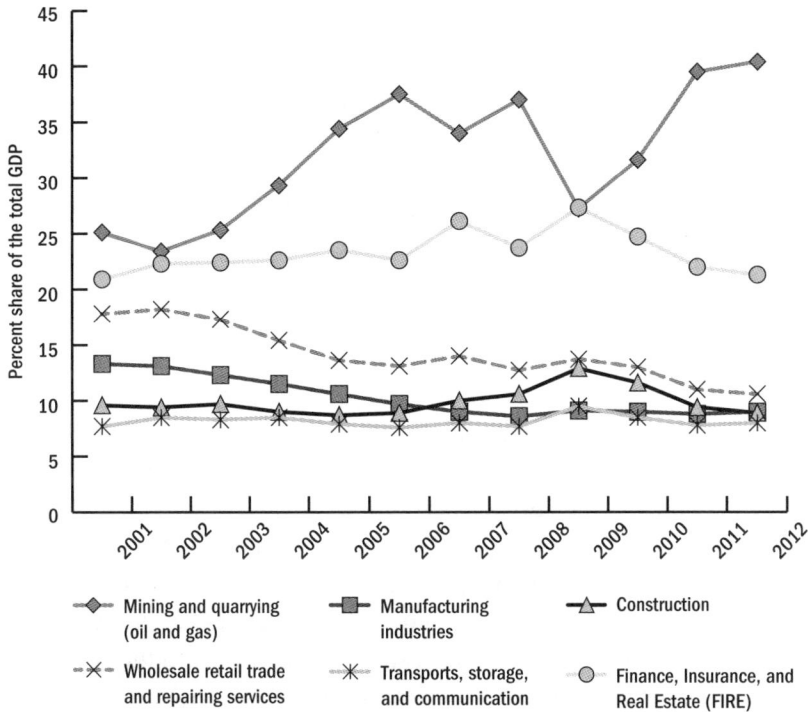

Figure 7.7. Contribution of the main economic activities to the UAE's GDP (2001–2012). Source: author's calculation, data from the Federal Competitiveness and Statistics Authority.

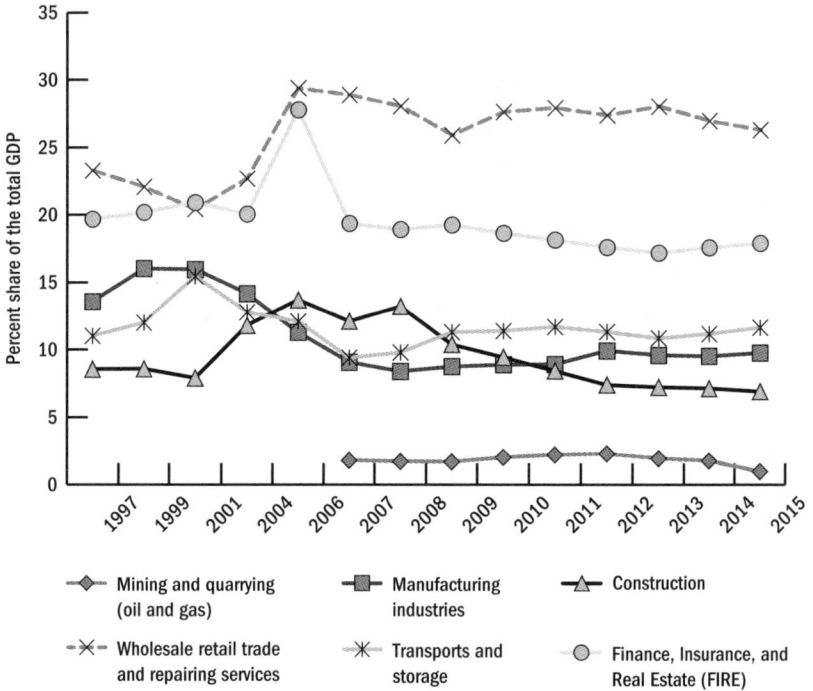

Figure 7.8. Contribution of the main economic activities to Dubai's GDP (1997–2015). Source: author's own computation based on data from Dubai Statistics Center.

As shown in figure 7.8, the pattern has been stable, with oil and gas a negligible element for Dubai, over the period from 1997 to 2015. Trade is consistently dominant (with 26.3 percent of GDP). Business services (finance, insurance, and real estate) follow at around 18 percent. Transportation and manufacturing come in a robust third. The overall picture bespeaks port and logistics.[27]

Dubai's niche (a giant one) is in handling container traffic, a realm in which Saudi Arabia had been the leader. Although in 1980 Dubai handled less than 5 percent of the container traffic entering the Gulf region, by 2011, it had more than a 40 percent share (table 7.2). With the construction of its ports, Dubai soon became the pillar for Arabian Peninsula trade with greater capacities and volume than its regional rivals, Saudi Arabia, Qatar, and Kuwait.[28] Dubai's success (as evidenced by Jebel Ali Port in particular) has led to emulation among its emirate neighbors

TABLE 7.2. Share of each port in handling the total throughput passing through the Middle East (Unit percent TEUs, 1980–2011).

Region	Port City	1980	1985	1990	1995	2000	2005	2011
Persian Gulf	Dubai	4.95	18.41	34.04	39.19	33.20	38.49	42.39
Red Sea	Jeddah	43.70	32.00	20.43	15.03	11.33	14.32	13.08
Arabian Sea	Salalah	NA	0.09	0.02	0.01	11.21	12.59	10.44
Persian Gulf	Sharjah	2.37	1.66	6.94	12.00	12.11	10.90	10.55
Persian Gulf	Bandar Abbas	NA	NA	NA	3.16	4.51	6.53	8.98
Persian Gulf	Dammam	19.5	11.96	8.63	5.26	4.93	4.52	4.87
Persian Gulf	Kuwait	13.2	11.38	4.62	4.11	3.37	3.40	NA
Red Sea	Aqaba	3.32	5.14	3.09	2.06	2.62	1.98	2.30
Red Sea	Aden	0.12	0.22	0.29	0.17	2.69	1.61	0.46
Persian Gulf	Abu Dhabi	0.95	1.21	1.70	4.65	3.69	1.72	2.51
Red Sea	Port Sudan	5.8	0.85	1.28	NA	1.02	1.61	1.51
Persian Gulf	Manama	4.67	4.91	2.79	1.88	1.92	1.28	1.22
Gulf of Oman	Muskat	1.44	5.27	NA	1.81	1.40	1.19	0.88
Gulf of Oman	Fujairah	NA	6.27	15.39	10.55	5.87	0.35	NA

Source: author, based on *Containerization International Yearbook* (1980–2011).

and hence fresh competition. With its new port of Khalifa (inaugurated in 2012), Abu Dhabi has had port volume growth of 37 percent over the 2012–2015 period. The emirate of Sharjah (located on the Gulf of Oman, the east coast of the UAE) has also emerged as a significant container port. Whereas in the 1970s Dubai handled more than 95 percent of total UAE shipping, that has come down to around a 75 percent share—albeit with a strong rise in volume (fig. 7.9 and table 7.3). Regional rivals Jeddah, Sharjah, Salalah, and Dammam are growing particularly fast.[29]

Dubai has replicated its UAE success in other parts of the world. The formation of a wholly owned subsidiary, Dubai Ports International FZE (DPI) in 1999, was an important step toward managing and controlling container terminals and other facilities beyond the national borders. Its first foreign project was Jeddah Islamic Port in Saudi Arabia in 1999. The year after, DPI took control over the port of Djibouti and Djibouti Airport, followed by the takeover of Visakhapatnam Port (India) in 2002, Constanta (Romania) in 2003, and Cochin (India) in 2004. At the beginning of 2005, DPI took a huge step with the acquisition of North Carolina–based CSX World Terminal LLC, a container terminal operator with operations and management in the United States, Asia, and Latin America.[30] Later in the same year, DPI merged with Dubai Port Authority (DPA) to form Dubai Ports World (DP World). The rapid expansion continued with acquiring (for $7 billion) the venerable British shipping

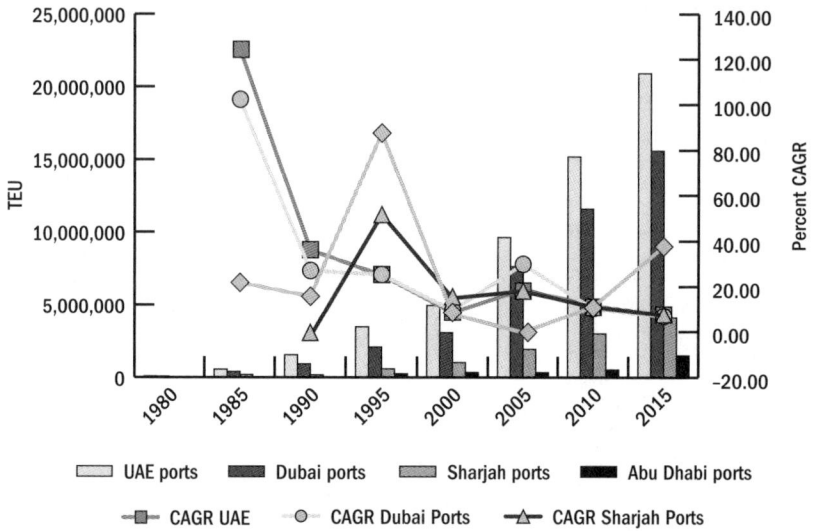

Figure 7.9. Evolution of the container traffic in UAE, Dubai, Abu Dhabi, and Sharjah (1980–2015). Source: author's own computation based on *Containerization International Yearbook* (several years) and the portal of local port authorities.

TABLE 7.3. Top ten world ports, 2014.

Rank 2014	Port	Country	(Million) TEUs 2014 (2000)	% CAGR (2000–2014)	Share (%) among World Total TEUs (2014)
1	Shanghai	China	35.29 (5.6)	14.05	5.2
2	Singapore	Singapore	33.87 (17.04)	5.03	4.9
3	Shenzhen	China	24.03 (3.99)	13.68	3.5
4	Hong Kong	China	22.23 (18.1)	1.48	3.2
5	Busan	S. Korea	19.45 (7.54)	7.04	2.7
6	Ningbo-Zhoushan	China	18.65 (0.9)	24.17	2.7
7	Qingdao	China	16.62 (2.12)	15.85	2.4
8	Guangzhou Harbor	China	16.16 (1.43)	18.91	2.4
9	Jebel Ali Port	UAE	15.25 (3.06)	12.16	2.2
10	Tianjin	China	14.05 (1.71)	16.23	2.1

Source: calculated from the *Containerization International Yearbook*; portal of World Shipping Council.

and logistics enterprise the Peninsular and Oriental Steam Navigation Company (P & O)—the world's fourth-largest port operator. DP World now has seventy-seven marine and inland terminals across six continents, making it third in size among world port operators. Beyond ports and their infrastructures, DP World is active in acquisitions, investments, and greenfield developments, especially those that can synergize with port functions, broadly conceived. Radically and well beyond any waterfront, Dubai port has escaped its boundaries and prior functional limits.

Conclusion

The Dubai model of development as a modern port integrated with free-trade zones has led to a dramatic increase in international trade and logistics, a basis for diversifying far beyond an oil-based economy. Dubai has been the first Arab Middle Eastern city to feature worldwide connectivity.[31] According to a prominent British-based index of world cities, Dubai ranks in the top ten of global cities, along with Hong King, Paris, Singapore, Shanghai, Tokyo, Beijing, and Sydney.[32] It is port development at the center of the Dubai dynamic. This is against the trend happening in the more established global cities, namely, London and New York, which, developing advanced producer services and related realms of the new urban economy, have had their port-based primacy erode.

An important asset for Dubai is its hub-strategy role. Not having evolved out of agriculture or manufacturing, Dubai's diversification is instead based in processing flows of people, goods, capital, and port-related know-how. Dubai's development powerfully exemplifies Manuel Castells's concept of the urban as not so much a series of places but a series of flows: "Flows, rather than places or organizations, become the units of work, decision, and output accounting," as Castells states it.[33] We can understand the spaces of flows as the key factor in defining what Dubai is—and places like it. Still unsettled, both in Castells's overall vision and certainly in the Dubai case, is the role of urban governance and planning for the improvement of civic life—a topic that repeatedly arises in this book's chapters. The Dubai hub-city model—in its UAE original version, as well as the exported variants—is a success as a terminal for the flows of products, capital, people, and goods of all kinds. Accomplishments of social inclusion do not seem to find a place to land.

NOTES

1 Pirenne and McCormick 2014 [1925].
2 Hein 2011; Meyer 1999; Hoyle and Hilling 1984; Konvitz 1978; Bird 1963.
3 United Nations 2005.

4   See the TV show *The Port That Built a City and a State*, by Helen Delich Bentley, www.worldcat.org.

5   Ng et al. 2014; Levinson 2010; Hoyle and Pinder 1981.

6   Akhavan and Mariotti 2015.

7   Ramos, 2010; Boodrookas and Keshavarzian, this volume.

8   Edney 1997.

9   See Fuccaro 2009, 58; Fattah 1997.

10 The United Nations (UNCTAD 1996, 3) describes an FTZ as "usually designated area at a port or airport where goods can be imported, stored or processed and re-exported, free of all Custom Duties. It is a free area which normally falls under the authority of the port or airport management."

11 Easterling 2012; 2014.

12 Jebel Ali Free Zone 2016.

13 Bagaeen 2007.

14 See for example Hvidt 2009.

15 Arvis et al. 2016.

16 EZW 2010.

17 Saidi et al. 2010.

18 In 1991, the authorities of the Port Rashid and Jebel Ali Port merged to form the Dubai Port Authority (DPA).

19 In 1999, Dubai Ports International (DPI) was recognized as an international port-management company, which later in 2005 joined DPA to form the Dubai Ports World (DP World).

20 Hoyle 1998; see also Fujita and Mori 1996; Gleave 1997; Hoyle and Hilling 1970; Omiunu 1989; Bird 1963.

21 See the six-stage consolidation model in Lee et al. 2008.

22 Akhavan 2015a; 2015b; 2017.

23 Dubai Statistics Center, various years, retrieved from www.dsc.gov.ae.

24 Dubai Economic Council 2012.

25 See also Ng et al. 2014.

26 See http://data.worldbank.org.

27 More detailed data are required to specify the role of the port cluster per se share in GDP.

28 Saidi et al. 2010.

29 Akhavan 2015b; 2017.

30 DP World Annual Report, several years 2007–2015.

31 Shin and Timberlake 2000.

32 GaWC 2016.

33 Castells 1989, 142.

REFERENCES

Akhavan, Mina. 2014. "Social Impact of the Economic Development in Emerging Global Cities of Middle East: The Case of Dubai." *Spaces and Flows: An International Journal of Urban and ExtraUrban Studies* 4, no. 3: 13–25.

Akhavan, Mina. 2015a. "Port Development and Port-City Interface Dynamics: The Case of Dubai Global Hub Port-city." PhD diss., Politecnico di Milano.

Akhavan, Mina. 2015b. "Port-City Relation in Dubai: Form an Entrepôt to the (Logistics) Hub of the Middle East." *PORTUSplus*, no. 5 (March), RETE Publisher. http://portusonline.org.

Akhavan, Mina. 2017. "Development Dynamics of Port-Cities Interface in the Arab Middle Eastern World: The Case of Dubai Global Hub Port-City." *Cities* 60, no. 1: 343–352.

Akhavan, Mina, and Ilaria Mariotti. 2015. "Investigating the Maritime Transport Structure of the Middle-East: How Competitive Is Dubai Hub Port-City?" Paper presented at the XVII Conference of the Italian Association of Transport Economics and Logistics. Milan Bocconi University, June 29–July 1, 2015.

Arvis, Jean-François, Monica Alina Mustra, John Panzer, Lauri Ojala, and Tapio Naula. 2016. *Connecting to Compete: Trade Logistics in the Global Economy*. Washington DC: The World Bank.

Bagaeen, Samer. 2007. "Brand Dubai: The Instant City; or, the Instantly Recognizable City." *International Planning Studies* 12, no. 2: 173–197.

Bird, J. 1963. *The Major Seaports of the United Kingdom*. London: Hutchinson.

Broeze, F. 1989. *Brides of the Sea: Port Cities of Asia from the 16th–20th Centuries*. Comparative Studies in Asian History and Society. Honolulu: University of Hawaii Press.

Broeze, Frank. 1999. "Dubai: From Creek to Global Port City." In *Harbours and Havens: Essays in Port History in Honour of Gordon Jackson*, Lewis R. Fischer and Adrian Jarvis, 159–190. St. John's, Newfoundland: International Maritime Economic History Association.

Castells, Manuel. 1989. *The Informational City: Information Technology, Economic Restructuring, and the Urban-Regional Process*. London: Blackwell.

Containerization International Yearbook. London: Emap Business Communications.

Dawson, Andrew H. 1996. "Cityport Development and Regional Change: Lessons from the Clyde." In *Cityports, Coastal Zones, and Regional Change: International Perspectives on Planning and Management*, ed. Brian Hoyle, 49–57. London: John Wiley & Sons.

DP World Annual Report, several years 2007–2015. http://web.dpworld.com.

Dubai Economic Council. 2012. *Dubai's Foreign Trade: Diversification, Challenges and Policies*. Reports. Government of Dubai. www.dec.org.ae.

Easterling, Keller. 2012. "Zone: The Spatial Softwares of Extrastatecraft." *Places Journal* (June), n.p. https://placesjournal.org.

Easterling, Keller. 2014. *Extrastatecraft: The Power of Infrastructure Space*. New York: Verso Books.

Edney, M. H. 1997. *Mapping an Empire: The Geographical Construction of British India, 1765–1843*. Chicago: University of Chicago Press.

Emirates Competitiveness Council. 2012. *Policy in Action: Dubai Trade—Building Competitive Advantage through Collaboration* 3 (January). n.p.: United Arab Emirates.

EZW (bimonthly newsletter). 2010. *Dubai Logistics Corridor Inaugurated by His Highness Sheikh Ahmed Bin Saeed Almaktoum* 24, no. 5. n.p. http://jafza.ae.

Fattah, Hala. 1997. *The Politics of Regional Trade in Iraq, Arabia, and the Gulf, 1745–1900*. Albany: State University of New York Press.

Fuccaro, Nelida. 2009. *Histories of City and State in the Persian Gulf: Manama since 1800*. Cambridge: Cambridge University Press.

Fujita, Masahisa, and Tomoya Mori. 1996. "The Role of Ports in the Making of Major Cities: Self-Agglomeration and Hub-Effect." *Journal of Development Economics* 49, no. 1: 93–120.

GaWC. 2016. "Globalization and World Cities: The World According to GaWC 2016." www.lboro.ac.uk/gawc/world2016t.html.

Gleave, M. Barrie. 1997. "Port Activities and the Spatial Structure of Cities: The Case of Freetown, Sierra Leone." *Journal of Transport Geography* 5, no. 4: 257–275.

Hayuth, Yehuda. 1982. "The Port-Urban Interface: An Area in Transition." *Area* 14, no. 3 (January 1): 219–224.

Hein, C. 2011. *Port Cities: Dynamic Landscapes and Global Networks*. New York: Routledge.

Hoyle, Brian Stewart. 1988. "Development Dynamics at the Port-City Interface." In *Revitalising the Waterfront: International Dimensions of Dockland Redevelopment*, ed. Brian Stewart Hoyle, D. Pinder, and S. Husain, 3–19. London: Belhaven Press.

Hoyle, Brian Stewart. 1989. "The Port-City Interface: Trends, Problems and Examples." *Geoforum* 20, no. 4: 429–435.

Hoyle, Brian Stewart. 1996. *Cityports, Coastal Zones, and Regional Change: International Perspectives on Planning and Management*. Chichester, UK: Wiley.

Hoyle, Brian Stewart, and David Hilling. 1970. *Seaports and Development in Tropical Africa*. London: Macmillan.

Hoyle, Brian Stewart, and David Hilling. 1984. *Seaport Systems and Spatial Change: Technology, Industry, and Development Strategies*. Chichester, UK: Wiley.

Hoyle, Brian Stewart, and D. Pinder. 1981. *Cityport Industrialization and Regional Development: Spatial Analysis and Planning Strategies*. London: Pergamon Press.

Hvidt, Martin. 2009. "The Dubai Model: An Outline of Key Development-Process Elements in Dubai." *International Journal of Middle East Studies* 41, no. 3: 397–418.

Jebel Ali Free Zone (Jafza). 2016. Official website of Jebel Ali Free Zone (Jafza). www.jafza.ae (accessed March 10, 2016).

Keshavarzian, Arang. 2010. "Geopolitics and the Genealogy of Free Trade Zones in the Persian Gulf." *Geopolitics* 15, no. 2: 263–89.

Konvitz, J W. 1978. *Cities & the Sea: Port City Planning in Early Modern Europe*. Baltimore: Johns Hopkins University Press.

Lee, Sung-Woo, Dong-Wook Song, and César Ducruet. 2008. "A Tale of Asia's World Ports: The Spatial Evolution in Global Hub Port Cities." *Geoforum* 39, no. 1: 372–85.

Levinson, M. 2010. *The Box: How the Shipping Container Made the World Smaller and the World Economy Bigger.* Princeton, NJ: Princeton University Press.

Meyer, Han. 1999. *City and Port: Urban Planning as a Cultural Venture in London, Barcelona, New York, and Rotterdam: Changing Relations between Public Urban Space and Large-Scale Infrastructure.* Utrecht: International Books.

Ng, Adolf K. Y., César Ducruet, Wouter Jacobs, Jason Monios, Theo Notteboom, Jean-Paul Rodrigue, Brian Slack, Ka-chai Tam, and Gordon Wilmsmeier. 2014. "Port Geography at the Crossroads with Human Geography: Between Flows and Spaces." *Journal of Transport Geography* 41: 84–96.

Omiunu, Francis G. I. 1989. "The Port Factor in the Growth and Decline of Warri and Sapele Townships in the Western Niger Delta Region of Nigeria." *Applied Geography* 9, no. 1 (January): 57–69.

Pacione, Michael. 2005. "City Profile: Dubai." *Cities* 22: 255–265.

Pirenne, H., and M. McCormick. 2014. *Medieval Cities: Their Origins and the Revival of Trade.* Princeton, NJ: Princeton University Press.

Ramos, Stephen J. 2010. *Dubai Amplified: The Engineering of a Port Geography.* Farnham, UK: Ashgate.

Saadi, Dania. 2013. *UAE's Khalifa Port and Jebel Ali Lead Way in Port Developments.* www.thenational.ae.

Saidi, Nasser, Aathira Prasad, Fabio Scacciavillani, and Tommaso Roi. 2010. "Dubai World Central and the Evolution of Dubai Logistic Cluster." *Economic Note* 10. Dubai International Financial Center.

Shin, Kyoung-Ho, and Michael Timberlake. 2000. "World Cities in Asia: Cliques, Centrality and Connectedness." *Urban Studies* 37, no. 12: 2257–2285.

Statistical Yearbook Emirate of Dubai (various years 1980–2011). Dubai Municipality. www.dsc.gov.ae.

UNCTAD (port section). 1996. *Unctad Monographs on Port Management.* New York and Geneva: United Nations.

United Nations. 2005. *Free Trade Zone and Port Hinterland Development.* New York: United Nations ESCAP.

8

Exporting the Spaceship

The Connected Isolation of Masdar City

GÖKÇE GÜNEL

"The first night of living in a Masdar apartment was hilarious. I didn't understand how anything worked: the stove, the lights, the bathroom fau-cet, the cabinets, and I couldn't figure out how to turn off the AC," wrote Laura Stupin on her blog in September 2010, just after moving into the new Masdar Institute campus.[1] Her studio apartment was situated at the center of Masdar City, inside a dormitory building she shared with her fellow students. "The Masdar Institute is the first part of the city to be completed, it includes the library, laboratory buildings, and the stu-dent residences," Laura continued, "and all these buildings fit together in a cube. And this cube is located in the middle of what is still a giant, flat, dusty, deserty construction site as progress on other phases of the city continues. It's quite a mind flip to be in such a strangely beautiful environ-ment, then look [out] a window and see flat dusty landscape stretching out to the horizon. It really feels like I'm living in a spaceship in the middle of the desert."[2]

Laura was in her mid-twenties and had moved to Abu Dhabi from the United States, after receiving her bachelor's degree from a private un-dergraduate engineering college in Massachusetts. Her ambition was to learn about renewable energy and clean technology at Masdar. In Septem-ber 2010, when she posted her blog entry titled "I Live in a Spaceship in the Middle of the Desert," she received unexpected attention from journalists and researchers around the world. Major media outlets, such as the *Guardian* newspaper, reviewed her comments.[3] Like the other students who had moved to Masdar, she was trying to make sense of her experience with Abu Dhabi's emergent renewable energy and clean technology infrastructures.

Figure 8.1. The Masdar Institute, a graduate level research center that focuses on renewable energy and clean technology, was designed by Foster + Partners. March 2014. Photograph by the author.

Masdar, meaning "source" in Arabic, was founded in May 2006 as a multifaceted renewable energy and clean technology company. It is widely known for Masdar City, the "futuristic" eco-city master planned to rely entirely on renewable energies by the London-based architects Foster + Partners (figs. 8.1 and 8.2). While the eco-city and its multiple infrastructures were central to Masdar's development, Masdar has also been investing in renewable energy through its other operations—Masdar Power, Masdar Carbon, and Masdar Capital—in an attempt to ensure Abu Dhabi will remain a significant player in the global energy industry well after its oil reserves run dry. Masdar Institute, the energy-focused research center, set up and supervised by MIT's Technology and Development Program, operates on a growing campus within the eco-city site. This campus was Laura's "spaceship in the desert."

This essay explores the intellectual origins of Laura's "spaceship in the desert," an urban-scale test bed whose design and construction were widely discussed in the UAE as well as the international media. I draw on seventeen months of ethnographic fieldwork with designers, scientists,

Figure 8.2. A computer rendering of the Masdar City master plan, which was circulated in the media between 2007 and 2010. Image by Foster + Partners.

and policy makers involved in its construction and maintenance. Masdar can be situated within a larger array of socio-technical projects that have taken place around the world. The test-bed logic is not unique to Masdar, but rather defines a new strategy geared toward confronting future urban, economic, and environmental challenges.[4] Projects like Masdar City offer a form of spatial and temporal management that render contextual concerns less significant and instead propose that all threats be dealt with in the same exclusive and technocratic manner, legitimizing the ongoing development of such "spaceships" around the world. In the United Arab Emirates, the spaceship in the desert affirms this notion of a context-free environment, absent from political or cultural constraints—an imaginary notion inconsistent with actual conditions. At the same time, these projects propose an optimistic and fun understanding of their interiors, stressing how residents will experience peace inside these spaceships even if the outside becomes difficult or impossible to inhabit.[5]

Since the 1960s, space technologies have inspired ecologically sensitive architecture, producing a blueprint for survival in a context of rising environmental concerns. As historians of science, such as Peder Anker and Sabine Höhler, note in their overviews of ecological design, the space program of the 1960s had considerable impact on the ways in which designers imagined and planned eco-friendly life on earth.[6] Buildings, perhaps best symbolized by the well-known Biosphere 2 project, would constitute self-regulating and decentralized systems with comfortable climatic conditions for humans, provide enclosed shelters for an impending ecological disaster, and perhaps serve as a means of escape from possible destruction on earth. Occupying buildings inspired by space technologies, humanity would behave like astronauts with clear outer space missions.

In these histories, the spaceship is a finite, technically sophisticated, and insular habitat for an exclusive group of beings facing an outside world of crises. In his book *Shipwreck with Spectator*, Hans Blumenberg explains how humans "prefer in their imagination, to represent their overall condition in the world in terms of a sea voyage."[7] The idea of the spaceship (much like the submarine that preceded it) then serves as an extension of the ship metaphor, demonstrating the inevitable boundaries of human activities, vilifying the space beyond human habitability, and producing the outside as a vacuum that should not be inhabited. As seas full of mythical monsters surround the livable environments on earth, the ship provides a safe interior space. Thanks to its strict boundaries, it acts as an ark or, as the German philosopher Peter Sloterdijk suggests, an "autonomous, absolute, context-free house, the building with no neighborhood."[8] This way, the ship puts forward an alternative environment of peace and rationality, standing in opposition to the destructive and irrational crises of earth.

In prioritizing enclosure for some over collective survival—the tension that underpins most space-faring movies—the spaceship also advances the principles of selection and endorses what Sloterdijk calls "exclusivity dressed up as universalism."[9] Despite saving only a very small number of those who suffer a metaphorical shipwreck, the spaceship insists on addressing the planetary-scale questions of survival in the unknown, the sustenance of the species beyond ecological disasters, and the preservation of an existing civilization albeit in highly limited and confined form.[10]

Figure 8.3. The Masdar Institute campus includes dormitories, a knowledge center, laboratories, and a sports facility. March 2014. Photograph by the author.

The Moon Landing

Inspired by this history of ecological architecture, Masdar City is intended to maintain the lives (and livelihoods) of its residents by relying on renewable energy and clean technologies, and performs the role of desert spaceship indeed. As onsite architects at Masdar City argued, this ecological mandate would assist Norman Foster, founder and chairman of Foster + Partners, in producing a legacy for himself. According to one of the onsite Foster + Partners architects, "Norman wants to be the Bucky Fuller of this century"—a point made, in essence, by Foster himself in interviews and publications.[11]

Buckminster Fuller conceived of the earth as a beautifully designed spaceship that lacks comprehensible instructions. To satisfy this need, he wrote *Operating Manual for Spaceship Earth*.[12] "We are all astronauts," Fuller asserted. "We have not been seeing our Spaceship Earth as an integrally-designed machine which to be persistently successful must be comprehended and serviced in total."[13] Since "no instruction book came with it," humankind was confronted with the challenge of self-instruction in order to successfully operate Spaceship Earth and "its complex life-supporting and regenerating systems." Earth was an operable technological object, fully accessible to humankind. Fuller not only wrote about his technocratic understandings of earth but also conceived many design and engineering projects illustrating his philosophy, such as the geodesic dome.

As a young architect, Norman Foster met Buckminster Fuller in 1971 to collaborate on the construction of the Samuel Beckett Theater in Oxford. The theater, which marked the beginning of their twelve-year relationship, was a subterranean building intended to be used as classrooms and exhibition spaces for St. Peter's College. It benefited from the geodesic, lightweight structures that made Fuller famous. Although it was never built, Foster claims this building had a significant impact on the later stages of his career, not only because it initiated his relationship with Fuller, but also in more formal ways: "I remember that Bucky made the comparison with a submarine because the structure of the building had to be resistant to water, like a seaworthy vessel. The building had to stand up to the ground water and other natural underground forces. So it's no coincidence that my later underground projects also take the form of ships and submarines."[14] Although none of their collaborative projects were built, in his Pritzker Prize biography, Foster says, "The thing about Bucky was that he made you believe anything is possible." Foster adds, "But perhaps the themes of shelter, energy and environment—which go to the heart of contemporary architecture—best reflect Bucky's inheritance . . . For me Bucky was the very essence of a moral conscience, forever warning about the fragility of the planet and man's responsibility to protect it."[15] For Foster, Fuller was what he termed "a green guru."

The legacy of the ship and the submarine continues to inform Norman Foster's design work. For instance, an article in the *Guardian* suggested that Foster's "reassuringly technical, graceful, silver, white, and immaculate" designs would be suitable for architecture on the moon.[16] More recently, Foster + Partners publicized renderings for a settlement on Mars, constructed by robots prior to the arrival of humans. "Designing for extra-terrestrial environments provides an exciting platform for experimentation that is at the front line of innovative technology," one of Foster's partners commented.[17]

In conversation with this lineage of outer space designs, Norman Foster also proposed that he understood practicing architecture in the Gulf to be similar to lunar exploration.[18] News commentaries, rather fascinated with the idea of constructing an eco-friendly city in the desert, accordingly state, "The inhospitable terrain suggests that the only way to survive here is with the maximum of technological support, a bit like living on the moon."[19] In his autobiography, the leading Emirati entrepreneur and businessman Easa Al-Gurg also demonstrates that Emirati rulers understood the desert as a moonscape by describing how Sheikh Rashid bin Saeed Al Maktoum of Dubai dismissed the moon landing as a hoax, arguing that the landscape looked like the empty terrain in Ras Al Khaimah, one of the emirates that make up the UAE. "Maybe it was filmed there," Sheikh Rashid said.[20]

Quite appropriately, the onsite architecture team at Masdar presented a slide show that included an image juxtaposing a lunar module with the gray, lightweight cladding of the laboratory buildings on the Masdar Institute campus. The laboratory facades were composed of insulating cushions, the architects explained, which shaded the interiors of the building and which were expected to remain cool to the touch under the desert sun (figs. 8.3 and 8.4). In December 2010, Fred Moavenzadeh, then president

Figure 8.4. The laboratory facades at Masdar Institute are composed of insulating cushions that shade the interiors of the building and remain cool to the touch under the desert sun. Photograph by Michele Nastasi.

of Masdar Institute, spoke on Richard Quest's CNN documentary about Masdar City and explained that when the United States wanted to send a man to the moon, it produced NASA. Now, when the United Arab Emirates is transforming and diversifying its economy, it is building Masdar City.[21]

The Frontier

The spaceship analogy reconfigured the desert as an undiscovered frontier from which a novel means of livelihood could emerge.[22] In this voyage, the frontierspeople of Masdar City would be in control, both abiding by the principles of the Abu Dhabi government and taking initiative to trigger a future of innovations in renewable energy and clean technology. In an ever-expanding geography, the students would act as astronauts—steering the spaceship and managing the successful institution of a new resource economy within oil-exporting Abu Dhabi.

In his book *Carbon Democracy*, Timothy Mitchell shows how conceptions of endless oil supplies enabled progress to be conceived as infinitely expandable and without any material constraints. In the mid-twentieth century, the cost of energy did not present a limit to economic growth, as oil prices continuously declined. Given how simple it was to ship oil across the world, this resource could easily be treated as inexhaustible. This belief in the infinity of oil also played a key role in producing "the economy" as an object, which could likewise expand without limit.[23]

In contrast to this history of oil, the Masdar City project acknowledges the fact that fossil fuels may eventually disappear. Nevertheless, the idea of resource infinity, this time enabled by renewable energy and clean technology, still characterizes the ways in which producers of the city imagine the future. In response to depleting oil resources, the eco-city promotes the infinity of sunlight and wind. The spaceship in the desert has the capacity to journey through endless space and confirm the vision of a boundless frontier where new types of resources await discovery.[24] As an exploratory vehicle, the Masdar City project is intended to challenge and resolve the problem of finitude. The frontier narrative also led the producers of Masdar City to conceptualize the present as a moment of potential while concentrating their efforts on constructing a future that would be incubated inside this enclosed space within the Abu Dhabi desert. Masdar City could give rise to a new generation of resource pioneers, who would hurdle through unbounded territory.[25] Accordingly, it was not only the space of the Abu Dhabi desert that awaited another discovery but also its temporality. The spaceship analogy spoke to a future of technical adjustments that would potentially emerge from this enclosed space, possibly allowing the eco-city to be replicated in other settings around the world.

Exporting the Spaceship

Alan Frost, the director of Masdar City, explained how the project's rationale had evolved during a presentation at the World Future Energy Summit (WFES) in January 2011: "When we started Masdar City, we thought it was an island, we thought that basically we were doing all these things people had not done before, we could do it all on our own, and then we come back and tell everyone about it. But you know what, that's not very healthy. . . . So, the lesson is that you cannot be an island."[26] The master-planned city, which would be fully constructed and thereafter sold and perhaps exported, reformulated its business plan after the economic crisis of 2008 and invited renewable energy and clean technology companies to start building their headquarters within its boundaries. This way, the city's growth would not depend completely on the funds made available by the Abu Dhabi government. "There is no point in doing something, which you can only do at Masdar. It has to be sustainable and it has to work for Abu Dhabi . . . Everything at Masdar City has to be translatable and repeatable around the world," Frost continued, inviting third parties to participate in this economic diversification project.

In its revised formula, Masdar City would constitute a test bed for multiple energy technologies that could later be purchased and used around the world. On top of this, Masdar City as a whole would be conceived as an exportable commodity, leading to the production of its replicas around the globe. The Masdar City configuration had to be mobile, traveling throughout the world. As a spaceship, the eco-city had the potential to further spread that technologically advanced environment in an undefined space and time. In other words, Masdar conveyed and emanated the promise to create that space and time for everyone else.

Nevertheless, Masdar Institute students, the frontierspeople of Abu Dhabi's emergent eco-city experiment, remained unsure about the translatability of Masdar City into other settings. As such, on February 1, 2011, they gathered in the Masdar Institute auditorium to stage a debate on whether "Masdar City is an elite enclave of sustainability, unsuitable for the rest of the world" or not. The graduate students, who came to Masdar City from many countries—including the United States, China, India, Egypt, Jordan, Iran, Turkey, and Iceland—were struggling with such questions and chose the context of a debate club performance as a way of thinking about them.

The team that perceived Masdar City as "an elite enclave of sustainability" argued how Masdar was "too unique" to be applied elsewhere. First, Masdar was very expensive. Which other country, other than the oil-rich UAE, would be able to devote $22 billion for an eco-city?[27] Second, they recalled how this project had been put together to contribute to the economic diversification of Abu Dhabi and perhaps would not be financially feasible or meaningful for other countries with different economies. Masdar City was expected to help the UAE transform its brand image from oil producer to technology developer and induce a perception shift, perhaps attracting foreign investments or facilitating the creation of local start-up companies focusing on renewable energy and clean technology. Third, the political climate of Abu Dhabi was working in favor of Masdar City by providing prolonged commitment and stability—the government often served as a steady source of financing for the project. "Well, other than that," the team arguing about the non-replicability of Masdar reiterated, "the concept of a green city has existed for a long time." In this understanding, Masdar City no longer comprised a vision that would unfold into the future. Rather, it remained an island contingent on a specific set of circumstances, only available within the United Arab Emirates. Abu Dhabi's oil capital, its future economic vision, and its political environment were thus perceived as preconditions for launching the spaceship.

In response, the team that defended the global applicability of Masdar City proposed that the eco-city should be understood and framed as a prototype: Abu Dhabi would shoulder the burdens of building the eco-city, and others would benefit. "Every new idea is expensive," one of the students underlined. "Think about the car: first rich people had it, and now it has spread around the world." Masdar City could become less expensive in an undefined future. It could be exported to other countries as a whole, in the same way that the car and its infrastructures had been exported. In the meantime, the experiments taking place at Masdar would be learning experiences for the students, researchers, and faculty, opening up global horizons for research on renewable energy and clean technology and eventually adapting them to other regions in bits and pieces.

At the end of the meeting, one student approached me to express his dissatisfaction at how none of the students in the debate teams had actually defined what Masdar City *was* or what exactly they expected to spread around the world: "No one talked about the personal rapid transit units or the motion sensors," he specified, pointing to the technological artifacts that seemingly defined the eco-city for him. In which of its materializations did Masdar inhere, and what would it pass on to the rest of the world, he wondered, and what exactly was the future that the spaceship promised?

Despite the student's skepticism, Masdar City's global horizons extend to new geographies, not only by incentivizing the production of new technologies at the Masdar Institute, but also by setting favorable trade and investment conditions through the institution of a free zone.[28] Masdar City now underlines its identity as a special and "smart" economic zone, promoting its capacities as "the city of possibilities," with perpetual potential, and inviting technology companies to come and build inside the 600-hectare area. Similar to others in the Gulf (see Mina Akhavan's chapter 7 and Steffen Hertog's chapter 12), this free zone creates a space where investors may avoid taxes and restrictions in moving capital, while relaxing requirements for UAE nationals to have majority stakes in business partnerships with foreign investors.[29] At the same time, some of the projects that Masdar Institute students discussed and built have been taken up by other energy and climate-change professionals in places with different climatic, economic, and social conditions than those found in the UAE—either through trade partnerships or the exporting of emergent technology. In southern Spain, Masdar partnered with Torresol, completing three solar plants. In the United Kingdom, Masdar professionals worked with the London Array project, inaugurated in 2013 by Prime Minister David Cameron, as the largest offshore wind farm in the world (over one hundred square kilometers).[30]

"Man with a Brush"

Abu Dhabi is perceived to be a perfect location for harnessing solar energy. However, according to an engineer at Masdar—let's call him Mahmood—this perception was not completely accurate. Mahmood was an Egyptian man in his mid-thirties and had recently finished his PhD at an American university. Wishing to be closer to home, he accepted a position at Masdar as his first job. As we chatted outside the solar power stations, he stated that high levels of dust and humidity not only blocked direct solar rays but also resulted in thick coatings on solar panels, diminishing their effective functioning. "Although we can't fix the first problem that easily, we have found a solution for the second problem." He continued, "We call it 'man with a brush'" (fig. 8.5).

While there was extensive research toward a solution for removing dust, humidity, and mud from solar panels in the UAE, during the time of our conversation, no technical solution had proved as effective as the use of low-cost labor. In Mahmood's narrative, the "man with a brush," a worker dedicated to gently wiping away dust and mud from the solar

Figure 8.5. "Man with a brush" clears the thick coatings on solar panels, which result from a mixture of dust and humidity, and ensures their efficacy. April 2011. Photograph by the author.

panels, became part of the picture mainly because he exposed the potential that is embedded in the solar panels. In some ways, "man with a brush" would allow for the proper functioning of not only the solar panels, but also the economic diversification outlined in the Plan Abu Dhabi 2030 (see chapter 6).

When I asked Mohammed, a Bangladeshi man who worked in the kitchen, serving the Masdar Institute president's guests and earning 600 dirham per month (roughly $160) in exchange for roughly two hundred hours of work,[31] if he knew why so many individuals and groups find this building worthy of a visit, he shook his head no. A professor in the institute had told him that solar panels provide energy to the campus. Daniel, an onsite architect with Foster + Partners, criticized the conception of renewable energy and clean technology within these compounds: "How could sustainability truly be targeted when there is this little attention paid to human capital," he told me, pointing to the harsh working conditions for large populations of migrant workers within the

United Arab Emirates. Daniel had spent most of his professional career in the United Kingdom, prior to moving to Abu Dhabi for the Masdar project, and also had experience living in Germany. "Sustainability is also about claiming some sort of justice, and making sure that what we build leads this very young country towards a better direction. It is also about some kind of equality."

In this context, however, the "man with a brush," who was essential to the construction and maintenance of the spaceship, functioned as a disposable tool, abandoned outside the technologically complex vessel.

Masdar City as an Idea

"Masdar is slowly helping to change attitudes about renewable energy and climate change in the Gulf and the Maghreb," an article in *Wired* magazine stated in December 2013, more than seven years after the launching of the Masdar project. "Across the region, governments have seen what has been achieved here, and have followed suit." Outlining the "shifting goalposts of Abu Dhabi's ambitious eco-city," the article quoted Bader al Lamki, the city's director of clean energy. "Six years ago, Masdar was the only initiative in this part of the world. Fast-forward six years, look around, and see Saudi Arabia going on full-speed, with 40GW of renewables as a target. And you see Jordan and Morocco and other countries in the MENA [Middle East and North Africa—ed.] region following the same path, because it's not only environmental, it's also economic."[32] In sum, the *Wired* article declared that while Masdar had given up many of its original aspirations, it still fostered transformation regionally and globally regarding renewable energy and clean technology initiatives. As one of my interlocutors told me, Masdar was not only its planned renewable energy and clean technology infrastructures: it was "an idea" that would spread around the world.

Perhaps here it is useful to interrogate and recap what kind of an idea Masdar City is. As a "spaceship in the desert," Masdar was "futuristic" and enclosed, moving toward a frontier of innovations to enable a new kind of future both for the UAE and for the planet. Its design did not necessarily seek to challenge the extreme levels of inequality in Abu Dhabi or elsewhere, but rather embodied them. Accordingly, the utopia or science fiction of Masdar remained an exclusive project that aimed to prolong the current social and political conditions by making use of technocratic solutions. The inhabitants of Masdar City, such as the students described above, became test subjects for the emergent city, responding to this prototype in real time. The producers of the city did not propose a new future for the whole of humanity but instead demonstrated that the social status quo was already a best-case scenario. In other words, Masdar City was a status quo utopia, which did not necessarily support the "man with a brush" or the many others who were not included in its strict boundaries.

A recent science fiction movie helps make the point. Released in 2014, *Interstellar* (by director Christopher Nolan) portrays a nearly uninhabitable world consumed by dust storms. Life becomes increasingly difficult for the film's protagonists as they lack breathable air and nutritious crops. Fast-forward to the final scenes of the movie, however, and the protagonists have arrived in a peaceful spaceship floating far away from earth, one that contains the same house, town, and lifestyle they occupied on earth. In preserving the status quo, the residents of the spaceship have left the rest of the earth to its collapse, celebrating the fact that they can inhabit technological dreams without attending to problems on earth in a collective manner.

In *Interstellar*, the American house, the baseball fields, and the beer bottles stand in as manifestations of what Sloterdijk, drawing on the 1970s work of the architecture office Morphosis, calls "connected isolation."[33] To construct an artificial lifeworld inside the spaceship, materials, designs, and building techniques have been imported, allowing the frontierspeople to fall back on their prior social lives and political conceptions. In a context of complete isolation, the absence of these attachments could perhaps facilitate the production of more radical transformations. But as Sloterdijk argues, "Previous and future space-islanders will remain comparable to their distant forefather, the imitator Robinson Crusoe, because like him, the cultural source on which they draw is exclusively the arsenal of brought-along patterns of meaning. Needless to say, conventional astronauts are far from being the pure consciousness of their island."[34] The inhabitants of the spaceship are bound by imported ideas that preclude the necessary shifts in perspective. Nothing new in terms of ideas or governance takes hold.

Despite the numerous technical adjustments they offer, contemporary forms of urban development, such as Masdar City, produce future scenarios that are akin to *Interstellar*, inviting future residents to both preserve existing social relations and survive ecological disasters inside serene and optimistic spaceships—so caringly cultivated and, as the Richard Brautigan poem goes, "all watched over by machines of loving grace."[35]

NOTES

1 This chapter is an adaptation of a previously published article "Inhabiting the Spaceship: The Connected Isolation of Masdar City." Many thanks to James Graham and others at *Avery Review* and Lars Müller for their permission to rework the essay for this volume. I also thank Harvey Molotch and Davide Ponzini for their invitation to participate in an NYU Abu Dhabi workshop on urbanism in the Gulf, which bore this set of essays. For a more extensive analysis of the Masdar City project, see Günel 2019.

2 Stupin 2010.

3 Vidal 2011.

4 Günel and Halpern 2017.

5 Günel 2019.

6 Anker 2010; also see: Höhler 2015.

7 Blumenberg 1996, 8.

8 Sloterdijk 2014, 237.

9 Sloterdijk 2014, 249.

10 The 1970s set the stage for innovative yet controversial conversations on what may be labeled "lifeboat ethics." For an example of these debates, see Hardin 1974.

11 For a video version of "Bucky Fuller & Spaceship Earth—Lord Norman Foster," see www.youtube.com/watch?v=aQzt_zJfouY.

12 Buckminster Fuller 2008. See also Anker 2010; Barber 2016.

13 Buckminster Fuller 2008, 52–54.

14 von Meijenfeldt and Geluk 2003, 130.

15 Tse Kwai Zung 2002, 2.

16 Glancey 2009.

17 Norman Foster takes on Mars: Reilly 2015; Frearson 2015.

18 Moon 2010.

19 Heap 2010.

20 Al-Gurg 1998. Easa Al-Gurg started one of the UAE's most prominent family businesses in 1960, after gaining considerable experience in the fields of banking and finance. He was an adviser to Sheikh Rashid, the late ruler of Dubai, and was also one of the people who attended the meetings in which the UAE was formed on December 2, 1971. Easa Al-Gurg also served as UAE ambassador to the United Kingdom and the Republic of Ireland for almost two decades, starting in 1991.

21 Quest 2010. Fred Moavenzadeh repeated this claim in an interview with *Wired* magazine in 2013, suggesting: "When you look at the whole concept of Masdar in the 21st century, it's the same as NASA in the 20th century . . . It has the same rationale, the same philosophy. NASA put a man on the Moon to show the strengths of the United States in that area of technology. And Masdar is being developed to show Abu Dhabi's commitment to clean air and technology." See Kingsley 2013. Interestingly, in 2015 the Dubai government set up the Mohammed bin Rashid Space Centre in an attempt to prompt economic diversification, scientific research, and technological complexity in Dubai and the wider UAE. So far, the center has conducted projects in collaboration with the South Korean space program and aims to send a probe to Mars. For more information, see http:// mbrsc.ae. Also see the *Guardian* article about the space center: Shaheen 2015.

22 Looking back at the Apollo space program (which the president of the Masdar Institute touched upon in Richard Quest's CNN documentary), David Mindell explains how President Kennedy had seized and mobilized the powerful mythology of the frontier in aiming for the moon. The term "frontier," originally meaning "border" or "borderline," obtained new meaning during the settlement of the American West in the eighteenth and nineteenth centuries. In this narrative, the heroic pioneers were headed to an unknown geography full of unpredictable dangers as well as antagonistic competitors, yet they would make use of self-control, self-reliance, and humility to open up this new frontier. See Mindell 2008.

23 Mitchell 2012.

24 For a longer exploration of this theme, see Williams 2008, 7.

25 As Sabine Höhler reminds her readers, "Appropriating space by compiling, registering, and neatly arranging the elements within it is a strategy not limited to the modern era of scientific collecting, archiving, and interpreting of the world. The procedure recalls the primal ship representing the inventory of the world, the biblical ark" (Höhler 2010). Also see Höhler 2015.

26 Presentation at World Future Energy Summit, Abu Dhabi, UAE, January 18, 2011.

27 For a review of these figures, please see "Work Starts on Gulf 'Green City,'" BBC News (website), February 10, 2008, http://news.bbc.co.uk.

28 Analyzing the ways in which the Abu Dhabi government builds and manages its transnational financial networks, Daniel Haberly argues that these capital flows are "both a response to the strategic and political vulnerability" of the UAE and "an attempt to leverage overseas investments to promote late development in an integrated global economy." Writing specifically about sovereign wealth funds, a key way in which Abu Dhabi manages its transnational investment strategies, he writes, "Host states often promote inward SWF investment to defend key firms from global financial market disruptions and help them gain preferential access to business opportunities with the investing state." At the end, companies such as General Electric, Bayer, Siemens, and BASF, receivers of sovereign wealth funds from the UAE, invest in special economic zones, such as Masdar City, and bring Abu Dhabi's capital back into the country under a different brand name. For a

rigorous analysis of how the Abu Dhabi government builds transnational financial networks, see Haberly 2014, 302.

29 Masdar City Free Zone website, www.masdarcityfreezone.com (accessed December 1, 2016).

30 For more details on these projects, see the Masdar Clean Energy website, www .masdar.ae (accessed December 1, 2016).

31 On labor conditions in the UAE, see Keane and McGeehan 2008; Khala and Alkobaisi 1999. For a recent account of struggles to protect immigrant rights in the Gulf, especially in Abu Dhabi, see http://gulflabor.org (accessed July 15, 2014).

32 Kingsley 2013 (accessed December 1, 2016).

33 Sloterdijk 2014, 294.

34 Sloterdijk 2014, 307–308.

35 Brautigan 1967.

REFERENCES

Al-Gurg, Easa Saleh. 1998. *The Wells of Memory: An Autobiography*. London: J. Murray.

Anker, Peder. 2010. *From Bauhaus to Eco-house: A History of Ecological Design*. Baton Rouge: Louisiana State University Press.

Barber, Daniel. 2016. *A House in the Sun: Modern Architecture and Solar Energy in the Cold War*. Oxford: Oxford University Press.

Blumenberg, Hans. *1996. Shipwreck with Spectator: Paradigm of a Metaphor for Existence*. Cambridge, MA: MIT Press, 1996.

Brautigan, Richard. 1967. *All Watched Over by Machines of Loving Grace*. San Francisco: Communication Company. http://allpoetry.com.

Buckminster Fuller, Richard. 2008 (original edition 1969). *Operating Manual for Spaceship Earth*. Rotterdam: Lars Müller.

Frearson, Amy. 2015. "Foster + Partners Reveals Concept for 3-D-Printed Mars Habitat Built by Robots." *Dezeen*, September 25, 2015. www.dezeen.com.

Glancey, Jonathan. 2009. "Man on the Moon: Norman Foster Prepares for Architecture's Lift-Off." *Guardian*, September 9, 2009. www.guardian.co.uk.

Günel, Gökçe. 2019. *Spaceship in the Desert: Energy, Climate Change and Urban Design in Abu Dhabi*. Durham, NC: Duke University Press.

Günel, Gökçe, and Orit Halpern. 2017. "Demoing unto Death: Smart Cities, Environment, and 'Preemptive Hope.'" *Fibreculture Journal*, no. 29. Computing the City, http://twentynine.fibreculturejournal.org/fcj-215-demoing-unto-death-smart-citiesenvironment-and-preemptive-hope/.

Haberly, Daniel. 2010. "White Knights from the Gulf: Sovereign Wealth Fund Investment and the Evolution of German Industrial Finance." *Economic Geography* 90, no. 3: 293–320.

Hardin, Garrett. *1974.* "Commentary: Living on a Lifeboat." *BioScience* 24, no. 10: 561–568.

Heap, Tom. 2010. "Masdar: Abu Dhabi's Carbon Neutral City." BBC News, March 28, 2010. http://news.bbc.co.uk.

Höhler, Sabine. 2010. "The Environment as a Life Support System: The Case of Biosphere 2." *History and Technology* 26, no. 1: 39–58.

Höhler, Sabine. 2015. *Spaceship Earth in the Environmental Age, 1960–1990*. London: Pickering and Chatto.

Keane, David, and Nicholas McGeehan. 2008. "Enforcing Migrant Workers' Rights in the United Arab Emirates." *International Journal on Minority and Group Rights* 15, no. 1: 81–115.

Khalaf, Sulayman, and Saad Alkobaisi. 1999. "Migrants' Strategies of Coping and Patterns of Accommodation in the Oil-Rich Gulf Societies: Evidence from the UAE." *British Journal of Middle Eastern Studies* 26, no. 2: 271–298.

Kingsley, Patrick. 2013. "Masdar: The Shifting Goalposts of Abu Dhabi's Ambitious Eco-city," *Wired*, December 17, 2013. www.wired.co.uk.

Mindell, David. 2008. *Digital Apollo: Human and Machine in the First Six Lunar Landings*. Cambridge, MA: MIT Press.

Mitchell, Timothy. 2012. *Carbon Democracy*. New York: Verso.

Moon, Timur. 2010. "Norman Foster: Building an Oasis." *National*, November 28, 2010. www.thenational.ae.

Quest, Richard. 2010. "World's Most Futuristic City." CNN, December 6, 2010. http://www.youtube.com/watch?v=IJjbqDq9_QE.

Reilly, Rachel. 2015. "Architect's Firm Reveals Their Award-Winning Vision for an Astronaut's Life on the Red Planet." *Daily Mail*, September 29, 2015. www.dailymail.co.uk.

Shaheen, Kareem. 2015. "Emirates Space Mission Hopes to Launch New Era in Middle East." *Guardian*, July 19, 2015. www.theguardian.com.

Sloterdijk, Peter. 2014. *Globes: Spheres 2*. South Pasadena, CA: Semiotext(e).

Stupin, Laura. 2010. "I Live in a Spaceship in the Middle of the Desert." *Rants and Rambles* (blog). September 25, 2010, http://squidskin.blogspot.com.

Tse Kwai Zung, Thomas. 2002. *Buckminster Fuller: Anthology for a new Millennium*. New York: St. Martin's.

Vidal, John. 2011. "Masdar City: A Glimpse of the Future in the Desert." *Guardian*, April 26, 2011. www.guardian.co.uk.

von Meijenfeldt, Ernst, and Marit Geluk. 2003. *Below Ground Level: Creating New Spaces for Contemporary Architecture*. Basel: Birkhäuser-Publishers for Architecture.

Williams, Rosalind. 2008 (original edition 1990). *Notes on the Underground: An Essay on Technology, Society, and the Imagination*. Cambridge, MA: MIT Press.

9

"Two Days to Shape the Future"

A Saudi Arabian Node in the Transnational Circulation
of Ideas about New Cities

SARAH MOSER

New master-planned cities are currently springing up across the Global South at an astonishing rate. Construction or at least planning has begun on over 150 new cities in Asia, the Middle East, Africa, and most recently, Latin America. Implementation budgets range from several billion to $100 billion, with build-out populations targeted from tens of thousands to several million. Despite their number and geographical spread, and the vast resources being directed toward them, little scholarly attention has been paid to the phenomenon. In particular, there has been little explanation of how ideas about new cities are circulating or why they are being adopted with such enthusiasm by ruling elites in the Global South. We do not know how they are adapted and shaped by local forces, much less with what concomitant consequences. The rich and heterogeneous body of recent scholarship on urban policy mobilities provides useful starting points for thinking about how and where such ideas circulate. Geographers are particularly concerned in recent years with examining flows and circuits between cities rather than cities as bounded objects.

Through an ethnographic investigation of an elite international meeting of major players in this new-city realm, I explore the mechanics of how urban policies, norms, and aesthetics circulate. My focus is on the Cityquest KAEC Forum, an elite, nonacademic new-cities-themed meeting held annually in Saudi Arabia. Jointly involved in its operations is the New Cities Foundation (NCF), a Paris-based[1] NGO formed in 2010. I participated in the KAEC Saudi meetings held December 2013,[2] 2014, and 2015. I attended sessions, mixed and mingled, and interviewed over a dozen CEOs[3] of new cities, as well as consultants, architects and planners, and other attendees. It is the only event to date that assembles leaders of new-cities projects, along with corporate players and leaders who aspire to create and sustain them. Cityquest Forum is an important node through which particular policies and assumptions are circulated and norms established. Since 2013, Cityquest has been held each winter in King Abdullah Economic City (KAEC, pronounced "cake"), the first of Saudi Arabia's new "economic" master-planned cities. Although itself still in infancy (with a population of only a few thousand), its eventual build-out of two million people makes it now among the world's most massive sites of investment and construction. It is a fitting backdrop for a discussion of mega urban projects that, even if at a smaller scale, might operate along similar lines elsewhere. The part of the site that has already been developed serves as a venue for showing and showing off what is set to come. The Saudi hosts reinforce a positive outlook through salubrious conference accommodations as well as advanced policy-think awareness. In part through projects like Cityquest KAEC Forum, the Saudis have taken on the mantle of experts on building new cities. It is an example of how Saudi Arabia, and Gulf places more broadly, has become an unexpected innovator and producer of urban policy, rather than passive recipient. Cityquest KAEC methods and substance embody a distinctive pattern of diffusion and enactment that complicates conventional thinking about patterns of North-South urban policy mobility.

Transnational Circulations in the Global South

While "policy transfer" scholarship emerged in political science, it has become an interdisciplinary approach adopted and modified by geographers, planners, sociologists, and anthropologists working from a variety of theoretical traditions, including poststructuralism, postcolonialism, and political economy. As has been pointed out by geographers in recent years,[4] scholarship in various disciplines departs in several significant ways from the "orthodox," "conventional" political science conceptualization of "urban policy transfer." First is the multidisciplinary approach that investigates policy assemblages, mobilities, and mutations. Second, rather than viewing policy transfer as a rational and voluntaristic adherence to "best practices," recent scholarship investigates how mobility happens through less logically coherent operations. It is structured by institutions and cultural contexts, which have an assortment of path dependencies, power hierarchies, and embedded assumptions.[5] Third, scholars are now interested in how urban policies are learned, translated, and mobilized, rather than imagining "fully-formed, complete policy packages" traveling around unchanged.[6] Urban policies transform as they circulate and arrive not as neat replicas of imported policies but as "policies-in-transformation."[7] This approach means that urban policy-mobility scholars are not interested in searching for evidence of global convergence or homogeneity,[8] so much as mapping how neoliberal agendas are extended across space.[9] They want to understand how urban policy is assembled from a variety of elements.[10]

One of the key emergent understandings is that urban policy mobility is not a linear route between discrete entities, but a nonlinear process in which policies get produced and reinterpreted along what can be very indirect meandering toward, at least at times, eventual implementation. Various agents escort them through diverse institutional contexts, as they are all the while mutating and evolving. Agents that circulate urban policy can include both nonhuman actors (plans, models, texts, images, cities themselves) and human actors, such as government officials on study trips and intergovernmental associations[11] and property developers and consultants.[12] As Bruno Latour's actor network theory (ANT) proposes (see also the introduction and Lieto, chapter 5), an array of human and nonhuman actors shape networks; both thus need to be considered in any study of urban policy mobilities.[13]

Charismatic and popular individuals are also significant in transferring ideas, as they may have wide connections internationally and, more importantly, they have a receptive (or at least docile) audience back home. The public's willingness to back imported urban ideas is intimately tied to the political legitimacy of a leader, as has been demonstrated in examples like the case of now-president Joko Widodo (Jokowi) when he was the mayor of Solo, Indonesia,[14] and Chandrababu Naidu in Hyderabad, India.[15] Dynamic personalities like these—as well as such recent leaders as Narendra Modi, Bashar Masri (developer of Rawabi, a new city in Palestine), Nursultan Nazarbayev in Kazakhstan, and Rafael Correa in Ecuador—have been able to muscle their utopian urban assemblages to fruition through a combination of power and personal popularity.[16]

Putting aside the somewhat imponderable dynamics of personal charisma, a phenomenon to which I had very limited access or intellectual basis for understanding, modes of policy circulation are more accessible for empirical research. Rather than giving urban policy mobilities themselves an aura of economistic necessity—"fetishized mobile objects or free-floating fields of transfer"[17]—they can be examined as being produced by the "social, spatial, institutional, ideological, and political contexts in which they are developed, applied, transferred, and adopted." In other words, we should treat the modes through which urban policy circulates as products of social processes, rather than inevitable and natural.[18] As an empirical matter and methodologically useful fact, "networks themselves are clearly also spatial formations that traverse particular places but in the process also require certain geographical anchors around which they can be organized."[19] As a key node in the urban policy circulation system, Cityquest KAEC Forum is worthy of focus. It is a place where ideas, values, and norms about new master-planned cities are presented, interpreted, reinterpreted, and transported back by conference attendees. In its personages, facilities, and choreography, it serves to normalize particular notions of what future urban development can and should be.[20]

New Master-Planned Cities

The current wave of new cities is almost exclusively a phenomenon of the (postcolonial) Global South, where leaders increasingly view the construction of new cities as an integral part of national economic development that can transition economies away from agriculture, manufacturing, or resource extraction toward a knowledge economy. For example, new cities in Malaysia, India, Morocco, and Ecuador, among others, are being constructed to jump-start high-tech industries and reduce dependence on prior (outdated) sectors.[21] In the Middle East (Abu Dhabi, Kuwait, Saudi Arabia), authorities see new cities as a way to diversify away from oil. In other cases (Nigeria, Angola, India, China), new cities are supposed to address housing deficits and inadequate urban infrastructure.[22]

New cities are also increasingly seen as a way to rebrand the country for foreign direct investment.[23] While the creation of architectural spectacles and "world-class" infrastructure is frequently used to broadcast that a country or city is open for business (see Ponzini, chapter 3), new cities—which may or may not contain such spectacle—are a somewhat different and, at times, even more dramatic way to advertise accomplishment. In their physical presence or ambitious planning, they also imply a business-friendly environment.[24] For their sponsors, the utterly new landscape will encourage a radical shift in direction.[25]

The current wave of new cities differs from precedents constructed after World War II in a number of significant ways. While such post–World War II new cities as Chandigarh and Brasilia (governmental capitals in these cases) were state-driven initiatives, funded largely by international aid, the current wave of new cities are corporate-state collaborations. Unlike their predecessors, they have little in the way of socialist-infused civic ambitions.[26] In this way, new cities bear a greater resemblance to the entrepreneurialism of colonial cities in their role as economic engines and spaces for the accumulation of capital. Governments collude with select corporations for mutual benefit. Again, similar to colonial-era cities, current new cities are not being designed to accommodate the poor as much as to earn profit and attract investment. Appropriately enough, critics argue that these new cities are neoliberal fantasies that, however much cloaked in sustainability and messianic economic vision, do little to address inequality, housing deficits, or other such social challenges. Instead, they are likely to exacerbate existing divides.[27]

Networks of politicians and consultants sell these versions of modernity around the Global South. There is indeed, as Tim Bunnell and Diganta Das[28] describe it, a "serial seduction" that moves the concepts, policies, and aesthetics around the world. Roving international architects, planners, corporate players, and consultants (often self-described globalists) carry the visions forward. Such institutions as the Asian Development Bank and the United Nations and various government officials further facilitate the process, including through grants and loans. For its part, Cityquest KAEC Forum brings a critical mass of new-cities partisans into direct contact with one another, perhaps for the first time and with the hope of sharpening goals, sharing insights, and sparking new initiatives.

At the Cityquest KAEC Forum

The Cityquest KAEC Forum focuses exclusively on issues related to new master-planned cities. While the meeting was initially intended to be hosted every second year in a different new-city project around the world, the Saudi collaborators (and financial backers) decided that, based on the success of the first Cityquest, they would host it on an annual basis for about four to five years, after which time it would pass to another new city as host. The tagline of the forum, "Two Days to Shape the Future," conveys the sense of importance the sponsors are attempting to project.

For its part, the New Cities Foundation, the cosponsor with King Abdullah Economic City of the forum, states its mandate is to "shape a better urban future for all by fostering urban innovation and entrepreneurship."[29] As a registered charity in the United States, France, Canada, and Switzerland, the NCF offers that it seeks to bring together stakeholders and function as a platform for discussing common challenges relating to growing urbanization and for developing, financing and sharing solutions. The NCF is headed by its founder, the wealthy[30] and well-connected John Rossant. Until recently, Rossant was the executive chairman of PublicisLive, the Geneva-based communications holding company that produces the World Economic Forum in Davos, among other global events. He is said to be a charismatic dealmaker with cultivated ties to rich and powerful individuals, including Saudis and others in the Middle East. The largest and most well known of the NCF's events is the New Cities Summit, a larger and more public conference than the KAEC Forum, but one that also aims to facilitate interdisciplinary solutions to urban problems. The summit is held in a different city each year: Paris in 2012, Sao Paulo in 2013, Dallas in 2014, Jakarta in 2015, and Montreal in 2016. Participants in the 2015 summit included "800 of the world's leading decision-makers, mayors, CEOs, entrepreneurs, thinkers, artists and innovators."[31]

Compared to the guest list of the New Cities Summit, the Cityquest KAEC Forum is far more exclusive, with only 120 to 150 attendees. It is by invitation only, and the NCF, in consultation with KAEC management and Saudi immigration authorities, carefully crafts the guest list. Aside from Saudi dignitaries who occupy important positions in developing the new economic cities, the key guests are CEOs of new cities being constructed around the world. Guests also include McKinsey consultants and high-level corporate players. Among a handful of "visionaries" and "thought leaders," are international starchitects, planners, and other public figures. Such individuals are invited to provide ten-minute TED talk–style lectures, or what the NCF calls "espresso shots of innovation." Deliverers of these "espresso shots" have included Benjamin Barber, author of *If Mayors Ruled the World*; a Silicon Valley high-tech billionaire; an artist who creates glow-in-the-dark pathways and roads; and Randolph Hencken, executive director of the libertarian Seasteading Institute. Rem Koolhaas provided what was billed as a "Master Class" on contemporary global urbanization, and John Rossant had a sit-down interview onstage with Daniel Libeskind. These characters provide some star power and offbeat excitement in an otherwise business-dominated event (figs. 9.1 and 9.2).

Saudi Arabia's strict entry restrictions mean that the only ways for most visitors to gain access into the country are as a religious pilgrim, on a business visa, or with a government invitation. It is unclear what percentage of applicants are denied a visa. Officially, Israelis, Jews, atheists,

Figure 9.1. NCF director John Rossant has an onstage conversation with Daniel Libeskind. Photograph by the author.

Figure 9.2. Many networking sessions provide opportunities for leaders, experts, and investors to mingle with builders of new cities. Photograph by the author.

gays, unmarried women, and others may be denied a visa. The opaque selection and vetting process has excluded participants whom the NCF wished to invite. As such, Cityquest serves as a platform that showcases the ideas, views, and opinions of a highly selective and vetted group. Around 90 percent of attendees are male. As a nonprofit organization, the NCF relies on funding from various corporations, including such oil and technology companies as Cisco, Bombardier, Schneider Electric, and Ericsson. Not surprisingly, the corporations are granted a prominent platform at the Cityquest KAEC Forum (as at the New Cities Summit). Company representatives give presentations on their technologies, specific projects they have worked on, and the many ways in which urbanization in the Global South can benefit from the products they sell. The Cityquest platform provides these select firms an opportunity to sell their vision of the future (in addition to their services and technology), serving to inflate the role of technology in new cities. Since no attendees are invited who challenge their assumptions or advocate for low-tech urban solutions, emphasis on commercial technology thwarts potential for alternative priorities.

Given the elite participation and the extensive resources of those individuals and their respective organizations, the Cityquest KAEC Forum boosts circulation for ideas and strategies to which it gives rise. Brought together at Cityquest, elite participants can engage in a direct and concentrated way in "practices of citation, allusion, comparison and competition"[32]—as well as bonding and fellowship. The powerful people in attendance, along with their somewhat less powerful supporting experts—helpfully seduced by the luxury of the venue—are given to adulation of one another. In terms of substance, they orient to high-tech for a new-cities environment, as a viable problem-free economic strategy for the Global South.

A Space for Mentoring, a Space for Seduction

One of the most important and exclusive meetings (exclusive within the exclusive) at Cityquest is a two-hour session designed as a platform for the Strategic Working Group, the CEOs of a handful of new cities that the NCF considers to be successful examples of projects underway. In the first Strategic Working Group meeting, the CEOs met to discuss how to help new cities become logistics hubs. CEOs of other new cities in their earlier phases were encouraged to sit in on the meeting to listen and learn. Among the core participants were the CEOs of King Abdullah Economic City (Saudi Arabia), Iskandar Malaysia, Tianjin Eco City (China), Lavasa (India), and Rawabi (Palestine). They shared their common successes and challenges related to their respective attempts to create logistics hubs from scratch. Leaders of cities in the very early stages—including Kabul New City (Afghanistan), Colombo Port City (Sri Lanka) and others—had the opportunity to listen in, ask questions, and get advice. They also discussed such topics as financing strategy and how to monetize city components, like parks, street trees, and sidewalks. There is also discussion of how to manage politicians and citizens' groups who resist projects, something they evidently indeed do. The Strategic Working Group creates, in effect, a hierarchy of new cities that establishes a mentor-mentee relationship among key individuals, ready to address issues on any such fronts.

In its various formats and venues, Cityquest validates the importance of the global revolution that is being advanced by the assumed

Figure 9.3. Welcome dinner: gourmet dining among luxury villas next to the Red Sea. Photograph by the author.

common agenda among its participants. A sense of the event's importance is communicated the moment the attendees touch down at the Jeddah airport. A red carpet welcomes guests to their first banquet on the eve of the conference, held at a party area around a large swimming pool set within a cluster of seaside luxury villas (fig. 9.3). It treats participants as would-be world changers.

The Saudi hosts provide extraordinary VIP treatment to all: world-class meals, luxuries appropriate to "world changers," including cultural spectacles. Staff is at their beck and call, subservient to visitors' desires. Participants are rubbing shoulders with global elites. The presence of Saudi royalty accompanied by armed guards add frisson. There are paparazzi to record personages like starchitects Koolhaas and Libeskind, the CEOs of Cisco, the dean of MIT's School of Planning, and others of high status.[33] It reinforces the sense that new cities have the seal of approval as a desirable and necessary model of development. At the end of the second day, each CEO is presented with a personalized trophy by a Saudi prince and John Rossant as a reward for attending and acknowledgment of their contribution to the new-cities phenomenon. Cityquest is spun as a meeting of the minds and a master class in advanced urbanization, while providing an unprecedented networking opportunity for powerful players in the new-cities world.

One of the dominant assumptions fostered at Cityquest is that corporations are and ought to be the main actors; only they are able to marshal the resources necessary for addressing problems on a massive scale. Beyond individuals working on state-driven new cities, no government officials are present; nor are representatives from the United Nations or other intergovernmental or citizens' organizations. Furthermore, while helping to address housing deficits, overcrowding, a lack of jobs, and so on, there is the proffered belief that corporations can make money in the process, so it is a win-win endeavor. The masses will gain housing and jobs; cooperating governments, which otherwise could not afford to execute projects, have a way to satisfy public needs. Significantly, despite a great deal of emphasis on the imagined benefits of new cities on urban populations, presenters offer up little evidence of actual success. Optimistic enthusiasm, with a sense of worldwide relevance, stands in for clear data or convincing case outcomes. Nevertheless, attendees gain reassurance that the steps they are taking align with other such efforts in various parts of the world.

The impact of the conference on some attendees was made clear during an interview I conducted with the mayor of a major West African city. While his country has yet to develop a new city, he felt new cities were an important and positive phenomenon and was excited and inspired by what he saw at Cityquest. When I spoke with him the following year, he had met with the president of his country, and plans were being drawn up for a new master-planned "finance city" that would ideally become the financial gateway into francophone Africa. While he acknowledged that they would need to find a low-cost way to build the city, drawing on local materials and methods, it was clear that a new city was seen as a necessary step for national economic development. He had returned to his country with ideas and expectations garnered from Cityquest.

Ismail Ibrahim, the CEO of Iskandar Malaysia, a massive special economic zone at the tip of the Malay Peninsula, was similarly influenced by Cityquest. As one of the members of the Strategic Working Group, Ibrahim offered to host the group in Iskandar Malaysia in March 2015. In my interview with him, he was inspired and impressed with Cityquest

Figure 9.4. CEOs of new cities start a site tour with an explanation of the master plan. Photograph by the author.

and the progress the Saudis have made in KAEC (fig. 9.4). He felt pressure to live up to both Cityquest and KAEC and expressed the need to "put on a good show" to impress the other CEOs who would visit Malaysia.

My interviews suggest that Cityquest helps to foster a sense of solidarity among CEOs who are embarking "together" on a great urbanistic adventure. Each type of attendee may have gained from specific contacts with counterparts from other regions. Public administration managers valued the opportunity to exchange experiences with other such administrators, more so than, say, with architects, planners, or politicians. They could get into details on common concerns, like the construction process, how to form and sustain public-private partnerships, how to manage political pressures, and how each project can fit into broader national development plans.

Saudis Take on the Mantle of New-Cities Experts

In urban studies and planning literature, Saudi Arabia has not, unlike neighboring Dubai for example,[34] been considered a place for urban innovation. Saudis are not conventionally viewed as having urban expertise to share, particularly with an international audience. The relatively little scholarship published over the past several decades on urban change in the kingdom has focused primarily on narrowly drawn technical issues relating to strategic planning tools and techniques,[35] managing city growth,[36] the proliferation of gated housing estates,[37] urban sustainability,[38] and Saudi cultural and religious needs in planning and architecture.[39] Despite the many master-planned industrial cities in Saudi Arabia (e.g., Jubail Industrial City, Yanbu, Sudair Industrial City, Rabigh) and a great deal of national experience constructing massive infrastructure projects, the scholarly literature does not reflect how Saudis are creating new urban environments and on a grand scale.

At Cityquest, Saudis have a prominent role on panels with topics like finance, logistics, governance, attracting residents and businesses, fostering entrepreneurialism, branding, transportation, and affordability. Of the sixteen sessions during the two-day event, Saudis were on stage as presenters for ten. They readily mingled among attendees at all venues. KAEC's CEO, Fahd Al-Rasheed, was himself a featured speaker. A Saudi national, educated at Washington University (BA) and Stanford University (MBA), Al-Rasheed travels to the most prominent venues, such as the World Economic Forum. He provides a young, sophisticated, and progressive face for the KAEC project. At Cityquest, he is a rock star who attendees jostle to meet. Many CEOs and other prominent attendees spoke to me with great admiration for Fahd Al-Rasheed's unwavering focus and commitment to KAEC, his skill in navigating a challenging political context, and his personal charisma. One CEO of an aspiring high-tech city testified that Al-Rasheed's insights were particularly useful and applicable to his new city: "Fahd emphasized that the master plan needs to be flexible and not set in stone. . . . It must be able to change and adapt to respond to market forces. We need to keep that in mind so we do not become slaves to our master plan but use the master plan as a vehicle for attracting entrepreneurs." Another CEO praised Al-Rasheed's presentation, suggesting that KAEC and its key proponent represented the right kind of model for his new city to follow: "We are not looking to Silicon Valley as an inspiration. . . . It is more valuable for us to take note of KAEC, Daedok Innopolis [South Korea], Tsukuba [Science City, Japan]. . . . These are state interventions, examples of entrepreneurial state projects. Fahd talks about the Saudi economy in the world even after oil. . . . This is what we are thinking about and planning for as well but we are a few years behind."[40]

Saudis are thus recognized not only as hosts, but also as experts. They are also at hand as potential investors in cities represented by the urban CEOs in attendance. During and after Cityquest, closed-door meetings were also set up between Saudi investors and urban development CEOs, who hoped to attract Saudi capital.

Normalizing New Cities as Economic Strategy

Cityquest normalizes neoliberal assumptions of urban development. It starts with a guest list that excludes citizen groups, academics, journalists, and others who do not support or personally profit from the construction of new cities. By holding the event in a fabulous setting, it makes palpable the possible material rewards that can follow from linking up with its assumptions and outcomes. The lack of debate and dissenting views presents a distorted view of who makes—or ought to make—decisions regarding the use of land and resources. As one attendee noted, while the word "resident" was used often, the word "citizen" did not come up once during the two days. Instead, urban megaprojects that are fundamentally undemocratic are presented as prescient, modern, and socially responsible investments—something to which leaders in emerging economies should aspire. When faced with professionals working on dozens of new-cities projects around the world, attendees gain the sense that their competitors are pursuing new cities and they will be left behind if they do not. The interpersonal dynamics reinforce a need to be "with it" by enlisting.

The rise of the so-called Asian Tigers and the lavish post-oil urban development in the GCC inspires the possibility of bringing other "miracles" into being. The Cityquest KAEC Forum sets up bold symbols of national pride and capability, with Saudi Arabia having a critical role. For better or worse, attendees of Cityquest are exposed to and inspired by alternatives to Western economic and urban growth models, whether capitalist or socialist-oriented. They can become agents that circulate versions of the hyped alternatives back home, even where conditions, especially financial ones, differ from those in Saudi Arabia. Further research will be needed to untangle the material impacts of Cityquest on new-cities projects and to determine how the cultivation of personal connections among those in attendance acts to reconfigure circuits of urban policy mobility.

NOTES

1 At the time of writing, the NCF had recently shifted its head office to Montreal.

2 I attended the first Cityquest KAEC Forum both as a scholar and as a consultant for the NCF. I authored the summary report for the NCF, Moser 2014.

3 New cities tend to be headed by CEOs or corporate heads rather than mayors or other elected positions, evidence of the shift from managerial to entrepreneurial roles for city managers. KAEC is in fact a corporation (Emaar the Economic City, or EEC) that is listed on the Saudi stock exchange.

4 Peck and Theodore 2010; McCann and Ward 2012.

5 Peck and Theodore 2010; Clarke 2012; McCann 2010.

6 Clarke 2012, 4.

7 Ward 2010; Ward 2006; McCann and Ward 2010; McCann and Ward 2012.

8 Peck and Theodore 2010.

9 Brenner and Theodore 2002.

10 McCann 2011.

11 Phelps et al. 2014; Pow 2014.

12 Bunnell and Das 2010; Percival and Waley 2012; Bunnell 2015; Lieto and Beauregard 2015.

13 McCann 2010; Farías and Bender 2010.

14 Phelps et al. 2014; Bunnell et al. 2013.

15 Bunnell and Das 2010; Das 2015.

16 Bhan 2013; Datta 2015; Koch 2014; Sherwood 2013; Moser 2012a.

17 Clarke 2012.

18 Burawoy 2000.

19 Collins 2011, 318.

20 My effort thus documents new patterns of circulation within the Global South and addresses McCann and Ward's concern with "how, why, where and with what consequences policies circulate globally."

21 Moser 2010; Moser, Swain, and Alkhabbaz 2015; Bunnell 2004.

22 Keeton 2015.

23 Moser 2010; Moser 2012b; Koch 2013.

24 Das 2015; Bunnell 2002.

25 Vale 2008.

26 Moser 2015.

27 Watson 2015; Watson 2009; Datta 2015.

28 Bunnell and Das 2010.
29 New Cities Foundation, www.newcitiesfoundation.org (accessed October 10, 2016).
30 Rossant maintains apartments in New York and Paris and a chateau in rural Normandy, the renovations of which were profiled in the *New York Times*; see Vaucher 2007.
31 Press release, New Cities Foundation 2014.
32 Roy and Ong 2011, 17.
33 My position as a professor at McGill University also plays a role in the legitimization of the new-cities agenda. My own ethical entanglements are part of a broader methodological discussion in a paper about the challenges of conducting research on new master-planned cities (forthcoming).
34 Elsheshtawy 2006; Elsheshtawy 2013; Acuto 2010; Kanna 2011.
35 Ghamdi 2005.
36 Mubarak 2004; Garba 2004; Aljoufie et al. 2013; Al-Hemaidi 2001.
37 Glasze 2006; Glasze and Alkhayyal 2002.
38 Alshuwaikhat and Aina 2006; Choguill 2008; Mandeli 2008.
39 Abu-Gazzeh 1995; Saleh 2004; Saleh 2002.
40 Personal communication, December 9, 2015.

REFERENCES

Abu-Gazzeh, Tawfiq. 1995. "Privacy as the Basis of Architectural Planning in the Islamic Culture of Saudi Arabia." *Architecture and Behaviour* 11: 93–112.

Acuto, Michele. 2010. "High-Rise Dubai Urban Entrepreneurialism and the Technology of Symbolic Power." *Cities* 27, no. 4: 272–284.

Al-Hemaidi, Waleed Kassab. 2001. "The Metamorphosis of the Urban Fabric in an Arab-Muslim City: Riyadh, Saudi Arabia." *Journal of Housing and the Built Environment* 16: 179–201.

Aljoufie, M., M. Zuidgeest, M. Brussel, and M. van Maarseveen. 2013. "Spatial-Temporal Analysis of Urban Growth and Transportation in Jeddah City, Saudi Arabia." *Cities* 31: 57–68.

Alshuwaikhat, H. M., and Y. A. Aina. 2006. "GIS-Based Urban Sustainability Assessment: The Case of Dammam City, Saudi Arabia." *Local Environment* 11, no. 2: 141–162.

Bhan, Gautam. 2013. "The Real Lives of Urban Fantasies." *Environment and Urbanization* 26, no. 1: 1–4.

Brenner, Neil, and Nik Theodore. 2002. "Cities and the Geographies of 'Actually Existing' Neoliberalism." *Antipode* 34, no. 3: 349–379.

Bunnell, Tim. 2002. "Multimedia Utopia? A Geographical Critique of High-Tech Development in Malaysia's Multimedia Super Corridor." *Antipode* 34: 265–295.

Bunnell, Tim. 2004. *Malaysia, Modernity, and the Multimedia Super Corridor: A Critical Geography of Intelligent Landscapes.* London: Routledge.

Bunnell, Tim. 2015. "Antecedent Cities and Inter-referencing Effects: Learning from and Extending beyond Critiques of Neoliberalisation." *Urban Studies* 52, no. 11: 1983–2000.

Bunnell, Tim, and Diganta Das. 2010. "Urban Pulse—a Geography of Serial Seduction: Urban Policy Transfer from Kuala Lumpur to Hyderabad." *Urban Geography* 31: 1–7.

Bunnell, Tim, Michelle Ann Miller, Nicholas A. Phelps, and John Taylor. 2013. "Urban Development in a Decentralized Indonesia: Two Success Stories?" *Pacific Affairs* 86, no. 4: 857–876.

Burawoy, M. 2000. "Introduction: Reaching for the Global." In *Ethnography Unbound: Power and Resistance in the Modern Metropolis*, ed. M. Burawoy, J. A. Blum, S. George, Z. Gille, T. Gowan, L. Haney, S. H. Lopez, S. O. Riain, and M. Thayer, 1–40. Berkeley: University of California Press.

Choguill, Charles L. 2008. "Developing Sustainable Neighborhoods." *Habitat International* 32, no. 1: 41–48.

Clarke, Nick. 2012. "Urban Policy Mobility, Anti-Politics, and Histories of the Transnational Municipal Movement." *Progress in Human Geography* 36, no. 1: 25–43.

Collins, Francis Leo. 2011. "Transnational Mobilities and Urban Spatialities: Notes from the Asia-Pacific." *Progress in Human Geography* 36, no. 3: 316–335.

Das, Diganta. 2015. "Hyderabad: Visioning, Restructuring and Making of a High-Tech City." *Cities* 43: 48–58.

Datta, Ayona. 2015. "New Urban Utopias of Postcolonial India: 'Entrepreneurial Urbanization' in Dholera Smart City, Gujarat." *Dialogues in Human Geography* 5, no. 1: 3–22.

Elsheshtawy, Yasser. 2006. "From Dubai to Cairo: Competing against Global Cities, Models and Shifting Centers of Influence." In *Cairo Cosmopolitan: Politics, Culture and Urban Space in the New Middle East*, ed. Diane Singerman and Paul Amar, 235–250. Cairo: AUC Press.

Elsheshtawy, Yasser. 2013. "The Global and the Everyday: Situating the Dubai Spectacle." In *The Superlative City: Dubai and the Urban Condition in the Early Twenty-First Century*, ed. Ahmed Kanna, 104–120. Cambridge, MA: Aga Khan Program at the Harvard University Graduate School of Design.

Farías, Ignacio, and Thomas Bender. 2010. "Introduction: Decentering the Object of Urban Studies." In *Urban Assemblages: How Actor-Network Theory Changes Urban Studies*, ed. Ignacio Farías and Thomas Bender, 1–24. London: Routledge.

Garba, S. B. 2004. "Managing Urban Growth and Development in the Riyadh Metropolitan Area, Saudi Arabia." *Habitat International* 28, no. 4: 593–608.

Ghamdi, Salem Mater Saeed. 2005. "The Use of Strategic Planning Tools and Techniques in Saudi Arabia: An Empirical Study." *International Journal of Management* 22, no. 3: 376–395.

Glasze, Georg. 2006. "Segregation and Seclusion: The Case of Compounds for Western Expatriates in Saudi Arabia." *GeoJournal* 66, no. 1–2: 83–88.

Glasze, Georg, and Abdallah Alkhayyal. 2002. "Gated Housing Estates in the Arab World: Case Studies in Lebanon and Riyadh, Saudi Arabia." *Environment and Planning B: Planning and Design* 29: 321–336.

Harrison, Philip. 2015. "South-South Relationships and the Transfer of 'Best Practice': The Case of Johannesburg, South Africa." *International Development Planning Review* 37, no. 2: 205–223.

Hogan, Trevor, Tim Bunnell, Choo-Piew Pow, Eka Permanasari, and Sirat Morshidi. 2012. "Asian Urbanisms and the Privatization of Cities." *Cities* 29, no. 1: 59–63.

Kanna, Ahmed. 2011. *Dubai: The City as Corporation*. Minneapolis: University of Minnesota Press.

Kanna, Ahmed, ed. 2013. *The Superlative City Dubai and the Urban Condition in the Early Twenty-First Century*. Cambridge, MA: Aga Khan Program at the Harvard University Graduate School of Design.

Keeton, Rachel. 2011. *Rising in the East: Contemporary New Towns in Asia*. Amsterdam: SUN.

Koch, Natalie. 2013. "Why Not a World City? Astana, Ankara, and Geopolitical Scripts in Urban Networks." *Urban Geography* 34, no. 1: 109–130.

Koch, Natalie. 2014. "Bordering on the Modern: Power, Practice and Exclusion in Astana." *Transactions of the Institute of British Geographers* 39, no. 3: 432–443.

Lieto, Laura, and Robert A. Beauregard, eds. 2015. *Planning for a Material World*. London: Routledge.

Mandeli, K. N. 2008. "The Realities of Integrating Physical Planning and Local Management into Urban Development: A Case Study of Jeddah, Saudi Arabia." *Habitat International* 32, no. 4: 512–533.

McCann, Eugene. 2010. "Urban Policy Mobilities and Global Circuits of Knowledge: Toward a Research Agenda." *Annals of the Association of American Geographers* 100, no. 5: 1–24.

McCann, Eugene. 2011. "Urban Policy Mobilites and Global Circuits of Knowledge: Toward a Research Agenda." *Annals of the Association of American Geographers* 101, no. 1: 107–130.

McCann, Eugene, and Kevin Ward. 2010. "Relationality/Territoriality: Toward a Conceptualization of Cities in the World." *Geoforum* 41, no. 2: 175–184.

McCann, Eugene, and Kevin Ward. 2012. "Policy Assemblages, Mobilities and Mutations: Toward a Multidisciplinary Conversation." *Political Studies* 10, no. 3: 325–332.

Moser, Sarah. 2010. "Putrajaya: Malaysia's New Federal Administrative Capital." *Cities* 27: 285–297.

Moser, Sarah. 2012a. "Circulating Visions of 'High Islam': The Adoption of Fantasy Middle Eastern Architecture in Constructing Malaysian National Identity." *Urban Studies* 49, no. 13: 2913–2935.

Moser, Sarah. 2012b. "Globalization and the Construction of Identity in Two New Southeast Asian Capitals: Putrajaya and Dompak." In *Rethinking Global Urbanism: Comparative Insights from Secondary Cities*, ed. Xiangming Chen and Ahmed Kanna, 169–189. London: Routledge.

Moser, Sarah. 2014. *Cityquest—KAEC Forum 2013 Report*. Paris: New Cities Foundation.

Moser, Sarah. 2015. "New Cities: Old Wine in New Bottles?" *Dialogues in Human Geography* 5, no. 1: 31–35.

Moser, Sarah, Marian Swain, and Mohammed Alkhabbaz. 2015. "King Abdullah Economic City: Engineering Saudi Arabia's Post-Oil Future." *Cities* 45: 71–80.

Mubarak, Faisal A. 2004. "Urban Growth Boundary Policy and Residential Suburbanization: Riyadh, Saudi Arabia." *Habitat International* 28: 567–591.

New Cities Foundation. 2014. "Jakarta to Host 2015 New Cities Summit: 'This Is Indonesia's Moment.'" Press release, November 6, 2014. www.newcitiesfoundation.org.

Peck, Jamie, and Nick Theodore. 2010. "Mobilizing Policy: Models, Methods, and Mutations." *Geoforum* 41, no. 2: 169–174.

Percival, Tom, and Paul Waley. 2012. "Articulating Intra-Asian Urbanism: The Production of Satellite Cities in Phnom Penh." *Urban Studies* 49: 2873–2888.

Phelps, Nicholas A., Tim Bunnell, Michelle Ann Miller, and John Taylor. 2014. "Urban Inter-referencing within and beyond a Decentralized Indonesia." *Cities* 39: 37–49.

Pow, Choon Piew. 2014. "License to Travel: Policy Assemblage and the 'Singapore Model.'" *City* 18, no. 3: 287–306.

Roy, Ananya, and Aihwa Ong, eds. 2011. *Worlding Cities: Asian Experiments and the Art of Being Global*. Oxford: Wiley-Blackwell.

Saleh, Mohammed Abdullah Eben. 2002. "The Transformation of Residential Neighborhood: The Emergence of New Urbanism in Saudi Arabian Culture." *Building and Environment* 37, no. 5: 515–529.

Saleh, Mohammed Abdullah Eben. 2004. "Learning from Tradition: The Planning of Residential Neighborhoods in a Changing World." *Habitat International* 28: 625–639.

Shephard, Wade. 2015. *Ghost Cities of China: The Story of Cities without People in the World's Most Populated Country*. London: Zed Books.

Sherwood, Harriet. 2013. "Rawabi Rises: New West Bank City Symbolizes Palestine's Potential." *Guardian*, August 8, 2013. www.theguardian.com.

Vale, Lawrence J. 2008. *Architecture, Power, and National Identity*. New York: Routledge.

Vaucher, Andrea R. 2007. "In Normandy, Buying and Restoring." *New York Times*, May 16, 2007. www.nytimes.com.

Ward, Kevin. 2006. "'Policies in Motion', Urban Management and State Restructuring: The Trans-Local Expansion of Business Improvement Districts." *International Journal of Urban and Regional Research* 30, no. 1: 54–75.

Ward, Kevin. 2010. "Towards a Relational Comparative Approach to the Study of Cities." *Progress in Human Geography* 34, no. 4: 471–487.

Watson, Vanessa. 2009. "'The Planned City Sweeps the Poor Away . . .': Urban Planning and 21st Century Urbanisation." *Progress in Planning* 72, no. 3: 151–193.

Watson, Vanessa. 2015. "The Allure of 'Smart City' Rhetoric: India and Africa." *Dialogues in Human Geography* 5, no. 1: 36–39.

Wood, Astrid. 2014a. "Learning through Policy Tourism: Circulating Bus Rapid Transit from South America to South Africa." *Environment and Planning A: Economy and Space* 46, no. 11: 2654–2669.

Wood, Astrid. 2014b. "The Politics of Policy Circulation: Unpacking the Relationship between South African and South American Cities in the Adoption of Bus Rapid Transit." *Antipode* 47, no. 4: 1062–1079.

Audacity, Work-Arounds, and Spatial Segmentation

10

Real Estate Speculation and Transnational Development in Dubai

YASSER ELSHESHTAWY

Dubai has become a byword for rampant speculation: an urbanity of excess based on spectacular and iconic structures that made questionable business sense. Such skeptical views seemed confirmed during the 2008 financial crisis and its aftermath, which left the city devastated and empty, its expatriate workforce fleeing in desperation to escape the crushing debt accumulated during the boom years. Yet in the wake of the crisis, it was left with an impressive legacy of projects and durable infrastructures that proved to be crucial in its ability to weather the economic downturn. There has been a reemergence of megaprojects and a return of real estate purchasers who buy even before ground is broken—off plan, as it is termed. Many halted projects were revived, others restructured. The downside is the continuous displacement of residents, destruction of "traditional" neighborhoods, and a fragmented urban form. Dubai represents capital accumulation, real estate speculation, and political power structures converging to create a distinctive city of the twenty-first century. It has potential—for better or worse—to become the blueprint for urban futures. Given such a potential, there is a need to step back and take stock of this city's rapid evolution.

It is an evolution that follows a logic and vision of sorts. This vision looks at the city as a provider of real estate. A few state-owned developers—that is, the ruling family—divide available urban land and sell it to high-worth individuals. The result is a fragmented urban fabric geared toward exclusivity, where livability and urbanity—in short, a sustainable urban environment—are issues that are dealt with, if at all, after the fact.

Modern (Post-1950s) Dubai: Plans and Projects

Approaching Dubai from the Al-Ain Highway in 1996 (when I first arrived in the UAE) presented the viewer with a memorable sight—a lone rising structure signals impending arrival. This was the thirty-nine-story World Trade Center, at that time one of only a few high-rise buildings in the region. The building was first dwarfed by the twin Emirates Towers and then by the Burj Khalifa (figs. 10.1 and 10.2). Within the span of four decades, the city transformed from a village-like existence to global-city status.[1] However dramatic and largely unprecedented in the world, there were indeed efforts made to plan the outcomes. At least initially, Dubai was in fact shaped by the vision of a master plan. This vision is still in evidence today, although it has given way to the great forces of real estate markets and land speculation.

Beginnings: The John Harris Master Plans (1959–1971)

In 1960, British architect John Harris drew the first master plan for Dubai.[2] He was introduced to Dubai's ruler, Sheikh Rashid bin Saeed Al

Figure 10.1. Dubai's changing skyline, 2004. Photograph by the author.

Maktoum, in 1959 by the British political agent Sir Donald Hawley. Harris rapidly won the ruler's trust and became the state's expert adviser on the new master plan. According to the UK-based *Times of London*, "He developed a means of working that wedded Sheikh Rashid's ambitions with an architecture both respected and respectful."[3] The choice of Harris was an interesting one given that he was relatively unknown and had no large practice. The Harris obituary seems to suggest that Sheikh Rashid approached the project with a somewhat modest rather than grand vision.

The situation of Dubai in the 1960s was quite primitive. The city had no paved roads, no utility networks, and no modern port facilities. Water was only available from cans brought into town by donkeys. Traveling to Dubai from London took several days in unreliable piston-engine planes with overnight stops. Communication was also difficult. There were few telephones, and cables were sent by radio.[4] The master plan developed by Harris aimed at rectifying this by fulfilling some fundamental needs: a map, a road system, and directions for growth. It called for the provision of a road system; zoning of the town into areas marked for industry, commerce, and public buildings; areas for new residential quarters; and the

Figure 10.2. Dubai's changing skyline, 2015. Photograph by the author.

creation of a new town center. These rather modest goals were in line with the emirate's limited pre-oil financial resources. It would be significantly modified with the discovery of oil in 1966.

In 1971, a new Harris master plan was introduced. The plan called for the construction of a tunnel (the Shindagha Tunnel) beneath Dubai Creek that would connect the city's two otherwise divided sides—Bur Dubai and Deira. The plan also called for construction of two bridges (Maktoum and Garhoud); in addition, the building of Port Rashid was also envisioned. A large area extending toward Jebel Ali was designated for residential use (now known as Jumeirah), and a further large area was reserved for industry. To the city's south, the plan dedicated additional areas to health, education, and leisure/recreation.[5] This phase also saw the creation of a series of landmarks, of which the Dubai World Trade Center was one. It was indeed the tallest building in the Arab world for the next twenty years and Dubai's first icon. The presence of Queen Elizabeth II at the opening of the building in 1979 heralded the start of Dubai's global prominence.

Overall Harris's architecture and planning principles did in many ways respect the past—not a typical modernist attitude. With Sheikh Rashid growing increasingly ill, decision making moved into the hands of his sons, which heralded a change in attitude under a period of rapid expansion.[6] Of particular note was the emergence of the city's growth corridor along Sheikh Zayed Road toward Jebel Ali. Dubbed the "new Dubai," this area emerged as the new commercial and financial center of the city. With dramatic changes in the city skyline, rapid developments emerged as a result of both increased resources and opportunities for alternative revenues for various stakeholders—the state, semistate developers, and the private sector. A main problem with these new axes of growth was fragmentation, resulting in a city composed of disjointed islands and archipelagos. Furthermore, the rapid proliferation of these projects necessitated an approach that would depart from any version of a "rigid" master plan.

Second Era: The Dubai Structural Plan (1995–Present)

Certainly, given the rapid development taking place, the old master plan proved insufficient. Competing developments, matters related to sustainability, and growing social and economic problems due to the increased influx of foreign laborers all contributed to the realization that a new plan needed to be adopted. Thus, in 1995 Dubai Municipality prepared a twenty-year plan—also known as the Structural Plan—with the main aim to be sufficiently flexible to accommodate shifting needs and opportunities.[7] The Structural Plan's concepts, based on a series of nodes and axes, account for much of the city's form as it appears today. In fact, many of the major megaprojects (e.g., the Palm Islands) do follow this plan to some extent.[8] Of course, the report was written prior to the city's remarkable real estate boom and the emergence of developers now of enormous consequence in capacities, political and economic, to shape uses of space and indeed the earth itself. Such companies as Nakheel, Emaar, and others were crucial in determining the city's growth pattern.

This was also the time when some of Dubai's most noted landmarks came into being: the sail-like Burj Al Arab, the ultramodern Emirates Towers, and, capping the extravagance of this phase, the supertall Burj Khalifa. This period also saw massive land reclamation and development of outlying and desert areas, along with waterfront sites. Hence, some of the great icons took shape: the Jumeirah Palm Island, Dubai Marina, and Jumeirah Beach Residence (JBR), a sprawling vertical residential complex overlooking the Gulf.[9] Besides these projects—which were actually built—still more were planned and excitedly promoted. This included Jumeirah Gardens—a massive mixed-use luxury development to replace an existing "traditional" neighborhood with still more reclamations and supertall towers.[10] The global downturn put a (temporary) halt to these projects.

The 2020 Urban Master Plan and Dubai's Reemergence

Linked to the great global downturn, many expatriates were forced to leave the city, and the value of real estate dropped by more than 50 percent. During the resulting enforced development "recess" came criticism of the helter-skelter patterns and the lack of a clear framework to guide future growth that a recovery would bring. Unlike its neighbor Abu Dhabi, Dubai did not have a governing body akin to Abu Dhabi's Urban Planning Council (UPC) that could act as a regulatory agency with overall vision and implementation authority. In cooperation with various governmental authorities and major developers, building on the 1995 structural framework plan, Dubai Municipality proposed the 2020 Urban Masterplan.[11] It adopts language and terminology common to such documents, including "utilization of existing infrastructure" and "preserving the environment, diversifying energy sources, being responsive to the socio-economic transformation and improving the legislative and governance framework to streamline planning process." The scheme was duly adopted, setting clear boundaries within which growth should take place. An aspect of the plan calls for specifications to "define urbanization parameters, and the expansion of future metropolitan and regional settlements." Of particular note is a priority to "consider infill redevelopment and revitalization opportunities." The plan also envisioned the formation of a supreme urban council, a regulatory agency modeled on its Abu Dhabi counterpart (UPC). This has yet to materialize.

With the introduction of the new master plan, came a revival of stalled megaprojects and a plethora of optimistic anecdotes about the return of traffic jams and other symptoms of comeback in various media reports. These accounts rely on the unexpected success of previously derided projects, as well as solid economic indicators of revival. For instance, the Burj Khalifa skyscraper, previously dubbed as a "great white elephant," came to anchor a thriving development called Downtown Dubai, a hotspot for the area's trendier inhabitants. The city's rapid transit, Dubai Metro, moves more than 300,000 people daily and is another heralded success.[12] The International Monetary Fund estimated that GDP was up by 4.1 percent in the first half of 2012 over the same period of 2011. For 2016, in the face of an oil price decline, the city's diversified economy provided strong GDP growth at 3.7 percent. The city's trade, transport, and tourism sector has been robust. And in a sure sign that the city is back to its old ways, in 2012 Emaar opened a sixty-three-story tower with 542 flats and sold them all on the first day.[13]

Another sign of revival was the substantial rise in property prices. According to Reuters, Dubai house prices posted the fastest year-on-year rise of any of the world's major markets in January–March 2015, for the fourth straight quarter—soaring 27.7 percent over the year (although this was not to be a steady pattern).[14] Annual economic growth is around

5 percent. Whatever goes on, Dubai continues to benefit from geopolitical troubles in the region, as it has throughout its modern history. The Arab Spring led to money inflows from Arab investors; their "flight of capital" is away from countries with political turmoil. Reliance on such fluctuating circumstances also makes the city vulnerable to financial implosion. Cash buyers, it has been estimated, account for 72 percent of transactions at the beginning of 2014—well above the rate of other major world cities.[15]

Authorities are aware of the danger of another bubble and have thus put mechanisms in place, such as higher transaction fees and placing a cap on mortgage lending, to try and restrain excessive price growth. Still, the market is far less restrictive than that found in other world cities.[16] In a sign of increasing anxiety, a large billboard appeared on the city's main artery, Sheikh Zayed Road, imploring people: "Keep Calm. There is no Bubble." Reflecting a sense of caution, a financial services officer notes: "Developers are more careful about launching big projects and tend to split them into more manageable pieces. That's all very rational. There is less speculative building, less of the 'build it and they will come' approach."[17]

Whatever the constraints or cautions, plans for Dubai real estate projects worth well over $50 billion were announced in an eighteen-month period, the last half of 2014 and the year 2015. Other reports project another $200 billion in development projects over the next decade. One of the biggest will be Expo 2020—a world's fair exhibition and accompanying developments, including a new city called Dubai South. A second giant is to be Dubai World Central, based on plans linked into the city's second airport (see chapter 7). Other notable projects include the extension of the Business Bay Canal to the Gulf, with accompanying towers and a beach park. And there are new projects, such as the Design District, attempting to replicate London's Shoreditch in the middle of the city; Mohamed bin Rashid City, a massive multiuse development; and a new aptly named Mall of the World. Many of these are infill developments, utilizing leftover land from the previous boom. Meanwhile, new "old" icons like Palm Jebel Ali and Deira and Dubailand are still incomplete. It remains to be seen how the ambitions for more and bigger will reconcile with the rhetoric of restraint.

Mapping the Growth: Magnitude, Land Use, and Developers

One of the issues that emerged during the financial crisis is the lack of reliable statistical data on business or socioeconomic conditions in Dubai. Among other absences were spatial maps based on reliable information on the impact of all these master plans and real estate developments. Analyses had to be based on anecdotal evidence or boosterish claims. To address the problem, I began, in 2010, a research project titled "Mapping Dubai: Towards an Understanding of Urban Form and Social Structure."[18] There are various scales, macro and micro, to my resulting study.

At the macro scale, I chronologically documented and mapped the city's population and growth within the urbanized boundary of the city. I quantified and mapped existing land uses. Next, I was able to spatially map developers, in terms of the locations of their projects. Finally, at the micro level, I carefully examined people's in situ street-level interactions. This helps us understand, through my "case study," the presence or absence of various forms of urbanism—as might result from the macro shifts in development patterns revealed in the quantitative data. These various strategies may well be applicable to other places in the world where interpolations, alternative sources, and indirect mechanisms are needed to fill in for more regularized and official data gathering.

Measurement and Mapping Growth

Historical maps do exist for Dubai, with the earliest published in 1822 by a British explorer and seafarer. Much later, in 1958, we have the master plan prepared by the British architect John Harris. In great detail, it identifies built forms in the 1950s. In addition to these maps, I used historical aerial photographs; although they do not allow precise plotting of buildings, they do help identify urban boundaries. Google Earth was available for more recent satellite imagery; its timeline function, in the case of Dubai, goes as far back as 1990. Overall, the following years had sufficient data and information for me to construct maps or augment prior ones: 1822, 1959, 1968, 1978, 1990, 2005, 2014, and 2020 (estimate). I established rates of growth graphically by placing urban form diagrams, drawn to the same scale, on a timeline. Another measure uses a mathematical formula that specifies two indicators: rate of growth (RG) and rate of change (RC).

Based on these analyses, we can observe significant variation over time in rates of growth. The city witnessed a massive rate of population increase from 1968 to 1978. Within this span of only ten years, the rate of change was an astonishing 1,200 percent. This declined to a still robust 135 percent increase from 1978 to 1990. The rise between 1990 and 2005 was 206 percent—a high rate attributed to the proliferation of various development projects, such as the Jumeirah Palm Island. At that point, the city more or less established its main contemporary boundaries and urban form. Growth became somewhat more moderate, at 59 percent from 2005 to 2016, with the financial crisis being a main factor in the slowdown. It is anticipated that this subdued rate will continue up until 2020.

In terms of the areal growth of the demarcated city, there have been three distinct phases: phase 1, from 1959 to 1978, with 11.1 square kilometers average growth per year; phase 2, from 1978 to 1990 at an average 6 square kilometers per year; and phase 3, from 1990 to 2014, at an average 20 square kilometers per year—the time of most rapid change.

Quantifying Existing Land Use—and Nonuse

The second phase of this project involved measuring, classifying, and quantifying existing developments as to their type of land use, such as gated communities, malls, parks, and so forth. In many cases, I could observe land use directly. In other instances, I went to such online sources as the Department of Economic Development (DED), Real Estate Regulation Agency (RERA), and developers. In addition, I used data (2011–2013) from the Dubai Statistics Center (a government agency). In instances where information was not available, Google Earth satellite imagery enabled identification of built versus unbuilt land areas, open parks, and special zones like worker housing camps. Additionally, Wikimapia and user-generated content formed another source of information. For instance, on Wikimapia users mark areas and buildings in terms of use, post photos, and add other descriptors. This aids in identifying specific land uses. Moreover, a GIS program was used for spatially mapping selected indicators, such as shopping malls, which was then used to calculate land area and identify percentage from overall urban area.

Beyond the specifics is one striking finding: a dominance of empty sites. This corresponds to the experience of simply driving through the city but confirms that impression and indicates its precise extent. Combining empty sites and those that are still in the planning stage—within the overall urbanized boundary of the city—53.2 percent of the city is unused space. Most is simply empty desert with little or no vegetation. Another significant finding is the preponderance of infrastructure projects. They occupy a large part of the city's overall urban area—about 14 percent. This includes both Dubai airport sites and the two major ports, Rashid and Jebel Ali. The city's focus on such developments since its inception is thus spatially in evidence. If one were to add the percentage of road networks and bridges, the infrastructure would further increase as a percentage of the city's overall area, perhaps reaching 25–30 percent (fig. 10.3).

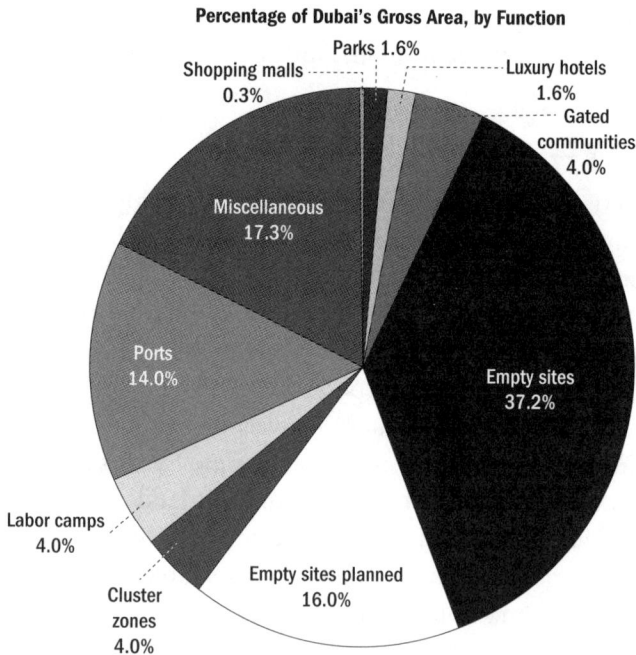

Figure 10.3. Land use indicators in Dubai's urban area, 2013. Source: Urban Research Lab, United Arab Emirates University.

Planned areas that have a very specific land use pattern, such as gated communities, labor camps, and special economic zones, occupy 4 percent each. Their location in areas and zones marked off and separated from each other affirms the city's reputation as an example of "splintered urbanism."[19] Perhaps the largest surprise is the modest footprint of shopping malls, which is about 0.3 percent of land area (the statistic that is used by planners in official city analyses). This seems to contradict the city's reputation as a major retail hub (see Molotch, chapter 11). Yet this statistic misleads because it merely refers to space occupied on the ground (inclusive of parking) without taking into account total or gross area of malls, which can be up to four stories high. Whatever the precise allocation considered as attributable to shopping, it exceeds what is given over to parks and green space. They come to about 1.6 percent of urban space, giving Dubai one of the lowest proportions of green space in the urban world (along with Istanbul, at 1.5 percent). Striking contrasts are London at 40 percent and Vienna at 51.[20]

Mapping the Developers

Property development quite famously tends to happen with large-scale projects, interlinked in complex and varied ways with the government (rulers and their kin) and prominent merchant families. The iconic Palm Island was developed by government-owned Nakheel. Downtown Dubai and Burj Khalifa are projects of the development giant Emaar (analyzed by Ponzini, chapter 3), a company initially government owned but later with public shareholders as well. This type of shared ownership (but with the government having the major stake) has become common for Dubai. There are also many privately owned entities, some belonging to well-established merchant families whose role has long been documented.[21] An example would include the family-owned Al-Futaim, based in Dubai but active in other parts of the world and involved in retail, automotive, and finance. Al-Futaim's key real estate project is Festival City, a major hotel and leisure complex overlooking Dubai Creek in one of the city's most prominent locations.

My goal was to comprehensively map these various developments, specifying the sponsor of each. This entailed creating a database that included all known projects and their developers. A tabular assessment included name of project, developer, description, and extent of acreage (hectares) of land area occupied (not total gross area).[22] Inspection of the mapped result (see figures 10.4 and 10.5) shows the extent to which new development increasingly carves up the city. The data reveal that of Dubai's overall area under development, 29 percent is being directly developed by state-owned and state-affiliated entities. Among those, developer Meydan has the largest stake at 23 percent, followed by Nakheel at 16 percent and Emaar at 14 percent. Aggregating existing and planned projects, Meydan came out the largest in terms of new projects because of the yet to be completed massive Mohammed Bin Rashid City (MBR), which will contain among its components the largest entertainment complex in the Middle East, Africa, and India. Among private developers, Al-Futaim has the largest stake at 62 percent of all such land—although, it should be noted, all private development comes to only about 1 percent of Dubai's urban area.

As per the pattern, none of these projects are done under the guidance of a specific master plan that regulates growth, establishes link-

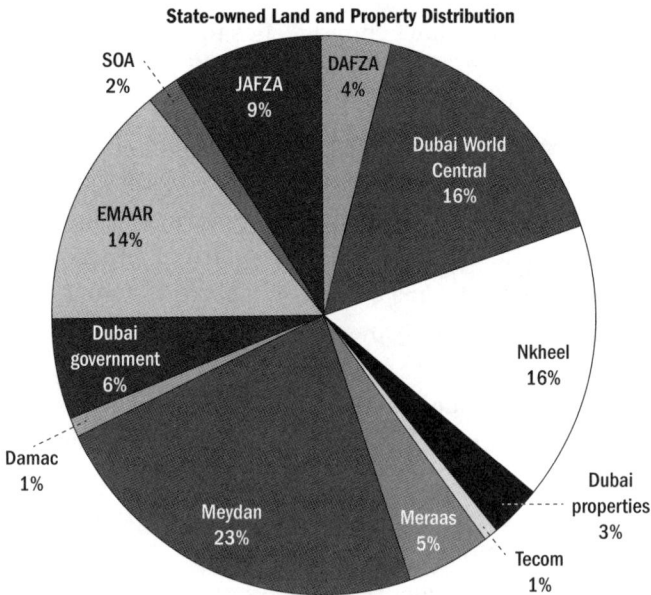

Figure 10.4. Developer distribution analysis: state-owned land and property distribution, 2013. Source: Urban Research Lab, United Arab Emirates University.

Private-Owned Land and Property Distribution

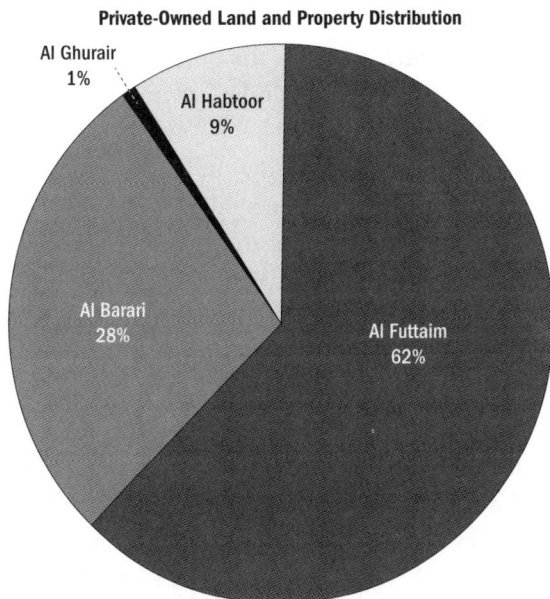

Figure 10.5. Developer distribution analysis: private-owned land and property distribution, 2013. Source: Urban Research Lab, United Arab Emirates University.

ages between various developments (roads or networks for pedestrians, for example), or makes overtures toward the creation of a viable public realm. The Dubai Structural Plan discussed previously lacks any enforcement mechanism since a regulatory agency, such as a Supreme Urban Planning Council, has not yet been formed. Instead, such matters are left to the discretion of developers who may or may not address them. Arguably, such an approach further intensifies the city's splintered urban patterning.

Case Study: Speculative Reverberations and Urban Displacement

Examining the Dubai phenomenon from a top-down perspective of master plans and quantification of urban form, reveals only part of the picture. In order to fully understand the impact of real estate speculation and project dynamics, a specific case study will help fill in the Dubai development paradigm. My focus is on the modest, low-rise district of Satwa, situated between the high-end district of Jumeirah and the ultraluxury towers of Sheikh Zayed Road. In its ramshackle appearance and informal architecture, it defies the conventional image of luxury Dubai. Walking through its streets and alleyways, one can experience a traditional place: Dubai as it used to be.[23]

Satwa has some of the oldest buildings in Dubai, where, over the years, it has evolved into a rich and diverse neighborhood—quite akin in its way to the low-rise old city centers we associate with places like Greenwich Village in New York or the Marais in Paris. It was initially home to locals who were given houses by the late Sheikh Rashid in the late 1960s in what was then the outskirts of the city. Built almost at once and in a context preceding the great flows of wealth to come, the housing is relatively modest. This explains the repetitive and standardized appearance of the residences. But as the city grew and residents came to prosper, locals moved out and a largely South Asian population moved in.[24] This did not happen in every part of the district though; indeed, at the far edge of Satwa, in the al-Wasl area, is Shabiyat al-Shorta; the so-called police neighborhood, until very recently was still occupied by Emirati nationals.

Satwa was slated for demolition to be replaced by a mixed-use development called Jumeirah Gardens. A scale model of the entire development was unveiled at the Dubai Cityscape exhibition in October 2008, occupying a large double-height room. It showed what developers had in mind: numerous skyscrapers forming a "mini-Manhattan" out of forms bending and reaching into fantastical shapes and assemblage. There was also to be a canal snaking its way through the mixed-use and residential buildings. Prior to this unveiling, residents of Satwa had been issued eviction notices, and buildings had been marked with green numbers, indicating their dreaded fate. Promptly, newspapers and filmmakers began lamenting the district's destruction. Portraying it as Dubai's version of, indeed, Greenwich Village, these reactions underscored the thirst for, and lack of, an authentic and vibrant urban living in the city. Media took up accounts of expatriates who had come to admire the district as representing a sense of authenticity that could not be felt elsewhere. A report in the English-language *Gulf News* described the district as "a tight-knit urban fabric, a dense conglomerate of houses shot through with narrow streets" that conceals "an assortment of urban riches."[25] It goes on to characterize the feelings of the more than 200,000 residents slated to lose their homes and businesses. Some buildings had already been demolished, and others were surrounded by construction fences. It was the 2008 financial crisis that put a halt to on what was planned for the district.[26] Satwa more or less remained intact. Previous residents came back, new ones moved in, and things returned to the way they were—at least for the present.

Just across the road from Satwa, a very different situation was unfolding at about the same time—one that may portend the eventual fate of Satwa as well. The previously mentioned Shabiyat al-Shorta neighborhood has been considered an extension of sorts for Satwa. Shabiyat al-Shorta is similarly composed of identical courtyard houses (from the 1970s) and was to house citizens, in this case Emirati employees of the police force. It too evolved over the years into a space that evokes old Dubai. But its fate has come closer to being irredeemably remade in the manner of Dubai's hyperdevelopment pattern—as already exists in the two mega developments that it is situated between. These are Downtown Dubai (with the Burj Khalifa as its centerpiece) and the Meeras City Walk residential and commercial complex. At present, the latter is at a considerable distance, but it represents only the first phase of the three that are planned.

The rhetoric accompanying this specific project—City Walk—usefully signals the transnational connection of stakeholders involved and the banal clichés that now permeate project depictions across the world. It is described as an "all-new outdoor lifestyle concept and destination where Dubai gets together," "the latest addition to the emirate's portfolio of luxury shopping destinations," and a "European style shopping strip."[27] The developer, Meraas, is under ownership of Dubai's ruler. Its upscale shopping and related facilities are slated to total over one million square feet. Contracts for the construction of its second phase, at an estimated cost of $250 million, have been awarded to the UK builder, Carillion (fig. 10.6). Lofty language aside, the immediate result is the displacement of the al-Shorta neighborhood residents, who are located at the edge of phase 2. Their houses will be demolished. In their place have come a skyline of cranes and a roadscape of billboards promising the good life. Published renderings show a generic luxury-shopping avenue with requisite global brands prominently featured. The only sign that this is in Dubai is a faraway view of Burj Khalifa and of a few token locals wearing traditional garb. (Nastasi's chapter 4 surveys how architectural images get deployed in such development schemes.) These images were themselves created by a transnational outfit, with offices in Dubai, Hong Kong, and London, called Place Dynamix. They describe themselves as a "placemaking consultancy," whose stated aim is "providing urban design, planning & landscape under a holistic approach that has the objective of creating great places and lasting value."[28]

The celebratory lingo obscures once again the development's severity in literally obliterating decades of urban built form. Much is lost in real and substantive neighborhood attachment, identity, memory, and of course sustainability. This became clear to me on a visit prior to its demolition. Appearing primarily as a curious ruin from a bygone era, most of its houses were abandoned and covered with graffiti and wild vegetation. Yet some were still occupied, and while I was walking among its dusty lanes, I met a resident who informed me that he too would soon have to leave. We stood in front of his house, which was completely surrounded by tended vegetation. He told me that his mother still watered the garden every day even though she knew that she would be moving soon; when neighbors asked her about why she kept doing this, she responded that she would continue to do so until the last day of their stay. This elderly local woman refused to accept that this would all be gone soon, continuing her daily routine.[29] Since my experience, the second phase has been completed with residents moving in and the original neighborhood becoming only a memory. A generic corporate landscape has been put in place, with the requisite street signage and furniture. Wide sidewalks and an upscale retail mix cater to a well-to-do clientele that is a far cry from the modest spaces and routine rounds of daily life it replaced (fig. 10.7).

Conclusion

The data of rapid change and intense speculation reinforce the impression of both material and social transiency. Even the new buildings, sparkling and profitable for a period, will likely not last long—they too will soon succumb to the inevitable march of progress. The example of Shabiyat al-Shorta embodies the speculative mind-set that has dominated Dubai's urban development paradigm. In typical neoliberal fashion, the city is not looked at as an egalitarian space for all but as a commodity.[30] The urban

Figure 10.6. The al-Shorta neighborhood in 2014, prior to demolition. Photograph by the author.

Figure 10.7. The projected replacement has become reality, May 2016. Photograph by the author.

planning structure of Dubai—in which there are no public hearings or input from city residents and in which the lines between public and private ownership are blurred—only intensifies these divisions. Outside investment is sought at all costs, and developments are accordingly mostly planned for transient residents and tourists. Indeed, as the city's rulers and decision makers clearly state, it is run like a corporation— Dubai, Inc. This is a depiction proclaimed with pride. And while this may allude to efficiency, transparency, accountability, and so forth, it also suggests a segregated and fragmented urbanity. As Peter Moore observes, "Over the years, the areas of the city occupied primarily by citizens have shifted, but the imperative to keep the locals away from the expatriates has remained. As the city has grown, new enclaves have opened to service this isolation of the citizenry, a tiny, ultra-privileged minority who are fearful of living in a city they did not build."[31] Works of fiction trade on the notion of the city as an alien space, permeated by anomie, where aimless individuals find temporary refuge. For instance, Joseph O'Neill's novel *The Dog* precisely highlights this vision of the city.[32]

Dubai is a place, one could argue, that shows how global capitalism is evolving to resemble just such a place. And while this may seem like an unnecessarily apocalyptic prediction—that Dubai will become a sort of dystopia that other cities will emulate—continued excess in the face of potential financial crisis and other future unknowns can make extreme pessimism appropriate.[33] One must also consider the substantive impact of Dubai's mode of development on the rest of the region and other parts of the world. This hyper-reliance on real estate as a major driver for city growth foretells a phenomenon I have dubbed "Dubaization."[34] Such impact can be made through direct intervention by Dubai-based developers in such places as Cairo or Rabat (see chapter 3) or through projects like the one that has been called "Dubai-on-Thames," the scheme that promises to turn the Battersea Power Station area—depicted by Nastasi in chapter 4—into "the largest retail and leisure destination in central London."[35] On the other side of Europe, it surfaces on the Belgrade waterfront where a UAE-based developer is building a Dubai-inspired project.[36] Fragile in its construction, the potential is for interconnected vulnerabilities.

It misses the mark to attribute the showy projects to sheikhs from the Gulf who turn quaint European neighborhoods into something alien.

Urban spectacle was not invented in the contemporary Gulf. London doesn't *have to* buy it. The more interesting, albeit modest, lessons would come from a focus on those neighborhoods and districts that somehow survive the onslaught of speculation. For London, Belgrade, or elsewhere in the urban world, including the Gulf, we need to refocus on spaces that have evolved organically over the years and that give their residents resilience. It is these sites that take us beyond the model of City, Inc., and offer a glimmer of hope.[37]

NOTES

1 Elsheshtawy 2010; Kanna 2013. See also Davidson 2008; Krane 2009; Davis and Monk 2007.
2 Elsheshtawy 2010.
3 *Times*, "Obituary, John Harris," March 21, 2008.
4 Lienhardt and Al-Shahi 2001.
5 Erhard 1987.
6 AlShafei 1997.
7 Municipality of Dubai 1995.
8 Maher Stino (personal communication, 2002), Egyptian city planner and one of the authors of the report, represented UNDP at the municipality.
9 Elsheshtawy 2004.
10 Elsheshtawy 2011.
11 Municipality of Dubai 2014.
12 "It's Bouncing Back," *Economist*, 2013, www.economist.com (accessed April 29, 2015).
13 "Edifice Complex," *Economist*, 2013, www.economist.com (accessed April 29, 2015).
14 Dokoupil and Menon 2014.
15 Data retrieved from www.oxfordbusinessgroup.com (Miami 59.8 percent, 90 percent foreign buyers all cash; U.S. average, 33 percent; UK 35 percent (2013), before crisis 10–15 percent, declining role of mortgage).
16 Hamdan 2013.
17 "Dubai to see $200bn invested in projects over next decade," *Arabian Business*, www.arabianbusiness.com (accessed April 29, 2015).
18 Research Grant, 2010, "Mapping Dubai: Towards an Understanding of Urban Form and Social Structure," National Research Foundation/United Arab Emirates University.
19 Graham and Marvin 2001.
20 Data source: www.skyscrapercity.com.
21 Al-Sayegh 1997.
22 This was accomplished through the GIS program Cartographica. Such an analysis allowed for measuring areas and determining percentages of distribution.

23 Elsheshtawy 2008.
24 Alawadi 2014.
25 Paradkar 2008.
26 Elsheshtawy 2011.
27 "Dubai Plans 250m Expansion of European Style Shopping Strip," Arabian Business (website), www.arabianbusiness.com (accessed April 29, 2016).
28 Place Dynamics website, www.placedynamix.com.
29 More on this can be found at the *Guardian*'s Urbanist Guide series, which also includes a video filmed in the al-Shorta neighborhood: Elsheshtawy 2014a.
30 Harvey 2009; Fainstein 2010.
31 Moore 2014.
32 O'Neill 2015.
33 Elsheshtawy 2011.
34 Dubaization website, http://dubaization.com.
35 Leech 2015.
36 Eror 2015.
37 Elsheshtawy 2013; 2014b.

REFERENCES

Alawadi, Khaled. 2014. "Urban Redevelopment Trauma: The Story of a Dubai Neighbourhood." *Built Environment* 40, no. 3: 357–375.

Al-Sayegh, Fatma. 1998. "Merchants' Role in a Changing Society: The Case of Dubai, 1900–90." *Middle Eastern Studies* 34, no. 1: 87–102.

AlShafei, Salem. 1997. "The Spatial Implications of Urban Land Policies in Dubai City." (Unpublished report) Dubai Municipality.

Davidson, Christopher M. 2008. *Dubai: The Vulnerability of Success.* New York: Columbia University Press.

Davis, Mike, and Daniel Bertrand Monk. 2007. *Evil Paradises: Dreamworlds of Neoliberalism.* New York: New Press.

Dokoupil, Martin, and Praveen Menon. 2014. "Dubai Faces Moment of Truth over Looming Property Bubble." Reuters, June 15, 2014. www.reuters.com.

Elsheshtawy, Yasser. 2004. "Redrawing Boundaries: Dubai, an Emerging Global City." In *Planning Middle Eastern Cities: An Urban Kaleidoscope in a Globalizing World. Routledge, New York*, ed. Yasser Elsheshtawy, 169–199. London: Routledge.

Elsheshtawy, Yasser. 2008. "Transitory Sites: Mapping Dubai's 'Forgotten' Urban Spaces." *International Journal of Urban and Regional Research* 32, no. 4: 968–988.

Elsheshtawy, Yasser. 2010. *Dubai: Behind an Urban Spectacle.* Planning, History and Environment Series. London: Routledge.

Elsheshtawy, Yasser. 2011. "The Prophecy of Code 46: Afuera in Dubai or Our Urban Future." *Traditional Dwellings and Settlement Review* 22, no. 11: 19–32.

Elsheshtawy, Yasser. 2013. "Where the Sidewalk Ends: Informal Street Corner Encounters in Dubai." *Cities* 31: 382–393.

Elsheshtawy, Yasser. 2014a. "An Urbanist's Guide to Dubai: 'A City Too Clean for Its Own Good?'" *Guardian*, May 13, 2014a. www.theguardian.com.

Elsheshtawy, Yasser. 2014b. "Searching for Nasser Square: An Urban Center in the Heart of Dubai." *City* 18, no. 6: 746–759.

Erhard, F Gabriel. 1987. *The Dubai Handbook*. Ahrensburg, Germany: Institute for Applied Economic Geography.

Eror, Aleks. 2015. "Belgrade's 'Top-Down' Gentrification Is Far Worse Than Any Cereal Cafe." *Guardian*, December 10, 2015. www.theguardian.com.

Fainstein, Susan S. 2010. *The Just City*. Ithaca, NY: Cornell University Press.

Graham, Stephen, and Simon Marvin. 2001. *Splintering Urbanism: Networked Infrastructures, Technological Mobilities and the Urban Condition*. London: Routledge.

Hamdan, Sarah. 2013. "U.A.E. Plans to Limit Lending to Home Buyers." *New York Times*, January 10, 2013. www.nytimes.com.

Harvey, David. 2009. *Social Justice and the City: Geographies of Justice and Social Transformation*. Athens: University of Georgia Press.

Kanna, Ahmed, and Aga Khan Program at the Harvard University Graduate School of Design. 2013. *The Superlative City: Dubai and the Urban Condition in the Early Twenty-First Century*. Cambridge, MA: Aga Khan Program at the Harvard University Graduate School of Design.

Krane, Jim. 2009. *City of Gold: Dubai and the Dream of Capitalism*. London: Macmillan.

Leech, Nik. 2015. "Welcome to 'Dubai-on-Thames.'" *National*, October 6, 2015. www.thenational.ae.

Lienhardt, Peter, and Ahmed Al-Shahi. 2001. *Sheikhdoms of Eastern Arabia*. Basingstoke, UK: Palgrave Macmillan.

Moore, Peter. 2014. "Boom, Bust and Boom in Dubai." Middle East Research and Information Project (website), June 9, 2014. www.merip.org.

Municipality of Dubai. 1995. *Structure Plan for the Dubai Urban Area (1993–2012)*. Dubai: Mimeo.

Municipality of Dubai. 2014. *Dubai 2020 Urban Masterplan*. Dubai: Mimeo.

O'Neill, Joseph. 2015. *The Dog*. New York: Vintage, Random House.

Paradkar, Shalaka. 2008. "Last Goodbye to Satwa." *Gulf News*, June 25, 2008. http://gulfnews.com.

11

Consuming Abu Dhabi

HARVEY MOLOTCH

How people consume is always a key element in shaping urban systems and constituting city distinction. Nowhere can this be more the case than in the Gulf, where it so prominently affects land use and structures social and political life. In particular, when it comes to Abu Dhabi, Doha, and Dubai—almost literally showcase cities in the plethora of the goods on view—the outsize role of consumption invites, indeed requires, a different sort of approach than is customary in urban analysis. Besides the bedrock heritage of urban studies, we also need material culture studies and related anthropological approaches[1] to grasp what goes on.

Oil to Consumption

Middle Eastern oil was discovered in Persia in 1908, in Saudi Arabia in 1938, and Abu Dhabi in 1958, where its flow began in 1964. Along the lines of the seven sheikhdoms that make up the present UAE, seven families were central to governance, with Abu Dhabi dominant, followed by Dubai. With power and wealth came privilege to consume. Although greatly concentrated in large and expanding ruling families, the massive oil wealth was not utterly monopolized. Instead, there was significant sharing among the anointed "citizens"—1.4 million at present in the UAE, about half a million (or 15 percent of residents) in superprivileged Abu Dhabi.[2] This contrasts, as one example, with oil-rich Equatorial Guinea, which, although the richest country in Africa, has average per capita income of less than $2 a day.[3] Oil-rich Trinidad, in a contrasting case, is a democracy with an inequality level about the same as the United States (Gini coefficient of 40.3). What is or is not a "resource curse"—or the distribution of benefits—thus has to do with institutional arrangements rather than being materially determined.[4]

As further part of that institutional arrangement in the Gulf is the translation of great aggregate wealth into mass consuming; whatever the conservative or "traditional" elements in the region, shopping is more than OK. Neha Vora refers to the result as a kind of "consumer citizenship."[5] Citizens partake of a "monarchical social contract," as Christopher Davidson helpfully puts it.[6] Given autocratic rule, there is "a trade of material distribution for quiescence."[7]

Some of today's richest UAE families descend from those who were monarchical opponents during the 1950s, including opposition members aligned with Nasserite pan-Arabism. For some of the rebels and for others of prominent standing, the regime granted exclusive rights to import lucrative product lines, some with a familiar luxury-brand ring—Cartier, Rolex, and Mercedes-Benz, as well as European franchises, like supermarket chains. Enterprises that started out this way have branched into such other fields as real estate and construction, forming some of the largest regional conglomerates.[8]

Abu Dhabi (the emirate with which I am most familiar) provided for souk-type retail clusters and shopping strips early on. There were officially designated "shopping festivals." Starting in the mid-1990s giant shopping malls arrived, which were to become "the quintessential urban form . . . across the Arab Gulf states."[9] Authorities facilitate with big-parcel, use-specific land assemblage.[10] As per the pattern, those close to the rulers or the rulers themselves have had large stakes.[11] The evolving product has come to include associated residential complexes, hotels, and related facilities, all now replicated (for example by the Dubai developer Emaar[12]) in other parts of the world (as documented in chapter 3). Dubai Mall receives more visitors annually than not only any other mall, but than any of the world's tourist destinations.[13]

Shopping in the Gulf has been called "the primary pastime of most men and women."[14] Although traditional dress may appear to the outsider's eye as uniform, distinctions exist in tailoring, fabric, color, and accessories—shoes, watches, and (especially for women) purses, perfume, cosmetics, and jewelry. Women nationals are expected to dress modestly (covered by the abaya over the body and the *shayla* [scarf] over the head), but such garments are themselves incorporated into the fashion system.[15] Whole wardrobes are replaced frequently and, given dust, changed within the course of a single day. Islamic women, often with exuberance, wear Western clothing when men are not present and, depending on the individual, when abroad. Children are dressed to be cute. Shopping is a craft—an avenue of human agency especially relevant in contexts where birth so influences status. The growing tourist economy provides avid buyers across many sectors. Merchant families and well-off expats—with more disposable income than their occupations would ordinarily provide—are robust participants.

House and Car

The two dominant consumption items in the UAE are critical shapers of urban form: the house and car. Let's begin with the home. The home is a primary basis for social standing and moral worth, not just in the Gulf, of course. Its appearance, layout, decor, cultural "fit," and affordances receive intense attention. Houses get filled up with much stuff—fabric, appliances, furniture, and artifacts. Urban houses are consumption machines—flagrantly different in this case from other types of shelter, including those from the nomadic past. Farah Al-Nakib argues that with the decline of old distinctions of Bedouin and merchant life, the size and extravagance of one's house replace occupation as the key status marker.[16]

In the case of the UAE, the existence of these extravagant homes and their particular configurations result from government policy going back to the country's founding or even before. Under the beneficence of the ruler, citizens receive allocations of land and or dwellings. Marriage (at least if to another national) creates eligibility. Residences vary in size and amenity with the changing prosperity of the country, land availability, and status of the beneficiary.[17] Starting with modest quarters at the time of the UAE's founding, much larger houses became common, sometimes involving a compound of sons, wives, and grandchildren grouped around a main structure. Provision can take the form of a physical dwelling, a grant to refurbish an existing house, and/or an interest-free mortgage. Citizens have some choice in the selection of the type of grant.[18] Also involved have been lotteries to determine who gets what and when. At least for some periods, the ruler not only gifts land for homes, but also land to develop for commercial use, including as residential income from noncitizens.

The government also subsidizes house utilities (for citizens, not for expats), further encouraging large houses and high-energy use. According to planning officials in Abu Dhabi with whom I have met, citizens prefer freestanding single-family houses, a pattern also observed for Oman[19] and Kuwait.[20] They typically avoid the high-rise clusters that attract affluent foreign nationals, in part because (as observed for a Kuwait project[21]) they provide insufficient gender privacy. Not only is there enthusiasm for single-family dwellings, but also for newly built versus "used" houses, with those better off thus likely helping to push city boundaries outward. Land development does not follow either strong zoning rules or the usual capitalist land-market discipline. Indeed, at earlier times, there was no property market at all, just gifts and inheritance. Given the open desert, there is extensive leapfrog growth as holders of development privilege enact their projects in a somewhat helter-skelter pattern. This creates vast swaths of empty space (as documented by Elsheshtawy in chapter 10).

The automobile is the consumer good of sprawl. From the urban beginning, a grid-based street system was designed to allow "swift traffic and easy navigation."[22] A government petrol subsidy (as much as two-thirds off market value[23]) and generous road and highway spending help further lock the car in. When land and housing grants are bestowed, congestion is not much considered and indeed can exacerbate problems. So, for example, recipients can use their grants only to build houses in the emirate from which they come. Thus, booming employment in Dubai and Abu Dhabi generates long-distance commutes (which can be well over an hour) for citizen-residents of perimeter sheikhdoms.[24] Cars themselves offer spaces for listening (and viewing) entertainment in air conditioning. With the heavy use of tinted glass, they also provide a way for women drivers and passengers to take off headscarves and adjust clothing in a private enclosure. Given large family sizes (although birthrates are now sharply declining[25]) and the big merchandise loads routinely ferried from malls, cars are typically large in dimension and engine size. Speeding fines can be waived by the authorities for privileged individuals.[26] Another part of the car-house system is heavy water use, to keep cars clean and highway plantings green and prettily colorful—"invariably" in the national colors (red and green), as observed of Bahrain's so-called

VIP roads.[27] For Abu Dhabi, highway landscaping uses over 21 billion cubic meters of groundwater annually—a total higher than for all uses across all of the United Kingdom (although less than for countries like France and semi-arid Spain).[28] As collateral national benefit, billboards prominently display rulers' faces (but rarely those of other persons), often with a patriotic message.

Largely omitted from this schema are amenities for the manual and service workers, mostly an afterthought in the urban spatial regime. They lack the houses and cars and often find themselves with only minimal public transit access. Frequently located in interstices and at the geographic margin, they make do with spartan quarters, picking up rides when possible, and using bits of leftover city space, including road shoulders and planted roundabouts for social gathering.[29] Vast worker camps, remote from other types of urban users and services, contribute a still more distinctive land use and mobility pattern. As pedestrians, the occupants must depend on irregular sidewalks (where they exist at all) and make-do street crossings, taking on risk from cars speeding down the wide boulevards.[30]

UAE car-related death rates are far higher than in other rich places; traffic deaths are more than threefold that of the United States and sevenfold that of the United Kingdom.[31] A sport among adolescent males is "joyriding" and "drifting"—making use of highway expanse to impress one another: "All we have is streets and cars" one of his Riyadh informants told the anthropologist Pascal Menoret.[32] This form of recreation is apparently not limited to Saudi Arabia, where Menoret did his fieldwork. He remarks that his Riyadh joyriders contrast their road styles with their counterparts, thought to be less skilled and daring, in other parts of the Gulf.

Skyline as Seduction

The much-remarked-on skylines of UAE cities (including, for example, in Nastasi's chapter 4) are arguably still another aspect of consumption—not just visual backdrop, but something imbibed and, at least in some ways, appreciated. Although Emirati do not often live within the supertalls, they do see them, and—given the flat landscape—from most everywhere. The fact that the skylines are so frequently used to brand UAE cities—"to suggest significance"[33] to the outside world—does not mean they do not also have an internal impact. They add some excitement and glamor to the shops, restaurants, and services they adjoin or house. With workers' camps separate from the glamorous malls, evidence of social exploitation and production effluvia do not intrude on the shopping experience.[34] Real estate spectacles (as explained by Ponzini in chapter 3) also help draw in foreign investors.

A striking analysis of "skyline seduction" comes from some distance away, from Delhi. Based on his extensive interviews and ethnographic work among both bureaucrats and poor residents, the anthropologist D. Asher Ghertner concludes that even for its most vulnerable residents, the emerging Delhi skyline gives pride.[35] Delhi's affluent social groups, as perhaps to be expected, take satisfaction in Delhi's "world-class" reconfiguration. But, as Ghertner also observes, those at the lowest rungs—occupants of slums set for demolition to make way for a more glamorous Delhi—also take pride in being a part of the transformation. Although concerned about what will become of them, these low-caste urban dwellers are not just resigned to their fate but see in it a collective "hope" (Ghertner's word) for the future. They somehow think, however vaguely, that as Delhi rises, so will they. If such a group can make a positive out of something so against their interests (as it appears to be), it is more than reasonable to think the dazzling UAE metropolis can operate similarly, at least for the citizens whose country is being daily built before their eyes.

Vagaries of Job

Sometimes it is work that takes citizens into and about their impressive buildings. Places of work, particularly where citizens have their offices, commonly have marble lobbies, stylish reception rooms, and other such amenities. We need to keep in mind that "work" and lifestyle are less separate from one another in the UAE than in other places. Emiratis do not don overalls and travel to industrial zones. For a good while, probably a generation, there have been, in the words of the founding documentarian of Gulf life, Frauke Heard-Bey, "almost no nationals who are manual laborers in the UAE." She published a first version of that assessment in 1982.[36] Nor are Emirati citizens likely to labor over what is a normal workday. One official estimate puts average annual working days at 180 in the

UAE public sector (where citizen employment is concentrated) versus 275 in the UAE private sector.[37]

Jobs are often allocated, directly or indirectly, on the basis of family or other status-based connections—wasta is the common term for connections that can be used to gain favor from higher-ups. Workplace position thus often derives from outside the workplace; jobs and sometimes the very creation of ministries and agencies that house them were a different way to distribute goods, another source of what Steffen Hertog calls (congruent with what goes on in land use) "administrative sprawl."[38] Citizen-employees receive important-sounding titles, cars, travel, drivers, and other perks. Seen this way, jobs are on the consumer side of the ledger—at least more so than in most other parts of the world. But, again by comparison, whereas the Western welfare system and its union base arose, at the end of the day, to enable people to work under better conditions (and yes, also have a decent material life), much about the Gulf welfare system entitles Emiratis not to work at all, or at least to work less.[39] "By and large" the Gulf regimes "do not put cash directly into the pockets of citizens"[40] but instead provide grants, loans, contracts, welfare, and jobs, and not just in the public sector. The sheikhdoms also subsidize nationals' private sector jobs if that is where they are employed.

According to Kamrava's report on Qatar,[41] all Qatari citizens are "guaranteed" salaries starting (in 2012 dollars) at $4,400 per month for high school graduates and $6,100 per month with a college degree. This much understates incomes since it is common for a single person to hold multiple positions and to participate in partnerships with foreigners who are not entitled, on their own, to hold a majority stake in a given enterprise.

Large-Scale Culture Imports

What about the import of costly cultural institutions? As with Hertog, who has weighed possible economic benefits (see chapter 12), I come up skeptical as to "rational" explanations. I consider the cultural stuff to be part of the consumption apparatus (which aligns with Hertog again). But unlike cars or clothing, they are consumption at the royal scale (recall Versailles or Schönbrunn). They have, it has been said, "stoked the vanity" of the ruling families, whose members pick them off the world-class shelf.[42] Plausibly an aspect of Gulf efforts at economic diversification, the museums can build the tourist industry. In Doha, the head of the Qatar Museums Authority (and sister of the ruling emir) is quoted as having the goal of making Qatar "the Mecca of Museums."[43] Tourism is consistent with still another goal often voiced, and that is raising citizens' cultural knowledge and world awareness. Fair enough.

But these institutions—let's start with the museums—are alien, both in development style and raison d'être. Quite beyond the type of art they will likely contain, the very idea of a museum "collection" is locally strange. So are the conventions of curation and conservation. In contrast to other parts of the world and also in the Middle East (e.g., Egypt, Lebanon), locals are not a museum-oriented constituency. Peggy Levitt in her survey of national museums around the world, notes in regard to Qatar efforts: "Everyone admits it's not easy to get Qataris to visit museums."[44] I doubt the evolving tourist profile looks very museum-like either.

As an architectural outcome, nothing could have been more successful than Doha's magnificent Museum of Islamic Art, opened in 2008. At the urging of its designer (I. M. Pei), it was constructed on a site built from the sea so that no adjacent structure could compromise its visual allure.[45] But it has had a somewhat modest attendance record: 212,000 visitors for the year 2012. To put that in perspective, New York's New Museum in SoHo, which is one-sixth as large, has 400,000 annual visitors; LA's Broad Museum had 400,000 within its first five months.[46] And Doha is building seventeen other museums, including a very large modern art center (designed by Jean Nouvel). Abu Dhabi's Louvre is about five times the size of the Whitney's new museum in Chelsea; the Abu Dhabi Guggenheim (now held back with money problems) is set to be seven times the size of the founding institution on Fifth Avenue. These are perhaps experiments to learn if glorious museums can feed economic development more generally—the vaunted "Bilbao effect."[47] But these Gulf city museums are repeats; in business-economics terms, they lack first-mover advantage, something discussed by Ponzini in chapter 3, albeit using different language.

Importing university campuses can be thought of as aligned with the founding sheikh's oft-repeated pronouncement, here taken from a large placard greeting travelers at the Abu Dhabi airport: "The best investment of our wealth is in creating cultured and educated citizens. We have to be swift and make our progress in education faster than our progress in any field."[48] Of the various academic campuses, the furthest along is the New York University campus (NYU Abu Dhabi), described in detail by Hilary Ballon in chapter 6. Sharing Saadiyat Island with the museum sites, it is unquestionably a cosmopolitan success, from the start becoming one of the most selective universities in the world. But the local payoff is not clear. After the government's multi-billion-dollar investment, and after five years of operation, Emiratis made up only 14 percent of the 2017 entering class. The sheikhdom provides the great majority of students with free tuition, room, board, and travel. NYU itself and its American-based benefactors make no financial outlay. Providing less by way of subsidy (compared to NYU Abu Dhabi), Qatar's six U.S. academic institutions in Doha (and one each from France and the United Kingdom) are all strikingly world-class architecturally and themselves heavily subsidized. Here too, it is not apparent how the campuses will yield up direct development benefits—although a larger proportion of students are region-based and/or paying tuition. Perhaps the campuses offer a further cultural amenity for high-skilled expats.[49]

Risks and Hazards

Part of the consumption matrix is careful management of its cultural and political textures. Retail can mean risqué clothing and T-shirts with disrespectful slogans, not to mention sex toys and condoms (Frederick's of Hollywood has an Abu Dhabi branch). To "protect the different communities from harmful influences" (as the law requires),[50] promotion of alcohol and tobacco is greatly constrained—but in ways where there are work-arounds to make it available to non-Muslims (as described below). Some types of product are more in the clear, like cars, motorcycles, athletic equipment, and other manly goods; horses and camels also get some wholesome play, in terms of international competitions (yes, camel racing). Doha's 2022 World Cup sponsorship (stadia and infrastructure costs of $140 billion!) is the most expensive illustration.[51] Nostalgia goods that evoke Emirati history, like baskets and objects of clay or leather, are also "politically safe" and readily sold at shops and heritage fairs.[52] Dense retail of most any sort, as with other tourist facilities, must be—without exception—maintained as secure from violence, but without conspicuous display of police power. Patrol must be discrete.

Museums, even in the context of the West's most sophisticated cities, have run afoul of those in authority. Displeasures from patrons, funders, or police have, over the years, interfered with shows at the Guggenheim, the Brooklyn Museum, and the Museum of the City of New York. Gulf authorities appear far more interventionist. Three ancient Greek statues, displayed as part of a 2013 Qatar Olympic exhibition, had to be removed because they were held to depict nudity.[53] In another Doha case, officials judged a monumental outdoor work of two contemporary soccer players (fully clothed) as excessively violent (they were removed).[54] At about the same time, albeit for uncertain reasons, the "annual" Doha Tribeca Film Festival ended after a four-year run.[55] Gulf cultural institutions are subject to what the *Financial Times* referred to as an "arbitrary, often unpredictable state interference in public speech" that "still hangs over the region's artists," as well as over art venues, like for example Art Dubai.[56]

Universities of course routinely risk opprobrium; professors give provocative lectures; student groups put on drag shows and organize demonstrations. It is going to be a challenge to contain these pulsations. At the other end of the political-cultural spectrum come objections from the institutional "home country" over labor practices and the implications of religious discrimination. Protesters picketed the Guggenheim and NYU in New York over Abu Dhabi labor practices,[57] which, along with visa denials for certain NYU professors, brought unwelcome coverage in the *New York Times* and the *Guardian*.

For their part, UAE citizens travel as tourists, investors, and, at times, for their education—using their world-class airports and airlines. Besides buying abroad, some Emirati have now experienced life on U.S. and British university campuses. Indeed, this may be another reason for the massive cultural investments. According to the American social scientist Calvert Jones, who has immersed herself in an Emirati elite setting, this younger group's "longing" and "nostalgia" for their college days[58] make them want to have such things back home. The massive cultural investments may not be simply economic, but also driven by sentiment.

Work-Arounds

Because of the notice they bring, Gulf work-arounds come into prominent view. Of direct relevance to our urban focus, the presence of problematic activities and types of people are spatially segregated. Some neighborhoods, beaches, hospitals, and even airport waiting areas are reserved for UAE citizens. Other spaces, like the labor camps, are no-go areas except for security personnel and their migrant workforce residents. High-end Western hotels, themselves typically spatially demarcated, routinely serve alcohol; working people's cafés never do. I was once in a hotel restaurant (at the middle-middle price level) where beer was served at our table from a porcelain teapot into dainty English-style teacups with floral patterns. There are distinct alcohol shops in malls, sometimes branded by a given supermarket chain, but accessed through separate routes (for example via an elevator serving it alone from the mall parking lot). They are otherwise Western-style wine and liquor stores bountifully stocked with wines identified by region of origin. Even here, sales are supposed to be limited to those who have procured special licenses to buy it (foreigners qualify). Everyone knows, at least in my Abu Dhabi experience, that when Westerners pay with cash, they are never questioned. One particular store, the Barracuda Beach Resort, routinely services Saudis who drive or fly in to stock up.[59]

As a routine matter, pork is sold. In the back of supermarkets (enterprises linked to non-UAE chains, like French-owned Carrefour) are doors unmarked except for the words, "For Non-Muslims Only." Step inside and you are in the midst of packaged pork products—meats that are familiarly pork, such as bacon and chops, but also items that I, at least, never knew had pork in them, like Pop Tarts and foods made with pork-based gelatin or lard. This is the "Pork Room," sometimes marked with those words, although not in figure 11.1. By law in Dubai, shoppers with pork products in their baskets have to go to a separate checkout stand, marked for pork.

There are the more usual elements of work-around that accommodate, albeit awkwardly and with caution (this is *not* Las Vegas), the usual demimonde—prostitution, drugs, gay sex, and gambling. Even in more puritanical Saudi Arabia, writes an expert on the country, "I was not only offered drugs and alcohol, but also 'woman for good time.' "[60] Some offenses are made difficult to prosecute because of offenders' rank or special circumstance, including being a tourist. Having a plethora of restrictions means they can be selectively relaxed or enforced, ad hoc, to spatially locate particular social types and activities.

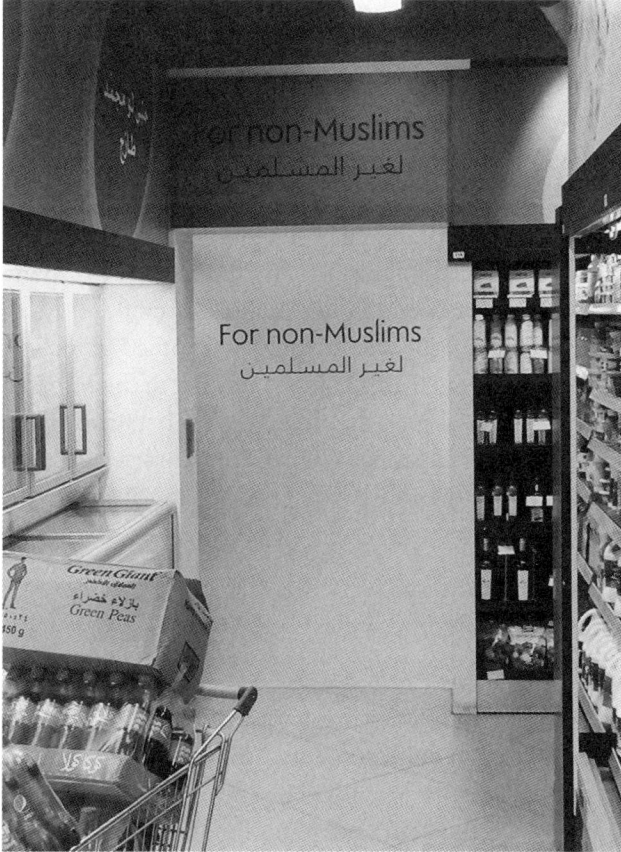

Figure 11.1. Pork room in rear of Spinney's supermarket, Saadiyat Island, Abu Dhabi, 2016. Photograph by the author.

Big houses, the hotel industry, shops, and highways—along with the construction to create it all—generate an enormous need for "help." "For every Emirati who works in the private sector, there are eighty-one foreigners," says Michael Herb.[61] "You need slaves to build pyramids," as one cryptic maxim puts it.[62] Standards—world-class standards—necessitate clean surfaces, crisp laundry, and dusting off desert sands. The high-consuming expats are also part of the agenda, compensated with high salaries, large living quarters, and access to cheap domestic labor—for a lifestyle otherwise above their station.[63] Much more than the production apparatus—which, in the case of oil, is capital intensive—this is a labor-intensive regime.

Gulf citizens do not take to heavy labor, waiting on people, or even routine white-collar jobs. There are also gender constraints. UAE women, with relatively low but rising rates of labor participation, are only in jobs considered appropriate; direct contact with men (as customers or even coworkers) can be problematic. Trying to sell the idea of work in the tourist industry to either men or women, a high-ranking employer spokeswoman announced, "Being hospitable was in Emiratis' blood." She is further quoted, "A person flourishes when in service to others, and servitude is nowhere to be found in hospitality. Through our work, we are trying to dispel this myth."[64] For anyone accustomed to life in the UAE, it does not seem like a myth; obsequiousness (from the foreign workers) seems the order of the day, as is the absence of Emirati women in anything resembling a service occupation. Having a temporary labor force of permanent outsiders is a grand work-around for the absence of a normal workforce.

Adjustments and Outcomes

Given all the complexities, including periodic demands for reform (and, in some cases, its limited achievement—such as in Kuwait[65]), what holds it all together, at least in my argument, is the massive consumption provided to certain segments. Yes, there has been open rebellion, not only in the early years of the country's founding, but also in sync with the Arab Spring. (A petition drive for reform in Abu Dhabi led to arrests and jailings.) Yet even when demands are "couched in elaborate terms of courtesy" (the words in the *Economist*'s reportage[66]), the result has been only symbolic citizen inclusion. In one sphere, appropriate perhaps in the high-gadget consumption environment, the UAE is "far in advance" of Western democracies—that is in e-government.[67] Government agencies provide direct access to official municipal offices for routine services and information. Perhaps it gives off at least an illusion of transparency.

As politically useful, authorities can sweeten the consumption pot, ratcheting up salaries, welfare payments, and household subsides. In the context of Arab Spring anxieties, Saudi Arabia provided a "bonus" of $130 billion in extra salary and welfare payments,[68] generating a very high year-on-year increase in consumer spending.[69] When King Salman ascended to the Saudi throne in 2015, another $32 billion was dispensed—even in the face of the falling oil prices. All this is in addition to unpublished "off-budget" programs privately controlled by the king. In an incisive assertion, Michael Herb says, referring to the Gulf oil states more generally, the ruling families protect "the interests of the expatriates from the citizens while, at the same time, encouraging citizens to cling to the ruling families as the defenders of Emirati identity in a country populated largely by expatriates."[70]

As always it is no small trick to keep things aligned so that one set of officials—say, in security operations—do not disturb the leisure, education, or retail sector. The agencies have to at least acknowledge one another's projects and proclivities. Parallel agencies in opaque pecking orders need to live and let live (see Hertog, chapter 12)—"colluding social hierarchies," in one observer's description of Dubai governance.[71] This is indeed a politics. The resulting settlement across diverse social, religious, and dietary orientations is thus not some fixed adjudication, but a dynamic encapsulation of alternative moral, political, and practical exigencies. Consumption does not just "reflect" the settlement but is an ongoing force in shaping it.

As long as the honey flows, the ruler provides marriage dowries, child allotments, health care, education, houses, businesses, land, travel, and enough money for people to live the kind of life that a great patriarch works out for his descendants. Embedded in the process, there are carrots and sticks, honors, celebrations, and discipline. It is a relationship of mutually reinforcing material and nonmaterial coherence, baked into the daily rounds and modes of urban life. The social practice of work-around handles tribulations as they might arise. Spatial segregation comes with the territory. The urban in these showcase cities is too distinctive to be classified as simply advanced or as simply reactionary. It has been, perhaps fittingly, termed an "alternative modernity,"[72] one that, I would say, has shopping at its distinctive core.

NOTES

1　See, for example, Douglas and Isherwood 1979; Miller 2012.

2　It takes only one "starter" male to spawn a very large set of descendants, given polygamy and affluence. Ibn Saud, the founder of Saudi Arabia (the only country to be named after a living person), is said to have yielded seven thousand descendants after "three or four" generations. See Mitchell 2011, 211.

3　Herb 2014, 188, citing IMF data.

4 Eibl and Hertog n.d.

5 Vora 2008, 379 as cited in Kanna 2011, 183.

6 Davidson 2008. See also Beblawi and Luciani 1987; Crystal 1995.

7 Hertog 2010, 18. In still more apologetic terminology, there is a democratic "deficit" (Heard-Bey 2005, 367).

8 See Crystal 1995, 8d as cited in Hanieh 2011, 12.

9 Al-Nakib 2016, 5.

10 Davidson 2008, 111.

11 For example, Sheikh Surur bin Muhammad Al-Nayhan was founding proprietor
of the Abu Dhabi Mall (Davidson 2008, 112).

12 Kanna 2011, 185.

13 Sophia 2015. Dubai Mall was invoked as a bright shining model for the troubled
New Jersey "American Dream Meadow Lands" project.

14 The quote is from Davidson 2008, 181, writing of Dubai.

15 Bucar 2017.

16 Al-Nakib 2016.

17 For an example of one recent program of the sheikh's orders to distribute houses
and land (including an image of what is to be built), see "Mohamed Bin Zayed
Orders Distribution of Houses and Plots of Lands to Citizens," www.uaeinteract.
com (accessed April 26, 2017).

18 Davidson 2015, 51.

19 Nebel 2014, 61.

20 Al-Nakib 2016.

21 Mahgoub 2008.

22 Menoret 2014, 18.

23 This is based on an estimate provided by Davidson 2015, 51 for the UAE in 2011.

24 MacLean n.d.

25 Official birthrate data, such as it is, has been critiqued as understating birthrates among nationals, since the "national" data is said to confound expatriate
birthrates, which are much lower with birthrates overall; see Davidson 2015, 115.
In the Saudi case, less confounded by expatriate family patterns, 80 percent of the
population was under thirty, Nolan 2013.

26 Davidson 2015, 150.

27 Doherty 2017, 113.

28 Abu Dhabi Environmental Agency, as cited in Dang et. al. 2017, 52; for United Kingdom and other countries, see World Bank, "Annual freshwater withdrawals, total
(billion cubic meters)," https://data.worldbank.org (accessed December 12, 2017).

29 Elsheshtawy 2015; Doherty 2017, 123.

30 Even in the U.S. context, pedestrians in areas designed for cars have high rates of
death from vehicles just as their jerry-rigged living spaces increase danger from
house fires (see Benediktsson 2017).

31 World Health Organization 2015.

32 Menoret 2014, 148.

33 Elsheshtawy 2010, 133.

34 See Vitalis 2006, 69, also Crot 2013.

35 Ghertner 2015.

36 Heard-Bey 2005, 372.

37 Fasano and Goyal 2004, 7 as cited in Herb 2014, 20.

38 Hertog 2010, 51. See also Herb 2014, 21.

39 The Saudi regime forced the private sector in 2011 to expand employment by 200,000 citizens, a boost of 35 percent in private employment in a single year (Herb 2014, 8).

40 Herb 2014, 18.

41 Kamrava 2013, 131.

42 Herb 2014, 118.

43 Adham 2008, 239.

44 Levitt 2015, 114.

45 Scharfenort 2014, 74.

46 "Over a Million Visit Museum of Islamic Art," *The Peninsula*, December 31, 2012, http://thepeninsulaqatar.com.

47 Ponzini 2011; Ponzini and Nastasi 2011.

48 Sheikh Zayed bin Sultan al Nahyan (undated). See "Welcome Message," http://emiratesnationalschools.com.

49 Lieto 2015.

50 Wam 2013.

51 Bromber 2014, 123.

52 MacLean n.d.

53 Doha News Team 2013.

54 Mackey 2013.

55 See "Doha Tribeca Film Festival," http://variety.com.

56 Gara 2012. See also Bharadwaj 2013.

57 Of media coverage, see, for example, Azimi 2016.

58 Jones 2015, 34.

59 Davidson 2015, 256.

60 Valentine, as quoted in review by Pelham 2016.

61 Herb 2014, 24.

62 Creischer and Siekmann 2014, 213.

63 Domestic workers are excluded from minimal protections now afforded to other workers. Dependent for room and board on their employer, they are under official "guardianship" of their employer. Although their lives are often depicted as arduous and even desperate, some are satisfied with their positions and dread, more than anything else, being returned to their country of origin (Parrenas and Silvery 2016).

64 Moukhallati 2015, 7.

65 Among the most dramatic displays of internal variation is the Bin Laden family whose vast wealth devolves from contracts to "build virtually every road in the

country" (Mayer 2001). Surviving Bin Ladens include graduates of Harvard and the University of Southern California, as well as devotees of disco, tennis, and lifestyles of the rich and famous (see Mayer 2001).

66 "Getting Twitchy about Democracy," *Economist*, 2011, www.economist.com (accessed April 5, 2016).

67 Davidson 2008, 165.

68 Kulish and Mazzetti 2016.

69 Davidson 2015, 214.

70 Herb 2014, 201.

71 Kanna 2011, 140.

72 Al-Rasheed, 282.

REFERENCES

Adham, Khaled. 2008. "Rediscovering the Island: Doha's Urbanity from Pears to Spectacle." In *The Evolving Arab City: Tradition, Modernity, and Urban Development*, ed. Yasser Elsheshtawy, 218–257. London: Routledge.

Al-Nakib, Farah. 2016. *Kuwait Transformed: A History of Oil and Urban Life*. Stanford, CA: Stanford University Press.

Al-Rasheed, Madawi. 2013. *A Most Masculine State: Gender, Politics, and Religion in Saudi Arabia*. Cambridge: Cambridge University Press.

Azimi, Negar. 2016. "The Gulf Art War." *New Yorker*, December 19–25, 2016: 74–79.

Benediktsson, Mike Owen. 2017. "Beyond the Sidewalk: Pedestrian Risk and Material Mismatch in the American Suburbs." *Mobilities* 12, no. 1: 76–96.

Bharadwaj, Vinita. 2013. "Artists and Shows Navigate Cultural Boundaries in U.A.E." *New York Times*, March 13, 2013. www.nytimes.com.

Bromber, Katrin. 2014. "The Sporting Way: Sport as Branding Strategy in the Gulf States." In *Under Construction: Logics of Urbanism in the Gulf Region*, ed. Steffen Wippel, Katrin Bromber, Christian Steiner, and Birgit Krawietz, 119–130. Surrey, UK: Ashgate.

Bucar, Elizabeth. 2017. *Pious Fashion: How Muslim Women Dress*. Cambridge, MA: Harvard University Press.

Creischer, Alice, and Andreas Siekmann. 2014. "Universalism in Art and the Art of Universalism: Thoughts on the 'Globalization' of the Art System, Taking the United Arab Emirates as Example." In *Under Construction: Logics of Urbanism in the Gulf Region*, ed. Steffen Wippel, Katrin Bromber, Christian Steiner, and Birgit Krawietz, 211–219. Surrey, UK: Ashgate.

Crot, Laurence. 2013. "Planning for Sustainability in Non-democratic Polities: The Case of Masdar City." *Urban Studies* 50, no. 13: 2809–2825.

Crystal, Jill. 1995. *Oil and Politics in the Gulf: Rulers and Merchants in Kuwait and Qatar*. Cambridge: Cambridge University Press.

Davidson, Christopher M. 2009. *Abu Dhabi: Oil and Beyond*. New York: Columbia University Press.

Davidson, Christopher M. 2012. *After the Sheikhs: The Coming Collapse of the Gulf Monarchies*. London: C. Hurst & Co.

Davidson, Christopher M. 2015. *The Vulnerability of Success*. New York: Columbia University Press.

Dang, Alice Y. Raphael Gernath, Filipe Mello Rose, and Beatrice Mercier. 2017. *Building Visions with Glass and Steel*. Dubai study report, Science Po Urban School.

Doha News Team. 2013. "Nude Statues Removed from Qatar Olympic Exhibition." *Doha News* (online), April 24, 2013. https://dohanews.co.

Doherty, Gareth. 2017. *Paradoxes of Green: Landscapes of a City-State*. Los Angeles: University of California Press.

Douglas, Mary, and Baron Isherwood. 1979. *The World of Goods: Toward an Anthropology of Consumption*. London: Routledge.

Easterling, Keller. 2014. "Zone: The Spatial Softwares of Extrastatecraft." *Places Journal* (online). https://placesjournal.org.

Eibl, Ferdinand, and Steffen Hertog. (n.d.) "Oil Is What You Make of It? Rents and Public Goods Provision in the Middle East and Sub-Saharan Africa." CPE MENA (Middle East and North Africa) concept paper, London School of Economics.

Elsheshtawy, Yasser. 2010. *Dubai: Behind an Urban Spectacle*. London: Routledge.

Elsheshtawy, Yasser. 2015. "Little Bangladesh—Mapping Abu Dhabi." Lecture given at NYUAD, Washington Square, September 25, 2015.

Gara, Tom. 2012. "Authorities Censor Art Dubai." FT.com, March 24, 2012. www.ft.com.

Garfinkel, Harold. 1967. *Studies in Ethnomethodology*. New York: Polity Press.

Ghertner, Asher. 2015. *Rule by Aesthetics*. Oxford: Oxford University Press.

Hanieh, Adam. 2011. *Capitalism and Class in the Gulf Arab States*. New York: Palgrave Macmillan.

Heard-Bey, Frauke. 1982. *From Trucial States to United Arab Emirates*. London: Acre House.

Heard-Bey, Frauke. 2005. "The United Arab Emirates: Statehood and Nation-Building in a Traditional Society." *Middle East Journal* 59, no. 3: 357–375.

Henry, Clement M., and Rodney Wilson, eds. 2004. *The Politics of Islamic Finance*. Edinburgh: Edinburgh University Press.

Herb, Michael. 2014. *The Wages of Oil: Parliaments and Economic Development in Kuwait and the UAE*. Ithaca, NY: Cornell University Press.

Hertog, Steffen. 2010. *Princes, Brokers, and Bureaucrats*. Ithaca, NY: Cornell University Press.

Jensen, Boris Brorman. 2014. "Masdar City: A Critical Retrospection." In *Under Construction: Logics of Urbanism in the Gulf Region*, ed. Steffen Wippel, Katrin Bromber, Christian Steiner, and Birgit Krawietz, 45–54. Surrey, UK: Ashgate.

Jones, Calvert. 2015. "Seeing Like an Autocrat: Liberal Social Engineering in an Illiberal State." *Perspectives on Politics*, 13, no. 1: 24–41.

Kahf, Monzer. 2004. "Islamic Banks: The Rise of a New Power Alliance of Wealth and Shari'a Scholarship." In *The Politics of Islamic Finance*, ed. Clement M. Henry and Rodney Wilson, 17–36. Edinburgh: Edinburgh University Press.

Kamrava, Mehran. 2013. *Qatar: Small State, Big Politics.* Ithaca, NY: Cornell University Press.

Kanna, Ahmed. 2011. *Dubai: The City as Corporation.* Minneapolis: University of Minnesota Press.

Keshavarzian, Arang. 2010. "Geopolitics and the Genealogy of Free Trade Zones in the Persian Gulf." *Geopolitics* 15, no. 2: 263–289.

Kulish, Nicholas, and Mark Mazzetti. 2016. "Saudi Royal Family Is Still Spending in an Age of Austerity." *New York Times,* December 27, 2016. www.nytimes.com.

Leigh, Nolan. 2011. "Under Reform? Saudi Arabia and the King's Dilemma." Brookings Doha Center Policy Briefing, May 2011.

Levitt, Peggy. 2015. Artifacts and Allegiances: How Museums Put the Nation and the World on Display. Oakland, CA: University of California Press.

Lieto, Laura. 2015. "Cross-Border Mythologies: The Problem with Traveling Planning Ideas." *Planning Theory* 14, no. 2: 115–129.

Luciani, Giacomo, and Hazem Beblawi, eds. 1987. *The Rentier State.* London: Croom Helm.

Mackey, Robert. 2013. "Qatar Removes Statue of Zidane's Head Butt after Complaints." *New York Times,* October 30, 2013. https://thelede.blogs.nytimes.com.

MacLean, Matthew. (n.d.) "Suburbanization, National Space and Place, and the Geography of Heritage in the United Arab Emirates." Unpublished MS, History and Middle Eastern and Islamic Studies, New York University.

Mahdavy, Hossein. 1970. "The Pattern and Problems of Economic Development in Rentier States: The Case of Iran." In *Studies in the Economic History of Middle East,* ed. M. A. Cook, 428–467. Oxford: Oxford University Press.

Mahgoub, Yasser. 2008. "Kuwait: Learning from a Globalized City." In *The Evolving Arab City: Tradition, Modernity and Urban Development,* ed. Yasser Elsheshtawy, 152–83. London: Routledge.

Mayer, Jane. 2001. "The House of bin Laden." *New Yorker,* November 12, 2001: 54–65.

Menoret, Pascal. 2014. *Joyriding in Riyadh: Oil, Urbanism, and Road Revolt.* Cambridge: Cambridge University Press.

Miller, Daniel. 2012. *Consumption and Its Consequences.* New York: Polity Press.

Mitchell, Timothy. 2011. *Carbon Democracy: Political Power in the Age of Oil.* London: Verso.

Moukhallati, Dana. 2015. "Drive to Recruit More Emiratis," *National,* November 3, 2015. www.thenational.ae.

Nebel, Sonja. 2014. "Tourism and Urbanization in Oman: Sustainable and Socially Inclusive?" In *Under Construction: Logics of Urbanism in the Gulf Region,* ed. Steffen Wippel, Katrin Bromber, Christian Steiner, and Birgit Krawietz, 55–69. Surrey, UK: Ashgate.

Parrenas, Rachel Salazar, and Rachel Silvery. 2016. "Domestic Workers Refusing Neo-slavery in the UAE." *Contexts* 15: 336–341.

Pelham, Nicholas. 2016. "In Saudi Arabia: Can It Really Change?" *New York Review of Books,* October 11, 2016. www.nybooks.com.

Ponzini, Davide. 2011. "Large Scale Development Projects and Star Architecture in the Absence of Democratic Politics: The Case of Abu Dhabi, UAE." *Cities* 28: 251–259.

Ponzini, Davide, and Michele Nastasi. 2011. *Starchitecture: Scenes, Actors and Spectacles in Contemporary Cities.* Turin: Allemandi.

Sato, Shohei. 2009. "Britain's Decision to Withdraw from the Persian Gulf, 1964–68: A Pattern and a Puzzle." *Journal of Imperial and Commonwealth History* 37, no. 1: 99–117.

Scharfenort, Nadine. 2014. "Off and Running: Qatar Brands for FIFA World Cup, and Life Beyond." In *Under Construction: Logics of Urbanism in the Gulf Region,* ed. Steffen Wippel, Katrin Bromber, Christian Steiner, and Birgit Krawietz, 71–90. Surrey, UK: Ashgate.

Sophia, Mary. 2015. "Dubai Mall Sees 80m Visitors in 2014." *Gulf Business,* February 10, 2015. http://gulfbusiness.com.

Valentine, Simon Ross. 2015. *Force and Fanaticism: Wahabism in Saudi Arabia and Beyond.* London: Hurst.

Vitalis, Robert. 2006. *America's Kingdom: Mythmaking on the Saudi Oil Frontier.* Stanford, CA: Stanford University Press, 2006.

Vora, Neha. 2008. "Producing Diasporas and Globalization: Indian Middle-Class Migrants in Dubai." *Anthropological Quarterly* 81, no. 2: 377–406.

Wam. 2013. "UAE Advertising Content Regulations Issued" Emirates247 (website), January 16, 2013. www.emirates247.com.

World Health Organization. 2015. *WHO Report 2015: Data Tables* (official report). Geneva: Mimeo.

12

A Quest for Significance

Gulf Oil Monarchies' International Strategies
and Their Urban Dimensions

STEFFEN HERTOG

The megaprojects that the Gulf's oil monarchies have pursued in the course of the post-2000 oil boom have variously been described as tools of economic diversification, vehicles of self-enrichment for ruling elites, attempts to deepen strategic alliances with the world's leading economic powers, or simply princely follies driven by surpluses too large for any government to handle rationally. This chapter works through various considerations to examine the related possibilities.

The Puzzle: International Ambitions and Local Enclaves

There is a subtle thread connecting a wide range of projects that has largely gone undiscussed to date but at least touched upon up in various chapters in this volume. It relates to a broader trend in Gulf Cooperation Council (GCC) cultural, economic, and foreign policies: during the last decade and a half, Gulf monarchies have been using their oil wealth to buy the accoutrements of "good citizenship" and "progressiveness" in the international arena through outward-oriented and costly activities. These include overseas investments in strategic assets like media and renewable energy, the hosting of humanitarian conferences, arts and film festivals, bidding for the world's leading sports events, generous aid policies, and support for international museums, higher education, and research institutions. The Gulf monarchies stand out among the world's small countries in the range and scale of their global "soft power" ambitions.[1]

Some of these policies have merely led to one-off events or involved checkbook transactions. In many cases, however, large-scale urban interventions were a critical component of the GCC countries' soft power initiatives. They have led to the building of international museums and universities, declarations of zero-carbon cities—often in enclaves that are disconnected from the rest of the urban fabric. Through the political economy of this process, local elites' ambitions are leaving their imprint on the region's urban landscapes. Stepping back, one can see the conjunction of two forces that are specific to Gulf rentier states: first, the oil-funded emergence since the 1970s of regulatory and spatial "enclaves" that are legally and geographically separate from the rest of local states and societies (as described, for example, by Mina Akhavan in chapter 7 in regard to ports), and, second, the increasing ambitions since the 2000s of Gulf rulers to make their small countries global leaders in the cultural, scientific, and normative realms.

The enclave model initially served purely commercial purposes or was used to co-opt critical groups in local society. With the recent emergence of soft power ambitions, however, new soft power enclaves have come into being that combine legal autonomy and spatial segregation with a global normative mission. Different from the older enclaves, they are separate from local society also in cultural and normative terms, giving rise to new social and political tensions.

Why Is It Worth Explaining?

The Gulf instinct to accompany new policies with new infrastructures might be natural: given state control over land, centralized decision making, limited political participation, and ample fiscal resources, most GCC rulers have faced few direct obstacles in doing so. International architects and planning firms are readily available to propose world-scale projects. They produce tangible, physical objects that give a semblance of policy "results" that might otherwise elude rulers.

Yet the nature of the projects poses a puzzle: almost invariably, the most daring and visible projects cater to Western-defined "liberal" international norms and tastes. They are developed predominantly with international partners, consultants, and contractors and have an audience—regardless of where specifically located—that is almost exclusively international. GCC citizens tend to be at best indifferent to new clean-energy projects, museums, or international universities. In some cases, they even appear hostile to them.

In his book about class, democracy, and diversification in high-rent GCC countries, Michael Herb argues that many nationals see the region's fast-paced, outward-looking economic development very critically—and in fact prevent it in the one country case in which they have a formal political say, Kuwait.[2] Their core concern in this is protecting their national and cultural identity—a hotly debated issue in the region—to which many of the region's soft power projects appear to pose a particularly visible threat.

As a result, leading proponents of "liberal" urban interventions like the Qatar Foundation (QF) or the Qatar Museums Authority (QM) have come under attack even in the tame local media. Columnists have called for the employment of more Qataris in the QM, and a poll in a journal published by the QF itself showed that a majority of readers think that Western education—which the QF has been introducing forcefully in the country—will water down Qatari identity.

At the same time, the ambition of the UAE and Qatar in particular to style themselves as beacons of cultural and scientific progress creates reputational risks in the international arena. It is quite likely that labor practices in Abu Dhabi and Qatar would have drawn less international attention were it not for Qatar's hosting of the 2022 FIFA World Cup, Expo 2020 in Dubai, or Abu Dhabi's highly visible Guggenheim, Louvre, and NYU campus projects.

The GCC countries remain largely unintegrated in international civil and human rights regimes, and their domestic political practices are at odds with international political and civil rights norms. In many ways, the higher profile they have achieved with their soft power initiatives has made their domestic noncompliance with important international norms more visible and problematic.

Historical Background: Elite Agency and State Building in the GCC

To understand state building and the shaping of urban space in the GCC, we need to recognize the disproportionate role of elite agency in the process. The existence and importance of individual ministries and public companies, of whole city quarters and sometimes whole cities, is often an outcome less of broader political processes than of the tastes, whims, and conflicts of—and among—a small number of princes and sheikhs. The key to understanding the role and shape of the huge Saudi Ministry of Defense with its military cities is knowing the role of Prince Sultan, who was minister from 1962 until his death in 2011; Abu Dhabi's state company and urban developer, Mubadala, is similarly inseparable from its patron, Crown Prince Mohammad bin Zayed; and the same is true with the Qatar Foundation and its patron, Sheikha Moza, the mother of Qatar's current ruler.

The reasons why elite agency looms so large in the creation of the institutions described in this chapter are themselves structural: the rentier status of GCC countries has given ruling families and their advisors a high level of political autonomy at critical junctures of state building.[3] Rulers had direct control over rapidly growing, externally derived state income and over state lands around and inside of rapidly growing cities.

They have also faced few organized constraints on their decision making. With the exception of Kuwait, GCC ruling elites do not face significant challenges from formal mechanisms of political participation. Similarly, traditional status groups that were able to negotiate with rulers in the pre-oil age, be they tribes or merchant families, have lost much of their cohesion and most of their social and economic autonomy in the course of rentier state building, when pretty nigh everyone in local society became dependent on state largess of one form or another.[4] The lack of organized resistance to the state and the extent of individual dependence on state largess is arguably the most pronounced in Abu Dhabi and Qatar.

Elite agency matters particularly during periods of high oil surpluses when new, uncommitted funds become available to those at the top. High autonomy and low short-term economic and political opportunity costs give elites much space for institutional experimentation—deploying the "patient money" mentioned in the introduction and elsewhere in this volume. There are no truly serious negative consequences of project failures in the short term, but a set of sociopolitical and cultural tensions may derive from their presence in the medium to long term.

"Hub and Spoke" State Building

But why have GCC policy experiments often taken the particular shape of institutional and spatial enclaves? Elite autonomy and surpluses have combined with two further factors to produce a fragmented institutional and spatial landscape in GCC countries: the need to accommodate various parts of the national population through public employment and, at least at times, the plural nature of leadership in Gulf monarchies.

GCC governments have felt historically compelled to share a substantial proportion of their wealth with their national populations. The most important channel for this has been employment in the public sector. This has meant the rapid growth of state institutions and in many cases recruitment with scant regard to institutional needs and substantive qualifications, often weakening the capacity of the new bureaucracies.[5] In some cases, elites have also used particular government institutions to co-opt specific social constituencies, such as tribesmen in particular sections of the security forces and religious interests in new educational and judicial institutions, especially but not only in Saudi Arabia. This has further reduced the coherence of the state apparatus.

Patronage employment has imposed constraints on administrative efficacy and coherence. As a result, in times of oil surpluses, ruling elites have often resorted to building yet more parallel, but more selectively recruited, more leanly staffed, and (even) better financed "pockets of efficiency" alongside the rest of the state, often functioning under their own laws and regulations.[6] These have been tasked with high-priority policies and projects, be it banking regulation, building of heavy industry, creation of free zones—or the building of soft power urban enclaves, the topic of this chapter.

The creation of new organizations for new clienteles and priority projects has often been accompanied by new, parallel urban infrastructures attached to the new institutions and their employees—a continuing process. When King Abdullah initiated judicial reforms in Saudi Arabia in the mid-2000s, one of the first follow-up announcements was that the government would create new "judicial cities" attached to the new courts. The main concrete consequence of the kingdom's still diffuse plans on atomic and renewable energy has been by the creation of the King Abdullah City for Atomic and Renewable Energy (KACARE). Similarly, the building of new city quarters and "cities" was a key component of the economic diversification projects initiated by Abu Dhabi's state holding and development company, Mubadala, in the 2000s. Institutional fragmentation has led to spatial fragmentation.

The creation of parallel institutional fiefdoms and spatial enclaves has been exacerbated by intraplate competition and the need to accommodate new generations within ruling families. In Saudi Arabia, following the death of its founder, King Abdul Aziz, his senior sons created or attained control of parallel security organizations in the Ministry of Defense and Civil Aviation, the Ministry of Interior, and the National Guard from the 1950s on, and all of these institutions subsequently created their own residential cities with their own large-scale housing estates, sports facilities, universities, and—often top-notch—hospitals outside of the weak public health system. Commoner-led agencies often replicated this pattern on a smaller scale as they found it difficult to rely on other line agencies for infrastructure and service provision, while themselves commanding sizeable surplus budgets.

Rent-financed state building in the Gulf oil monarchies has been both top-down and deeply fragmented, serving very different political purposes and social clienteles: tribes, the modern middle classes, technocratic elites, religious groups, high-skilled expatriates or low-skilled expatriates of different nationalities, and so on. Most of these operate in their own urban enclaves—often, though not always, attached to different state institutions—and live according to very different social rules and sometimes laws.

The Gulf's oil monarchies present an unusual mix of quite powerful central states that can reach deeply into individuals' lives (as modern nation-states do) and the parallel existence of social, ethnic, and legal enclaves (a characteristic of premodern empires). The GCC monarchies never experienced a historical moment—such as a struggle for independence (with the partial exception of Kuwait's occupation by and liberation from Iraq in 1990/91) or a social or industrial revolution—that would have molded different social groups into a more integrated whole. Instead, the oil booms have in many ways led to further segmentation. The recent soft power projects are just one particularly visible output of a larger process of enclave building.

The Institutional Framework for Urban Enclave Projects

The soft power projects draw on an older model of commercial enclaves that has existed since at least the 1970s in the shape of free- trade zones (FTZs) and other spatially segregated infrastructures (again, see Akhavan's chapter 7 for an elaboration). These commercial enclaves themselves are just one subtype of state-created enclaves, which as mentioned can also include military cities, ministerial compounds with their own education and health systems. This chapter does not engage with such other enclaves in detail, however, as they are less relevant as a model for the soft power projects.

GCC Free Zones

The basic institutional principle that enables the development of commercial enclave projects is the existence of parallel regulatory spheres that are separate from the rest of government in both formal and informal ways. The purpose usually is to circumvent the constraints and inefficiencies of the existing state apparatus.

Dubai was the first economy in the region to introduce free zones. Dubai's zones are regulatory enclaves that not only allow tariff-free imports and full foreign ownership of businesses, but also enjoy unusually far-reaching legal autonomy. They have their own company licensing regimes and are not subject to core parts of the national labor legislation: workers in the zones do not labor under the country's controversial sponsorship system, and companies are not subject to Emiratization rules (requiring that citizens be hired as part of the workforce). The Dubai International Financial Centre (DIFC) even has its own separate laws and court system, mostly staffed by retired British judges.

Different from most other emerging markets, many free zones in the GCC are located in central urban areas (e.g., DIFC, Dubai Healthcare City, and JLT Free Zone in Dubai; twofour54 in Abu Dhabi; QFC in Qatar). They are often tied to large-scale developments that provide office space as well as luxury real estate for predominantly foreign buyers, who typically are not allowed to acquire property outside of the zones. The zones have moved far beyond the geographic model of remote industrial enclaves or international logistics hubs that the region's first free zones followed in the 1970s and 1980s and that still characterize most free zones in the rest of the world.

Free zones are not only spatial enclaves with their own infrastructure, but constitute parallel economies and, in many ways, governments. They are, in effect, offshore. Their swift administration and outward orientation contrasts with the much less accessible "onshore," even in a supposedly business-oriented economy like the UAE. Administration outside of the free zones is often slower moving, and business is largely reserved to nationals. UAE onshore foreign ownership must not exceed 49 percent, a provision more restrictive than in any other GCC country. New federal company legislation issued in 2013, after more than a decade of discussion, was supposed to liberalize it but, in the end, failed to do so. Onshore business is only possible through joint ventures with (often silent) national partners. Larger businesses are mostly in the hands of traditional merchant families. National "ownership," both in an economic and in a spatial sense, is larger outside of the enclaves.

State-Owned Enterprises

Another vehicle that has helped build enclave projects in the GCC is the state-owned enterprise, an entity that sometimes overlaps or even is identical with the free zones. State-owned enterprises (SOEs) have been the primary tool of economic diversification in the GCC—although in many cases they are tasked with developing projects that do not have a primarily economic rationale, such as hospitals, universities, museums, and stadiums. They typically are outside of the purview of government agencies formally in charge of such kinds of facilities.

While the region also has its share of overstaffed and inefficient SOEs, the GCC's top SOEs typically concentrate a critical mass of genuine managerial expertise, otherwise lacking in many government bodies.[7] The leading Gulf SOEs are led by close confidants of rulers that also have modern managerial training; Khaldoon Al-Mubarak of Abu Dhabi's Mubadala, the state-owned holding company tasked with numerous strategic projects, is perhaps the most prominent example: he holds an economics and finance degree from Tufts but is also from a prominent family and personally close to Crown Prince Mohammed bin Zayed (as a result of partially growing up at the ruler's court after his father, a UAE ambassador to France, was killed in 1984). Mubadala has served as the prime vehicle for the development ambitions of the crown prince and was created at a time when he reportedly did not yet have full control of Abu Dhabi's general budget and overseas assets. Other GCC SOEs and state holdings are often similarly affiliated with specific ruling family factions.

As per the pattern, leading SOEs operate separately from the rest of the government, with independent budgets and their own more competitive and less egalitarian salary and HR structures. They often enjoy de facto monopolies and other regulatory privileges; UAE SOEs for example are exempt from the country's corporate governance code.

It often is autonomous SOEs or companies with strong shareholding by ruling family members that organize public space: State-owned airlines for example control important parts of urban space with their own segregated housing for expatriate employees. Companies like Mubadala and Aldar in Abu Dhabi, Emaar and Nakheel in Dubai, or Diar and Barwa in Qatar develop new city areas or whole new cities—and in many cases also are owners and regulators of the new spaces. Infrastructure outside of SOE-controlled urban enclaves is typically the responsibility of less nimble onshore agencies, such as municipalities or departments of transport, housing, social affairs, and other conventional governance units.

Successes and Spread of the Commercial Enclave Model

Dubai's commercial enclaves, whether more traditional free zones or regulatory free zones cum urban megaprojects like the DIFC, by and large fulfill their function successfully. Depending on the source, between a quarter and a third of Dubai's GDP is generated in free zones, and many of them—not just the ports—obtain top spots in international rankings given out by the relevant global associations. While the attempt to create a new international stock exchange through Nasdaq Dubai has failed, the DIFC has become one of the region's foremost hubs for consulting and banking more broadly. Its courts have become a go-to destination for litigants who want to avoid not only the UAE's but the whole MENA region's opaque onshore court systems. While the DIFC courts were initially perceived as based on shaky legal grounds (requiring an amendment to the UAE federal constitution as well as memoranda with local courts to enable enforcement of verdicts), their extraterritorial arbitration services drawing on British common law—rather than the aging Egyptian-French system practiced onshore—have proven durable. Dubai's ruler, Mohammad bin Rashid, has managed to build a wholly separate judicial system while keeping Dubai as an integral part of the UAE.

Dubai's model of large-scale free zones disconnected from the rest of the city has been copied all around the region (and other parts of the world): Abu Dhabi now has four free zones that in principle allow 100 percent foreign ownership. It has recently created the Abu Dhabi Global Market—modeled on the DIFC and located on Sowwah Island, an urban megaproject developed by Mubadala. Bahrain, Oman, and Qatar have also created various special economic or free zones, usually in combination with large-scale, state-developed office and residential projects catering to foreign demand. The Qatar Financial Centre (QFC), set up in 2005 just one year after the DIFC, goes perhaps the furthest in providing separate regulatory structures, operating under its own labor and immigration rules as well as its own court and arbitration system. Different from DIFC, companies registered with QFC do not have to be physically present in it.

Saudi Arabia has also started following the Dubai model of developing integrated residential and commercial communities, as in the King Abdullah Financial District in Riyadh and the King Abdullah Economic City near Jeddah (the setting for Moser's analysis of elite conferencing in chapter 9).[8] Different from Dubai, however, these new projects have not been able to acquire proper free zone status due to the resistance of established government agencies. Together with the much stronger cultural constraints on expatriate life in Saudi Arabia, this has dampened their economic prospects.

Saudi Arabia does in fact have its own successful tradition of SOE-led enclave development, but this has centered on one industry: the national oil company, Aramco, which has inherited its corporate culture and organization from its previous American owners. It is by far the kingdom's most efficient institution,[9] enjoying a high level of operational autonomy. It controls separate American-style residential cities with their own educational and health infrastructure in which English is the language of work and where women have been allowed to unveil and drive—measures the kingdom's conservative religious lobby had, until recently, been able to block for the rest of the country.

Saudi Arabia has also built two world-scale "industrial cities" in Jubail and Yanbu since the 1970s, which are regulated by a separate Royal Commission. These places have their own training institutes, hospitals, and utility company. On its inception in 1974, the Royal Commission, operating under the patronage of then minister of interior (and later king) Prince Fahd, was given an explicit mandate to avoid other government bureaucracy. Most of the production facilities of Saudi Arabia's mostly state-owned chemicals giant SABIC are located in Jubail and Yanbu.[10] These are purely function-oriented company towns that lie far from established cities. Their governing authorities have no ambition to provide high-class or any kind of spectacular real estate (residential or commercial) for either locals or foreigners.

The New Soft Power Enclaves

Adapting Dubai's free zones to still more ambitious goals, neighboring sheikhdoms have pushed the model much beyond its purely commercial purpose.[11] The new soft power enclaves in Abu Dhabi, Qatar, and Saudi Arabia are not just about offering international business a hospitable environment. They use oil rents to create separate cultural and normative spheres that operate in parallel to the rest of state and local society. They circumvent not just logistical or administrative constraint but also local societies' cultural and normative barriers. By the same token, their intended audience and the tastes they cater to seem to be international more than domestic. They range from audacious renewable energy projects to museums, universities, and research centers.

Renewable Energy

While in principle a good case can be made for the use of solar power in the Gulf, some of the region's ambitious renewable energy projects outside of Dubai were conceived without any obvious commercial rationale. The most ambitious of them, Masdar City in Abu Dhabi, was announced in 2006 as the world's first zero-carbon city (detailed in Günel's chapter 8).[12] It appears clear that Masdar's wider zero-carbon target was set before its commercial feasibility was assessed. Its purpose was symbolic, and the audience, international.

The Foster-designed project, administered by a daughter company of Mubadala, has been repeatedly scaled back, and the Masdar Free Zone seems to have attracted few international tenants so far. One important local tenant is the Masdar Institute, an enclave university whose motto is "Learning to change the world." Another key tenant on the edge of the Masdar City campus is the International Renewable Energy Agency (IRENA), the hosting rights for which Abu Dhabi managed to win thanks to an intense international lobbying campaign among developing countries, beating competition from Germany and Austria. The 32,000-square-meter IRENA headquarters is billed as the "greenest office building in the UAE."

The professed environmental ethos of Masdar is dramatically at odds with ingrained onshore energy consumption habits, building practices, and industrial structures that Gulf regimes have to date left largely untouched. Electricity for national households remains highly subsidized in most GCC countries, encouraging excessive levels of demand and very high carbon footprints. The *New York Times* architecture critic Nicolai Ouroussoff has termed Masdar a gated community that reflects "the growing division of the world into refined, high-end enclaves and vast formless ghettos where issues like sustainability have little immediate relevance."[13] While "ghetto" might not capture the nature of the often very affluent UAE onshore, its social and ecological distance from Masdar could hardly be larger.

Saudi Arabia's King Abdullah City for Atomic and Renewable Energy (KACARE), announced as a separate administrative entity in 2010, has received less international press than Masdar City. In addition to researching and developing renewable energy in the kingdom, it has the relatively mundane task to develop civilian nuclear energy. It does however follow the GCC enclave model in that it was created in parallel to existing government agencies in charge of domestic energy matters and in its plan to build a separate "sustainable city" near Riyadh. Its publicly announced $109 billion plan to deploy forty-one GW of solar capacity by 2032—amounting to a third of total Saudi electricity generation by then—also seems to have been an outward-oriented signal as much as a concrete plan for internal development. It comes at a time when the kingdom has come under increasing pressure in the context of international climate negotiations.

The solar capacity target date has since been pushed back to 2040. Saudi Arabia continues to provide domestic fuel and electricity at low prices and has been slow to develop a clear regulatory framework for renewable substitution. Like the King Abdullah Economic City, KACARE has run into resistance from other agencies in an institutional landscape that is older and more cluttered and where decision making is relatively less centralized than in the kingdom's smaller neighbors.

Museums

Perhaps the most discussed—and most clearly noncommercial—soft power enclaves in the GCC are the new museums. The biggest already established institution is the I. M. Pei-designed Museum of Islamic Art in Doha, administered by the Qatar Museums Authority (QM), which operates in parallel to the older Ministry of Culture, Arts and Heritage. QM was created in 2005 and since 2006 has been headed by Sheikha Mayassa, born in 1983 and a sister of the current ruler, giving it a particularly high profile.

Above we referred to some of the flak that the QM has attracted in local media. While one might imagine Islamic art to be of interest to the local population, at least anecdotally the museum draws limited crowds of mostly expatriates (for some of the numbers, refer back to Molotch's chapter 11). The wider activities of QM, including the Doha Tribeca Film Festival and the installation of sculptures by international artists (several of which were removed after local protests over their depicting nudity and violence), reveal an alignment with international rather than local tastes.

This alignment is even more visible in the case of the Guggenheim and Louvre projects in Abu Dhabi, led by the state-owned Tourism Development and Investment Company (TDIC).[14] The museums have run over budget and been much delayed, with the latter finally opening in 2017 and the former still on hold. They are part of a broader bid to make Abu Dhabi a hub for high-class international tourism, and also—similar to Masdar—to brand it as a progressive state on a par with leading Western cultural and economic capitals. Given the huge cost of the projects, the commercial rationale seems quite speculative, while the branding aspect thus far has mostly backfired as the projects have attracted much critical attention from international labor rights advocates (see, again, Molotch's chapter 11).

As a result of criticism from Human Rights Watch and others, developers involved with the museum projects have pledged to adhere to labor standards above and beyond those that generally apply in the UAE— separate standards that themselves confirm the enclave nature of the projects. It is however not clear how well they can be enforced given that the subcontractors on the projects are mostly onshore businesses potentially deploying some of the same workers in other projects with lower standards.

A further reaction to improve the lot of workers on high-profile construction projects has been to build new, separate housing enclaves for them to replace substandard worker housing, a task undertaken by big SOEs like Diar in Qatar and Zonescorp and Arabtec in Abu Dhabi. At the same time, the Qatari Ministry of Municipality and Urban Planning has published maps with no-go areas for single expatriate workers, delineating where they are not to be housed, facilities like shopping malls they are not to enter, or public event venues they are not to attend. The response to international criticisms of exclusion and local demands to preserve national identity seems to be, albeit with some ambivalence and uncertainty, increased regulatory and spatial segmentation.

Universities and Research

The final main area of urban soft power enclaves is that of new internationally branded and outward-oriented university projects. The Gulf has had separate, private universities for children of expatriate residents for several decades, notably in Bahrain and in Dubai's International Academic City. These have had limited international visibility however; they are purely teaching institutions and operate on a commercial basis.

QATAR FOUNDATION

Qatar has taken the lead on outward-oriented enclave universities in its Education City, a campus operated by the Qatar Foundation—a sprawling institution under the control of the current emir's mother, Sheikha

Moza, that, similar to the QM under her daughter Sheikha Mayassa, has pursued a broader agenda of high culture, research, and community development with strong international involvement.[15] The institution is not bashful about its ambitions of international leadership; its motto is "Qatar Foundation—Encouraging the people of the world to start thinking." It regularly hosts high-profile international conferences about education and welfare issues at which it awards international prizes; in 2010, it signed a 170 million Euro sponsorship deal with the FC Barcelona, placing its name on the shirts of Barca players (since then replaced with the name of Qatar Airways).

The foundation's Education City houses large branches of substantial universities: Georgetown, Texas A & M, Carnegie Mellon, Northwestern, France's HEC Paris, University College London, Weill Cornell Medical College, and Virginia Commonwealth University. They are grouped as a large compound of individual campuses, each designed by an important architect. Professors are almost invariably expatriates, as are the majority of students, a subject of some discontent in Qatari society and a result of both a small local population and an onshore schooling system that—despite reform attempts led by RAND and the Supreme Education Council, of which Sheikha Moza used to be vice chair—does not sufficiently prepare students for academic work. Education City exists in parallel to the older Qatar University, which caters mostly to local students and has a higher proportion of local faculty. In addition to Education City, the Qatar Foundation also controls Qatar Science & Technology Park (QSTP), a free-trade zone that was inaugurated in March 2009. Until recently, it was also working on the creation of Qatar Space City, at Al Khor north of Doha, a $3 billion project to take passengers into space. QF has undergone severe budget cuts with the lower oil prices and has announced no major new initiatives.

NYU ABU DHABI CAMPUS

The most visible and controversial international university enclave in the region to date has been NYU Abu Dhabi. Different from the relatively narrow disciplinary focus of the various Education City transplant universities, NYUAD was conceived as a full liberal arts college offering a range of disciplines. Even more than the Education City institutions, it has been outward-oriented, recruiting its students almost exclusively outside of Abu Dhabi through a costly process that involves flying all prospective candidates over to Abu Dhabi for interviews and initially hosting them in local hotels. (They are now housed on campus.) NYUAD's permanent campus is located at Saadiyat Island and was developed by Mubadala (see Ballon, chapter 6). Saadiyat is also the location of the Guggenheim and Louvre transplant museums, as well as a number of planned high-class residential, entertainment, and tourism projects—one of which Mubadala bought in June 2013 from loss-making TDIC.

The very costly NYUAD project—pursued at a time when funds for some of the UAE's traditional onshore state universities were frozen or cut—has been much discussed in the international media. It has come under fire from NYU faculty in New York, one of whom, a Professor of Social and Cultural Analysis, Andrew Ross, was denied entry to Abu Dhabi in early 2015 after his criticisms of labor practices on the campus construction site were widely circulated in his publications and reports to the press. Ross himself has pointed out that a liberal arts university that is supposed to engage critically with social and political issues in the surrounding society cannot function in a segmented enclave.[16] He has also publicly doubted the viability of the agreement between NYUAD and the Abu Dhabi government that is supposed to guarantee free speech on campus, giving students and faculty a form of extraterritorial status that privileges them over onshore residents and citizens of the emirate.

KING ABDULLAH UNIVERSITY OF SCIENCE AND TECHNOLOGY

In 2009 Saudi Arabia, a country whose social practices in most ways are even more at odds with Western campus life, created its own high-profile, outward-oriented enclave university: King Abdullah University of Science and Technology (KAUST), endowed by then King Abdullah with a reported $20 billion and located on a new campus outside of Jeddah with its own large-scale housing, schools, stadium, golf course, and hospital.[17] The development of KAUST was entrusted to enclave SOE Saudi Aramco, and it initially operated separately from the Ministry of Higher Education.[18] KAUST is the only institution outside of the Aramco compounds in the Eastern Province where "Aramco rules" have applied—that is, women can unveil and mix with men—made possible only by direct royal patronage of the project. It is, as might be expected, a source of some controversy in Saudi society, particularly among the religious lobby. Three sons of former King Abdullah (d. 2015) continue to serve on KAUST's board, reflecting its continued links to this particular branch of the ruling family.

KAUST has also come under strong criticism from a Saudi princess who has blamed it for catering to foreign elites rather than Saudis. It is currently headed by a former president of Caltech, has mostly expatriate faculty, and a majority of its (generously funded) students are foreigners. Saudis by statute are not allowed to constitute more than 50 percent of the student body. Like KACARE, KAUST is more of a hybrid institution that combines an outward-oriented mission of international leadership with significant local tasks of building technology and engineering capacity in critical areas like energy and renewables. It has a relatively larger national student population to recruit from than the transplant universities in Abu Dhabi and Qatar.

The spectacularization of its architecture and the scale of international outreach—and PR activities around its launch—suggest the importance of international tastes and audiences in the conception of the institution. It has only weak links to existing Saudi universities. If the purpose had only been to improve local research capacity, it is not clear why this could not have been accomplished by strengthening a relatively success-ful established institution like the King Fahd University of Petroleum and Minerals in the Eastern Province, which is more selective than other Saudi universities and has traditionally been the main local recruiting ground for Aramco.

Commonalities across the Enclaves

There are further urban developments that reflect GCC regimes' inter-national ambitions—involving sports and media—which do not need to be discussed in detail but which are of significance. The list includes the Formula One infrastructure in Bahrain and Abu Dhabi, FIFA 2022 in Qatar, and Abu Dhabi's twofour54 media city and free zone (the associated international film festival that came to be terminated). All these follow the same template already illustrated in some detail: ambi-tious architecture, integrated residential and commercial infrastructure that is physically segregated from the rest of the urban landscape, and direct patronage from rulers or senior princes. There is administrative and often legal separation from the rest of the state, a leading role of autonomous local SOEs and international consultants in their development, an ambition to cater to an international rather than a local audience, and questionable commercial viability. No project of these kinds existed before the early 2000s; now dozens of them occupy prized positions in the geographic and institutional landscape.

Outcomes

The second-generation soft power urban enclaves have either had no commercial ambitions at all, as is the case with the transplant universities, or have, to date, been unsuccessful in realizing them. Using soft power facilities to spin-off significant business returns, particularly with related real estate, has not met success. By 2011, foreigners had bought only sixty-two apartments in Qatar's free zones (established through a 2004 law), and for several years now the Qatari government has pondered the plan to reintegrate the QFC into the emirate's onshore financial market (QFM), due to lack of business. Many of the leading state-related companies that have been the primary drivers of enclave projects have required government bailouts, despite privileged access to lands and contracts as well as (in several cases) part ownership by members of the ruling family. Cases include Barwa in Qatar as well as Abu Dhabi's Tourism Development and Investment Company (TDIC), Aldar, and Sorouh (the latter two of which were merged in 2013 in the wake of significant losses). Many of the more ambitious urban and free zone projects announced since the mid-2000s have either been downscaled or abandoned since the early 2010s.

The most ambitious and multifaceted operator among the region's SOEs, Abu Dhabi's Mubadala (developer, almost incidentally, of NYUAD), has also incurred losses in several years. More important, it appears that it has only one main source of profits, the hydrocarbons-focused Dolphin project, which has allowed it to import gas cheaply from Qatar and resell it more dearly on international markets. Its other business divisions have been weighed down by bold but ill-timed international acquisitions in semiconductors and commodities as well as costly aerospace manufacturing projects. These were to enable Abu Dhabi to leapfrog into a position of international technology leadership. A good share of Mubadala's local revenue seems in fact to have derived from the enclave projects, based on land grants and exclusive development contracts with government, rather than through technological know-how or innovation.

Results from soft power enclaves with noncommercial objectives are by nature harder to evaluate, regardless of possible success. But evidence from places like Masdar and weak enrollments of nationals in the new universities do not display much by way of local impact or international reputation. Attempts to build R & D, high-tech capabilities and world-class universities have been undercut by deficient local education systems that the enclave projects have done nothing to fix—or try to work around. (NYU does offer additional "gap year" pre-university training for locals in the area.) And while some of the enclaves pursue such advanced social and environmental policies as building to a high (LEED) environmental standard, this usually is a result of centralized decisions by the SOE developer in charge and does not seem to have spilled over to onshore institutional practice, at least not so far. Cultural projects have found little by way of local audience and created controversy among international labor advocates.

Even if local spillovers are not intended, the social and cultural messages that the new soft projects embody are more difficult to contain than the offshore economic activities in traditional free zone enclaves. While often met with indifference from onshore national society, some of the enclaves have also created local friction in otherwise politically placid societies.

Why Does It Happen?

So we are back to the questions with which we began. Why do regimes pursue ambitious soft power enclave projects in the face of what arguably are long odds of success and potentially considerable social, economic, and political costs? Conventional explanations based on economic and strategic rationality do not work well: we have seen that the commercial rationale of many projects is questionable. At least for the small, rich sheikhdoms of Abu Dhabi and Qatar, the long-term viability of their states would be more easily secured with accumulating diversified overseas assets that could generate a permanent revenue stream—which had been happening to an important extent during the post-2000 boom but could have happened on a larger scale were it not for the huge local outlays involved with many of the enclave projects.

One might argue that commercially questionable large projects based "at home"—and thus under the rulers' political control—provide a good opportunity for rent-seeking elite. While this might be true for some of the projects, it would be much easier to pocket the money through less visible infrastructure contracting and land deals that do not involve high-profile clean energy, research, and culture projects that expose the country to international scrutiny. Rulers of the sub-Saharan African petro-states like Equatorial Guinea, Gabon, and Angola have managed to enrich themselves colossally without going through the trouble of building international universities or museums.

Some scholars think that building large-scale projects with Western involvement gives foreign powers a stronger stake in the survival of GCC regimes. This is probably true when it comes to the energy sector and defense contracting. Western stakeholders in museum, university, or renewable-technology projects however would appear to have little influence over Western security strategies—and if anything, the increased attention devoted to the Gulf in the wake of its soft power policies has made the public defense of GCC-Western alliances harder.

This chapter proposes a more constructivist, if still preliminary, explanation of the soft power strategy. The GCC track record is most consistent with local ruling elites' quest for social recognition and status in international society, even if there is no immediate strategic rationale for such recognition. (Even Saudi leaders seem to have ambitions in this regard [see Moser, chapter 9].) Building soft power infrastructure is best understood as a quest to acquire post-oil statehood that would give the rentier monarchies an international identity and status independent of their role as hydrocarbons producers. The ambition that shines through all of the projects is Gulf elites' desire for their states to be taken seriously—to be seen as able to exert some sort of non-oil cultural and economic leadership.

This elite-driven ambition appears analogous to what happens in the second and third generation of many family business dynasties around the world. While the first-generation founders build family wealth, subsequent generations often realize that wealth as such does not buy respect. Hence, the offspring (including daughters) and wives of the sons branch out into charitable, cultural, and civil-society activities to acquire social and cultural capital for their family—think of the Rockefellers, Vanderbilts, or Langhorne/Astors in the United States. The large autonomy that their inherited wealth provides makes this strategy easy to pursue, particularly for family members not directly involved in the core business. Like U.S. business dynasties, Gulf ruling families have a particular penchant for endowing buildings and infrastructure, physical monuments that permanently embody their social standing.

This explanation relies much on leadership psychology and agency. There is some existing research demonstrating the importance of GCC leaders' personal world view and desires on how they shape their educational and cultural policies: Based on her having embedded in a sheikh's family compound, Calvert Jones[19] has documented how GCC rulers' personal experience and infatuation with liberal education in the West induces them to pursue local reform projects that appear at odds with the GCC social and political status quo. Whatever their inclination, and however it came to evolve, it is indeed the political autonomy of ruling sheikhs and the oil cycle that together best explain the timing and degree of experimentation with soft power enclaves in the region. The lack of organized political resistance and the extent of individual dependence on state largess is the most pronounced in Abu Dhabi and Qatar, which have also seen the most daring soft power enclave experiments. The one GCC country with strongly organized social constituencies that have access to formal decision making, Kuwait, is also the one case with no large-scale soft power projects and limited economic diversification initiatives more broadly: parliament and organized interests in the public sector have made sure that most state resources are instead used for distribution to the middle-class citizenry.[20]

Given the post-2014 oil price environment, we should expect few new large-scale projects in the foreseeable future. Almost no major new projects have been announced since the recent plunge of oil prices and some existing ones—notably at the Qatar Foundation—have been put on hold or are being downsized. When GCC rulers face "normal" fiscal constraints, their political choices become more normal too, and their urban strategies, less experimental and ambitious.

Conclusion: What Is Special about GCC Soft Power Enclaves?

The Gulf's soft power enclaves are not the only spaces in the region that function according to their own rules and cater to specific social clienteles. They seem to leave local society behind in a particularly stark and visible fashion, however. In the GCC context, it is difficult to imagine elites pursuing their hypermodern cultural and educational ambitions in anything but an enclave fashion: GCC countries are social, legal, and economic late developers; most of onshore society was untouched by modern education, media, and consumption until a few decades ago. Nationals have seen dizzying social and demographic change; concern about the loss of national identity, Westernization, and rule by expatriates is acute particularly in the high-rent countries, the UAE and Qatar.[21] These countries' onshore political and social structures provide little fertile ground for the experiments they host to take root. Tensions between the enclaves' sociocultural missions and onshore norms have repeatedly come to the surface. Enclaves are easier to separate from the rest if they limit themselves to commercial activities; cultural and educational activities that are at least in principle predicated on openness and diffusion risk friction with citizens.

All this suggests that the new urban enclaves would be hard to export to other jurisdictions where elites have less fiscal and political autonomy, where local societies are larger and better organized and the needs of the onshore therefore more difficult to circumvent. It is telling that the one country that has attempted to adopt several of the aspects of the Gulf enclave model is Kazakhstan: it has actively consulted Dubai in its plans to create a DIFC-style financial center with its own court system (see Ponzini, chapter 3). Its attempts to host the winter Olympics and the FIFA World Cup are reminiscent of Abu Dhabi's and Qatar's soft power events and infrastructure strategies. Astana hosted Expo 2017, while Expo 2020 will be in Dubai. Kazakhstan's economy is heavily based in oil and gas (and some other mineral resources). It is an authoritarian, family-controlled rentier state with a short history of independence. If the GCC template can be fully replicated anywhere, it might be there. But Kazakhstan's potential dims with oil price decline. Even in the Gulf, economic realities are imposing new constraints and the advent of new cultural megaprojects might be coming to a close.

NOTES

1 The only comparable case with similar high-profile "branding" projects might be Kazakhstan, a case I hope to investigate more closely in future research. On this, see the works by Natalie Koch: http://nataliekoch.com.
2 Herb 2009; 2014.
3 Mahdavy 1970; Crystal 1995; Luciani 1987; Beblawi and Luciani 1987.
4 Crystal 1995; Hertog 2010b.
5 Hertog 2016.
6 Geddes 1996; Hertog 2010b.
7 Hertog 2010a.
8 Moser, Swain, and Alkhabbaz 2015.
9 Lippman 2004; Hertog 2008.
10 Hertog 2010b.
11 My analysis in this chapter only deals with soft power initiatives that have a clear spatial and urbanistic dimension. Others—such as the UAE's Mars mission, the operations of international charities, and humanitarian conferences and organizations—are not discussed here.
12 Cugurullo 2013.
13 Ouroussoff 2010.
14 Ponzini 2011.
15 Sheikha Mouza also is chairperson of Msheireb Properties, a state-owned entity in charge of redeveloping central Doha (a project formerly known as Dohaland).
16 Ross 2011.
17 Koch 2014.
18 "Saudi Aramco as a National Development Agent Recent Shifts," Peace Building (website), www.peacebuilding.no (accessed April 26, 2016).
19 Jones 2015.
20 Herb 2014.
21 Herb 2014.

REFERENCES

Beblawi, Hazem, and Giacomo Luciani, eds. 1987. *The Rentier State*. London: Croom Helm.

Crystal, Jill. 1995. *Oil and Politics in the Gulf: Rulers and Merchants in Kuwait and Qatar* (updated). Cambridge: Cambridge University Press.

Cugurullo, Federico. 2013. "How to Build a Sandcastle: An Analysis of the Genesis and Development of Masdar City." *Journal of Urban Technology* 20, no. 1: 23–37.

Geddes, Barbara. 1996. *Politician's Dilemma: Building State Capacity in Latin America*. Los Angeles: University of California Press.

Herb, Michael. 2009. "A Nation of Bureaucrats: Political Participation and Economic Diversification in Kuwait and the United Arab Emirates." *International Journal of Middle East Studies* 41, no. 3: 375–395.

Herb, Michael. 2014. *The Wages of Oil: Parliaments and Economic Development in Kuwait and the UAE*. Ithaca, NY: Cornell University Press.

Hertog, Steffen. 2008. "Petromin: The Slow Death of Statist Oil Development in Saudi Arabia." *Business History* 50, no. 5: 645–667.

Hertog, Steffen. 2010a. "Defying the Resource Curse: Explaining Successful State-Owned Enterprises in Rentier States." *World Politics* 62, no. 2: 261–301.

Hertog, Steffen. 2010b. *Princes, Brokers, and Bureaucrats: Oil and the State in Saudi Arabia*. Ithaca, NY: Cornell University Press.

Hertog, Steffen. 2016. "The Post-WWII Consolidation of Gulf Nation-States: Oil and Nation-Building." In *The Emergence of the Gulf States*, ed. John Peterson, 323–351. London: Bloomsbury.

Jones, Calvert. 2015. "Seeing Like an Autocrat: Liberal Social Engineering in an Illiberal State." *Perspectives on Politics* 13, no. 1: 24–41.

Koch, Natalie. 2014. "The Shifting Geopolitics of Higher Education: Inter/Nationalizing Elite Universities in Kazakhstan, Saudi Arabia, and Beyond." *Geoforum* 56: 46–54.

Lippman, Thomas. 2004. *Inside the Mirage: America's Fragile Partnership with Saudi Arabia*. Boulder, CO: Westview Press.

Luciani, Giacomo. 1987. "Allocation vs. Production States." In *The Rentier State*, ed. Hazem Beblawi and Giacomo Luciani, 63–82 London: Croom Helm.

Mahdavy, Hussein. 1970. "Patterns and Problems of Economic Development in Rentier States." In *Studies in the Economic History of Middle East*, ed. M. A. Cook, 428–467. Oxford: Oxford University Press.

Moser, Sarah, Marian Swain, and Mohammed H. Alkhabbaz. 2015. "King Abdullah Economic City: Engineering Saudi Arabia's Post-Oil Future." *Cities* 45: 71–80.

Ouroussoff, Nicolai. 2010. "In Arabian Desert, a Sustainable City Rises." *New York Times*, September 26, 2010. www.nytimes.com.

Ponzini, Davide. 2011. "Large Scale Development Projects and Star Architecture in the Absence of Democratic Politics: The Case of Abu Dhabi, UAE." *Cities* 28, no. 3: 251–259.

Ross, Andrew. 2011. "Human Rights, Academic Freedom, and Offshore Academics." *Academe* 97, no. 1: 14–17.

Conclusion

From Gulf Cities Onward

HARVEY MOLOTCH AND DAVIDE PONZINI

Examining the Gulf expands our understanding of how contemporary cities and urban societies come to be built and sustained. Repeatedly in our chapters, extremes and distinctions in the Gulf—heights of buildings, demographic incongruity, and the contrast of traditions with cosmopolitan ambition—offer up lessons applicable to other places. Gulf reality enlightens us about the challenges and tensions central to urban functioning more generally. These considerations point to the possibilities for achievement as well as cautioning against myopic excess. For those of us in the West (and other places too), we can take our findings (and method) from the Gulf and try them on for "fit."

We learn, as we anticipated in our opening chapter, that the classic urban theories—Marxian, neoclassic-economic models, or otherwise—do not always work. All the efforts toward a universalistic explanation fall short. We also see in a clear way that the doctrine of city-hinterland symbiosis, as inherited from past urban analysis, fails to come through. Chicago has been called "nature's metropolis,"[1] given that its natural surrounds provide a base for its industries (e.g., meat, ores, and grain). Other than oil, Gulf cities have no such regional symbiosis. Though geographically small, Abu Dhabi and Doha are near the peak of the urban wealth hierarchy, even as they lack significant manufacturing or agriculture sectors. As with Las Vegas before them, they do not arise from a productive hinterland. Again, we caution, Gulf cities are not isolated examples; they point to others. Stand-alone cities based on technology, recreation, innovation, and education now abound across the world.

Rather than a great metropolis, some cities can cohere as outposts or specialized enclaves. Corporations populate them for use as knowledge-economy research-and-development sites. Affluent people can use them as a second (or third or "nth") home. Thanks to the affordability of contemporary travel (and in the case of the Gulf, governmental priority investments in airlines), world capitals are no longer so far-flung or isolated, including the exploding metropoles of India and China. Etihad, Emirates, and Qatar Air are consistently ranked among the top airlines in the world. Putting it most extravagantly, as fitting the subject, the whole world is an air-mode suburb to places like Abu Dhabi, Dubai, or Doha. Other cities may replace, or at least supplant, them in the Gulf or elsewhere in the next urban firmament. We now have a glimpse of how they might emerge.

A key method we have used—again, useful for anywhere—has been to *follow the buildings*. More specifically, built form and infrastructure clue us in to the politics, organizational structures, and cultural patterns that made these burgeoning cities possible and that they, in turn, alter and reinforce. We can get at least a tracer on how things spread, build, and meld. Especially in contexts where information is guarded or otherwise hard to come by, physical structures are not just visible, but often (as in the Gulf) publicized as proud accomplishments. Buildings teach about how innovation, invention, and creativity operate—along with mimicry, suffering, and environmental loss. In the restrictive Gulf context, we get a glimpse of complex systems of authority, partnerships, and subcontracting beneath it all. Physical structures, here as elsewhere (the great gift to archaeology), serve as evidentiary residues.

In concrete research terms, we can see some payoffs. Yasser Elsheshtawy has shown what you can do with buildings and land when even the basic data found for most cities is not available. He has patiently pieced together data from different sources and used site visits to posit and draw his own conclusions. He also notes, as do we, the frenetic pace of transition: the flood-lit, nonstop, twenty-four-hour-a-day schedules under which work goes on. Gökçe Günel has made close examination of the Masdar complex, exploiting its own promotional materials and the physical access she's gained to the site itself and to other expats—some enthusiastic for the project, others skeptical. They may not be the most central figures, but they were willing to talk. Through Hilary Ballon's analysis of the NYU project, especially as a physical apparatus, we benefit and gain insight from the direct experience of someone near the top, but it is through the buildings and the plans that we can get a clear glimpse of how authority and institutions link up. From what happened at its desert site, we see how the institutional relationship refracted back on the New York "host" institution itself, including who sits on its board of trustees and how the university got reconfigured. Beyond these examples, virtually all the chapters work through what is on the urban ground, up and down and across geographies.

The Open Gulf

The openness we witness in the present-day Gulf is nothing new and—at least, in historical terms—does not present an inherent contradiction that somehow needs working out. Actual histories contradict any claims made about Gulf cities being discrete from the rest of the world or from one another. So we hesitate to put forth any notion that there is, in the contemporary moment, a single Gulf city model. As we have learned from Alex Boodrookas and Arang Keshavarzian, the Gulf cities examined herein (along with others in the region) are positioned in a region of meldings—of religions, ancestries, commerce, and customs. Amale Andraos, in her chapter, has used the architecture of her native Beirut to illustrate the varied and multisourced histories that have long characterized the Middle East urban. So-called Arab architecture *is* the result of interactions across the region as it has interacted with the design schemes and cultures in other parts of the world. You can *see* it in the buildings. To betray this reality, in her view, risks kitsch or—especially as doctrine moves into political and ideological realms—mayhem and national catastrophe. And, of course, the contemporary spectacles presented and examined have no Arab pedigree; whether high or low, they too are amalgams.

The historical Arab city—like Islam itself—has an open and indeterminate structure. Such cities represent "a fully decentralized and *ex post facto* system of land use and governmental regulation over space,"[2] as the sociologist Janet Abu-Lughod explained a generation back. It is a system based on custom, family lineage, and ad hoc judgment of private and collective well-being. As Abu-Lughod, writing about prior and non-UAE Arab cities elaborates, there are "juridical distinctions between Muslims and/or citizens and outsiders [. . . and] segregation by gender."[3] It is thus eminently plausible that any contemporary version of an "Islamic city" would, if tradition were followed, also apportion rights and privileges by virtue of status in the larger system, rather than simple market dealing. In this understanding, modern Gulf cities are amalgams of the new and the old, the local and foreign. Land was the basis of riches first prior to oil, then from oil, and consistently after—as we have seen from some of our chapters—from other forms of rent. Land use becomes built in to the social and political sorting system and taken for granted in the institutional matrix. Urban development, which accompanied nation formation in the UAE and Qatar almost from the outset, generated its own system of returns. Before thinking this totally odd as a source of power and wealth, we might remind ourselves that George Washington, the "father of his country," was one of the richest landholders in the British Colonies, one whose fortunes benefited from the formation and stability of the country he fought to create. So, again, what we see in the Gulf may be extreme, but not unique.

Besides bringing things in, the Gulf sends things out. Gulf cities are not simply repositories but—based on their export of capital, design, and organizing capacities—influence the outside world. Of all non-oil industrial development, one of the most striking homegrown successes is Dubai's port (see Mina Akhavan's chapter). It processes not only vast freight tonnage but develops modes of organizing surrounding urban space and exports logistical capacities. In architecture and engineering, Gulf projects—often by designers from Paris, New York, and London—also travel out. As manifested in the Gulf, often with regional finance and development, the outsiders' designs can go on to be replicated, imitated, or knocked off across the Gulf, the Middle East, and beyond. Some designs, in effect, return to the West, with changes wrought by the different political, social, and climactic conditions they then encounter. Technologies, as part of the process, also come and go; whatever the motivation to build tall and fantastic, it means pumping concrete to unprecedented heights. Keeping a glass high-rise tower cool in the desert provides the knowledge-base wherewithal to keep a building cool anywhere. Creating decorative fountains that outdo plumbing and electronic precedents may also travel in a similar pattern—just as the fountains of Versailles advanced the history of world plumbing. Even decorative elements, we are reminded from the history of glass making and metallic gilding, can be a basis for far-reaching innovations in other realms like electronics.[4]

Gulf trends go out to nonaffluent areas as well, including Egypt, Morocco, Turkey, and other Middle Eastern and African countries. The tastemakers, engineers, and investors in the Gulf (see Sarah Moser's chapter on this) create packages readied up for ambitious cities even in economically marginal parts of the world. Gulf cities are also developing new ways to satisfy the tastes of wealthy consumers now emerging from China, Russia, and Africa as they come as tourists or otherwise intersect with Gulf interests. Such people's tastes and proclivities used to be of little consequence for most of the world, but that has changed. They are shoppers and investors looking to create tourist and other industries on their own turf. As Gulf projects get copied, they get larger or smaller, lose some pizazz, or change in other ways. Design, development, and finance, as always interdependent, come and go and constitute aspects of the global transnational.

Lessons for Hybridity

This gives us, at ground level, a way to witness the urban hybrid—in a place that, as officially part of the Muslim world, is sometimes rendered as anything but. Hybridity has become an au courant cliché, bandied about with little substantive content. The connotation usually is one of diversity—within a country, community, or even within a person. Gulf city hybridity is a particular variant that does not typically stand in for the phenomenon but is indeed a significant instance of how it can work. If residential or work sites were mapped, many Gulf city districts would surpass Greenwich Village in the variety of faces, languages, and origins of the people. But it is a very different form of diversity—or "heterogeneity," as termed in classic urban sociology.[5] The idealization of the likes of Jane Jacobs makes little sense here. Gulf cities are diverse because of the needs of the government and the locally affluent elites, which require a pool of construction laborers, professionals, and service workers. As such, diversity itself is neither a government priority nor even acknowledged as an asset; instead it is a necessary encumbrance. Given foreigners' lack of rights and privilege, it represents, to borrow another term from Manuel Castells, a kind of "perverse integration."[6] Workers are cheap and so is their transit.

There are exceptions to even this limited type of diversity. Shi'ites are subject to exclusion (several NYU faculty have been kept out of the UAE apparently on those grounds), and there has also been, according to Adam Hanieh, a decision to dampen immigration from non-GCC Arab states out of fear of dangerous ideas that might come along with it.[7] So the demographic and cultural mix is a complex matter, and certainly not a result of any idealized vision of "huddled masses yearning to breathe free." Again, lest we get carried away with a version of Gulf exceptionalism, let us be reminded that the U.S. system, for example, relies on labor coming in from Mexico and Latin America, just as it has always depended on worker-migrants from poor parts of the world—and their severe treatment or, at best, marginal accommodation.

Urban Work-Arounds

Through the research and writings of our various authors, we return to the phenomenon of the work-around—something we raised in the book's introduction and that we bump into repeatedly in the chapters that followed. However true it may be that contradictory beliefs and practices recur in all societies, once again the Gulf brings them out more clearly. We can see their manifestations—and how they are managed. They are assiduously and consequentially worked through. Some sociologists have regarded rules as negotiated more or less ad hoc; rules, laws, and so-called norms always exist in the presence of counterrules, counterlaws, and counternorms.[8] Work-arounds are the institutional means for making things happen. Examining them closely comprises a heuristic for understanding any place or society: define it not by some master "ideal type," distinctive great force, or ineffable cultural wellspring; instead, define it by its work-arounds. They reveal the real mechanisms that secure continuity and also (potentially at least) points of vulnerability. If the work-around should somehow falter, all bets are off. With the Gulf cities as our guide, we thus learn something to apply to many—maybe to all—settings: know them by their work-arounds.

In Gulf environments, those work-arounds aid in overcoming blockages, frustrations, or limits. They accommodate the absence of conventional capitalist markets, interest-bearing debt, or open access to trading in real estate. They address moral and religious difficulties, including parochial contradictions as well as some dicta, like stoning, abhorred in the world outside. There are concessions, exemptions, deviations, and other types of fitted (almost bespoke) adjustments. Each in itself is a rational response to conditions at hand, yielding a world of multiple rationalities. We learn from the Gulf how inconsistency and segmentation (so stressed by Steffen Hertog in chapter 12) can be made unnoticeable—and *not* "cry out" for reconciliation. Maybe not forever, but for a very long time, contradiction can go on.

Put in the kind of macro terminology to which it stands so much in contrast, we might say that the work-around is hegemonic—reaching through all analytic levels and across all places. In titling his first book *Complexity and Contradiction in Architecture*,[9] Robert Venturi was asserting that even "great" architecture (*especially* great architecture) combines elements that are not "supposed" to be together, as in his own provocation of putting an oversize Ionic column in a modern structure. In the Gulf, we find the inconsistencies both in built forms and in organizational, political, and social realities. In conceptual terms, their presence is not necessarily antagonistic to explanation, but can be its basis. Assemblage happens.

Geographic separation—by social class, occupation, ethnic background, or economic function—operates, as we have seen, as a key mechanism. Spatial exceptionism was by no means invented in the Gulf. Europeans practiced it for centuries; charters and edicts marked off specific locales for each guild or particular group, Jewish ghettoes most notably.[10] South African apartheid, with its multiple categorizations and emplacements by "race," is still another famous and infamous example. Gulf urbanism then represents another such real specificity with its own distinctive format of rights, duties, and privileges, distributed along functional as well as essentialist criteria. The Gulf extends, elaborates, and makes the separations formal as to who can be where and what is allowable in given demarcated spaces. Creating geographic zones of exception is so extensive in the Gulf that it is sometimes hard to think of laws and administrative apparatuses as fundamentally applicable to a given country or city within the country, as opposed to specific districts and their functions. Parts of cities, in some instances cumulating to great shares of it, are set aside for special privileges or constraints.[11] The overall pattern of ad hoc permission and exception enables authorities to choose who and what will be favored with privilege and rent. For owners as well as residents, cartography becomes destiny.

Each name of so-called component cities has an adjective to express its hoped-for homogenous purpose: Education City, Technology City, or Humanitarian City (the latter to service the administrative needs of regional NGOs). Geo-demarcations can enhance access to a greater or lesser degree of free speech (greater at NYU Abu Dhabi, for example) or tax benefit, or more or fewer forbidden foods and drinks. Lacking the economic and social diversity ordinarily associated with the terminology, the word "city" here throws us off—these are not just an approximation of what a city is, but almost the opposite. In fashioning inclusions or exclusions, authorities do not need to satisfy a voting public, political parties, or civil-society institutions. Various projects are under the ownership, sponsorship, or protection of citizens, expats, foreign investors, monarchs, or combinations thereof. Even in Europe and the United States, where there is legal transparency along with judicial and legislative oversight, the plethora of special districts and their administrative complexity hinders scrutiny. In the Gulf, autocratic rule and secrecy further mystify arrangements—in a sense, making secrecy more obvious than it is in the West with its systems of offshore accounts, creative accounting, and financial subterfuge.

There are more routine precedents from the United States and other democracies where the comingling of official resources and private gains are mystified, often by the complexity of administrative structures. There can be urban renewal zones, business improvement districts, and model city precincts—whatever their public-spirited rationale, they in fact distribute and redistribute benefits. Outside the official rules, there is a history of de facto as well as de jure restrictions against African Americans, Native Americans, Jews, and Americans of Italian, Asian, and other extractions. Many borders between and within U.S. territories were created to facilitate their development as rent-yielding investments—or to foster control over what went on within them. Counterparts exist elsewhere, of course, including the City of London (i.e., its financial district, akin to the ersatz cities in the Gulf), a hoary instance of autonomous exception. China's special economic zones have been engines of its economic boom, most massively in the case of Shenzhen and then spreading to many other places in adapted forms. The open-market Chinese trading zones follow on, however ironically, from the "concessions" forced on China by the colonial powers in the nineteenth century.

The Greatness of Money

What can't be assumed for any society is the availability of the mother of all work-arounds: wealth to disperse and to tide over. Money, being fungible, can be applied across settings and specific to needs at hand, including those not anticipated. Vast "backup" money helped the GCC regimes weather the economic reversals of 2008 and perhaps even exploit them, as Elsheshtawy notes. Before the crash, real estate speculation, fed in part by investors from other parts of the world, had run rife. Changing the name of the world's tallest building from its original Burj Dubai to Burj Khalifa marked the ruler of Abu Dhabi's (Khalifa bin Zayed Al Nahyan) putting up the money to rescue the project from the financial disaster the Dubai ruler had on his hands. This recapitulates or at least reminds us of the capacity for elite readjustment: shared power and, to some degree, income among the various emirates. Living standards and privilege were sustained across the GCC with economic downturns; they were also, in most of the countries, almost impermeable to the 2011–2013 Arab Spring.

Money may not buy happiness, but it does buy lots of stuff and, as several of our authors (and others) indicate, a quiescent populous. It qualifies indeed as a work-around. In much academic scholarship, consumption comes up as trivial, a way in which people foolishly fritter away resources in a losing battle to find meaning or keep up status displays. This may also be the case in our Gulf cities, but it is central to the political economy. Affluent consumption offers up all the seductions preached and practiced in the cosmopolitan world centers. This is not a consumption inspired by social consciousness, of the sort once proclaimed in the socialist block. It is not aimed at meeting "basic needs" with products of functional simplicity, as preached in some Western design schools of the past. Instead, it feeds and feeds off all that the world's fashionable emporia can offer. In the presence of this great assortment of luxury goods, those in high-up levels are a new form of citizen, weak in political power but rich. Consumption fixes a day-to-day good life and gives substance of a sort for daydreams and aspirations. It keeps people attentive to something (products) and busy with arrangements of what to buy, where to get it, and how to deploy its use. Even in places outside the Gulf region where there is much ado about democracy, elections, and rights to debate, we can be reminded of the significance of consumption as intricately connected with governance and stability.

Mighty wealth carries the potential for mighty initiatives. As with the glorious buildings, money configures impressive ventures that convey national purpose and certainly the appearance of attainment on the world economic stage. Some of them bespeak going beyond real estate and retail to indicate more basic economic productivity. As one such example of homegrown success is Dubai's port enterprise (documented by Akhavan in this book). No doubt with the right mix of partners and consultants, the regime in effect got out in front to leverage its particular capacities—water, open space, location and, über alles, capital. The homegrown version was a base for far-flung foreign replication (albeit also including outright purchase of other conglomerates). It is an instance of deliberate assemblage. The locality operates as a center for putting together complementary elements that can then be replicated as combinations in other places. As when mall developers (at a more modest level) scheme up their tenant mix and layouts, synergy does not "arise" but is plotted. So can other types of combining create wealth in place. Often outside the routines (and constraints) of usual governmentality, ports and airlines have the special benefit of being able to operate without confronting local mores. Further, they do not need a local milieu to grow and prosper—apart from what is put in as part of the ensemble.

The larger lesson is that we are seeing how a place, a Gulf city in this instance, can originate a configuration and be the geographic base while all the rest remains an open question: where, what, and with what effects should a combination occur. The resource is the funding and the capacity to organize—to *assemble*, pulling in as Gulf cities have the habit of doing, the elements from wherever they are needed and largely without ideological or religious constraint. The creativity, the value added, is in managing the portfolios: what to buy, where to go for supply, how to configure, and where to deploy. Movement of people is similarly a manipulation of inputs, temporary in most cases. They are inputs, not citizens. We have a distinctive development imaginary and a way to think of future world enterprise.

In extreme terms, but also on the horizon, we can see the "seasteading" phenomenon—the creation of floating settlements outside normal governmental reach. Such "sea-based micro nations"[12] would be liberated from conventional bureaucracy and protected from rising waters above which they could forever float.[13] Silicon Valley libertarians, like PayPal billionaire Peter Thiel, are financial backers.[14] It is a further move toward exception—or to put the same result in the phrase of a key advocate, to create a "start-up country."[15] It has absurdity but takes its place in a history of unconventional accomplishments.

The Gulf, in its physical configurations, including massive landfill and island building, portends—perhaps even models—the logistically ambitious. Masdar and Saadiyat are pushing envelopes. They use deliberate internal juxtapositions, along with institutional arrangements, that are distinct from the usual nation-state set-ups. The new cities under development in Saudi Arabia (described by Moser), like King Abdullah Economic City, take it up another notch. Underway is the building of cities the size of a Washington, D.C., but up from scratch rather than over the several hundred years of evolution that it took to build the U.S. capital. Subsequent to Moser's fieldwork comes the Saudi announcement of a $640 billion (!) investment for a still bigger city project, dubbed Neom. Announced in front of a substantial portion of the global business elite (3,500 in number) who were then being hosted in Riyadh (in a high-end luxury setting),[16] the scheme far surpasses Masdar in its zero-emission and other technological ambitions. The Saudi project CEO is a German national, the former chief of Alcoa and before that of Siemens. These actors make no small plans.

Why Have a Country?

Our Gulf project enables us to pose a question (though not a "finding" from the book) that would otherwise not arise. Seldom since earliest times of modern political theory (e.g., with Hobbes) or later concerns of theories from utopian socialism do we have reason to ponder so basic an issue. But perhaps oddly in light of all the splendid accomplishments and exercise of state authority, some basic facts about certain of the Gulf states invites attention to the counterfactual: instead of forming the emirates as a nation, the sheikhs might have just, to put it crudely, taken the money. Gulf investment funds now approach $1 million per capita in the case of Abu Dhabi, albeit lower in other Gulf countries (like Saudi Arabia).[17] If the data were in terms of wealth *per family* (just nuclear family), the numbers would hugely inflate. If so much had not been spent on all the infrastructure and cultural institutions as they were in Qatar, Dubai, and Abu Dhabi, the citizens would be richer still. This point is strikingly made by Steffen Hertog in the prior chapter.

The magnitudes of wealth raise the question of why, at the moment of original formation, the "decision" was made to have a country at all. With citizen populations, a fraction of the numerators used in the per capita calculations just mentioned, there was—at least in economic retrospect—no reason to create a country at all. Every person could have used the wealth to live an affluent life in Paris or London, not to mention Bali or Mexico. Such a historical route would have obviated all the rigmarole of labor importation, intraregional quarrels, and conquest of harsh climate. Carbon footprints would have been greatly reduced. But evidently, more goes on than calculations of monetary return when humans—elite or otherwise—create their futures. As Hertog argues, there is something bound up with a "search for significance." The European monarchs built Versailles and Schoenbrunn before there were mass tourist industries upon which to calculate the basis for the outlays. For the orders lower down (but still included), it may be appropriate to think of having a state as inflecting a general prestige—flags, seats at tables, visits from important dignitaries, and such.

Of course, we don't know why "they" did what they did when forming a country rather than arranging to go away in affluence. Nor is it likely that they—any more than the leaders of the Western countries (or the authors of this chapter in deciding to write it)—"really" knew what motivated their actions. The various sheikhs did take somewhat different paths, especially in the earlier decades—some avoiding ambitious wealth-generating investments and others embracing the chance to make it big. And their situations materially varied (oil or no oil), but so did more idiosyncratic dispositions (Dubai's ruler being more risk taking and developmentally oriented than, for example, Abu Dhabi's). Something that was capricious at the outset may be later portrayed as "strategy," in part to better conform to the precepts of economistic rationality.

Perhaps most important, and more in line with conventional political thinking, having a state helps to protect wealth, not just for the rich against the poor, but more generally to preserve efficacy of contracts, deeds, patents, and passports. States can be helpful in such regards. Not having a state at all makes people more vulnerable to arbitrary economic power, bigotry, even genocide. Although we can't manage to assign weights to these various explanations, at least we can say that the special conditions (wealth endowment in particular) help bring such a big "why" to the forefront.

As we have also described, another use for the state is to mount vast economic initiatives, notably, creative ones with the potential for worldwide impact, including benign impact. Even as pollution powers on, the Gulf agenda includes over-the-top techno-utopian projects, again bewildering in their own way. Gulf actors now both avoid the subject of climate change and avidly confront it. The hunt is on, apparently (but who can be sure), for the means to transform the economic base of Gulf cities while saving the earth. The bet, if there is one, is that energy alternatives can be brought online at just the optimal moment, when wealth has been sucked from oil but commercial energy made newly available through the government's initiatives. As part of the bet, there must be patent controls or some other mechanism (foreign direct investments? international treaties?) to capture the rewards for the Gulf country of origin. The GCC countries need to step out of one boat and into the other without tipping into the sea. But, to repeat the refrain, all this may be overthinking what may turn out to have been another ego-driven enterprise that really makes no economic or even political sense. Whatever challenge for the GCC, this is no ordinary "management problem"; it connects into survival issues for much of the world.

Limits of Enactment

Gulf rulers and their expert consultants are unanimous in their intentions to "diversify" the economy. But intentions are likely not enough. Here's why: segregated enclaves and spaces of exception run counter to urbanism's generative potential. They do not leverage the buzzing complementarities of the city. Ongoing accomplishment—which can have legs to carry it into the future and across space—depends on imagining and daring from life in situ. There also needs to be social trust and tolerance, at least some experts argue.[18] The knowledge industry arises through inputs that are unanticipated and with outputs that are also unanticipated. Staging the city as an archipelago of special districts may help in implementing individual megaprojects, but such a tactic does not portend synergy.[19]

Nor is it helpful that so many people in the Gulf are temporary. This militates against the building up of knowledge empathies, across groups, professions, and institutions. While they are together, expats share clubs, restaurants, golf courses, malls, marinas, and schools for their children. An unintended feature of these Gulf cities is that they provide havens for professionals from other parts of the Middle East, including places where they would have had less ability to pursue careers and live with stability and safety. Given their internal diversity, such communities may have a special richness, however inadvert their creation. (The NYU Abu Dhabi campus community of students and staff forms a truly fertile ground of rich interactivity.) We might refer to them as "collateral communities," and they are indeed a resource. But they themselves are temporary. Otherwise, there is not much backup from emplaced cultural and social capital. The scene is thin, not thick.

Importing "off the shelf," whether a technology, a group of people, or a building design, comes up short. Drawing again on lessons from the built environment, we know that icons best work in the initial version but not, almost by definition, as replication. The Parthenon sitting on the Greek Acropolis is not the same when repeated in the city of Nashville, Tennessee (as has been done). Moving London Bridge to Lake Havasu City, Arizona, is a mere folly. Ironically enough, the Eiffel Tower has more paying visitors than any monument on earth, but its replica does not work well as a landmark in Paris or Texas, or as a hotel attraction in Las Vegas or Macao. More generally, Michele Nastasi's photographs, backed up by the writing of Davide Ponzini, tell us that the very act of travel changes the meaning and impact of even the "best" designs. No matter how well done, repetition erodes, in both economic and aesthetic terms, "first-mover" advantage—eventually dwindling down to boredom or kitsch.

Gulf precedent for self-starting innovation is not strong, even in the fields of technology, where issues of censorship and social exclusion might be less of a liability. Masdar does register several patents each year,[20] but U.S. universities register hundreds per year. Under the Masdar brand, construction is underway on apartment buildings, shopping facilities, and a handsome prototype for an environmentally advanced single-family house (the Eco-Villa). Critics will call out the narrative as mere "green washing"; in the meantime, we have still another demonstration of the ability to build and market real estate. Creating the smartest of smart-city experiments makes an inspiring sci-fi scenario (spaceships in the desert, as Gökçe Günel calls them out)—a hopeful way, perhaps, to blunt concern over consumption-dependent economies, high carbon footprints, and low productivity of nationals—but not an actual city on its own.

The urban practitioners are themselves hired hands; their spirits are not indigenous. They are paid to give advice, but their projects are often shelved because they are not usable in the practical context of the Gulf or because they are simply not in line with what the elite client might desire. For its part, public administration typically does not transfer complex information and learning across comparable places and projects. Simplified policy narratives and catchwords ("world class," "sustainable," "smart," "spectacular") are not sufficiently meaningful. Gulf cities compete with one another around such claims but, we suspect, engage in only limited mutual learning. Speed is the essence, itself a point of pride in its accomplishment. Even though much gets done,[21] it does not encourage the thinking through of problems of overbuild or conflict with existing uses or other projects coming along at the same time. Projects race ahead of institutional ability to guide them.[22] There is little time for sedimenting of local knowledge, let alone building a local-specific planning culture rooted in civic engagement. This also means that decisions about what to build and how can defy simple planning logic, or even economic feasibility. Without provision for political engagement—or even residents' knowledge—any so-called intelligence of democracy is thwarted. Indeed, decision makers and rulers may simply deny urban problems, making redress even less likely. Such problems are acute in other cities—of the Far East in particular, but also in the Western world, where access to usable planning knowledge is continuously debated. But here the issue is more clear-cut.

To extend the point: every innovation, no matter how daring, rests on a prior layering that is complex and precisely fitted to its situation—including past experiences of complaint and satisfaction. Whether a building, a painting, or a mousetrap, an unseen background gives productive coherence. In the Gulf, there is a kind of patina deficit—a shortage of built-up elements that create, ironically, conditions for innovation. Always dependent on what already has been, usually from somewhere else, Gulf actors are behind, even if only slightly. It is thus not, as crude stereotype would have it, that these places are "mired in the past." Quite the contrary, they seem more mired in the present—almost hidebound to it. And not all of it is pretty.

Complexity of the Global: One Great Elephant among Us

For many, in the Gulf and elsewhere, the most noticeable aspect of urban life is the presence of "migrants." But our Gulf cities, it might be said, do not really have migrants. It is more apt to say that migrants *are* their population. As Nelida Fuccaro depicts the "multi-cultural world" of Manama's earlier pearling era, it is a "town of foreigners."[23] And this, it looks like, is going to be so for a while. The "outside population," either the same individuals or their substitutes, are an essential aspect. From the standpoint of the sending country and the families of those left behind, these Gulf cities are the global workspace; people travel large geographic and cultural distances to be "at work." They commute to a different world. We can observe that, through a combination of the security apparatus and the fragility of their status, these workers of the world cannot unite.

The Gulf breaks up the convention—or what is left of it[24]—of identifying citizenship with the lands on which people are housed, even for generations. There are worlds of compromised status for those who migrate; they have an agreed upon status but only very contingent rights. Germany's guest worker program (Gastarbeiter), initiated with a 1955 treaty to import temporary labor from Italy, was followed by similar German agreements with Spain, Greece, Turkey, and parts of North Africa. As reported in 2017,[25] workers from Bulgaria and Romania now rotate on temporary contracts into and out of Western Europe—"replaceable cogs in a tireless machine," as the *New York Times* coverage termed them. Migrations from the Middle East and Africa further stimulate EU countries toward various versions of acceptance, repulsion, or expulsion.[26] The modern U.S. system has tended toward the informal ("don't ask, don't tell") while also policing the Mexican border. In effect, entitled citizens benefit from the exploitation of foreign labor. Whatever else their terrible deprivations, Gulf workers are, compared to their U.S. counterparts, more likely to at least "have papers" and hence a legal identity.

An irony, noted by Hertog in the prior chapter, is that the reason we know about severe conditions in the urban Gulf is through the very spectacle that attracts Western attention. The starchitects' ebullient attractions and the global glitter of the institutions and companies involved—Louvre, NYU, Sorbonne, and Guggenheim, but also Cartier, Four Seasons, and Ferrari—in effect get the injustices *branded*. They are made articulable and scandalous. The local paper of the Guggenheim, NYU, and Human Rights Watch is the *New York Times*. This paper (along with the *Guardian*) has been responsible for the major exposés. The continuing protests among NYU students and faculty, along with New York art activists, has aided and abetted the coverage. News and opinion pieces contrast the prestige partners' creations with the abject difficulties of those who build them.

There are long-standing dilemmas of what stance to take. Fundamental moral and analytic questions remain: To what degree do Gulf cities *cause* global inequality or is it that they *display* it? Gulf cities (thank you again) help guide us to a question that might otherwise not be so pressing. Exposure does bring the possibility of reform. We can note that a positive response (while again no panacea) has been given by Gulf authorities—now confirmed by Human Rights Watch,[27] as well as the NYU administration. Some reforms have taken place. Results are not stunning, but the "room" has grown, quite literally. While reports from Doha in 1980 evidenced thirteen workers per room, later exposés reported a far fewer number; standards in place limit occupancy to four per room:[28] hardly luxury, and maybe even still not decent, but an improvement. The publicity in the metropolitan core likely garnered amelioration—another manifestation of local-global connectivity.

Again, a different approach we might take—something other than straightforward critique—is to use the Gulf to *see*. Resisting ready explanation through the traditional paradigms, Gulf cities force our attention to state-structured mobility and the conditions of its occurrence. These are not above-mentioned peoples yearning to breathe free, but people looking for an income. It is obvious for those who have contact with them in the Gulf that many of these exploited workers greatly fear being deported. Gulf wages are lifelines for the families they have left behind. Some are saving for a return to build a house or start a business or, in the interim, to educate a child. In one of the few reliable surveys we have of Gulf workers—conducted by the Yale sociologist and former dean at NYU Abu Dhabi, Ivan Szelenyi[29]—Gulf workers have mixed evaluations of their experience. But 45.9 percent reported being satisfied with the wages they received, and 53.5 percent said they would return to the UAE for work (10.8 percent responded "maybe"). This survey of workers was conducted after their return to Pakistan. Here is another chance to learn about—or, at least, be reminded of—what goes on less noticeably in other parts of the world. The Gulf, so often a poster child for exploitation, may be showing us something more relevant—that is, not how bad off workers in the Gulf are but how horrible life is in, say, Pakistan.

When we look and think closely, intervention becomes too complex for a simple protest, precisely because of all the interconnections. Certainly, pressure needs to be exerted for labor rights, higher living standards, and environmental reform. But we are dealing with a world of difficulties, not simply a stand-alone problem in one urban region. Given the entanglements, do we strive to bring down the Gulf apparatus as unjust in and of itself? It helps meet the needs of those at the desperate end of the global wealth continuum. Do we, in effect, pry off their fingers as they cling to the Gulf city? Wary of any perfunctory solution, conceptual or political, we are left to further reflect on Robert Venturi's insistence that direct and honest focus always reveals complexity and contradiction.[30] Getting to it is, in a way, the litmus test for having found reality. We need to face up to his reminder, which we have come to stridently support, that we have an "obligation toward the difficult whole."[31]

NOTES

1 The term is from the main title of William Cronon's book *Nature's Metropolis: Chicago and the Great West* (1992).

2 Abu-Lughod 1987, 172, italics added by authors.

3 Ibid.
4 On this example, and many others, see Smith 1981.
5 Hannerz 1980; 1996.
6 Although his meaning is somewhat different, Manuel Castells suggests the term in his *End of Millennium* (2010, 73).
7 Hanieh 2011, 63.
8 Zimmerman 1970.
9 Venturi 1966.
10 Duneier 2016.
11 See, for example, Human Rights Watch 2015a.
12 Sorkin 2017.
13 Morozov 2017.
14 For a description of the "Seasteading Institute," see www.seasteading.org.
15 Gelles 2017, 8.
16 Hubbard and Kelly 2017. See also MacMah 2017.
17 Demographic data are kept secret. For relevant estimates, see www.swfinstitute. org; Winckler 2015.
18 Among others, see Florida 2002.
19 Malecki 2000.
20 For a Masdar patent enumeration, by year, see http://stks.freshpatents.com. On Masdar, see also Reiche 2010.
21 For a prideful government summary of what has been accomplished, see Crown Prince Court 2011.
22 For an insightful description of how almost all megaprojects in the 2000s in Abu Dhabi did not follow a comprehensive city plan or land use regulations, see Samarrai 2016.
23 Fuccaro 2009, 231.
24 Sassen 2015.
25 Alderman 2017.
26 For a recent effort to grapple with the complexity, see Sassen 2015.
27 Human Rights Watch 2015b; 2015c.
28 Adham 2008, 229.
29 Szelenyi 2017.
30 Venturi 1966.
31 Venturi 1966 (the quote is the title of the book's last chapter).

REFERENCES

Abu-Lughod, Janet L. 1987. "The Islamic City—Historic Myth, Islamic Essence, and Contemporary Relevance." *International Journal of Middle East Studies* 19, no. 2: 155–176.
Adham, Khaled. 2008. "Rediscovering the Island: Doha's Urbanity from Pears to Spectacle." In *The Evolving Arab City: Tradition, Modernity and Urban Development*, ed, Yasser Elsheshtawy, 218–257. London: Routledge.

Alderman, Liz. 2017. "Europe's Thirst for Cheap Labor Fuels a Boom in Disposable Workers." *New York Times*, December 11, 2017. www.nytimes.com.

Castells, Manuel. 2010. *End of Millennium: The Information Age: Economy, Society, and Culture*. New York: Wiley.

Cronon, William. 1992. *Nature's Metropolis: Chicago and the Great West*. New York: Norton.

Crown Prince Court. 2011. *United Arab Emirates: 40 Years of Progress Retrospective Analysis of Key Indicators*. Abu Dhabi: Mimeo. www.cpc.gov.ae.

Duneier, Mitchell. 2016. *Ghetto: The Invention of a Place, the History of an Idea*. New York: Macmillan.

Elsheshtawy, Yasser. 2010. *Dubai: Behind an Urban Spectacle*. London: Routledge.

Florida, Richard. 2002. *The Rise of the Creative Class: And How It's Transforming Work, Leisure and Everyday Life*. New York: Basic Books.

Friedland, Roger, Frances Fox Piven, and Robert R. Alford. 1977. "Political Conflict, Urban Structure, and the Fiscal Crisis." *International Journal of Urban and Regional Research* 1, nos. 1–4: 447–471.

Fuccaro, Nelida. 2009. *Histories of City and State in the Persian Gulf: Manama since 1800*. Cambridge: Cambridge University Press.

Gelles, David. 2017. "Floating from Science Fiction to Blueprint." *New York Times* (international edition), November 15, 2017, 8.

Hannerz, Ulf. 1980. *Exploring the City: Inquiries toward an Urban Anthropology*. New York: Coflumbia University Press.

Hannerz, Ulf. 1996. *Transnational Connections: Culture, People, Places*. New York: Taylor & Francis.

Hubbard, Ben, and Kate Kelly. 2017. "Saudi Arabia's Plan to Move Past Oil: Big Goals and Hurdles." *New York Times*, October 26, 2017, A12.

Human Rights Watch (website). 2015a. "UAE: A Move to Protect Migrant Workers: 'Contract Fraud' Measure Can Deter Forced Labor," November 1, 2015a. www .hrw.org.

Human Rights Watch (website). 2015b. "UAE: NYU's Labor Rights Provisions Break New Ground," February 3, 2015b. www.hrw.org.

Human Rights Watch (website). 2015c. "Migrant Workers Rights on Saadiyat Island in the United Arab Emirates," 2015 Progress Report, February 10, 2015c. www.hrw.org.

Jones, Calvert. 2015. "Seeing Like an Autocrat: Liberal Social Engineering in an Illiberal State." *Perspectives on Politics* 13, no. 1: 24–41.

MacMah, Lauren. (n.d.) "Saudi Prince's Bold Plan for a $640b Futuristic Megacity." News.com. www.news.com (accessed December 10, 2017).

Malecki, Edward. 2000. "Creating and Sustaining Competitiveness: Local Knowledge and Economic Geography." In *Knowledge, Space, Economy*, ed. John R. Bryson, P. W. Daniels, N. Henry, and Jane Pollard, 103–119. London: Routledge.

Morozov, Evgeny. 2017. "Google's Plan to Revolutionise Cities Is a Takeover in All but Name." *Guardian*, October 21, 2017. www.theguardian.com.

Reiche, Danyel. 2010. "Renewable Energy Policies in the Gulf Countries: A Case Study of the Carbon-Neutral 'Masdar City' in Abu Dhabi." *Energy Policy* 38, no. 1: 378–382.

Samarrai, Kais. 2016. "The Evolution of Abu Dhabi's City Urbanization and the Sustainability Challenge." In *Shaping Cities: Emerging Models of Planning Practice*, ed. Mohammad Al-Said and Rahul Mehrotra, 98–118. Berlin: Aga Khan Award for Architecture/Hatje Cantz.

Sassen, Saskia. 2015. *Expulsions: Brutality and Complexity in the Global Economy*. Cambridge, MA: Harvard University Press.

Smith, Cyril Stanley. 1981. *A Search for Structure*. Cambridge, MA: MIT Press.

Sorkin, Andrew R. 2017. "An Oasis for Global Capital." *New York Times*, October 24, 2017, B1, B4.

Szelenyi, Ivan. 2017. "Pakistani Guest Workers in the United Arab Emirates." *Demográfia* (English edition) 59, no. 5: 5–47.

Venturi, Robert. 1966. *Complexity and Contradiction in Architecture*. New York: Museum of Modern Art.

Vogel, Frank. 1997. "Islamic Governance in the Gulf." In *The Persian Gulf at the Millennium*, ed. Gary Sick and Lawrence G. Potter, 249–296. New York: Palgrave.

Winckler, Onn. 2015. "How Many Qatari Nationals Are There?" *Middle East Quarterly* 22, no. 2: 1–14.

Zimmerman, Don H. 1970. "The Practicalities of Rule Use." In *Understanding Everyday Life*, ed. Jack D. Douglas, 221–238. Chicago: Aldine.

ACKNOWLEDGMENTS

We thank our two home universities, New York University and Politecnico di Milano, for their steadfast support. The NYU Abu Dhabi Institute funded workshops in which our authors (and other scholars) engaged in fruitful intellectual exchange. Additional Institute aid helped offset editorial and production costs. For events in New York, we gratefully acknowledge the support of the NYU Institute for Public Knowledge (IPK) and the NYU Sociology Department.

Our chapters were written in conjunction with two exhibitions centered on the architectural photography of Michele Nastasi, held in Abu Dhabi and New York. These exhibitions, focusing on urbanization in the Gulf region, both reflected and further inspired our authors' thinking. The outcome represents a synthesis of imageries and infographics to make substantive intellectual points. We are grateful to the Politecnico Department of Architecture and Urban Studies (Farb Fund) for its financial support as well as for research and editorial assistance. We also express our appreciation for the NYUAD Akkasah Center for Photography's sponsorship of Nastasi's further fieldwork in the Middle East. Nastasi's photographic research has been a central part of our larger intellectual endeavor.

In producing this book and its related exhibitions, we have collaborated with exceptional colleagues and assistants: Mina Akhavan, Luca Astorri, Riccardo Balzarotti, Celeste Calzolari, Martha Coe, Anita De Franco, Zachary Jones, Maryam Karimi, Rossella Locatelli, Liana Mandradzhieva, Fabio Manfredini, and Matteo Poli. Thank you! We benefitted as well from a close and valuable reading of our text by Bernadette Baird-Zars. Others who read and critiqued our various texts include Paul DiMaggio, Eric Klinenberg, and Andrew Ross. Farah Al-Nakib, Francesca Arici, Nelida Fuccaro, and Nasser Rabbat provided close and thoughtful readings. Chapter 7 benefitted particularly from suggestions made by Stephen Ramos; other sections in the book similarly gained from his insights and intelligence. We owe a special debt to Kais Samarrai, former head of the Abu Dhabi Urban Planning Council. From the outset, he was a generous participant and contributor—to our events and panels as well as in reading our work. His knowledge and wisdom have been a unique resource.

The key person to most all our endeavors was the late Hilary Ballon, the former NYU Deputy Vice-chancellor for Abu Dhabi and University Professor in the NYU Wagner Graduate School of Public Service. She believed in our mission from the start, including the critical orientation to which honest intellectual engagement must be open. She represents that and more: scholar, teacher, and builder. This book is dedicated to her memory.

ABOUT THE CONTRIBUTORS

Mina Akhavan is a Research Fellow and Adjunct Professor at Politecnico di Milano. Her research focuses on the role of port cities at local, regional, and transnational scales. Her publications include articles in the journal *Cities* and in the *International Journal of Transport Economics*. Her PhD, from the Politecnico di Milano, focuses on spatial planning and urban development. She has been a visiting researcher at CNRS-Gèography Cités, Paris 1.

Amale Andraos is Dean of Columbia University's Graduate School of Architecture, Planning and Preservation (GSAPP). She is cofounder of WORKac, a New York–based architectural and urban practice with international reach. Andraos has taught at the Princeton School of Architecture, Harvard Graduate School of Design, University of Pennsylvania Design School, and American University in Beirut. Her publications include *Architecture and Representation: The Arab City, 49 Cities, The Farm!* and numerous essays. Andraos has received more than twenty awards for her distinguished work in the United States and elsewhere in the world.

Hilary Ballon was founding Deputy Vice-Chancellor of NYU Abu Dhabi. She was University Professor of Architecture and Urban Studies at NYU, before that Professor at Columbia University. Her books include *The Greatest Grid: The Master Plan of Manhattan, Robert Moses and the Modern City*, and *New York's Pennsylvania Stations*, along with other prize-winning scholarly publications. Besides her career in academic administration, she was a national leader in advancing digital technologies for the humanities.

Alex Boodrookas is a PhD Candidate in the joint History and Middle Eastern Studies Program at NYU. His dissertation is on migration and citizenship in the twentieth-century Persian Gulf.

Yasser Elsheshtawy is a leading authority on Middle Eastern cities, paying particular attention to informal urbanism, urban history, and environment behavior. His books include *Planning Middle Eastern Cities, Dubai: Behind an Urban Spectacle*, and *The Evolving Arab City*. Currently an independent writer and researcher, and Adjunct Professor at Columbia University, he was Professor of Architecture at United Arab Emirates University, Al Ain, where in addition to teaching, he also ran the Urban Research Lab. He served as curator for the UAE Pavilion at the 15th Venice Architecture Biennale in 2016.

Gökçe Günel is Assistant Professor in the School of Middle Eastern and North African Studies at the University of Arizona. Her book, *Spaceship in the Desert: Energy, Climate Change and Urban Design in Abu Dhabi*, focuses on renewable energy infrastructures, more specifically on the Masdar City project. She has been a Cultures of Energy Mellon-Sawyer Postdoctoral Fellow at Rice University and an ACLS New Faculty Fellow and Lecturer at Columbia University.

Steffen Hertog is Associate Professor in Comparative Politics in the Department of Government at the London School of Economics and Political Science. He was previously Kuwait Professor at Sciences Po Paris, Lecturer in Political Economy at the University of Durham, and Postdoctoral Research Fellow at Princeton. His books include *Princes, Brokers and Bureaucrats: Oil and State in Saudi Arabia* and (with Diego Gambetta) *Engineers of Jihad: The Curious Connection between Violent Extremism and Education*.

Arang Keshavarzian, Associate Professor of Middle Eastern and Islamic Studies at New York University, is the author of *Bazaar and State in Iran: The Politics of the Tehran Marketplace*. His essays on the political economy of Iran and beyond have appeared in the journals *Politics and Society, International Journal of Middle East Politics, Geopolitics, Middle*

East Report, and *Economy and Society*. His current research focuses on competing and interdependent geographic spaces and scales in the Persian Gulf during the twentieth century.

Laura Lieto is Associate Professor of Urban Planning at the Department of Architecture, University of Naples Federico II. Her areas of interest are critical urban theory, urban informality, and transnational urbanism. Her recent publications include the volume *Planning for a Material World*, co-edited with Robert Beauregard. She has additionally published widely, in Italian and English, in international urban journals. She has been visiting professor at GSAPP, Columbia University.

Harvey Molotch is Professor of Sociology at New York University, where he has conducted research on city growth, urban security, industrial design, and sociology of the environment. Before coming to NYU, he was Visiting Centennial Professor at the London School of Economics and Chair of Sociology at the University of California, Santa Barbara. His books include *Urban Fortunes* (with John Logan), *Where Stuff Comes From*, and a volume on urban security, *Against Security*.

Sarah Moser is Assistant Professor in the Department of Geography at McGill University. Her research examines how national, religious, and ethnic identities shape cities in Southeast Asia and the Muslim world more broadly, as well as how cities across Asia are looking to the Global South rather than to the West for inspiration regarding architecture and urban identity. She has published widely on urban issues and recently co-edited (with Xiangming Chen and Ratoola Kundu) the *Research Handbook on Asian Cities*.

Michele Nastasi is a researcher and a photographer of architecture and cities. From 2007, he has been editor of the architectural review *Lotus international*. His works have been exhibited in venues such as the MIT Museum in Boston, New York University (galleries at Washington Square and Abu Dhabi), and the Venice Biennale. His books include (with Davide Ponzini) *Starchitecture: Scenes, Actors, and Spectacles in Contemporary Cities* and *Suspended City: L'Aquila after the*

Earthquake. He has taught architectural photography at Politecnico di Milano.

Davide Ponzini is Associate Professor of Urban Planning at Politecnico di Milano and was Visiting Professor at TU Munich in 2017. He has also been a visiting scholar at Yale, Johns Hopkins, Columbia, and Sciences Po. His research focuses on planning theory, urban and cultural policy, contemporary architecture, and the urban environment. Among recent publications, he is co-author (with Pier Carlo Palermo) of the book *Place-Making and Urban Development: New Challenges for Planning and Design* and (with the photographer Michele Nastasi) *Starchitecture: Scenes, Actors, and Spectacles in Contemporary Cities.*

INDEX

Page numbers followed by *f* indicate photographs; page numbers followed by *m* indicate maps; page numbers followed by *t* indicate tables, charts, or graphs.

Abadan, Iran, 40–42, 44
Abdul Aziz (king of Saudi Arabia), 281
Abdullah (king of Saudi Arabia), 280, 291
A blocks (NYU Abu Dhabi), 164–166
Abu Dhabi: Aldar Properties, 89–91; automobiles as consumption item in, 259–260; consumption adjustments and outcomes, 268–269; consumption in, 256–269; free zones, 285; housing as consumption item in, 258–259; jobs in, 261–262; large-scale cultural imports, 262–264; museums, 50, 288–289; NYU Abu Dhabi (*see* NYU Abu Dhabi); skyline as seduction, 260–261; unskilled/semi-skilled labor, 267–268; urban planning in, 50. *See also* Masdar City
Abu Dhabi Global Market, 285
Abu Dhabi Investment Council, 15
Abu Dhabi National Bank, 112, 113, 114*f*
Abu Dhabi Plaza (Astana), 89–91
Abu-Lughod, Janet, 302–303
ACA (Arab Center for Architecture), 67–69
actor network theory (ANT), 11, 132–133, 215
Adjaye, David, 74
Africa, 223
Agbar Tower. *See* Torre Agbar
agriculture, 5
Ahmadi, Kuwait, 40–43
AIF (Arab Image Foundation), 67–68

Aishiti Foundation (Beirut), 74–75, 74*f*
Ak Maktoum airport (Dubai), 179
Al Bandar (Abu Dhabi), 119, 120*f*
alcohol, 264, 266
Aldar Properties (Abu Dhabi), 89–91
Al-Futaim, 245, 246
Al-Futtaim Carillion, 156
Alissa, Reem, 42–43
Al Sayegh, Ahmed Ali, 90
al-Wasl (Dubai), 248
American University of Cairo, 163, 167
Anglo-Iranian Oil Company, 42
Anglo-Persian Oil Company, 47
Anker, Peder, 197
ANT. *See* actor network theory
Apollo space program, 210n22
Arab architecture, 302
Arab Center for Architecture (ACA), 67–69
Arab city, concept of, 58–59
Arab Image Foundation (AIF), 67–68
Arab nationalism, 67
Arab Spring: in Abu Dhabi, 268; and Arab cities, 58; and investment in Dubai, 241; Saudi response to, 268; and visions of Islam, 66–67
Arabtec, 289
Arab Village (Ahmadi), 41–43
Aramco, 42, 285, 291, 292
Arbid, George, 71
architectural renderings, computer-generated, 107–108

Arquitectonica, 121
Arts Center (NYU Abu Dhabi), 168, 169
Asian Tigers, 226
assemblage, 11
Astana, Kazakhstan, 89–91, 297
automobiles, 259–260
Awali, Bahrain, 40

Bahrain: free zones, 285; private
    universities, 289
Bahrain Pavilion at the Fourteenth Venice
    Architecture Biennale, 71
Bahrain Petroleum Company (Bapco), 4
Bank of China Tower (Hong Kong), 111,
    112, 113*f*
Barber, Benjamin, 219
Barcelona, Spain, 83–84
Barthes, Roland, 134, 138
Battersea Reach (London), 119, 120*f*
Baudrillard, Jean, 80
Beasley, Larry, 152
"Beaubourg effect," 80
Bedouin Kuwaitis, 42
Bedouins, 64
Beirut, Lebanon, 13–14, 71–75
Bilbao effect, 263
Bill, James, 4
Bin Laden family, 271–272*n*65
Blumenberg, Hans, 197
"boundary objects," 107, 139
branding: architecture and, 37, 59, 60, 82;
    of injustices, 316; Masdar City and,
    203–204; museums and, 288–289; new
    cities and, 217; skylines and, 109, 260
Braudel, Fernand, 12
Brautigan, Richard, 209
British imperialism, 36, 47, 65
Broadway Malayan, 119
Brutalist architecture, 119
Bunnell, Tim, 217
Burj Al Arab Hotel (Dubai), 59, 59*f*, 239
Burj Khalifa (Dubai), 101*f*, 106*f*, 124*f*; and
    Downtown Dubai, 240; and Dubai

Structural Plan, 239; and Dubai World
    Trade Center, 236; Emaar and, 88–89;
    money as factor in renaming of, 308;
    and spectacularization, 15, 79; as
    subject of photography, 123, 124
Burj Mohammed bin Rashid Tower
    (Abu Dhabi), 89, 118, 118*f*

Cameron, David, 205
Campus Center (NYU Abu Dhabi), 164,
    166, 168
Capital Gate (Abu Dhabi), 118, 119*f*
Carbon Democracy (Mitchell), 201–202
Carillion, 249
Carrefour, 266
cars, as consumption item in Abu Dhabi,
    259–260
Castells, Manuel, 12, 189, 305
CBD. *See* West Bay Central Business
    District
centers, in Arab modernization process,
    69–75
centrality model, 4–5
Central Market (Abu Dhabi), 89–90,
    117–118, 118*f*
Central Park (New York City), 123, 124*f*
Central Plaza (NYU Abu Dhabi), 164
Centre Georges Pompidou (Paris), 80
Chalcraft, John, 42
Charles, Prince of Wales, 86
Chicago School of Human Ecology, 4
China, special economic zones in,
    307–308
Chrysler Building (New York), 15
City Life Hadid Residences (Milan), 119,
    121, 121*f*
Cityquest KAEC Forum, 213–227, 219*f*,
    220*f*, 222*f*, 223*f*; about, 218–221;
    and new master-planned cities,
    216–217; normalization of neoliberal
    assumptions of urban development,
    226–227; Saudi progress in new-cities
    expertise, 224–226; Saudi treatment of

attendees, 221–224; and transnational circulations in global South, 214–216

City Walk (Dubai), 249

climate change, 142, 205, 207, 312

commercial enclaves: commonalities, 292–293; success and spread of, 284–286

"company towns," 40, 69–70

Complexity and Contradiction in Architecture (Venturi), 306

component cities, 307

computer-generated images, 107–108

concentric zone hypothesis, 4

"connected isolation," 208

consumption, 24–25, 256–269; in Abu Dhabi, 256–269; adjustments and outcomes in Abu Dhabi, 268–269; automobiles, 259–260; housing, 258–259; oil wealth and, 256–258; political economy and, 308–309; risks and hazards, 264–265; work-arounds, 265–268

container shipping, 176, 186–187, 188*t*

context: building identity between past and future, 64–67; and representation in Arab and Gulf cities, 58–75

Corm, Georges, 67

Corniche (Abu Dhabi), 166

countries, reasons for existence of, 310–312

"creative" places, 8

Crinson, Mark, 41

cultural institutions, 262–264. *See also* museums; *specific institutions*

culture, Gulf development trends and, 6–7

Das, Diganta, 217

Davis, Mike, 36

Debord, Guy, 81

decontextualization, 99

Delhi, skylines in, 261

Dell, Edmund, 49

density, as design element, 162–166

Design District (Dubai), 241

Didi-Huberman, George, 127*n*15

DIFC (Dubai International Financial Centre), 282, 284–285

displacement, speculation and, 247–250

diversity, hybridity and, 304–305

Dog, The (O'Neill), 252

Doha, Qatar, 15, 83–84, 116–117, 263–265. *See also specific buildings*

Doha State Hospital, 45

Doha Tower, 83, 84, 116–117, 117*f*

d'Olivo, Marcello, 68

Dolphin project, 293

domestic workers, 271*n*63

Downtown Dubai, 240, 245

Doxiadis, Constatinos, 49

DPI (Dubai Ports International FZE), 187

DP World (Dubai Ports World), 187–189

Dubai, 236*f*, 251*f*; 2020 Urban Masterplan, 239–241; Burj Khalifa (*see* Burj Khalifa); commercial enclaves, 284–285; diversified economy of, 185–189; Emaar Properties, 87–89, 88*m*; foreign real estate holdings, 15; free zones, 176–178, 282; GDP growth, 240; growth and diversification in, 180–184; growth patterns, 185–189; John Harris master plans, 236–238; land use indicators, 244–245, 244*t*; main contributors to GDP, 185*t*, 186*t*; malls in, 45; mapping developers, 245–247; mapping growth of, 242–245; measurement and mapping growth, 242–243; modal split of international trade, 183*t*; as model for Kazakhstan's soft power projects, 297; Palm Islands, 50; as port city, 175–189, 179*t*, 309; post-1950s plans and projects, 236–241; private-owned land and property distribution, 247*f*; quantifying existing land use/nonuse, 243–245; real estate speculation and transnational development in, 235–253; skyline, 123–125, 124*f*, 125*f*, 236*f*, 237*f*;

Dubai (continued)
speculative reverberations and urban displacement, 247–250; state-owned land and property distribution, 246*f;* Structural Plan, 238–239; top trading partners, 184*t*; and urban planning, 46, 48; value of total foreign trade, 182*t*
Dubai Cityscape, 248
Dubai Fountains, 124*f*
Dubai International Financial Centre (DIFC), 282, 284–285
Dubai Logistics Corridor, 179
Dubai Mall, 257
Dubai Marina, 239
Dubai Metro, 240
Dubai model of port-city linkage, 178–180
Dubai Opera House and Cultural Center, 61
Dubai Ports International FZE (DPI), 187
Dubai Ports World (DP World), 187–189
Dubai South, 241
Dubai Statistics Center, 243
Dubai World Central (DWC), 179, 241
Dubai World Trade Center, 236, 238

EAA (Executive Affairs Authority), 151, 156
Easterling, Keller, 177
East Plaza (NYU Abu Dhabi), 168*f*
Education City (Qatar), 289
Electricité du Liban building (Beirut), 69
elite agency, 278–279
Elizabeth II (queen of England), 238
Emaar Properties (Dubai), 87–89, 88*m*, 245
Emaar Square (Dubai), 88
Emirates Towers (Dubai), 236, 239
enacted, cities as, 6, 11, 304–305, 312–315
enclaves: cities as specialized enclaves, 301; colonial planning of, 44; in Dubai, 252; as inimical to generative potential of urbanism, 312–313; institutional framework for, 282–284; Masdar City

as, 203–204; oil companies and, 40, 69–70; outcomes of, 293–294; and soft power initiatives, 277, 280–297
Equatorial Guinea, 256
ethnography, 37
Executive Affairs Authority (EAA), 151, 156
Expo 2017 (Astana), 297
Expo 2020 (Dubai), 241, 297
exporters, Gulf cities as, 303–304

fabric, in NYU Abu Dhabi design, 166–169
Fahd (prince of Saudi Arabia), 286
False Creek (Vancouver), 87
Fathy, Hassan, 68
FC Barcelona, 290
Festival City (Dubai), 245
financial crisis (2007–2008), 79, 87, 235
Financial Times, 46
Florida, Richard, 8
foreign direct investment, master-planned cities and, 217
fortuitous etatisme, 6
Foster, Lord Norman: and Abu Dhabi development, 90; and Central Market, 117; Buckminster Fuller and, 199–200; and the Gherkin, 114; on Gulf architecture, 200; and Hearst Tower, 111; and Masdar City, 199
Foster + Partners, 61, 89, 90, 199, 200
Foucault, Michel, 134, 139
fragmentation, transnationalism and, 38–43
free-trade zones (FTZs), 176–178, 282–283
Friedman, Thomas, 65
frontier mythology, 210*n*22
Frost, Alan, 202, 203
Fuccaro, Nelida, 4, 35, 39, 41, 315
Fuller, Buckminster, 199–200

garden city movement, 44
Garhoud Bridge (Dubai), 238

gated neighborhoods/communities, 4, 69–70

Gate Towers (Abu Dhabi), 121, 122f, 123

GCC. *See* Gulf Cooperation Council

Gehry, Frank O., 60

gender roles. *See* women

Gherkin, the (London), 114, 115f

Ghertner, D. Asher, 261

global financial crisis (2007–2008), 79, 87, 235

Google Earth, 242, 243

Grabar, Oleg, 66

Great Britain: and Dubai free-trade zone, 177; and Gulf building boom, 48–49; and Gulf urban planning, 44–45; imperialism, 36, 47, 65

Greenwich Village, New York City, 157, 170, 248

Griesemer, James, 107

Gruen, Victor, 45

guaranteed salaries, 262

guest worker programs, 315–316

Guggenheim Museum (Abu Dhabi), 60, 263, 288–289

Gulf Cooperation Council (GCC): elite agency and state building in, 278–279; free zones, 282–283; "hub and spoke" state building approach, 280–281; soft power initiatives, 276–277 (*see also* significance, quest for); state-owned enterprises, 283–284

Gulf exceptionalism, 35–36

Gurg, Easa Al-, 200

Haberly, Daniel, 210n28

Hadid, Zaha, 61, 121

Hanieh, Adam, 305

Hariri, Rafik, 72

Harper's Weekly, 109

Harris, Jill, 45

Harris, John, 45, 236–238, 242

Hawley, Sir Donald, 237

Heard-Bey, Frauke, 261

Hearst Tower (New York City), 111, 112f

Hencken, Randolph, 219

Herb, Michael, 267, 269, 278

heritage. *See* tradition–modernity binary

High Line (NYU Abu Dhabi), 161f, 163, 164

Hinchcliffe, Tanis, 43, 49

HKR Architects, 90–91

Höhler, Sabine, 197

Hong Kong skyline, 110f

housing: as consumption item in Abu Dhabi, 258–259; for workers, 23, 40–41, 260, 289

Hoyle, Brian, 180

"hub and spoke" state building, 280–281

hub-city model, 189

Humanities Building (NYU Abu Dhabi), 163f

Human Rights Watch, 316

hybrid cities, 16–19; and European-style piazza for Jubail City, 136–140; hybridity and the urban, 131–136; hybrid urban metabolism of Masdar City, 140–142; and NYU Abu Dhabi, 147–170; origins of, 132–133; origin stories and myths, 133–136; photography and circulation of spectacular architecture, 99–126; planning for, 130–143

hybridity: and diversity, 304–305; evolution of concept, 132–133; and the urban, 131–136

Ibrahim, Ismail, 223–224

iconic building: and image, 59–60, 102–103, 107, 116–119, 123, 126; and urban spectacle, 83–86, 89–90, 92; uses of, 15, 17, 238–241, 245, 313

iconic space, 138

images: computer-generated, 107–108; learning from, 102–103; photography and circulation of spectacular architecture, 99–126; representation for Arab city, 67–69

income: average vs. median, 10; of foreign workers, 317; in oil-producing countries, 256; in Qatar, 262
industrial atmosphere, 7
inequality, Gulf cities' role in, 316
innovation, Gulf culture and politics as inimical to, 314–315
intelligence of democracy, 92, 313–315
institutional identity, 149–150
International Academic City (Dubai), 289
International Building Code, 153
International Renewable Energy Agency (IRENA), 287
Interstellar (movie), 208
Iran: and Anglo-Persian Oil Company, 47; John Harris's work in, 45; sterling holdings, 49
Iraqi Public Works Department, 40
Iskandar, Malaysia, 223
Islam: architectural motifs in Louvre Abu Dhabi, 63; architectural motifs in Masdar, 62; architectural motifs in NYUAD, 160–163, 167, 170; and Gulf development trends, 6–7; and historical Arab cities, 302–303; mosques as public space, 137; and tradition-modernity binary, 65–66; and women's clothing, 257–258
Italy, Qatari projects in, 86–87
Izenour, Steven, 1, 102

Jacobs, Jane, 8, 260
Jebel Ali Free Trade Zone (JAFZA), 178
Jebel Ali Port, 177
Jeddah International Airport, 61
Jeddah Islamic Port, 187
jobs. *See* labor
Jones, Calvert, 265, 296
Jubail City, Saudi Arabia, 136–140, 286
judicial cities, 280
Jumeirah (Dubai), 238
Jumeirah Beach Residence (JBR), 239

Jumeirah Gardens (Dubai), 239, 248
Jumeirah Palm Island (Dubai), 239

KAEC (King Abdullah Economic City), 88, 214, 285. *See also* Cityquest KAEC Forum
Kanna, Ahmed, 35, 37, 64–65
KAUST (King Abdullah University of Science and Technology), 291–292
Kazakhstan, 89–91, 297
Kennedy, John F., 210*n*22
Khalifa bin Zayed Al Nahyan, Sheikh (emir of Abu Dhabi), 308
Khoury, Bernard, 71, 73
Khuzestan, Iran, 47
King, Anthony, 44
King Abdullah City for Atomic and Renewable Energy (KACARE), 280, 287–288
King Abdullah Economic City (KAEC), 88, 214, 285. *See also* Cityquest KAEC Forum
King Abdullah Financial District (Riyadh), 285
King Abdullah Petroleum Studies and Research Center, 61
King Abdullah University of Science and Technology (KAUST), 291–292
Kingdom Tower (Jeddah), 79
knowledge industry, enclaves as inimical to, 313
Koolhaas, Rem, 36, 61, 79, 91, 219, 222
Kuwait: democracy in, 6; lack of soft power projects in, 296; land ownership in, 47; land speculation in, 48; spatial segmentation in, 42–43; sterling holdings, 49; urban planning in, 44–45
Kuwait City, 6, 44, 46–48, 259, 296

labor: in Abu Dhabi, 261–262, 267–268; Aramco and, 42; and building construction/maintenance, 81; and consumption infrastructure, 24,

267–268; in Dubai, 180; fragmented structure of, 130; and GCC free zones, 282; guest worker programs, 315–316; Gulf citizens and, 268; in Jebel Ali Free Trade Zone, 178; in Masdar City, 205–207; and museum projects, 289; in ports, 176; as source of diversity, 304–305; spatial separation of housing for, 23, 40–41, 260; at universities, 265, 291; U.S. system, 305, 315–316
laboratory, city as, 9–10
labor camps, 40, 70, 260, 261
labor communities, 41
labor protests, 42, 265
labor standards, 289
La Défense (Paris), 113, 114, 115*f*
Lakeshore Drive Apartments (Chicago), 104*f*
Lamki, Bader al, 207
land economics, 4, 39
landscaping, water use and, 260
land speculation. *See* speculation
land use planning, 4–5, 23, 84–86, 91, 152–153, 238–245, 256, 260–262, 302–303
Las Vegas, 1–3, 102, 300, 313
Latour, Bruno, 11, 215
Learning from Las Vegas (Venturi, Scott Brown, and Izenour), 1, 102
Levitt, Peggy, 263
Libeskind, Daniel, 219, 219*f*, 222
Lienhardt, Peter, 39, 41
Livingstone, Ken, 85
London, England, 85, 86, 307
London Array project, 205
Louvre Abu Dhabi, 62, 63, 63*f*, 263, 288–289

Mahdavy, Hossein, 6
Maktoum Bridge (Dubai), 238
Mall of the World (Dubai), 241
malls. *See* shopping malls
Malthouse, Kit, 86
Manama, Bahrain, 4, 39, 315

Mangera, Ali, 62
"Mapping Dubai: Towards an Understanding of Urban Form and Social Structure," 242
Marina Bay Sands (Singapore), 121, 122*f*, 123
Marina District (Saadiyat Island), 158, 159
Marshall, Alfred, 7
Marx, Karl, 5
Marxian analysis, 5
Masdar City, Abu Dhabi, 50, 196*f*, 206*f*; debate over replicability of concept, 203–204; desert as frontier, 201–202; hybrid urban metabolism of, 140–142; as idea, 207–209; lunar module design parallels, 199–201; solar power and low-cost labor in, 205–207; as source of innovation, 314; symbolic vs. commercial success of, 286–287; symbolism in design of, 61–62; as test bed for renewable technologies, 202–205; as urban test bed, 194–209
Masdar Free Zone, 287
Masdar Institute, 194, 195*f*, 198*f*, 201*f*, 287
Mayassa, Sheikha, 288
Mecca, 79
Megaproject: and urban design, 142–142, and urban development, 20, 23, 214, 226, 235, 239–240, 249, 313–314; and urban spectacle, 85, 88, 91, 178–179; and enclaves, 276, 284–292, 297, 313–314
Menoret, Pascal, 260
Meraas, 249
Meydan, 246
migrants: as population of cities, 315–317; as source of diversity, 304–305. *See also* labor
Mindell, David, 210*n*22
Ministry of Municipality and Urban Planning (Qatar), 289
Minoprio, Spencely, and Macfarlane, 44–45

Mitchell, Timothy, 201–202
Moavenzadeh, Fred, 200–201
modernity, tradition vs. *See* tradition–modernity binary
modernization: oil companies and, 41; old and new centers in process of, 69–75
Mohamed bin Rashid City (Dubai), 241, 246
Mohammed bin Rashid Al Maktoum (ruler of Dubai), 285
Mohammed bin Rashid Space Centre, 210n21
Mohammed bin Rashid Tower, 89
Mohammed bin Zayed al Nayhan, Sheikh (crown prince of Abu Dhabi), 150, 151, 152, 279, 283
money, as work-around, 308–310
Moore, Peter, 252
Morphosis, 61, 208
mosques, 137
Moza bint Nasser, Sheikha, 279, 289–290
Mubadala: economic diversification projects, 281; financial losses, 293–294; Mohammad bin Zayed and, 279; and NYUAD, 18, 151, 153, 154, 156, 291; and Sowwah Island, 285; as state-owned enterprise, 283–284
Mubarak, Khaldoon Al-, 283–284
Mubarak bin Sabah Al-Sabah, Sheikh, 47
Munir, Hisham, 68
Murray, Stuart, 139
Museum of Islamic Art (Doha), 15, 83, 263, 288
museums: as prestige projects, 50; as soft power enclaves, 288–289; and tourism, 263. *See also specific museums*
myth: building identity between mythical past and futuristic utopia, 64–68; and hybrid cities, 133–136; and Jubail City piazza planning, 137–139. *See also* tradition–modernity binary
MZ Architects, 117

Nakheel, 245, 246
Nakib, Farah al-, 42, 43, 47, 258
Nasser, Gamal Abdel, 67
National Bank of Abu Dhabi, 112, 113, 114f
National Commercial Bank of Jeddah, 70
National Museum of Qatar, 61
"native towns," 41
Nazarbayev, Nursultan, 90
neoliberalism, 36, 217, 226–227, 250–252,
Neom (Saudi new city project), 310
New Cities Foundation (NCF), 213, 218
New Cities Summit, 218
"new frontier," Gulf cities as, 43–46
New Gourna project (Luxor), 68
New York City, 109, 110, 176
New York Journal, 109
New York Times, 316
New York University. *See* NYU Abu Dhabi
Nolan, Christopher, 208
Nouvel, Jean: Burj Qatar tower, 116; Doha Tower, 83; Louvre Abu Dhabi, 62, 63; National Museum of Qatar, 61, 83; Torre Agbar, 83, 114
NYU Abu Dhabi (NYUAD), 147–170, 155f, 157f, 161f, 163f, 167f, 168f, 264; density, 162–166; as fabric, 166–169; local framework, 150–153; public access and security, 169–170; site selection for, 157–159; and soft power, 290–291; speed of design/construction process, 153–157; as walkable campus, 160–161, 162f

off-budget programs, 269
oil: and consumption in Abu Dhabi, 256–258; discovery in Abu Dhabi, 256; and Dubai free-trade zone, 177; effect on economic thought, 201–202; and Gulf state structures, 6; and hybrid cities, 135; and rentier state theory, 37; as source of funding for soft power initiatives, 279–281; urban construction by oil companies, 40–43

oil prices, soft power projects and, 296, 297
oil shock (1970s), 49
OMA, 61
Oman, free zones in, 285
O'Neill, Joseph, 252
openness, in present-day Gulf, 302–304
Operating Manual for Spaceship Earth
    (Fuller), 199
Orientalism (Said), 9, 36, 63–65, 76n11,
    134–135
Ott, Carlos, 112
Ouroussoff, Nicolai, 287

Palm Islands, Dubai, 50, 239, 245
pan-Islamism, 66
patronage employment, 280
Pei, I. M., 15, 83, 111, 263, 288
Pelli, César, 86
Peninsular and Oriental Steam Navigation
    Company (P & O), 188
Pensee et Politique dans le Monde Arabe
    (Corm), 67
photography: and circulation of
    spectacular architecture, 99–126; and
    computer-generated images, 107–108;
    identity of images and difference of
    places, 111–125; learning from images,
    102–103; paradoxes of the skyline,
    108–110; rhetorical figures, 103–107
Piano, Renzo, 85
place, identity of images and, 111–125
Place Dynamix, 250
Plan Abu Dhabi 2030, 152
Plaza Hotel (New York), 15
Poland, 46
policy transfer scholarship, 214–215
pork products, 266
"Pork room," 266, 267f
Porta Nuova (Milan), 15
port cities: Dubai, 175–189, 179t, 309; and
    Gulf economy, 39; share of each port
    in total Middle Eastern throughput,
    187t; top ten world port hierarchy, 188t

Port Rashid (Dubai), 177, 238
prostitution, 266
public relations, 41
PublicsLive, 218

Qasimi, Sheikh Sultan bin Muhammad
    Al-, 151
Qatar: free zones, 285; guaranteed salaries
    in, 262; museums in, 263; National
    Museum of Qatar, 61; projects from
    international designers, 83; soft power
    urban enclaves' lack of business
    success, 293
Qatar Faculty of Islamic Studies, 62, 62f
Qatar Financial Centre (QFC), 285
Qatar Foundation (QF), 278, 289–290
Qatar Holding, 15, 87
Qatar Investment Authority (QIA), 84–87
Qatar Ministry of Municipality and
    Urban Planning, 289
Qatar Museums Authority (QM), 263,
    278, 288
Qatar Science & Technology Park
    (QSTP), 290
Qatar Space City, 290
Qatar University, 290
Qatari Diar, 84–87, 86m, 289
QF (Qatar Foundation), 278, 289–290
QFC (Qatar Financial Centre), 285
QIA (Qatar Investment Authority), 84–87
QM (Qatar Museums Authority), 263,
    278, 288
QSTP (Qatar Science & Technology
    Park), 290
Quest, Richard, 201

Rafael Viñoly Architects, 153–156, 158–159,
    167, 170
Ramos, Stephen, 48
Ras Al Khaimah, UAE, 61–62
Rasheed, Fahd Al-, 225–226
Rashid bin Saeed Al Maktoum, Sheikh,
    200, 236–238, 248

rate of change (RC), 243
rate of growth (RG), 243
real estate speculation. *See* speculation
religion: and Gulf development trends,
    6–7; Solidere and, 73. *See also* Islam
renewable energies: King Abdullah City
    for Atomic and Renewable Energy,
    280, 287–288; as means for projecting
    soft power, 286–288. *See also* Masdar
    City
rentier state theory, 37
representation: in Arab and Gulf cities,
    58–75; building identity between
    past and future, 64–67; of images
    for Arab city, 67–69; old centers and
    new centers in Arab modernization
    process, 69–75
RG (rate of growth), 243
rhetorical devices, of architects and
    photographers, 103–107
Riyadh, Saudi Arabia, 1–2, 48
RMJM, 117, 118
Ross, Andrew, 291
Rossant, John, 218, 219, 219*f*, 222
Royal Clock tower (Mecca), 79
Royal Commission of Jubail and Yanbu,
    136, 286

Saadiyat Island, Abu Dhabi, 50, 60, 264.
    See also NYU Abu Dhabi
SABIC, 286
Safdie, Moshe, 121
Said, Edward, 64, 65
Salam, Assem, 73
Salman bin Abdulaziz Al Saud (king of
    Saudi Arabia), 268–269
Samuel Beckett Theater (Oxford),
    199–200
Sasaki Associates, 158
Satwa district (Dubai), 247–250
Saudi Arabia: Cityquest KAEC Forum,
    213–227; commercial enclaves,
    285–286; European-style piazza for

Jubail City, 136–140; industrial cities,
    286; land ownership in, 47; modern
    architecture in, 69–71; parallel
    institutional fiefdoms in, 281; racial
    segregation in, 42; renewable energy
    projects, 287–288
Saudi Aramco. *See* Aramco
Schuyler, Montgomery, 109
science and technology studies (STS), 132
Scott Brown, Denise, 1, 60, 102
Sears Towers (Chicago), 105*f*
"seasteading," 310
security, at NYU Abu Dhabi, 169–170
Sexton, John, 150
Shabiyat al-Shorta (Dubai), 248, 249
Shard, the (London), 15, 86
Sheep Meadow, Central Park (New York
    City), 124*f*
Sheikh Zayed Road (Dubai), 238, 241
'Shindagha Tunnel, 238
Shipwreck with Spectator (Blumenberg),
    197
shopping malls: in Abu Dhabi, 90,
    121–122, 257; in Dubai, 45, 88, 257; and
    land use, 244, 245; in Mohammed bin
    Rashid Tower, 89; work-arounds in,
    266
Shorta (Dubai), 249, 251*f*
significance, quest for, 276–297, 311;
    commonalities across the enclaves,
    292–293; elite agency and state
    building in GCC, 278–279; GCC
    Free Zones, 282–283; "hub and
    spoke" state building approach,
    280–281; institutional framework
    for urban enclave projects, 282–284;
    international ambitions and local
    enclaves, 276–277; and museums,
    288–289; new soft power enclaves,
    286–293; outcomes of soft power
    urban enclaves, 293–294; renewable
    energy projects, 286–288; state-
    owned enterprises, 283–284; success

and spread of commercial enclave model, 284–286; and UAE skylines, 260; uniqueness of GCC soft power enclaves, 297; universities and research, 289–292; and world-scale projects, 277–278

Sinan, Mimar, 66

Sir William Halcrow and Partners, 49

Skidmore, Owings, and Merrill, 15, 70

skyline: Abu Dhabi, 260–261; Doha, 83; Dubai, 236f, 237f; paradoxes of images, 108–110; in photography, 123; polarity of image, 127n15

skyscraper, 4, 34–35, 79, 236–237, 240, 248; architecture of, 60–61; photography of, 83–86, 107, 109–111, 116–119, 124

Sloterdijk, Peter, 198, 208

SOEs (state-owned enterprises), 283–284

soft power. See significance, quest for

solar power: and low-cost labor in Masdar City, 205–207; in Saudi Arabia, 287–288

Solidere (Beirut), 71–73, 72f

souk, 137

spatial exceptionalism, 306

spatial segmentation, 23–24, 306–308; in Abu Dhabi, 266, 269; in Kuwait, 42–43. See also work-arounds

spectacularization, 14–15; Aldar Properties, 89–91; architectural/urban spectacles, 80–82; and branding of injustices, 316; connotations of spectacles, 80; Emaar Properties, 87–89, 88m; Gulf cities' origin role in, 91–92; Gulf vs. European architecture, 82–84; of KAUST architecture, 292; mobilities of urban spectacle, 79–92; photography and circulation of spectacular architecture, 99–126; Qatar Investment Authority, 84–87; and UAE skylines, 260–261

speculation, 308; in Dubai, 247–253; in Kuwait, 48; in Manama, 39; and urban displacement in Dubai, 247–250; urban planning and, 48

sprawl, automobiles and, 259–260

Squire, Raglan, 49

Stanek, Łukasz, 46

Star, Leigh, 107

starchitecture (star architecture), 10, 15, 38, 65, 219, 222, 316; and urban spectacles, 82, 86, 91–92, 99, 111–112, 114–117, 121

state(s): reasons for existence of, 310–312; as tool for enhancing monarchical rule, 5; urbanism and formation of, 46–49

state building, 278–281

State Department, U.S., 169

state-owned enterprises (SOEs), 283–284

Storper, Michael, 7

Strategic Working Group, 221, 223

Structural Plan (Dubai), 238–239, 247

STS (science and technology studies), 132

STS/ANT, 132–133

Stupin, Laura, 194

suburbanization: "company towns," 69–70; in Kuwait, 42–43; in Saudi Arabia, 42

Sultan (prince of Saudi Arabia), 279

sustainable technologies. See Masdar City

symbolism, in architecture, 61–62

Symphony of Lights (Hong Kong), 110f

Szelenyi, Ivan, 317

Tange, Kenzo, 70

taxation, free-trade zones and, 5, 177

TDIC. See Tourism Development and Investment Company

Tehran, Iran, 45

terrorism, 169

Thiel, Peter, 310

Tornado Tower (Doha), 117, 117f

Torre Agbar (Barcelona), 83–84, 114, 116, 116f

Torresol, 205

tourism: employment of women in, 268; heritage tourism, 36–37; in Qatar, 263; Saadiyat Island and, 158

Tourism Development and Investment Company (TDIC), 153, 158, 159, 288, 291

trade, 36–37. *See also* free-trade zones; port cities

tradition–modernity binary, 23; in Beirut, 71–72; building identity between past and future, 64–68; and history of Gulf cities, 36–37. *See also* work-arounds

transnational circulations: and Cityquest KAEC Forum, 213–227; in global South, 214–216; from Gulf cities, 303–304

transnationalism, 12–16; and Cityquest KAEC Forum, 213–227; context and representation in Arab and Gulf cities, 58–75; in Dubai, 235–253; Gulf cities as "new frontier," 43–46; and history, 35–51; mobilities of urban spectacle, 79–92; old centers and new centers in Arab modernization process, 69–75; urban construction by oil companies, 40–43; urbanism and formation of the state and global, 46–49

transshipping, 177

Trinidad, 256

Tschumi, Bernard, 75

2020 Urban Masterplan (Dubai), 239–241

UniCredit Tower (Milan), 86–87

United Arab Emirates. *See specific locations*

United States: immigration system, 316; special districts in, 307

U.S. State Department, 169

universities: importing Western academic campuses, 263–264; lack of success as soft power enclaves, 294; pressures from government authorities, 265; as urban soft power enclave, 289–292. *See also specific universities*

Unknown Soldier Monument (Baghdad), 68

untraded dependencies, 7

urban centers, in Arab modernization process, 69–75

urban design, 44, 111, 136, 141, 211, 250

urban enclaves. *See* enclaves

urbanists/urbanism, 37, 41, 46–49

Urban Masterplan (Dubai), 239–241

Urban Planning Council (Abu Dhabi), 152–153

Urban Structure Framework Plan (Plan Abu Dhabi 2030), 152

urban test bed(s), 19–22; and Cityquest KAEC Forum, 213–227; Dubai as, 175–189; Masdar City as, 194–209

Vehicle, The (Zaatari), 68

Venturi, Robert, 1, 60, 102, 306, 317

Viñoly. *See* Rafael Viñoly Architects

Vitalis, Robert, 42

Vogel, Frank, 7

Vora, Neha, 37, 257

wages. *See* income

walkable environment, NYU Abu Dhabi as, 160–162

Washington, George, 303

wasta, 262

water use, 259–260

wealth, as work-around, 308–310

welfare system, in UAE, 262

West Bay Central Business District (CBD), Doha, 83, 116–117, 117f

WFES (World Future Energy Summit), 202

Wikimapia, 243

Wilson, James, 40, 41, 44

Wired magazine, 207

women: in American compounds in Saudi Arabia, 285; in Aramco compounds, 70, 291; automobiles and, 259; in colonial cities/company towns, 41; in

Dubai, 18; and shopping in Abu Dhabi, 257–258; in UAE labor force, 268
work-arounds, 23; in Abu Dhabi, 265–268; manifestations of, 305–308; wealth as, 308–310
workers. *See* labor
workers' housing, 40–43, 69–70, 243, 248–250, 289, 315–316
World Cup (Doha, 2022), 264
World Future Energy Summit (WFES), 202

World Trade Center Abu Dhabi, 89
World Trade Center Dubai, 236, 238

Yamasaki, Minoru, 70
Yanbu, Saudi Arabia, 286
Yvars Bravo, Ada, 62

Zaatari, Akram, 68
Zayed bin Sultan Al Nahyan, Sheikh (emir of Abu Dhabi), 151, 153
Zonescorp, 289